PFLAUM / STANDARD
38 West Fifth Street, Dayton, Ohio 45402

James Michael Lee
The Flow of
Religious Instruction

A SOCIAL-SCIENCE APPROACH

Library of Congress Catalog Card Number 72-97171
ISBN 0-8278-9058-3
Pflaum/Standard
38 West Fifth Street
Dayton, Ohio 45402
© 1973 by James Michael Lee
Printed in the United States of America

90058/S2M-1-373

To
Ernest, Julia, and Sally Lundstrom

CONTENTS

PREFACE

Nun sei bedankt, mein lieber Schwan!
Zieh' durch die weite Flut zurück,
Dahin, woher mich trug dein Kahn,
Kehr' wieder nur zu uns'rem Glück:
Drum sei getreu dein Dienst getan!
Leb' wohl! Leb' wohl, mein lieber Schwan!
—Richard Wagner[1]

It was during my 1970-1971 sabbatical year in Vienna that I commenced work on this book. In my sunny top-floor apartment overlooking the Bennoplatz, I spent many happy hours reading and making preparatory notes. Sometimes I would supplement my reading by attending lectures at the university. Walking up its sweeping stone staircase to the *Hörsäle* or strolling in the courtyard amid the busts of renowned professors of its glorious past seemed to place the lectures in a broader historical and affective context. Often I would take leisurely walks through the Vienna Woods, sometimes to the Kahlenberg or to the Leopoldsberg, mulling over and mentally rearranging the numerous elements of the book on which I was embarking. But books are planned best in a situation in which cognitions and affects and lifestyle realities are mingled in a grand symphony. Vienna provided me with just such a situation. There were the glorious balls in majestic old Viennese palaces where one danced away those special evenings under dazzling crystal chandeliers in full expectancy that at any moment Franz Josef himself would enter. On other nights the opera beckoned—and there is no place in all the world where the opera is such a total event as it is in Vienna. On weekends, thanks to my *gelber Blitz*, there were long days and soft nights to spend gently rummaging around the many old churches and castles which abound in the Austrian countryside. Back in Vienna, little Balkan restaurants with their piquant food and lively music provided a warm, flavorful atmosphere highly promotive of deep and productive conversation. It was my good fortune to be able to spend *den heiligen Abend* and Christmas day in the little Austrian village of Oberndorf where in 1818 Josef Mohr and Franz Gruber composed and played "Silent Night" for the first time, and where to this day a little brass band goes from house to house on Christmas Eve playing this loveliest of all carols. Snow fell heavy on the ground both days. Then came the springtime, and what can compare with enjoying a *Heurige* in the Wienerwald?

It was in such a personalistic atmosphere that this book had its origins. As I progressed in my work during that year, I often reflected on how Vienna—for me at least—encapsulated so much of what I was writing about. Life in Vienna surely illustrated the powerful effect which a particular environment has on learning. It also demonstrated rather forcefully that a fruitful learning situation is one which is multidimensional rather than unidimensional. Moreover, the life, the times, and even the very stones of St. Stephen's Cathedral seemed to shout the essential difference between religion and theology.

The Flow of Religious Instruction is the second volume of my trilogy on religious instruction. It is the goal of this trilogy to lay a basic, comprehensive, and systematic foundation for a thoroughgoing social-science approach to religious instruction.

The first volume, *The Shape of Religious Instruction,* sets forth the basic principles out of which issue the next two volumes. Therefore a reading and an understanding of *The Shape of Religious Instruction* is necessary for a proper and full grasp of the contents of this present volume.

The thesis of the present book is that attention to and control of the teaching act together constitute the most direct and most practical way of improving the quality of religious instruction. Consequently the thrust of this book is highly practical: it is targeted toward the enhancement and improvement of religion teaching. But it assiduously eschews any kind of cookbook or Mr. Fix-It approach. Indeed, nothing is more destructive of true and authentic practicality than cookbook formulas and Mr. Fix-It prescriptions. What *The Flow of Religious Instruction* includes, therefore, is a set of generalized, effective pedagogical guidelines which (1) are derived both from the facts of learning and the facts of teaching, and (2) are anchored in sound theory of instruction. This kind of treatment enables the religion teacher to augment the effectiveness of his pedagogy regardless of the conditions or setting in which his instructional activities take place.

One of the major factors hindering the growth and development of religious instruction is that for centuries it has had no identity as a field in its own right. All too often religious instruction was considered a second-class enterprise or a messenger boy for theology. But beginning in the 1960's and continuing into our own decade, religious instruction is becoming emancipated from theology. In the process it is developing its own ontological and professional identity. It is my earnest hope that by concentrating on the dynamics of the flow of religion *teaching,* this volume will accelerate the emancipation process. Thus this book can serve as a springboard for the growing number of religious educators and educationists who are focusing their efforts on developing a more effective religious pedagogy. A natural result of such a concerted effort is that new research interest and technical development will ensue. Without sophisticated empirical research and development, there can be no real or viable future for religious instruction.

Few sectors of life more glaringly exhibit the scandal of Christian disunity than does religious instruction. In a world becoming more and more a single mosaic, the splitting of Christianity into walled-off factions and denominations surely must be a continual reproach and rebuff to that Lord whose Last Supper plea was for Christian unity. If religious instruction is to be faithful to its Christ, prophetic to its church, and true to its people, then it must be authentically and broadly ecumenical. To this end, each volume of the trilogy endeavors to be ecumenical in approach and concern. Authors, examples, and situations are drawn from a variety of Christian confessions.

A writer, like any other kind of teacher, operates within a situation characterized by a host of interacting variables. Singularly important among these variables are people. In conceiving, writing, and refining this book, I received the help of many persons on both sides of the Atlantic. During the first year of research and reflection, many persons in Vienna helped me a great deal. Great is my debt in this regard to Heinrich Heyszl von Heyszenau. Other persons who shaped the setting for the book's origins include Hubert and Cornelia and Diana Aich, Alix Blaschka, Michael Bujatti, Karl and Fritzi Garnitschnig, Marian Heitger, Helvig Habsburg von Lothringen, Gábor von Littasy, Barbara Prutscher, Alexandra Reininghaus, Alice Szecsen, Willy Stehno, and Peter and Jutta Trautmansdorff von Weinsberg. In the second year when most of the actual writing was done, my colleagues and students at the University of Notre Dame and elsewhere gave me much of their valuable time and effort. I am especially thankful to Willis Bartlett, chairman of Notre Dame's department of graduate studies in education, for his constant encouragement and support both of my own research in particular and of the religious instruction program in general. J. Duane Beals, Dennis Mooney, Frank Ruetz, Joseph Shenher, Brian Simpson, John van der Beek, and Jack Welch critiqued portions of the manuscript. In addition to commenting on large segments of the work, Norine Dugan and Ellen Dunn provided much needed background assistance through typewriting. Robert O'Gorman's perceptive analysis caused several portions of the manuscript to be altered. The ecumenical thrust of the book was enhanced through the careful, scholarly critiques made by Morton Trippe Kelsey from mainline liberal Protestantism and by Harold Burgess from evangelical Protestantism. I am particularly grateful to Walter Doyle whose well-honed analytical scalpel made visible some previously neglected or overlooked features of the inner dynamic of the book's structural anatomy. Incalculable is my debt, as always, to Pobdwm, treasured partner in so many scholarly explorations in the apostolate.

Notre Dame, Indiana   *—James Michael Lee*
April 28, 1972

1. Richard Wagner, *Lohengrin,* Act I.

PROLOGOMENON

"I'll ask the government for orders."
When Rieux met Castel, the Prefect's remark was still rankling.
"Orders!," he said scornfully. "When what's needed is imagination."
—Albert Camus[1]

THE RANGE OF TEACHING

A Definition of Teaching

In previous centuries philosophers typically defined teaching or instruction as the process by and through which learning is caused in an individual in one way or another.[2] Contemporary specialists in the teaching-learning dynamic define teaching as the deliberative process by which changes are effected in the learner.[3] This modern conceptualization of teaching represents an operationalizing of the traditional philosophical notion. By this I mean that teaching is now identified as the overall act which causes a change in an individual's behavior. In other words teaching is a process which effects a behavioral change of some sort in the learner as the result of a particiular experience or set of experiences which the learner undergoes. There are many kinds and varieties of behavioral change: it can comprise cognitive change, for example, learning the ten commandments; affective change, for example, acquiring a deeply felt appreciation of liturgical celebration; conative change, for example, developing the will power to attend church services on a regular basis; and lifestyle change, for example, performing charitable acts as a matter of course.[4]

THE SETTING FOR TEACHING

The teaching process, whether it be the teaching of religion or the teaching of any other area of human activity, is a generalized process of effecting behavioral change in the learner. *Teaching is teaching regardless of the setting in which this process is being carried out.* Religious instruction is *fully* religious instruction whether it takes place in a formal or informal setting, whether it takes place in a school setting, a home, a church, a restaurant, or a youth club. Religious instruction qua instruction occurs in an environment in which one or more persons consciously and deliberatively structure a situation in which desired learning outcomes can and do take place. The fundamental principles and strategies of effective teaching remain basically the same whether the locus of teaching is in a formal or informal setting. There is no such thing, strictly speaking, as formal or informal religious instruction; rather there is the one process of religious instruction adapted to formal and informal settings, such as the classroom or the home.

For centuries both Catholic and Protestant church officials have explicitly or implicitly equated religious instruction with formally structured learning settings such as the religion period in the church-related school or the Sunday School and CCD program. Beginning with the late 1960's and continuing to the present, this age-old identification of religious instruction with formal settings has been brought into question. In many third-world countries, school-centered religious instruction is fast disappearing due to the nationalization of denominational schools, or in instances of certain non-Christian countries to the abolition of Sunday as the day of rest.[5] In the United States and Europe, parochial school closings and/or renewed interest in the role of the nuclear family and peer-group associates have led to a growing reassessment of the value of school-centered religious instruction. There is much merit in the recognition that the teaching process is not school-bound. Yet, unfortunately, a great deal of scientifically unsupported nonsense is currently circulating about the alleged incompatibility of formal instructional settings and effective religious teaching-learning— witness, for example, Gerard Sloyan's statement that "in general, when they [religion teachers] begin to teach religion formally they spoil everything," after which he urged the elimination of formal religious instruction in Catholic schools.[6] Other persons similarly advocate a "deschooling" of society, commonly for reasons which seem to stem from a well-meaning but frothy mixture of nostalgia and unreality.[7] From the social-science perspective, such arguments for the actual crippling disadvantages or outright hopelessness of either formal religious education or schooling itself are usually based on *a priori* assumptions or "hip-pocket data."[8] It is, of course, possible that these assumptions may be valid. However, until empirically controlled research studies are conducted into the relative effectiveness of religious instruction done in formal versus informal settings, it would appear premature and overhasty to consign religious instruction in formal settings to the rubbish basket of history.[9] Based on both the scant research data on the teaching of religion and from easily extrapolatable data from teaching areas akin to religion, I suspect that the problem of weak religious learning stems far more from ineffective pedagogical practices than from the general setting in which the activity of religious instruction takes place. Ineffective teaching will still be ineffective whether it is carried out in a formal or informal setting. The solution to ineffective religion teaching rests not so much in the switching from formal to informal sites but rather in the sharpening of the pedagogical process itself. Direct attack on the problem is always a more effective tactic than an indirect attack such as simply switching settings. The teaching-learning process itself, rather than its location in formal or informal settings, is the crux of the issue.

Education in a formal setting—a term typically coextensive with schooling—is "a system of complex, planned, organized, systematic, purposive, deliberative, and interrelated learning experiences which in concert bring about the desired behavioral changes in the person."[10] The purpose of schooling is to render the learning process more efficient and effective by means of supplying the learner with a consciously planned set of expanding and reinforcing experiences which are intended to have a more powerful effect than do either the ordinary life experiences or informal educative experiences in changing the individual's behavior in a given direction. Religious instruction in a formal setting represents a situation structured to harness in one milieu all we know about what produces the most effective and efficient learning. Yet I suspect that if one were to analyze those effective educational programs taking place in informal settings, one would soon discover that the basic pedagogical principles and activities in operation in these settings are similar to those employed in effective educational programs occurring in formal settings. Adaptation in teaching practices will vary, of course, according to whether the setting is formal or informal, but the fundamental pedagogical practices will be present in both types of milieux. The religious instruction movement should not be diverted from its primary focus by cheap panacea proposals like totally deschooling religious instruction or completely eliminating religion classes in formal settings. *It is primarily through deep, penetrating, and unswerving attention to the teaching-learning dynamic and the improvement of all that is involved therein that the teaching of religion will be rendered optimally effective and fruitful.*

What I have just stated is in no way to denigrate the axial importance of religious instruction in so-called informal settings. To be sure, in our own age, large segments of our population receive helpful and valuable learning experiences from religious instruction programs in informal settings such as the Marist House experiment in Indiana,[11] as well as from other sources like the mass media which only incidentally treat of religion. Actually there are instances when religious instruction in an informal setting might prove more effective than would be the case in a formal setting. Moreover, religious instruction for individuals of nonschool age, notably preschool children and adults, is at last beginning to receive that degree of attention and programatic effort due to these important yet hitherto neglected sectors of the Christian community. For preschoolers and adults alike, religious instruction probably should be and doubtless will be carried on more extensively in informal than in formal settings. However, in our growing appreciation of the highly beneficial and significant effects of religious instruction carried on in informal settings, we should not lose sight of the valuable role which religious instruction programs in formal settings have played and will continue to play in even larger measure in the world. Admittedly, any number of persons have achieved a high degree of religiosity even though they never attended a religion class in a formal setting. It may even be argued that for certain individuals it is more beneficial to a heightening of their religiosity if they never attend a religion class in a formal setting or attend them only at certain levels. Nonetheless, it would appear that religious instruction in a formal setting can have a significant and beneficial effect on the religious behavior of the learners, provided of course that the religious instruction is of superior quality.[12] From the point of view of setting—that is to say the origin and situation of educative experiences—what is needed in religious instruction today and tomorrow is a carefully-planned articulation between all the agencies providing religious instruction. Religion classes in formal settings, early childhood experiences in the family environment, peer-group and near-group milieux in a downtown house reserved exclusively for this purpose, discussion clubs (the "rap joints" of the early 1970's), adult education programs of divers sorts are just a few of a long list of enterprises which should begin to collaborate actively in furnishing a broad and effective network of religious experiences for Christians of all ages. Religious instruction provided in formal settings such as in the religion class, in the church-related school, or in the Sunday School will continue to exercise an important function; yet to be truly effective, these programs must forge a dynamic and integrative relation with nonschool educative experiences.[13]

The process of effective religious instruction is basically the same no matter when or where it is carried out. *Consequently, the analysis of the process of teaching religion which I shall make in this volume will hold valid for religious instruction in all sites and settings*—in schools, in the home, in nonschool agencies, in peer-group clubs, and so forth.

THE PURPOSE OF RELIGIOUS INSTRUCTION

*Ronny's religion was of the sterilized [English] Public
School brand, which never goes bad, even in the tropics.
Wherever he entered, mosque, cave, or temple, he retained
the spiritual outlook of the Fifth Form, and condemned as
"weakening" any attempt to understand them.*
                                                    —E. M. Forster[1]

In large measure, the pedagogical practices used by an individual
teacher will be an outcome of what he holds to be the primary
proximate purpose of religious instruction. One cause of the present
confusion in religious instruction quite possibly is a hazy or unclear
notion of its primary proximate purpose.

Three primary purposes of Christian education in general, and
religious instruction in particular have been proposed, namely, the
intellectualist position, the moralist position, and the integralist
position.[2]

The Intellectualist Position

The intellectualist position holds that the primary proximate
purpose of religious instruction lies in the intellectual development
of the learner in matters pertaining to religion. Strict intellectualists
maintain that knowledge of religion and the intellectual processes
attendant upon that knowledge constitute the only true and
legitimate proximate purpose of religion class.[3] Moderate intellectualists believe that knowledge and related intellectual processes
constitute the primary but not exclusive purpose of religious
instruction. "In the concrete," writes Neil McCluskey, quoting
Robert Henle, "teaching activity may be carried out so as to
promote virtue . . . ," yet McCluskey himself concludes that "despite
its importance, this secondary aim must remain incidental and
subordinate to the primary activity of teaching."[4] For the intellec-

tualists, religious instruction is aimed primarily or exclusively at handing on to the learner the accumulated knowledge of doctrines and understanding of values which help to form the faith commitment of the church or denomination.

The Moralist Position

In contrast to the intellectualist position, the moralist viewpoint contends that the primary proximate purpose of religious instruction consists in making the student more virtuous. Religious knowledge in this view is decidedly secondary and ancillary to religious virtue; knowledge and understanding are brought into the teaching situation only to the extent that they promote virtue. Kevin O'Brien, a vigorous proponent of this position, encapsulates at least one sector of the moralist position when he observes that the church-related school, and therefore *a fortiori* religious instruction, should teach the learner to do all for the love of God; "knowledge without moral formation," he notes, "is simply a weapon in the hands of a criminal." O'Brien adds that the world should not worry so much about educating a poor, devout, but intellectually backward savage in some distant land, because "he has in his will charity which is superior to all knowledge in this life."[5]

The Integralist Position

In another volume[6] I propose a third position, one which applies both to the church-related educational enterprise in general and to religious instruction in all its forms in particular. This stance, which I term the integralist position, regards the primary purpose of religious instruction as the fusion in one's personal experience of Christianly understanding, action, and love coequally. By coequally is meant that the development of each of these outcomes is sought by the process of religious instruction coextensively with the others—all within the contextual fabric of personality development. Christian living, or lived religion, is "the confluence of the thoughts, emotions, desires, and overt actions of a person to form an integrated behavioral pattern" and mode of one's human existence.[7] Religious instruction, according to the integralist position, aims at enabling the learner to actualize in a harmonious, integrated, developmental, and self-fulfilling way all five dimensions which have typically been identified as comprising religious behavior: the ideological dimension, that is religious belief; the ritualistic dimension, that is religious practice; the affective dimension, that is religious feeling; the intellectual dimension, that is religious knowledge and understanding; and the consequential dimension, that is religious effects.[8] For the integralist the aim of religious instruction is to empower the learner to act in the interests of God: God as he is in himself; God as he is in the Church; God as he is in the community of men; and God as he is in the learner. To the intellectualist the integralist responds that the real Christians are not necessarily the people who know or even notionally believe the right things, but rather the people who live the kind of life which Christ lived. To the moralist, the integralist answers that a Christian lifestyle devoid of or deficient in a pervasive intellectuality is neither human life nor human style, and hence can scarcely be considered Christian.

Social-science survey data suggest that Christian parents (those typically neglected figures vis-à-vis institutionalized religious instruction programs) appear to regard the integralist position of overall Christian living as the primary proximate purpose of religious education. The data in Reginald Neuwien's national survey on Catholic schooling suggest that the overwhelming majority of parents whose children attend Catholic schools believe that Christian living constitutes the primary purpose of these institutions, and *a fortiori* of the religion program conducted there.[9] The nationwide study by Greeley and Rossi of both "average" and "intellectually and liberally elite" Catholics came to precisely the same conclusion.[10] The Donovan-Madaus investigation of the opinions of both Catholics and non-Catholics in a large New England archdiocese revealed that regardless of their faith, the Christian parents surveyed viewed Christian living as the most important outcome of church-related in-school or out-of-school educational programs.[11]

Religious Instruction and the Three Positions

The stance which the teacher or curriculum builder takes on the primary proximate purpose of religious instruction is no mere abstract position nor speculative gymnastics. On the contrary, the position taken on the primary proximate purpose of religious instruction will vitally affect every phase of the concrete ongoing religious education program in general and the religious instruction activity in particular. What the curriculum builder or teacher or parent does in the concrete is to operationalize in a specific instance the overall primary proximate purpose. Thus the primary proximate purpose deeply affects which particular pedagogical practices are to be chosen and which are to be rejected for a given religion class. For example, the intellectualist will tend to select a primarily transmissionist strategy, stressing chiefly or even exclusively verbal and cognitive practices. An integralist, on the other hand, will typically opt for a primarily environmental strategy, emphasizing product-process, cognitive-affective, verbal-nonverbal, action-oriented practices as they intersect in a prepared, educationally-oriented, total environment. The mature teacher consciously radicates his own pedagogical practices in the broad framework of the primary proximate educational objective he wishes to achieve. As I shall discuss at length later in this book, it is only by consciously incorporating educational practice within the broad framework of theory that there can result an optimally effective and cohesive set of concrete instructional activities.

My own position on the primary proximate purpose of religious instruction is the integralist one. My belief that Christian living constitutes the purpose of religious instruction pervades every aspect of this book and serves as one of the three major points of departure for the social-science approach to religious instruction. The other two major points of departure are the way in which a person does in fact learn, and secondly, the way in which a teacher does in fact facilitate learning.

THE DIMENSION OF RELIGIOUS INSTRUCTION

*I realize today that nothing in the world is more distasteful
to a man than to take the path that leads to himself.*
                                            —Hermann Hesse[1]

TEACHING RELIGION OR TEACHING THEOLOGY?

A Clarification of Goals

What is the dimension of religious instruction? Is the dimension
religion or is it theology? Put another way, is teaching religion the
same as teaching theology? The answer to this all-important question
has critical practical implications for each and every phase of the
religious instruction enterprise. Yet all too few religious educationists and educators[2] have addressed themselves to this crucial
question; even more regrettably, few seem to have raised this
question to themselves. It is my strong conviction that unless and
until the religion teacher (or curriculum builder) faces and resolves
this pivotal question there will be a lack of consistent and focused
thrust to his pedagogical work.

Gabriel Moran, one of the few religious educationists to have
addressed himself squarely and maturely to this question, declares
that the teaching of religion and the teaching of theology are
identical, since "both pertain to the communication, understanding
and assimilation of Christian faith."[3] I believe Moran is incorrect on
this point, a fact which will be borne out by an analysis of the
distinct nature of both theology and religion.[4] Theology is a
speculative science encompassing "the methodological elaboration of
the truths of divine revelation by means of reason enlightened by
divine faith."[5] Theology, as Emil Brunner observes, is the science of

faith, a systematic reflection about faith in its relation to the Word of God. Born in and through faith, theology represents an attempt to attain intellectual clarity as to what the church has to proclaim and what the Christian has to believe.[6] This is the nature of theology, and hence specifies its general method and the kind of results it attains in the speculative and practical orders. The actual product results of theological reflection may indeed be at variance, as for example, the affirmation or denial of the Virgin birth; nonetheless both the so-called "old" and "new" theologies employ the same general kinds of investigative methodologies and attain the same general kinds of speculative results.[7]

In contrast to the speculative, intellectual science of theology, religion comprises the lived behavior of an individual within the context of his ongoing relationship with God.[8] This context is a combination of two elements: (1) the individual's lived perception of his own relationship with God, and (2) the creedal and ritualistic behaviors that the institutionalized religious group of which he is a member declares to constitute de facto the overall framework of one's right relationship with God. For believers in a new testament religion, religion is Christian living within the context just specified.

Religion and theology are, then, distinct entities; Christian living and thought concerning God are not the same thing.[9] Theology is a mode of reflection, while religion is a mode of living, as Edward George Bozzo succinctly reminds us. The two are of course related, but they are nonetheless distinct entities.[10] Theology, then, is dependent upon religion but is not identical to religion.

Theology is a speculative, intellectual, academic discipline; when it is taught it makes no special confessional demands upon the learner. Consequently Kenneth Eberhard, the theologian, rightly affirms that one unfortunate digressionary development in recent times is that "theology has too often been conceived as 'character building' or 'strengthening the faith,' rather than as knowledge."[11] To be sure, the very basis for the inclusion of theology departments in government-operated secular universities in America and in other lands is that the nature and goal of theology is knowledge and not religious living. Further, the ultimate foundation of academic freedom for theological programs (and for theologians) in church-related universities is that theology is an objective intellectual academic discipline and hence is not part of the pastoral mission of the bishop, clergy, or church elders.

The Role of Theology

What I have written in the foregoing section in no way disparages or minimizes the vital role which theology plays in every phase of the process of religious instruction. The point I am making is that theology ceases to play its crucial function in the religious instruction dynamic when it ceases to be theology. Theological science has its speculative and practical branches. The theologian is concerned with the practical order, but in a way proper and distinctive to theological science. In his scientific activities vis-à-vis the practical order, the theologian must remain a theologian if he is to insert the yeasting effects of theology into the dough of that practical world. Practical or pastoral theology must, of course, be relevant, but it cannot be truly relevant unless it is truly theology. Now theology is a discrete science with distinctive methodologies and with circumscribed procedures of verification and explanation. Once the theologian departs from these methodologies and procedures, what he says about the practical order might indeed be relevant, but if so, it is for reasons other than those of theology. Theology investigates and expounds that which it believes to be the practical consequences of the Christian faith for the church and its individual members; it is there that its proper function ceases. If theology is to fulfill its crucial function for the church, observes Paul Tillich, it must declare the truth of the Christian message, and then interpret this truth for every new generation and every new culture.[12] To effectively perform this dual function, theology must be authentic and faithful to itself as a cognitive science investigating God. It is a sham theology which attempts to perform the task of all sciences and of all human activities. There is a point at which theology becomes so broad in its effort to be practical that it ceases to be theology. Even the newest of the new theology perceives its task not as simply to address itself to ideas of the past, but from ongoing living Revelation to generate new ideas on what should and must be done in the present and the future as theology views this task. Some and possibly much of the new theology will be done in action-oriented milieux and will also be more directed to the practical consequences of theology. Nonetheless, such theology must remain theology, a distinct cognitive science, if it is to have its unique impact on the consequential order. Theology is not metaphysics or history or cultural studies or biology; theology is theology.[13] Practical theology is the theology of the church's practice; it is not identical to or coextensive with that practice.

Religious Instruction as Ontologically Distinct from Theology

Theology reflects cognitively on religious experience; religious instruction is the concrete activity which enables the learner to have present and future religious experiences. The religion teacher, then, serves as a kind of existential mediator between God and the learner in the actual concrete situation. This type of activity is beyond the scope, range, and capabilities of theological sciences.[14] The religion teacher serves not only as a kind of mediator between God and the learner but also as a kind of existential mediator between theology and life in a way unavailable to a theologian as theologian. To mediate is to create between two realities facing or opposing one another an existential link which neither previously possessed, although each had a tendency toward it.[15] Mediation establishes and maintains between two realities an ontological relationship which would not exist without the mediational activity.[16] Religious instruction is the active concrete process of existentially mediating theology and concrete reality. Religious instruction is neither singly incarnating theology in the real flesh-and-blood world, nor is it singly bringing to consciousness the relationship to God which characterizes all flesh-and-blood reality. In other words, religious instruction is not just an offshoot of theology on the one hand, or merely flesh-and-blood living on the other hand. Rather, *religious instruction is a new entity, composed of both theology and the practical order in a new ontological reality.*[17] An appropriate analogy would be one from chemistry. Religious instruction is a compound, not a mixture, formed from theology and life-experience. (In chemistry, a compound is a combination of two or more elements or ingredients which when combined form a new substance with properties quite different from those of the original ingredients. A mixture, on the other hand, is a combination of two or more elements or ingredients which when combined do not form a new substance but retain their separate existences and properties no matter how thoroughly they are commingled). In the case of religious instruction, this practical order comprises the way a particular learner or group of learners actually do learn, the texture of the learner's culture, and the art-science of the pedagogical process. The facilitation act itself is the mediator. Religious instruction, like all other forms of mediation, is thus a dynamic conception. Theology and the practical order are reconciled to each other, in all the richness implied in the notion of reconciliation. As mediator religious instruction does not stand between theology and practical life; instead, it fuses them together, empowering both to actively share in a new ontological form toward the making of a genuine and authentic religious experience for the learner.

The Three Historical Stages of Religious Instruction

Religious instruction as mediator represents the third and most highly developed stage of conceptualization concerning the relation of theology to life. The first stage, held historically until the end of World War II in most Protestant circles, and until the late 1950's in the Catholic sphere, viewed religious instruction as a messenger boy for theology.[18] According to this view, religious instruction is a sort of errand boy by whom the wisdom and understandings acquired in theological science can be delivered to the man in the street. Thus religious instruction was regarded as a combination of two elements: (1) a watering down (usually phrased as "adapting") of theology to make it comprehensible to the man in the street, and (2) a treating of religious instruction as mere methodological messenger boy to deliver theological goods, as intact as possible under the circumstances, from the theologians to the man in the street or to the learner in the class.[19] Very likely one major reason for this centuries-old view of religious instruction arose from the fact that it was the theologians—typically untrained in social science—who by and large formulated the theory and often controlled the practice of religious instruction.

The second stage in the relationship between theology and religious instruction can be called the translation stage. By this is meant that religious instruction is conceived to be a translation of theology back into the truth it arose from and represents, where it can be learned in life and in relationships.[20] Like the messenger boy stage, the translation stage treats religious instruction as a branch of theology. However, it represents an advance in sophistication over the messenger boy level in that this stage regards the relationship of theology to religious instruction as a two-way street, in contrast to the one-way street posited by the messenger boy approach. In this conceptualization both theological science and life simultaneously insert their dimensionalities into religious instruction according to the distinct modes of theology and of life, all within the general outlook and thrust of theological science.

One practical result of both the translation stage and particularly the messenger boy stage was that for centuries the enterprise of religious instruction revolved around a method-content duality.[21]

At various times in the history of religious instruction, either the method or the content gained the upper hand, ordering the other unto it. The consequence was misplaced emphasis, lack of dynamic equilibrium, and often inefficient religion teaching. The conceptualization of the mediation stage heals the artificial breach created in religious instruction. In the subsumptional process which is mediation, method and product content cease to be separate entities to be applied to each other in varying degrees of intensity. Rather, they now enter that new, sophisticated, and unified relationship which I discuss in *The Shape of Religious Instruction.* Viewing religious instruction as an ontological mediatorship distinct from, yet at once subsuming both theology and the practical order will give rise to a new stage in religious instruction. And it is the social-science approach which of its nature is uniquely fitted to provide the overall framework for ushering in this new era.[22]

Why is it that for so many decades emphasis has been placed on the process of religious instruction as either messenger boy or translator for theology? The basic answer to this puzzle lies in what might be termed the typical traditional theological speculative outlook. Method and product content are regarded as two real, actual entities in themselves, with method at the service of product content. But such a view ignores the fact that "method" as such and "product content" as such are separate only as thought categories. They do not exist as real concrete beings. In the actual teaching-learning dynamic, method and product content cease to exist as separate entities—or more accurately, the thought categories merge in the concrete act of religious instruction. In the actual teaching-learning situation, one cannot simply teach (method); rather, one teaches something (method and product content). Conversely, in religious instruction something (product content) is taught (method). It is the actual teaching-learning dynamic itself which mediates method and product content. In this concrete dynamic, method and content cease to simply add their own properties to the act, but take on in addition the new dimensionalities of a religious instruction compound. Hence the age-old method-content duality never really existed except in the heads of religious instruction theorists.

Religious Instruction as Helping to Enrich Theology

The enterprise of religious instruction has a prophetic role to play vis-à-vis theology considered in itself (as distinct from the theology which is intermingled in the religious instruction act itself). One aspect of this prophetic role is that religious instruction pushes forward the boundaries of theological science per se. The teaching church is not composed of theologians alone; it includes all the people of God—and in a special way, religion teachers. Yet beyond this, religious instruction plays a uniquely prophetic role relative to theology inasmuch as its very work consists in a here-and-now, deeply existential theologizing.[23] Religion teachers are forging their own theology in the real-life situation. The result of this theologizing and this theology done by religion teachers in the context of the teaching-learning dynamic can serve as a valuable and vivifying input to the theologian. The high-level theologian does his theology from a double seat, as it were: from his seat in the quiet of his study, reflecting and bringing to conscious awareness new insights into and interpretations of the Good News; and from his seat in life where the waters of the world wash over him and swirl through him. Nevertheless, because of the undeniable fact that professional theologians as a class tend to live in milieux somewhat isolated from the hurly-burly of the world, the life in which the professional theologian sits tends to comprise only a small portion of life as a whole, and an unrepresentative portion at that. How immersed is the professional theologian in all facets of concrete life, the sordid and the sublime, the ordinary and the extraordinary, the regular and the irregular? Does not the average religion teacher and parent often sit more in the nitty-gritty of life than does the professional theologian? On the negative side, this undeniable fact sometimes causes the workaday religion teacher and parent to be a bit skeptical about the realness and indeed practicalness of the professional theologian's attempt at practicality. In other words, to constitute a valid methodology, the theologian's setting in life must be done in all those segments which are representative of the totality of life. Sitting in only some sectors of life will bias the theologian's findings vis-à-vis all of life and hence the generalizability of the results of his theological inquiry. On the positive side, the variegated waters of life in which the religion teacher sits enable him to do that kind of theologizing which can supply fresh and cleansing insights to the professional theologian vis-à-vis his development of a well-rounded practical theology.

The Role of Theology vis-à-vis Religious Instruction

Religious instruction is a form of pastoral work; it is not a branch of theological education. What then is the proper role of theology in the teaching of religion? I have already stated some of the vital functions which theology plays as it suffuses all areas of religious instruction. This notion of "suffusing all areas of religious instruction" provides the initial clue to my further exploration of this relationship. According to the theological approach to religious instruction, the teaching of religion in every aspect from starting point through to goals is completely determined by theology. In the operationalizing of this total normative function of theology, religious instruction becomes basically a way to pump life into the transmission of theology from teacher to learner.[24] Putting it another way, the process of religious instruction is entirely circumscribed by theology, because religious instruction is conceived simply as a mode of theology. The social-science approach takes the opposite view, a view based on the previously-mentioned concept of theology suffusing all areas of religious instruction. Thus the nature, form, and thrust of the theology that comprises an indispensable aspect of the mediational process which is religious instruction take on the hue and texture appropriate to its role in furthering the teaching-learning of religion. The shape and form of the theology employed in the act of teaching religion are not determined by what will cause more effective learning of theology but what will cause more effective learning of religion. In the religious instruction act, therefore, theology is thrusted toward facilitating Christian living rather than being thrusted toward itself. Does this mean that theology becomes a handmaid to religious instruction? My analysis of the mediational character of religious instruction suggests that quite the opposite is the case. There could be no mediational character of religious instruction if the original theology input were anything but theology at its fullest and purest. Yet as it exists in the dynamic of the mediational context, theology clearly becomes targeted toward something outside itself; it becomes targeted toward the goal of the entire mediational process of which it itself formed an original and present ingredient.

Both theology as a science distinct from religious instruction and theology as incorporated into the mediational activity of teaching religion have an additional role to play in furthering the work of religious instruction.[25] Theological science brings the process of religious instruction to wider significance and meaning by making it more conscious of its role in the history of salvation in general and in the here-and-now revelational dynamic in particular.

While religious instruction is not theological education, it is among many other things a process of being educated in theology. Theological instruction is the acquisition of certain knowledges and understandings which serve as a means to living, whereas religious instruction suggests an activity geared to the facilitation of Christian living. Faith or hope or charity is not kindled by theology; they are facilitated by the process of religious (I do not say theological) instruction. Theological instruction is the reflection on and exploration of the nature and operations of revelation: religious instruction is the activity in which the revelational process is being enabled and lived. Religious instruction includes an abundance of theological product and process contents located in and mediated through that living of flesh-and-blood Christianity which comprises religion class. Revelation is not merely a set of doctrinal propositions deriving from the bible or from church authorities. Revelation is also, and more importantly, action, event, and encounter—as Gabriel Moran reminds us.[26] It is in the teaching-learning act of religion, rather than in theological science as such, that action, event, and encounter occur. Revelation is relation, and it is in the religion class in both formal and informal settings that existential relation between man and man, and between man and his environment takes place.[27]

To educate faith, to educate hope, and to educate charity in such a way that they are dynamically incorporated into the individual's lifestyle is the work called religious instruction. Theology provides the requisite speculative basis for the kind of faith, hope, and charity which the religion teacher will attempt to facilitate in the learner. By contrast, the work of religious instruction consists in the process itself of enabling faith, hope, and charity, all facilitated in such a manner as to be incorporated into the personal lifestyle of the learner. Theology forms one necessary speculative grounding; religious instruction is the actual process which mediates these theological foundations with the practical order (culture, learner personality, and so forth) in the very dynamic of teaching-learning itself.

The Need for a Taxonomy of Religious Behaviors

If religious instruction is to successfully accomplish its task of facilitating Christian living, then it is absolutely imperative that Christian living be defined operationally. Which specific behaviors and bundles of behaviors go to form Christian living? After all, if religious instruction consists in the modification of the learner's behavior along religious lines, then it is essential to know which are the terminal religious behaviors that are sought from the learner. One of the things which has most hampered the entire enterprise of religious instruction over the centuries is that there has been no taxonomy of religious behaviors. By taxonomy here I mean an overall classification system of the totality of those behaviors recognized as specifically religious. The behaviors enumerated in this classification system are placed in hierarchical order according to their presumed or demonstrated level. This hierarchical ordering is done both for type groups of religious behaviors as well as for the particular behaviors falling within these type groups.[28]

The primary purpose of a taxonomy of religious behaviors is to identify in operational terms those outcomes which the religion teacher or curriculum builder wishes to facilitate. At the present time without such a taxonomy, intended religious outcomes in the learner are often conceived of in vague terms which do not suggest what specifically is to be learned, much less what is to be taught or how. For example, a typical desired outcome might be "to really understand the Mystical Body." Now what in the concrete does "really understand" mean in this case? How does the teacher or the learner know when the learner has "really understood"? By intuition? By the so-called "feel of it"? Or again, another typical outcome might be "to deeply appreciate Jesus's call to union at the Last Supper." What does "deeply appreciate" mean? What is the learner doing internally or externally when he is "deeply appreciating"?

The forming of behavioral objectives is an essential first step in the development of a taxonomy of religious behaviors. Even after such a taxonomy is constructed, the religion teacher and curriculum builder will still need to construct behavioral objectives for each basic learning experience. But over and above that which the development of specific behavioral objectives accomplishes, a taxonomy classifies these behaviors into a system which delineates discrete religious behaviors in an hierarchical order. The function of this kind of ordering is to give added meaning to heretofore isolated behaviors by enumerating them both separately and as they stand in relationship to other previously unconnected behaviors within a broad framework. Such a functional relationship is ultimately required for effective teaching and curriculum building. Teaching and also curriculum building are goal-directed behaviors, hence the clearer and more operationally defined is the pedagogical goal, the potentially more effective will be the teaching and curriculum building.

Some Practical Ramifications

An operationalizing of the distinction between religious instruction and theological instruction has real and far-reaching implications for the way in which religion lessons are taught in the concrete order. Let me select four major practical ramifications which result from the teaching of religion being viewed as religious instruction rather than as theological instruction.

First, religious instruction is lifestyle-oriented; theological instruction is cognitively oriented. In other words religious instruction is directly geared to changing the learner in all the aspects of his lifestyle which are related to religious behavior, for example, his knowledge, understandings, affects, values, ideals, overt behaviors, and so forth. Religious instruction in this view is the deliberative process of facilitating Christian living in the learner. In contrast theological instruction is aimed at developing the learner's knowledge and understanding of both theology itself and of a theological worldview. Thus Gabriel Moran, one of the most mature and sophisticated advocates of the view that religious instruction is basically theological instruction writes that "the work of the catechist [religion teacher] is a work of helping men to attain an understanding of the Christian life." He views as ultimately "disastrous" the work of any teacher or school which sets about enabling students to encounter Jesus.[29]

Second, religious instruction is learner-centered whereas theological instruction is subject-centered. To be learner-centered means that decisions on what to teach, how to teach, and when to teach will be rooted in the learner as he is as a goal-directed person in the here-and-now situation. The psychological laws of learning in general and the way in which the teacher can most effectively facilitate learning within the instructional environment provide both the point of departure and the pedagogical practices for the teaching-learning act. To be subject-centered means that these same instructional decisions will be radicated in the nature and structure of the subject to be taught, in this case theology. Gabriel Moran as well as many other thoughtful proponents of the thesis that religious instruction is in reality theological instruction have a difficult time reconciling (as far as concrete instructional and curricular decisions are concerned) the following notions: the learner learns in a definite way; revelation happens in the *hic-et-nunc* experience of the learner; theology is basically what is to be learned in religion class.[30]

Third, religious instruction is based on educational processes while theological instruction is founded on logical processes. By this I mean that religious instruction is ordered according to how the learner does in fact learn, and from this base are selected those teacher behaviors and the sequencing of things to be learned which will most effectively facilitate this learning. For example, the bible might be read and studied in a nonchronological fashion by learners who wish to make it relevant to their own needs, hopes, fears, strivings, and loves. Or the bible might be read in chronological order by learners who wish to see how things fit into an historical context. The decision of what is to be learned is jointly made by the learner and the teacher.[31] Theological instruction, on the other hand, is ordered around the internal logical structure of theological science; this determines the mode and sequencing of things to be learned. To illustrate: the bible would be read and studied in a logically consistent fashion, for example, historically (chronological order of events), topically (the development of the idea of God among Jews in pre-Christian times as evidenced from selected passages in various books of the old testament), or thematically (the variations of the biblical notion of prayer). There is no room in theological instruction for any decision-making role for the learner in curricular matters. Thus Gabriel Moran writes that to permit the learners to play a significant role in the formation of the religion curriculum represents "an abdication of adult authority and responsibility."[32]

Fourth and finally, religious instruction is environment-centered whereas theological instruction tends to be transmission-centered. Consequently religious instruction utilizes as its basic pedagogical strategy a purposively structured learning environment where all the aspects of that environment—learner, teacher, materials, socioemotional climate, and so forth—mutually interact in a way which optimally effect desired outcomes in the learner. The learning environment becomes a laboratory in which the learner learns Christian living precisely by and through his living of Christianity. Theological instruction, on the other hand, typically uses as its basic instructional strategy the transmitting of the matter to be learned as directly as possible from teacher to learner, usually by means of teacher talk. In this vein Gabriel Moran writes that "[religion] classrooms are places for teachers who because they have understood something can convey it to another by speaking to him and with him." And again Moran notes that the religion teacher's task lies in "evoking by his words the student's consciousness of his faith and vocation."[33]

Theory and Practice in Teaching Religion

Even the most casual observer of the contemporary religious education scene in Europe and especially in the United States will notice that while the vast majority of religion teachers adhere to the theory that religious instruction is theological,[34] nonetheless these same teachers utilize pedagogical approaches which flow directly from social-science theory. For example, these teachers will use affective and even some lifestyle-oriented educational practices; they will employ role-playing, field trips, in-class celebrations, and so forth. Yet truly effective use of any pedagogical practice is dependent upon its being consciously grounded in the very theory or approach which both gives birth to this practice and explains how and when this practice most efficaciously can be employed. The function of a theory is to specify relationships among practices in order to explain and predict the consequences of the practices themselves. A theory, then, gives guidance to the teacher as to the basic reason why one practice will work in one situation but not in another. Practices are like tools in a toolbox; the teacher can possess all the tools, including the most modern ones, yet be unable to use them effectively. It is theory which provides the explanatory framework for utilizing the tools, and will provide the clues as to when to use or not to use a particular tool.[35] The tools which the teacher will put into his pedagogical toolbox will be determined by his theory of the capability of tools.

Perhaps an illustration will help clarify the derivative relationship of particular pedagogical practices in a religion class to basic religious-instruction theory. Religious educators who subscribe to the theological approach to religious instruction often explicitly or implicitly advocate the "blow theory," that is, the teacher really cannot have very many effects on learner outcomes in religion class because "the Spirit blows where he wills" (John 3:8).[36] By contrast religious educators who support the social-science approach to religious instruction operate on the theory that the teacher's behaviors can and do have a great many effects on learner outcomes in religion class because an individual is shaped and nurtured by the environment with which he interacts.

I firmly believe that one major cause for the relative inefficacy of much of contemporary religious instruction lies in the fact that most religion teachers hold one theory of religious instruction while at the same time they utilize pedagogical practices drawn from another highly-conflicting theory. Consistency in the relationship between theory and practice is absolutely indispensable for the effectiveness, expansiveness, and fruitfulness of a practice in any domain whatsoever. I will return to this central point quite frequently throughout this book.

Religious instruction viewed as theological instruction corresponds to the intellectualist goal of religion class which I discussed in the preceding chapter. Conversely, religious instruction viewed as religious instruction fits in with the integralist goal of religion class. The religious instruction view—which is grounded in the social-science approach developed in *The Shape of Religious Instruction*—regards the purpose of religious instruction as consciously modifying the learner's total behavior pattern along religious lines. In other words the purpose of religious instruction is to facilitate Christian living. The theological instruction view—which is grounded in the traditional theological approach to religious instruction—is nicely summarized as to its purpose by Gabriel Moran, one of its most articulate and gifted proponents:

> The purpose of theology is not to stir up religious feelings, but neither is theology simply a neutral collection of truths. Theology can bring before the Christian mind some particular aspect of revelation that needs special emphasis, and it can work out the logical structures in the movement of understanding and the process of development.[37]

The intellectualist goal in this position is clearly evident from Moran's statement.

Conclusion

This chapter has dealt with three ontologically separate but highly interrelated areas, namely theology, religion, and religious instruction.[38] Religion (Christian living) constitutes the goal of religious instruction. Religious instruction is the facilitation of religion (or more operationally stated, religious behavior) in an individual. Theology forms one indispensable content of both religion and religious instruction.

TOWARD A TAXONOMY OF THE TEACHING ACT

"The Boy's Uncle made me Real," he said. "That was a great many years ago; but once you are Real, you can't become unreal again. It lasts for always."
— Margery Williams[1]

The Relationship between Product Content and Educational Practice

The carrying out of the teaching task is commonly referred to as "method." However, as I shall indicate a little further on, method, properly considered, represents only one phase or element of the totality of instructional practice. Accordingly, it is more precise and to the point to use the term "educational practice."

Educational practice is not and indeed cannot be separated from subject matter. John Dewey explains this by observing that instructional practice "means the arrangement of subject matter which is most effective in use; ... it is simply the effective treatment of material."[2] Conceptually one can make an abstract distinction between product content and the way in which this content is taught. However, in the actual reality of the concrete here-and-now teaching-learning act, material and practice cannot be ripped asunder. The notes on a musical scale (product content) are the same for everyone; but it is the arrangement of these notes (process content) by Beethoven or by the Beatles which makes the difference in what one hears.

To go one step farther, instructional practice is far more than the arrangement of the product content. Educational practice is itself a content, a process content. This notion of educational practice as process content will be a theme which will undergird and permeate much of this book.[3] Subject matter and educational practice (product content and process content) are both vital components of the mediational entity that is the act of religious instruction. Product content and process content as forces in the teaching-learning dynamic each interact with the other in a kind of shaping way. Marshall McLuhan explores this interaction in depth and suggests that process content has shaped product content much more than the world has suspected. His analysis of the effect which the linear process involved in Gutenberg typeset has had on Western thought is particularly pertinent in this regard. McLuhan's examination of hot and cool media (process contents) and their effects on the type of material presented on the electronic media are similarly relevant. It is the process content inherent in media (itself a process) which so intimately and exquisitely interacts with the material (product content) that makes some radio or television or telephone presentations effective and others ineffective.[4]

There is no such thing then as "straight product content" or "straight process content" in the teaching-learning situation. Everything which occurs in the concrete teaching-learning situation is content. So when I speak of process content or of product content, I employ these terms as conceptualizations of something which occurs in the religion lesson. These conceptualizations are useful in that they serve to illumine what can and should take place in an effective religion lesson.

Instructional practice considered solely in and of itself is a process content and as such it teaches values. Indeed, it often happens that instructional practice teaches values much more effectively than does the product content of the lesson. A pertinent example might be the teaching of the doctrine of the Mystical Body (product content) which features autocratic teaching procedures (a process content). Process content is typically far from being the "subtle content" which Michael Warren seems to believe it is.[5] Rather, it is a powerful and quite often a very manifest content, one which learners are particularly sensitive to and influenced by.

The separation of product and process contents is, as Gabriel Moran suggests, a false dichotomy from the point of view of the existential religion lesson itself.[6] For this reason Moran perceptively notes that "the confident statement made [by most Catholic religious educationists] that the catechetical movement has passed from an early methodological phase into the really important concentration on 'content' shows the continuing failure to see the whole issue."[7] The whole issue is, of course, the dynamic interpenetration and interrelationship between product and process contents which take place at every moment in the teaching-learning act. My discussion earlier in this book of religious instruction as a mediational act is particularly germane here. John Dewey expresses it nicely when he observes that instructional practice is not antithetical to subject matter but rather is antithetical to random and ill-considered action.[8] From one standpoint much of the erroneously perceived separation of instructional practice and subject matter is rooted in an equally false separation of means and ends in pedagogical activity. Sara Little skillfully addresses herself to this false separation:

> But there is also an inadequacy in views which speak of methods, organization, Christian education, always in terms of means and ends. The terminology makes the structure, the dynamic movement seems to be quite extraneous to the content with which it deals. Such a separation is comparable to what Tillich deplores as the separation of technical and ontological reason, and to what A. E. Taylor has in mind when he says "The hard and fast distinction between ends and means, effect and instrument, a distinction in fact borrowed from the realm of industry, if taken over seriously, is as pernicious in the theory of art as it is in the theory of morals."[9]

Why is it that for so many centuries Catholic religious educators have incorrectly posited a fundamental separation between what they typically have termed "content" and "method," or more precisely between product content and instructional practice? I would suggest that one major factor contributing to the erection of this false dichotomy is the outmoded notion of religious instruction as messenger boy for theology. Theologians have for ages treated religious instruction as a sort of errand boy by whom the wisdom and understandings of theological science are to be delivered to the multitude.[10] Under this antiquated rubric, not only was the unified fabric which is the religious instruction act torn apart into theological content and the instructional practice, but also instructional practice was looked upon as being in all ways subservient to its theological content. Apropos of this, Josef Goldbrunner, a theologically-oriented religious educationist in Germany, could write that the proper relationship of instructional practice and theological content is that educational practice "must serve" theological content.[11] On this side of the Atlantic, Michael Warren takes a similar stand when he declares that "the proper place" of instructional practice is in a decidedly secondary capacity to theological content.[12] While conceding that instructional practice is crucially important, Frank Norris, an American theologian, still sees it as "subordinate" to theological content.[13] Johannes Hofinger, a European theologically-oriented religious educationist, views instructional practice as the art of "interpreting the [theological content] of the message."[14] In an earlier chapter, I indicated that the view of instructional practice as messenger boy belongs to the first and most primitive stage of the relationship between theology and religious instruction. It is only by an awareness of and an acting upon the third and most sophisticated stage of the relationship between religious instruction and theology that the unwarranted breach between theological content and instructional practice will be healed. It is only through the actualization of the third stage, the mediation stage, that the fabric of religious instruction will be restored to that wholeness so necessary for its optimal fulfillment.

Most Catholic as well as Protestant religious educationists have traditionally held that theology exercises *the* normative role in the religious instruction act.[15] This view is a direct outgrowth of the antiquated notion that instructional practice is both separate from and subordinate to theological content in the religious instruction act. Theological imperialism of this kind leads to patently silly conclusions such as postulating the normative function of theology over all key variables in the learning process, ranging from the most effective method of teaching reading to the way human learning actually takes place. James Smart goes so far as to state that one of the major tasks facing religious educators today is the establishment of theological benchmarks against which every phase of religious instruction can be constantly measured.[16] With the realization of the third and mediational stage of the relationship of theology and religious instruction, the entire issue of normative function takes on a vastly different and—I might add—decidedly more sensible cast. In the mediational stage theological content and educational practice are subsumed in a new entity, the religious instruction act itself. Therefore, it is the religious instruction act, the totality of the entire ongoing process of the teaching act, which serves as the guiding norm. Theology as a norm is indeed present according to its mode of presence in the subsumptional act of religious instruction.

The Teaching Act

Beginning with the 1950's, a new area of study opened up within the field of education. This new area concentrates on the dynamics of the teaching act per se. Prior research and critical investigation of teaching centered on such variables as teaching effectiveness, teacher personality, materials of instruction, and so forth. The new area promises to be exciting and fruitful, for it represents a plunge into the very heart of the teaching dynamic rather than limiting the focus of attention to input and output variables exclusively. It is anticipated that attention to the inner constituent, flowing dynamic of the teaching act will in the end enable us to be in a position to enhance pedagogical effectiveness.[17]

Regrettably no one appears to have carefully examined the teaching act from the vantage point of hierarchical classes of pedagogical behavior considered in itself. One step in this direction was taken by Pierre Babin who distinguished between method as a general direction which teaching follows and method as a specific set of pedagogical procedures.[18] But as far as I am aware, there has not yet been developed any taxonomy identifying and classifying discrete categories of teaching behavior logically arranged on a generality-specificity continuum. I strongly believe that a taxonomy of this type is urgently needed for at least four reasons: (1) to come to a deeper knowledge and understanding of the teaching-learning act; (2) to design an optimally effective instructional practice; (3) to develop more effective modes of teaching; and (4) to help insure a consistency among all the levels of the teaching act so that each level will reinforce the others instead of working at cross-purposes. An important by-product of such a taxonomy is that it will liberate many religion teachers from the notion that instructional practice is just a bag of pedagogical tricks.

Elements of a Taxonomy

I should like to propose a tentative taxonomy of the instructional process. This taxonomy is preliminary and consequently sketchy. There are six categories in this taxonomy. Ranging from the most general to the most specific these categories are: approach, style, strategy, method, technique, and step. All six might be and indeed usually are present in any given pedagogical operation. Further all six, from approach right on down to step, comprise a unitary flow in the teaching act. The combination of all six makes up the teaching act, the teaching-learning dynamic. This taxonomy classifies solely the pedagogical act per se with no reference to the product content involved. Since it is free of any specific product content, this taxonomy is indeed an abstraction. But for purposes of pedagogical analysis, design, and research, this property of being free of any specific product content is useful in that it serves as a model into which any kind of pedagogical operation, whether it be religion teaching or language teaching or science teaching, can be situated. In the following few paragraphs, I will indicate in a very brief and sketchy way the primary features of a taxonomy of the instructional act considered in itself. The taxonomy enumerates discrete classes within the instructional act, beginning with the most general and ending with the most specific.

Approach is the primary, fundamental orientation of the teaching-learning act. It flows naturally out of the context of a theory. An approach provides the most fundamental matrix which conditions the direction which the teaching-learning act will take in its actuality and in its operations. The approach underlying and permeating the teaching-learning act cannot be directly observed; it can be inferred by synthesizing the diverse activities involved in a particular instructional act. In religious instruction the two principal approaches are the theological approach and the social-science approach. The theological approach, as Michael Warren notes, suggests that all instructional practice "must be based on adequate theology."[19] The problems here are legion. Who is to determine "adequate theology"? In the end it is faith (and for a Catholic also the magisterium) which determines which theology is "adequate." This accounts for the long procession of papal statements over the decades declaring that this or that form of instructional practice is "approved" or not. At bottom it is hard for the theologically-oriented religious educationist who wishes to be consistent to escape the conclusion that there is a "Christian instructional practice" just as there is a "Christian dentistry" or a "Christian farming." Indeed James Smart, a theologically oriented religious educationist, appears to espouse a "Christian instructional practice." The other religious educationists, Johannes Hofinger on the Catholic side and Randolph Crump Miller on the Protestant side seem to take a position somewhat similar to Smart's, though not as clearcut or definitive. Hofinger states that there is an abiding danger that religious education will "appropriate techniques of teaching which are fully in accord with profane subjects, but meaningless or even harmful in religious formation."[20] Miller asserts that the view of revelation with its theory of knowledge will "determine" the choice of instructional practice employed as well as the theological content.[21] A theological approach to religious instruction, if it is consistent with itself, will be basically uninterested in developing new forms and modes of instructional practice or of verifying those forms of instructional practice currently in use. On the other hand, the social-science approach to religious instruction considers instructional practice to be of extreme importance in its own right since for this approach religious instruction is fundamentally a form of teaching. In the social-science approach religious instruction is the facilitation of learner behavior along religious lines. A social-science approach to religious instruction regards as central to its work the development of new empirically-tested forms of instructional practice, and the verification of those forms presently in use.

Style is the basic overall pattern or mode which serves as the indicator of the specific direction which the activities of the teaching-learning act will take. Style is the main thread with which the cloth of the concrete teaching-learning act is woven. It is from this thread that strategies, methods, and techniques at once flow from and return to. There are many examples of style as mode in religious instruction, including the following pairs of opposite patterns: teacher-centered versus learner-centered; didactic versus heuristic; logical versus psychological; theological-content-directed versus experience-directed; preservation-oriented versus reconstruction-oriented.

Strategy is the comprehensive, systematized, concrete scaffolding on, around, and through which are placed the more specific methods and techniques of the teaching-learning act. Strategy provides the overall plan and concrete operationalized blueprint for the deployment of pedagogical methods and techniques. Primary examples of strategy include the transmission strategy, the discovery strategy, and the structured learning strategy.[22]

Method is the internally ordered set of pedagogical procedures which are arranged in discrete generalized bodies or classes. Method serves to furnish the larger tactical unit of the teaching-learning act. Examples of method are problem-solving, teacher-pupil planning, socialized teaching, individualized teaching, and affective teaching.[23]

Technique is the concrete, tangible, specific way in which a pedagogical event is structured in a given teaching-learning situation. Technique functions as a specific procedure which is actualized in a definite instructional circumstance. Lecturing and telling, role-playing, project, discussion, and panel are all examples of technique.

Step is the highly specific behavior unit or behavior sequence through which the here-and-now instructional practice is enacted. Step is the most directly observable feature of the pedagogical act and serves as the particularized antecedent teacher behavior upon which depends the particularized consequent learner response. Examples of step include such specific teacher or student behaviors as praise, asking questions, offering verbal support, and giving directions. Because the effective exercise of step is most immediate to the workaday teacher, and because the systematic investigation of teaching steps has been the most neglected area in pedagogy, there has been considerable research in recent years into this most specific and focused of all the taxonomic categories. As a result of this research, very specific pedagogical behavior units and behavior sequences have been identified and coded. Typical of such units and consequences are the pedagogical step clusters of Ned Flanders, Edmund Amidon, Arno Bellack, B. Othanel Smith and Milton Meux, Marie Hughes, Charles Galloway, and Karl Openshaw. I shall do no more than mention them here; the second half of Chapter 9 will be devoted to a discussion of the specific pedagogical behaviors grouped in the step category of the taxonomy.

Function of the Taxonomy

There seems to be a continuous clamor on the part of religion teachers for universities and workshops to provide them with new pedagogical practices which they can apply directly and immediately in their own teaching situations. Gerard Sloyan incisively observes that a consequence of this demand is that religious instruction is looked on as the pill which outstanding European and American religious education experts dispense liberally to the waiting teachers.[24] Small wonder, then, that religious education as a field is held in such low esteem and why it is difficult to develop it into a profession. It seems paradoxical that religion teachers talk so passionately about the teaching act as being highly creative, artistic, expansive, and free from scientific restraints, while at the same time wanting religious instruction specialists to provide them with a set of pedagogical recipes which they can follow without deviation in their own teaching situations.

At least five causes of this "pill mentality," "recipe mentality," or "Mr. Fix-It" mentality can be identified. The first cause is traceable to the rupture of instructional practice and subject matter as posited by most of the theologically-oriented religious educationists who hold that religious instruction is basically a messenger boy for theology. The separation of instructional practice from subject matter reduces all instructional practice to a set of cut-and-dried steps, a sort of fixed routine.[25] This position debases educational practice into a mechanistic affair, and in the end renders it impotent. Only in its role as an integral force in the subsumptional dynamic of the teaching act can instructional practice be effective. To appreciate this is to eschew any Mr. Fix-Itism. In this connection Robert Gagné points out a fundamental pedagogical law: "different kinds of change (learnings) have different instructional requirements."[26] A second reason for the "recipe mentality" is the difference which exists among teaching circumstances. Some teaching practices work well under certain circumstances yet are ineffective in others. This is not due to any deficiency in the practice. By its nature practice is circumstance-bound. Not all pedagogical environments are uniform. A third cause of the "pill mentality" is that learners, even in similar circumstances, are nevertheless different from each other to some degree. Thus a practice might be effective for one learner but not for another in the very same lesson. The teacher who utilizes a pedagogical practice like a cookbook formula ignores individual differences in pupil learning.[27] A fourth cause is the difference in teacher personality. Effective pedagogy calls for, among other things, a complementarity of teacher personality and the pedagogical practices he utilizes. This is not in any way to sacrifice the importance of instructional strategy on the altar of teacher personality, rather it is to affirm that there must be congruence between the teacher's overall behavior pattern and his instructional behaviors. The fifth and final cause is the all-too-human tendency to seek easy solutions to difficult problems. Teaching is a complex, multi-faceted affair. The busy workaday religion teacher, generally overwhelmed by too many classes containing too many students, naturally tries to find relief in shortcut solutions which prove in the end to be no solutions at all.

Like this book the taxonomy focuses on educational practice qua instructional practice. Unfortunately instructional practice in the full and global sense of this term has been slighted and even mocked in the past. Part of this is traceable to the old notion of religious instruction as messenger boy for theology; what messenger boy is more valuable than the sender of the message itself? Part is due also to the customarily low repute which has characterized the general educational enterprise in the United States and Europe until the late

1960's. Yet as George Leonard trenchantly observes, "We ridicule [teachers] for preoccupation with 'method' when no really workable methods have been provided them and, indeed, that is what they most desperately need."[28] From a theological vantage point, Pierre Babin remarks that to underestimate the value of instructional practice "is to refuse that 'fundamental method' which is God's Incarnation. It was in the plan of God that he would redeem man by becoming one with and using what was in man."[29]

In light of the axial importance of instructional practice, why is it that religious educationists have consistently neglected both to do empirical research on and to design instructional practice? As of this writing André Godin's words in 1962 still hold true: "Not a single study has been published as a dissertation at the master's or doctoral level which has taken for its object the evaluation of the pedagogical effectiveness of a method of religious instruction ... and has demonstrated (from the point of view of religious results among those taught) the superiority of this method over another."[30] If empirical research on an output variable such as effectiveness of religious instruction is so grossly neglected, what may be said of less manifest (but crucially important) aspects of religious instruction such as the very pedagogical dynamic itself? Indeed the monumental 1971 comprehensive handbook *Research on Religious Development*,[31] which reviews virtually all the available empirical research on the topic, is not even able to index a single entry on the teaching of religion, so sparse is the research. As Godin himself observes, religious educationists and curriculum builders "discuss with intelligence and depth the theological pertinence of a religious pedagogy, all without any reference at all to a demonstrated effectiveness of a particular instruction or a specific form of teaching or pedagogical method on the religious level. If a new [curricular or teachers'] manual appears on the market, the teachers who are supposed to use it content themselves most of the time with expressions of satisfaction (sometimes equivocal)."[32] Curriculum programs and religion series produced by Catholics seem to be virtually devoid of the necessary empirical support on the alleged educational outcomes which these materials are supposed to produce.[33] By virtue of both his worldview and the operating principles of his discipline, the religious educator who believes religious instruction is a mode of theology is typically unconcerned with empirical verification of instructional practice, or in fact with instructional practice itself. To a social-science-oriented religious educator, however, instructional practice and the empirical verification of all its phases are of central concern.

One important practical and immediate benefit deriving from a taxonomy of the instructional act such as the one I propose is the highlighting of the fact that each level of the teaching dynamic is rooted in the one next highest on the taxonomic scale. By means of the taxonomy, the religion teacher can radicate his technique in method or strategy, thereby developing a technique which will be effective in his here-and-now lesson. In this way he will heighten the level and degree of his practicality without becoming a cookbook teacher. Utilization of the taxonomy reduces the undue specificity which results from exclusive concentration on technique or step alone, while at the same time making more applicable the very strengths inherent in specificity itself.

To be optimally fruitful and effective an instructional practice must in one sense be an instance of a wider pedagogical law. For example, there is a law which states that instructional behavior which is reinforcing tends to enhance learning. Practice enfleshes this law in such a manner as is determined by the kind of learning to be facilitated. Thus the law is generative of all sorts of specific steps and techniques. To the extent that a practice is a concrete extension of a law, to that extent is it effective. Conversely, the specific instructional circumstance plus the specific behavioral outcome to be facilitated indicate the nature and kind of technique which is appropriate in a given teaching situation. A pedagogical practice, therefore, grows out of the combination of a pedagogical law and a particular pedagogical situation. Both pedagogical law and pedagogical practice have their roots in general overall pedagogical theory. It is in this sense that theory is the most practical thing in religious instruction.[34] It is constant nourishment in the soil of theory which is the death of any kind of Mr. Fix-Itism.

LEARNING THEORY AND TEACHING THEORY

NORFOLK: "You lay traps for me."
MORE: "No, I show you the times."
—Robert Bolt[1]

The Nature and Usefulness of Theory

In the preceding chapter I suggested that pedagogical steps, techniques, methods, and so on can be rendered optimally fruitful by rooting these in an overarching theory. This is a cardinal point, for on it hinges much of the success or failure of the teaching of religion.

A theory is a set of interrelated facts and laws which present a systematic view of phenomena by specifying relations among variables in order to explain and predict the phenomena.[2] Theory is eminently practical precisely because it specifies the relationships which exist among variables. By indicating these relationships, theory has a threefold usefulness: (1) it explains how and why seemingly disparate and unconnected facts are related or integrated; (2) it permits inferences to be drawn about phenomena which cannot be observed directly; (3) it enables predictions of phenomena. One can grasp immediately from this analysis of the function of theory how essential and practical theory is for the workaday religion teacher in his here-and-now lesson. A theory of learning, for example, enables the teacher to take what appear to be isolated bits of the learner's behavior and place them into an intelligible pattern which more adequately describes the way in which the learner as a total person operates. Such a global explanatory system also makes it possible for him to make inferences about the way the learner behaves when he is outside of class and hence not being observed by the teacher. Because of all this, theory enables the religion teacher to predict that one pedagogical practice rather than another will be effective in achieving a desired learning outcome.

The significance of theory, therefore, lies primarily in its fruitfulness, not in its validity.[3] Thus by its essence a theory is practical. It generates new practices, new explanations, new discoveries. Small wonder, then, why the eminently practical Lenin could make one of his most seminal and celebrated statements: "Without a revolutionary theory there can be no revolutionary movement."[4]

A theory is a systematic way of looking at the teaching-learning dynamic in order to organize what is known about it in a way which will furnish practical guidelines to the religion teacher's behavior, clues to the learner's behavior, and directions for valid evaluation of instructional outcomes. Most religion teachers seem to hold implicit rather than explicit theories about the nature of human personality, learner behavior, and instructional practice. Nonetheless, the instructional decisions which the teacher makes throughout the religion lesson are strongly influenced by the theory he holds on human personality, learner behavior, and instructional practice. His decision in a given situation on whether to give praise or reproof, to use a logical or psychological process, to employ a transmission strategy or a structured learning situation strategy, to use teacher-student planning, or to lecture or role-play—all these practical decisions will represent a conscious or unconscious enfleshment of a theory in the here-and-now situation.

The effective religion teacher interprets by means of theoretical knowledge the events which occur in the teaching-learning situation. It should be emphasized that the teacher's interpretation of what happens is important because he responds to the meaning of what he observes rather than to the happening itself. His interpretation of the events which occur in the lesson results from a combination of the theory of instruction to which he consciously or unconsciously subscribes, and his own practical experience which refines and sharpens this aspect of the theory. B. Othanel Smith contends that "teachers fail because they have not been trained calmly to analyze new [instructional] situations against a firm background of relevant theory. Typically, they base their interpretations of behavior on intuition or common sense."[5] In other words, one major cause of the religion teacher's failure is the lack of theoretical equipment by which to understand at the deeper levels what is really taking place in the religion lesson.

To teach is to predict. A teacher elects to employ pedagogical technique X rather than pedagogical technique Y because he predicts that X will be more effective than Y in producing a desired outcome in the learner.[6] Therefore, at bottom the teacher is an hypothesis maker. He hypothesizes that technique X is more predictive of desired learner outcomes than is technique Y. Now it is instructional theory which provides the base and the ground for generating and verifying hypotheses. From a theory can be developed many alternative hypotheses of effective methods and techniques, the implementation of which can be verified or rejected because of their effectiveness or ineffectiveness in the religion lesson.

A sound theoretical base can suggest strategies, methods, techniques, and steps which will prove more effective than those the religion teacher is presently using. Very practically it guides instructional practice so that sheer trial and error is reduced. So much of religious education literature abounds in the recounting by all kinds of religion teachers of methods and techniques they have found useful. But unless these methods and techniques are radicated in basic theory, they remain a welter of jumbled data of little or no use except to the individual teachers who proposed them in the first place. A theory not only enables the religion teacher to discover and explain the relevance of his strategies and techniques, but to invent new ones.[7] A theory generates pedagogical invention because it provides the overarching framework (the Scholastic "universal") which of its very nature breeds new, yet connected, pedagogical inventions. Further, even when teachers do stumble accidentally on useful new pedagogical methods or techniques, they can launch new hypothesis-oriented instructional practices which in the end will significantly enhance the effectiveness of their own teaching.

Training programs for religion teachers, consequently, must include both theory and practice. Without a grounding in and permeation by theory, instructional practices become an assortment of isolated tools in a toolbox. Tools in a carpenter's toolbox are useless unless the person using them is aware of the basic theories of physics and mechanics, and utilizes them within the structures of these theories. So it is with the pedagogical toolbox. Paolo Freire draws our attention to the fact that practice needs theory to illuminate it.[8] Indeed in the ultimate sense practice requires theory to make it really work now and especially over the long term. Many theologically-oriented religious educationists, having little or no acquaintance with the growth of theoretical knowledge in pedagogy, are prone to reduce the instructional aspect of the training of religion teachers to the development of a few teaching methods and techniques.[9] Yet the unhappy fact is that the teacher who is inadequately grounded in theory will typically interpret events that occur in the lesson in terms of common sense concepts which have come from the experience of his culture and are permeated with outmoded ideas about human behavior.

Theory makes a great deal of difference as to the nature and kind of practice. A review by Buford Stefflre and Kenneth Matheny of the pertinent empirical research on the counseling encounter indicates that the counselor's theoretical orientation does make a difference in his practice of counseling.[10] In terms of religious instruction, it makes a great deal of difference in the actual ongoing situation whether the teacher's theoretical framework is one of theological science or of social science. For example, a teacher will teach a lesson quite differently if he views teaching as simply opening the pedagogical windows to let the Spirit blow where he wills (John 3:8), or, on the other hand, as purposeful behavior in which the teacher and other environmental variables exert predictable influences on the learner. A parent operating out of a Christian Science framework will suggest very different practices for a boy suffering from appendicitis than will a surgeon operating out of a natural science theory. An individual who views spiritual direction as a form of theological work will engage in far different kinds of practices than a person who considers spiritual direction as religious counseling and hence a mode of psychology. One who classifies church finances as a branch of theology will use quite different practices than will someone for whom they are a form of business administration.[11] I believe that instructional behaviors deriving from a social-science approach rather than from a theological approach represent the major hope and opportunity for a bright future for religious instruction. To be sure, the adoption of an instructional theory deriving from a social-science approach requires first a change in worldview. But I suspect that as effective religion teachers examine deeply their own pedagogical behaviors, they will find that they are working out of a social-science theory rather than out of a theological theory. For those teachers who pursue this discovery to its logical and existential conclusion, the adoption of a social-science approach is close at hand.

A theory does not specify which pedagogical steps or techniques are to be employed in a given teaching-learning situation. If it did, it would no longer be a theory. But this does not mean that a theory is useless; quite the opposite. A theory would be of no value if it did supply a specific practice for a specific circumstance. A physician uses a theoretical framework in diagnosing a disease, but he cannot prescribe a specific treatment directly from this theory. Intermediate stages of specificity exist between theory and step. It is precisely here that the taxonomy of instructional behaviors which I formulated in Chapter 4 comes into full play. This taxonomy fills in each major intermediate stage between the general approach and the specific step thereby helping to insure that the particularized practice incorporates as fully as possible the richness inherent in the theory which gives rise to the approach. Further, the taxonomy enables the instructional designer and curriculum builder to provide the teacher with a hierarchical set of pedagogical behaviors which will maximize the effectiveness of his lesson. Thus the taxonomy with its carefully-ordered stages helps bridge the here-and-now gap between theory and practice. It makes theory practical and practice theoretical, mediating the riches of every stage of the instructional repertoire.[12]

To teach religion is to facilitate religious learning. Therefore a theory of learning is highly relevant to, and indeed necessary for the exercise of effective educational practice.

THEORIES OF LEARNING

Theological and Social-Science Theories of Learning

Theories of learning have historically served as a major implicit or explicit source from which religion teachers have drawn their own instructional behaviors. Since the overwhelming majority of Protestant and Catholic religion teachers consciously embed their instructional behavior in the theological approach rather than in the social-science approach, the theories of learning out of which they operate are perforce theological in nature. Hence when Randolph Crump Miller states that "the existing structure of religious education needs only to have a satisfactory theology inserted beneath it and it will be securely founded"[13] he is articulating what most religion teachers take as the underlying principle of religious education. Every aspect of religious education, including the learning theory out of which it flows, is based on theology, and in many ways is theological in nature. The result of all this is a so-called

"Christian learning theory." Since the product content of religious education is supposedly different and unique with respect to all other areas of human learning,[14] then the learning theory on which such an education is grounded must also be unique. And unique it is. In its fundamental form this learning theory usually states that it is God who is the basic and essential teacher. The way in which the learner learns, therefore, is not for the teacher to decide or to plan for; rather it is for God to take care of in his own ineffable, mysterious, and deeply noncommunicative way. The teacher simply opens the door. Advocates of the theologically-oriented learning theory historically have proposed one or other person of the Trinity as the teacher. In recent years this role has been awarded to the Holy Spirit.[15] With the Jesus Christ Superstar movement of the 1970's, Jesus might well make a comeback as the "Master Teacher" (as he used to be called before the Holy Spirit movement). To be sure, the Holy-Spirit-as-principal-teacher movement in the twentieth century was given enormous prestige because Karl Barth supported it.[16] Religious education is, as Wayne Rood argues, "siding with God" rather than teaching product content to learners or helping them to modify their behavior along religious lines.[17]

There are many serious problems with a theologically-based learning theory. It is fuzzy and vague. It gives very little if any practical help to the teacher. Nor does it really assist us in understanding why a learner behaves in a particular way at a particular moment. But most serious of all is the fact that it is a learning theory based on prior theological positions rather than on human behavior. Consequently, as William Williamson suggests, a theologically-based learning theory is unsupportable, impractical, and indeed useless.[18]

A theory of learning grounded in learning itself is as helpful to teachers as it is obvious. It is parsimonious in that it dispenses with the *deus ex machina* of the theologically-oriented learning theory. Because it is derived from the facts of human behavior and the laws governing it, a social-science oriented learning theory is eminently beneficial to the religion teacher working with his here-and-now learners. What I am emphasizing is that learning theory is important to the religion teacher because it will assist him a great deal in enhancing the effectiveness of his own teaching. Indeed there is no teacher alive who does not radicate his instructional behaviors in some theory of learning. Every aspect of one's teaching is colored and suffused by an underlying theory of learning. Norman Wallen

and Robert Travers sadly observe that theories of learning underlying a teacher's instructional behaviors typically are based on a
philosophical-theological approach or on the self-gratification needs
of the teacher.[19] For his teaching to be effective, the religion
teacher needs to utilize a learning theory which is constructed on a
scientific, empirically-verified knowledge of the dynamics of learning.

Before briefly discussing learning theory and its relevance to the
teaching of religion, I should like first to point out that learning
itself is a hypothetical construct.[20] By this I mean that learning is a
reality which is presumed to exist because it is inferred as a
generalization from specific changes in an individual's behavior.
Performance and learning, then, are distinct. Performance is an
observable measurable response to some antecedent behavior or
stimulus. Learning, on the other hand, is a generalization or
hypothetical construct indicating that a performance or series of
performances has occurred. We cannot observe learning directly; we
can only observe performance. For the teacher the importance of
the construct "learning" in relation to performance is that it answers
the question: Of what worth is performance? Conversely, the
construct "learning" is assumed to be one of the major determinants
of performance. Therefore, if the religion teacher wishes to enhance
the learner's performance in a given cognitive, affective, or lifestyle
sphere, he must first know the conditions, the factors, and the
contingencies which elicit the desired performance. The function of
teaching is to most effectively elicit a desired performance. To
accomplish this task efficiently, the teacher must know the conditions, the factors, and the contingencies which comprise learning.
And an understanding of learning is impossible apart from an
understanding of learning theory.

Learning Theory Helps the Teacher

Learning theory can assist the religion teacher in myriad practical
ways. At this juncture I shall content myself with identifying only
two of these ways. First, learning theory can provide much-needed
information as to the nature of each performance act and of the
conditions affecting this act. Every single performance act contains
in microcosm the whole of the problem of learning. It brings into
play the question of which paradigm or paradigms of learning may
be in operation at that particular moment. Any and all of the
variables which might conceivably affect a particular performance

are potentially in the ascendancy. Learning theory suggests to the teacher which variables are truly the ascendant ones at a given moment. Second, learning theory guides the religion teacher in selecting those variables which will aid him in structuring that kind of learning situation which will most effectively promote the desired performance. In other words, learning theory helps the religion teacher to formulate an effective educational practice and to interrelate the component parts of this practice so as to produce a desired performance act or learning outcome.

A knowledge of the discrete variables affecting learning and the placement of them together in a series of identifiable instructional behaviors provide one indication that a social-science-based learning theory is superior to a theologically-based one. A theologically-based learning theory suggests that variables like grace, divine-human encounter, and openness to a full response to divine initiative are central to religious learning. But since the religion teacher is powerless to arrange such variables into a set of instructional behaviors, he is left directionless by a theologically-based learning theory. A learning theory based on social science, on the other hand, suggests that the various classes of performance behaviors which learners display differ in their stimulus and response characteristics and indeed in the ways in which stimulus and response are related or structured. Depending on these characteristics, the conditions promoting different categories of performance behavior will vary.[21] Identification of the characteristics of discrete performance behaviors and also of the conditions most promotive of these behaviors in learners furnish the religion teacher with an armamentarium for educational practice. Knowing that certain factors such as praise, fatigue, environmental press, anxiety, and socioeconomic status tend to elicit certain kinds of performance acts under certain conditions enables the teacher to devise and employ those instructional behaviors designed to bring about the desired learning outcomes. In no way does this deny the effects of God's grace or the divine-human encounter. As a matter of fact, these two variables are always present—but always present according to the mode of terrestrial reality, in this case, the realities of praise, fatigue, environmental press, and so forth. Grace and divine-human encounter are not things laminated on to terrestrial reality, rather they suffuse terrestrial reality according to the mode of that reality. What this means in terms of the teaching of religion is that God's grace and the divine-human encounter tend to be rendered most operative in terrestrial situations which are most true to themselves. If teaching at its truest and most authentic level is to optimally promote learning, then in and through the conditions which constitute effective teaching will God's grace most fully flow and take effect. It is a social-science-based learning theory, drawing from data on how learning actually takes place and how it can be most effectively promoted, which helps teaching to be true to itself. I suspect that a theologically-based learning theory is constructed on a defective theology of the nature and relationship of the natural and supernatural.[22] One can only speculate whether there are not some strands of Occasionalism, Docetism, Manichaeism, and Jansenism subtly interwoven into a *learning* theory which attempts to be theologically based.

Limitations of Learning Theory for Instructional Practice

Until the late 1950's and early 1960's, it was assumed by virtually all educationists that teaching consisted simply in the teacher's application of learning theory to individual learning situations. (It should be noted that religious educationists rarely if ever have concerned themselves with this issue.) Even well into the 1970's this notion has remained the prevalent one. Thus A. Morrison and D. McIntyre write: "Since all teaching is concerned with changing the behavior of pupils in one way or another, one may view the professional expertise of a teacher as consisting largely of his skill as a type of applied psychologist."[23] Educational psychologists strongly advocate this position. David Ausubel comments in a similar vein that the basic principles of teaching are nothing more than special derivatives of educational learning theory. He likens such principles to products of an engineering type of practice based on whatever modifications of learning theory are required by either practical difficulties or by additional new variables involved in the teaching task.[24]

I take sharp issue with those who maintain that teaching is merely a form of applied learning theory. To be sure, the nature of teaching is heavily dependent on learning, since to teach is to cause learning in another person. Nonetheless, teaching has its own set of unique behaviors. Teaching and learning are reciprocal activities with reciprocal task descriptions. These reciprocal activities are, of course, highly related and in the actual teaching-learning dynamic exert a mutual influence on one another. Notwithstanding, we employ the phrase "teaching-learning act" to simultaneously indicate the separateness, the relatedness, and the reciprocity of the two functions. The instructional experience constitutes a single social activity which includes both teaching and learning components.[25] As I remark elsewhere, teaching is rooted in learning, and learning is rooted in teaching; the two work extremely closely in the ongoing instructional act.[26]

Many are the reasons why there must be a theory of teaching independent of a theory of learning. Teaching is not the same as being taught. Taking a watch apart is not the same as putting it together.[27] Theories of learning deal with the way an individual learns; theories of teaching deal with the ways in which one person influences another to learn. A teacher must know how to shape the variables which facilitate learning; such knowledge and skill cannot be derived automatically from knowledge about the learning process. "Farmers need to know more than how plants grow. Mechanics need to know more than how a machine works. Physicians need to know more than how the body functions. Teachers need to know more than how an individual learns."[28]

Theories of teaching center around three major complementary constituents: (1) a knowledge of the conditions and the variables most highly correlated with the acquisition of specified learning behaviors; (2) an understanding of the principles involved in most effectively structuring the pedagogical situation so as to bring about the specified learning behaviors; (3) concrete skills in structuring this kind of pedagogical situation.

A theory of instruction, in short, is concerned with how best to facilitate what one is learning rather than merely describing it. Some of learning theory is of little or no relevance to the teacher; however, most if not all of teaching theory is of relevance to him. When I say this, I am in no way implying that theories of learning are not pertinent to theories of teaching. As I stated above, a theory of teaching has three necessary constituents, one of which is learning theory. But a theory of teaching is not just learning theory standing on its head. Rather, a teaching theory includes elements drastically different in kind and genre from a learning theory, for example, facilitational skills. In Nathaniel Gage's words, "Although theories of learning are necessary to the understanding, prediction, and control of the learning process, they cannot suffice in education. The goal of education—to engender learning in the most desirable and efficient ways possible—would seem to require an additional theory of teaching."[29]

Scholars—frequently educational psychologists—who contend that teaching is merely an application or enfleshment of theories of learning attempt to rebut argumentation for a separate theory of teaching by an appeal to the pure-science-applied-technology model. Thus Ernest Hilgard remarks that "the relationship between learning theory and educational practice is that between any pure science and its technological applications."[30] Hilgard takes pains to note that in any process of application there is more involved than the theory from which this application allegedly derives. "Thus, one does not move directly from astronomy to navigation without concern for tides, prevailing winds, and the location of lighthouses; investigations of heredity in fruitflies do not lead immediately to applications in animal husbandry without concern for the resistance of cattle to disease, the desirable characteristics determined by the market, and many other considerations."[31] It would seem that Hilgard is a bit too simplistic in his analysis of the relation between the process of application and the theory from which it flows. At bottom, the problem lies in what Robert Glaser succinctly states as "the relationships among basic science, applied science, and the development and the process that leads to the methods and technology which can be used by the practicing educator."[32] It is precisely in terms of the linear relationships among basic theory, applied theory, and technology that the notion of "teaching as applied learning theory" breaks down. To be the truly all-nurturing theory of teaching, pedagogical practice must be a direct and unilinear outgrowth of basic learning theory. If the teaching act contains in itself essential ingredients which flow from another basic theory, then it is safe to say that teaching is derivative from several basic theories. A theory explains and predicts all the phenomena under its scope; phenomena which are explained by more than one theory quite obviously belong to more than one theory, and to receive adequate nourishment they must have their roots sunk deep into those theories which feed them explanation and prediction. If learning theory were the sole basic theoretical source of instructional behavior, then it could supply an all-sufficient explanation of the facilitational process itself. However, learning theory cannot do this, as virtually all the proponents of the notion "teaching as applied learning theory" admit.

Let me use an analogy here. A farmer needs to know how plants grow, how they depend on the soil, the water, and the sunlight. So too does a teacher need to know how children learn, how they depend on motivation and reinforcement. But a farmer also must know how to farm—how to till the soil, to plant the seed, to eliminate harmful weeds and insects, to harvest the crops and get them to market. Likewise a teacher must know how to structure the learning situation, to properly pace his lesson, to make continuous evaluations, to facilitate transfer of learning.[33]

Perhaps another analogy might further clarify the point I am making. In building a laboratory in which high-energy experiments will be conducted, Hector MacDonald, a scientist, requires an insulating material that will withstand a certain electrical voltage. General data on the desired physical and chemical properties are fundamental for supplying the answer to this problem. The skill in installing the material in a way that all the variables are accounted for comprises the technology. The explanation of which chemical and physical properties are necessary constituents of the insulating material in order for it to perform its task adequately is applied theory. In this case applied theory suggests which materials should be selected for the insulating material and which should be rejected. Finally, the question of why do particular materials have the properties they do comprises basic theory. Chemistry theory explains questions such as why one material has more electrical conductivity than another; physics theory explains questions as to the atomic structure and atomic forces present in materials of different conductivity. Hence both the applied theory and the technology involved in the installation of the correct insulating material flow not from one but from two basic theories, chemistry and physics theory.

To return to the analogies Ernest Hilgard uses, navigation does not derive its practice from astronomy theory alone. Meteorology theory plays a vital role as well. Similarly animal husbandry does not derive its practice exclusively from heredity theory; ecology theory is also decisive.

The import of the last few paragraphs is that while instructional practice does indeed derive much of its fruitfulness from learning theory, nonetheless there are other basic theoretical frameworks in which it is radicated. The combination into a new entity of those few basic theories from which instruction derives is a theory of teaching.

TOWARD A THEORY OF TEACHING

Teaching is distinct from learning. Therefore, what are urgently needed are not just theories of learning but also theories of teaching.

Yet in the field of education the development of theories of teaching has been woefully neglected. Volumes have been devoted to theories of learning, but there is scarcely a book devoted to theories of teaching. In the area of Christian religious instruction, a rigorous analysis of the teaching act has been neglected or ignored, probably due to incredibly vague or naive pedagogical "hip-pocket theories" such as "to teach religion is to side with God,"[34] or "religion teaching is first and foremost a work of the Spirit who blows where he wills."

Teaching Theory Helps the Teacher

While both are essential, nonetheless teaching theory is more helpful to the religion teacher than is learning theory. Learning theory of its nature means that the teacher must *infer* what he needs to do pedagogically from what he is told about learners and the learning process. Teaching theory makes explicit how the teacher behaves pedagogically, why he should behave in one way rather than another, and what are the differential effects of various pedagogical behaviors.[35]

A theory of instruction explains the constituent subject matter content of the teaching act. It explains to the teacher why teaching step A is successful and why teaching step B is unsuccessful in a given set of conditions. Further, a theory of instruction enables a teacher to predict when and under what circumstances teaching step A or B or Y will effect the desired learning outcome. The principal advantage of a theory is that it serves as a guide to present and future practice. Without theory educational practice is a blind man; theory is the guide who leads the blind man to the most efficient way to his destination. Sanford Erickson notes in this connection that "a theory of instruction is really a statement about the procedures that enhance the learning process; it provides a rationale for the way a teacher functions as the director of this process."[36] The religion teacher is basically an hypothesis maker in that he hypothesizes that method or technique A will work more successfully than method or technique B in this particular lesson. A theory of instruction helps here because should the teacher's hypothesis be rejected (step A proves to be a disaster), the theory provides the most effective overall structural framework for locating the false propositions underlying the formulation of the original hypothesis.[37] A realistic and scientifically viable theory of teaching gives prominent place to how and under what conditions the pedagogical variables in a given lesson can be so structured as to result in the optimal facilitation of desired learning outcomes.

The kind of instructional practice which the religion teacher employs does indeed make a difference in the resulting kind and type of learning outcome. But this difference has been obscured by the lack of an adequate theory of teaching. A theory of teaching points up conceptual, process, and outcome differences all along the line of pedagogical practice.[38] The lack of a guiding teaching theory in religious instruction has resulted in religion teachers forming their own "hip-pocket theories" selected randomly from a wide variety of sources including the Sunday sermon, the latest book in theology, the way they themselves were taught as young persons, their concept of revelation, "how-to-do-it" tips found in the local religious education newsletter or journal, and their own notion of God. Such a melange of sources boils down to a kind of tasteless religious instruction stew which, when served to a learner, proves not to be filling and often causes pedagogical indigestion. Because they are neither integrated nor scientifically-based, hip-pocket theories of instruction blur the causative connection between a particular educational practice and its result. Certain learning outcomes are desired, but without a guiding scientific theory, it is difficult to select the particular educational practice which will effect these outcomes. A good example of this is the development in the late 1960's of "encounter catechetics" or "happening catechetics." In these instances there was no structuring of the learning situation, and the lesson was allowed to ramble aimlessly along, all in the name of "happening" and "the Spirit blows where he wills." Religion teachers were amazed to find that such lessons resulted not only in inadequate learning of product content but in the acquisition of process content which was quite different from that hoped for by the religion teacher. Further, the teachers using pedagogical practices of this sort were astounded to discover that after a certain number of "encounters" or "happenings," the students objected and began demanding that the teachers teach.

An adequate teaching theory enables the religion teacher to bring his various pedagogical behaviors to a higher level of meaning and significance. Lacking a theory of instruction, the religion teacher has typically been unable to generalize principles of instruction from specific instances of lesson interaction.[39] An example of a failure of this type is a book by John Murphy which takes the form of a diary of what Murphy perceives occurred in the high school religion class which he taught. At the end of the book, Murphy attempts to give broader meaning to the classroom events and to derive from them general principles of instruction. But Murphy fails in his attempt precisely because he has no guiding theory of teaching into which he can insert the various teacher-learner behaviors.[40] In contrast is the work of Louis Smith and William Geoffrey who also kept a log of the events which transpired in the latter's classroom. These men consciously build the events into a kind of teaching theory. The result is a book of significance and practical help to teachers.[41] Generalized principles of teaching are necessary as tentative guiding formulations for future and predictive instructional behavior.

A teaching theory teases out all of the significant pedagogical variables affecting learning and relates them vertically and horizontally to each other. This has many advantages for the religion teacher, not the least of which is that it enables him to see clearly that teaching is a form of behavioral chaining rather than some fuzzy, quasi-mystical event. Isolation of the independent and dependent variables (the cause and effect) in the teaching act assists the religion teacher to attribute a student's learning of a particular outcome to some specific set of independent (causative) variables, rather than to amorphous and supersweeping forces, for example, the Spirit blowing or the enigmatic dynamism of the person-to-person encounter. To be sure, the Spirit does influence everything in the world, but this fact tells the religion teacher nothing *in concreto* about how to teach his lesson.

Functions of a Theory of Teaching

Like all theory a theory of instruction has two major functions. First, it makes the teaching act intelligible vis-à-vis its context within a larger body of systematic and coherent relationships. It formulates general explanations which encompass and link many different teaching-learning behaviors. A theory of instruction enables the religion teacher to understand and to make sense of what happens in the lesson. Second, a theory of instruction provides a means for the teacher to discover which specific set of pedagogical variables interacts in such a way during the lesson that the outcome of this interaction can be accurately forecast. Prediction, of course, flows as a consequence from explanation.

Jerome Bruner has identified two additional functions of a theory of instruction. First, it is prescriptive in that it sets forth rules about the most effective way of producing a desired learning outcome.

Second, it is normative in that it establishes the criteria for successful teaching and states the conditions for meeting them.[42] (Parenthetically I hasten to observe that the normative function of a teaching theory serves as an undergirding for the statement I made earlier in this book, that is, that it is the educational process itself, and not theology, which exerts *the* normative function on religion teaching.) In one sense Bruner's two functions are extensions of or other ways of looking at the functions of explanation and prediction.

Features of a Theory of Teaching

Bruner has further identified four major features of a theory of instruction.[43] First, it suggests which experiences most effectively dispose an individual to learning—learning in general or a particular type of learning. For example, what kinds of relationships with people and things in the environment prior to religion class tend to make the individual willing and able to learn when he enters the religion class? Second, a theory of instruction suggests the manner in which the product and process contents to be learned should be structured so that they can be most readily acquired by the learner. Optimal structuring in this case depends on the nature of the product and process contents themselves. Third, a theory of instruction suggests the most effective sequences in which the product and process contents to be learned are made available to the learner. These sequences suggest when, and to some extent how, the teacher should decide to structure a given pattern of learning situations. Finally, a theory of instruction suggests the nature and pacing of rewards and punishments in the overall teaching-learning dynamic. The more the learner is involved in the learning situation, the more the rewards and punishments become intrinsic to the learning task itself. Rewards and punishments, such as praise and reproof, do produce differential effects in learners.

It should be noted that a theory of instruction can only suggest pedagogical practices in each of the four areas listed in the preceding paragraph. By its very nature a teaching theory cannot specify in detail which particularized pedagogical steps or techniques or methods a teacher should employ in a given instructional situation. What a teaching theory does is to suggest which general kinds of pedagogical practice are likely to be the most effective in certain instances; it remains the work of the teacher to operationalize these suggestions in terms of which specific steps and techniques and methods he will use with a particular group of learners in a particular situation. It is the art of the practitioner which brings theory about practices and specific practices together in order to help learners. A teaching theory generates pedagogical practice; it does not produce this practice automatically. It is the teacher in the concrete instructional act who fashions a set of specific pedagogical behaviors from the major interactive clusters of the overarching instructional theory.

To be valid and viable, a theory of instruction must be based on scientific, empirically-controlled facts and laws of both learning and facilitational behaviors. A valid and viable theory of instruction cannot be founded on untested assumptions or on theological *a priori* statements. A theory of instruction explains and predicts that kind of human behavior called teaching; if it is to do its job, it must perforce be congruent with the facts describing human behavior and the empirical laws governing human behavior.

A Theory of Teaching and Instructional Practice

Once a theory of instruction is developed and put in order, the principles and practices of teaching will flow from it. In turn instructional practice will enrich and expand the theory of instruction so that it will have greater and greater explanation and prediction. This closed-loop feedback system is illustrated in the following diagram:

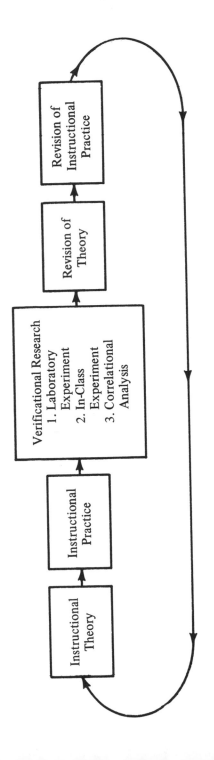

I must emphasize that what I have written in the second half of this chapter by no means denigrates either learning theory itself or its great usefulness to a theory of instruction. What I have been underscoring is that a theory of teaching is not the same as a theory of learning. To be sure, a theory of teaching strongly integrates appropriate and relevant aspects of learning theory. But to utilize learning theory, evenly strongly, is not to be totally dependent upon it. Valid learning theories do offer teachers one feasible point of departure for discovering general laws and methods of effective teaching formulated in terms of both mediating variables and cause-effect relationships. An adequate theory of learning is a necessary but not a sufficient condition for the improvement of instruction.[44] Laws of learning provide one general direction for discovering effective teaching principles; they do not of themselves indicate what these principles are. In summary, then, a theory of teaching suggests how a teacher can teach effectively while a theory of learning suggests how a learner can learn effectively.

Put another way, learning theory is a different kind of theory than teaching theory. Learning theory is a type of event theory while teaching theory is a form of praxiological theory. Event theory deals with occurrences while praxiological theory is concerned with appropriate means or practices to attain what is believed to be desirable or valuable.[45] Only confusion results when praxiological theory is equated with or reduced to event theory.

The Facts of Learning

Both teaching theory and learning theory draw heavily from the *facts of learning*. By facts of learning I mean empirically observed and tested performance phenomena of behavioral change. A fact *eo ipso* is a proven datum and is not tentative. But a theory, however significant and useful it may be, remains a tentative explanation of phenomena; consequently it must be revised when new facts come in. Hence the facts of learning, the hard data, are primary. As such, facts of learning are crucial and axial both to teaching theory and teaching practice. After all, teaching is the facilitation of learning. To deploy his facilitational skills effectively, the teacher must know how the learner does indeed learn. An inquiry into the facts of learning has the further advantage of enabling the religion teacher to understand the real phenomena of learning rather than to utilize untested assumptions derived from folklore, theological *a priori* propositions, or amorphous quasi-mystical sources. It is to a consideration of some facts of learning relevant to religious instruction that I now turn.

SOME KEY FINDINGS ABOUT LEARNING

*"Every one has to do what he can do according to
how it can be truly done."*

—Ernest Hemingway[1]

The Nature of Findings

Looking at statements on religious instruction made over the centuries by ecclesiastical bodies or individual theorists, one gains the impression that one manifesto or pronunciamento has followed another without being primarily rooted in the facts of learning. Perhaps this empirical rootlessness accounts for much of the ineffectiveness and indeed unreality which has characterized so much of religious instruction in the past. Religion is learned according to the way the learner learns and not after the manner of its own existence.[2] The focus of this chapter is to provide a brief overview of some of the more significant research findings about human learning so that the religious educator can root his teaching in essentially proven empirical data about the way learning actually does occur.

For the sake of usefulness, I have decided to present the facts of learning within the broader framework of general findings about learning.[3] These findings represent empirically-supported generalizations drawn from relatively homogeneous clusters of hard data. The advantage of presenting findings rather than simply facts in this book is that findings suggest a wider applicability and hence a higher order of usefulness to the teaching-learning dynamic than is the case with bald facts.

Empirically-verified generalizations about the way people do in fact learn in no way minimizes individual differences. Findings are not inherently automatic or uniformly applicatory; they do not operate at the same time and in the same way in all learners. Rather, these generalizations function with differing force at different times, depending on the nature and circumstances of the concrete learning situation. Human behavior is far more viable, and therefore less predictable, than that of other species. Nonetheless, these findings, properly understood, do indicate the way learning typically does take place.

In reviewing some major findings concerning human learning, I should like to underscore a point I make in the previous chapter: learning is at bottom a hypothetical construct. Learning, therefore, is an inference drawn from observing specific behavioral changes in the individual. Ernest Hilgard remarks in this connection that "learning must always remain an inference from performance, and only confusion results if performance and learning are identified."[4] The benchmark, then, is performance or behavior; if the individual does not exhibit a specified performance, if he does not behave in a particular way, then one can infer that the person has not learned.[5] Learning, therefore, may be defined as that form of self-activity through which behavior is changed by means of experience.[6]

It might be argued that there is some learning which is not visible or which does not otherwise manifest itself in performance. This might well be true. However, until an individual performs a particular behavior how can one say that he has learned? It cannot be validly assumed, much less demonstrated, that learning has taken place if the individual has not evinced this learning in some observable fashion. To say that learning is both nonvisible and visible is to make room for every sort of charlatan and fakir who claims he has truly acquired some particular learning outcome.

Effective religion teaching is that which focuses on performance and behavioral change rather than on learning as such. In the final analysis, performance is all the religion teacher has to work with.

Religious Learning and Secular Learning

The findings on learning and behavioral change which I discuss in this chapter are of extreme importance to the religious educator since they suggest how an individual learns religion. A person learns religion basically the same way as he learns so-called "secular" reality. The learner is an integer; he does not possess one complete set of faculties by which he learns "natural" phenomena, and a second complete set by which he learns religious phenomena. I know of no corpus of empirical data which indicates that the learning of religion differs essentially from the learning of any other kind of reality. Indeed, Ronald Goldman's research investigation concluded that "religious thinking employs the same modes and methods as thinking applied to other fields."[7] One cannot help but wonder why so many religious educationists and educators erroneously assume that religious learning is basically different from "secular" learning. In any event, such an attitude has prevented religious instruction from achieving optimal effectiveness.

Applicability to Religious Instruction

The findings on learning presented in this chapter provide data which religion teachers and curriculum builders can use in designing instructional environments and in enhancing the teaching-learning process. Religious instruction is in constant need of curricula and teaching methods which make maximum possible use of the wide range of the findings on learning. When this is done, remark Norman Wallen and Robert Travers, there may be some hope of building a curriculum and a set of educational practices which are definitely and markedly superior to others which have not been thus systematically designed.[8] As I observe elsewhere, "the teacher [and curriculum builder] must also understand the complex factors affecting the student during the actual learning process. These ongoing factors constitute the dynamics of learning and help to explain the manifold modifications and differences in learning which are constantly taking place at every moment in every learner or group of learners."[9]

There are many areas of learning which are relevant for religious educators. For reasons of space, I have limited myself to ten major areas on which to focus attention. There will be some inevitable overlapping in the data supporting the various findings. This is to be expected since man is an integer. Learning processes have commonality as well as specificity.

Finding #1: Early family life and background constitute the most powerful, the most pervasive, and the most perduring variable affecting virtually all phases of an individual's learning.

Early childhood experiences in the home exert an enormous and in many ways an indelible influence on the individual's entire life. A review of the pertinent empirical research by Jeffrey Keefe concludes that by the age of six (and possibly even earlier) the child's basic personality structure is already formed; subsequent experiences which the individual undergoes merely amplify, reinforce, or expand these basic personality configurations.[10] This also holds true for one's deeper attitudes and values. Bernard Berelson and Gary Steiner summarize the research data on this point by observing that attitudes and beliefs (including religious beliefs) are "inherited from one's parents; people learn them early and the learning persists into adulthood."[11] Psychologists of the Freudian and neo-Freudian school are among the first to assert that by the age of four the child's basic personality structure is already formed. By this they mean that prior to the age of four the deepest impressions have been recorded; thereafter reimpressions or surface impressions are registered. One of the classic Freudian proofs derives from the act of attempting to recall one's earliest memories. Rarely can one's recollection go back farther than the age of three-and-a-half or four.[12] Clinical research by John Bowlby,[13] René Spitz,[14] and Bruno Bettleheim[15] provides strong empirical evidence that one's basic evaluation of self as well as one's basic outlook toward others have their prefiguration in infant experience. A review of the research by Bernard Berelson and Gary Steiner concludes that "the weaker an infant's or child's identification with his parents, the less developed and less strong his personality or ego is apt to be."[16] Data from nearly 1,000 longitudinal studies have been examined and interpreted by Benjamin Bloom who indicates that the most rapid growth of intelligence takes place before the age of four; what the child learns in these years largely determines his future cognitive achievement.[17]

The research is reasonably clearcut in its conclusion that the average level of a person's moral conduct is the same in early childhood as in later life. This suggests that the basic forces of moral character develop very early.[18] Lawrence Kohlberg's review of the research indicates that "experimental measures of resistance to cheating or stealing do not increase significantly from nursery school to high school."[19]

An individual's emotional life is likewise formed basically within the context of his family environment. Ira Gordon's survey of the research has shown that fear and anxiety are learned behaviors stemming from interaction with one's parents, particularly in infancy and in early childhood.[20] An investigation by Robert Sears and his associates concludes that the more the child feels rejected by his parents, the more dependent a personality he is likely to be and become.[21] Empirical research investigations have also shown that prolonged separation of the child from its mother and from a secure home environment (such as with hospitalized or institutionalized children), especially up to about age 30 months, but also from ages 3-5 years, appears to lead to serious emotional and mental retardation.[22]

Severe emotional disturbance, aggression, antisocial behavior, and crime tend to result from the defective texture of the family milieu in which the individual grows up. Reviewing the pertinent empirical research, Robert Peck and Herbert Richek conclude that "in emotionally disturbed adolescents, it seems rather definitively established that unhealthy parent-child relations have been antecedent to the emotional illness."[23] The research suggests that "severity of socialization (i.e., highly rigid or highly critical practices by parents) seems to make for generalized anxiety in later life."[24] An investigation by Wesley Becker disclosed that children who are unable to control their aggression tend to come from families in which both parents are maladjusted emotionally, quarrel with each other, and deal arbitrarily with the child.[25] Kurt Lewin and his associates conducted an investigation which revealed among other things that the more rigid the family structure, the more difficult it is for an individual to move from childhood to adulthood.[26] Boyd McCandless concludes from his review of the research that overcontrolling parents who employ predominantly nonlove-oriented control and socialization techniques are the most likely to bring up children who are rigid and authoritarian.[27]

Physical and psychological punishment administered by parents to their children has a significant impact on the child's present and future personality structure. An investigation by Robert Sears and his associates has discovered that the more severely boys were punished for aggression by their mothers, the more aggressive they were in preschool environments.[28] An investigation by Leonard Eron and his associates indicated that children reared in homes exercising considerable physical discipline are more likely to be aggressive within the school setting; although, interestingly, such children may or may not exhibit aggressive behavior at home.[29] Donald MacKinnon's study of one group of college students who cheated on examinations and another group which did not cheat found that the parents of the dishonest ones were more likely to employ physical discipline than the parents of the honest students; conversely, the parents of the honest students were more likely to use rational, affective, or psychological devices to induce conformity among their offspring than did the parents of the cheaters.[30] It would also appear that academic underachievers tend to come more from punitive home environments than do normal achievers or overachievers.[31] Benjamin Fine concludes from his review of the research that the most important single factor in producing juvenile delinquents is the home milieu; ("almost 90 percent of those traits which characterize a delinquent appear before he is eleven".[32] Conversely, the research shows that an emotionally satisfying family life tends to facilitate the development of law-abiding self-concepts in the child.[33] A study by Alfred Baldwin and associates of the effect of parental attitudes on the behavior of offspring revealed that the parental attitude cluster "acceptant-democratic" seems to facilitate psychological growth the most.[34] In short, the research tends to agree with the data from the Peck-Havighurst investigation: the personality and character of an individual prove to be almost a direct reproduction of the way in which his parents have treated him.[35]

The socioeconomic status of the family in which the child is reared also exerts a powerful influence on the offspring's personality configuration. A study by John Coster disclosed that the high school student from a low-income family is less likely than other students to enjoy the family's strong interest and support, something which tends to be productive of academic and indeed of economic achievement.[36] Robert Havighurst and Fay Breese concluded from their investigation that the level of the family's socioeconomic status affects the offspring's basic use of his intelligence as well as the patterns of his overt behavior.[37] A study by Eleanor Maccoby and her associates found that upper-middle-class and upper-class parents tend to be more permissive in child-rearing, while lower-middle-class parents are prone to favor authoritarian or prescriptive regimens.[38] It will be recalled that authoritarian home practices lead to deleterious effects on the child. Summing up the research, Jo Ann Stiles and Boyd McCandless observe that, generally speaking, the child growing up in a lower-class family has not learned to value the approval of adults since he has so seldom experienced it at home.[39]

Significance of finding #1 for the teaching of religion. If finding #1 suggests anything, it is that the religion teacher's role must be regarded as basically a reinforcer and amplifier of the family's work in the religious sector. Religion teaching by nonparental agencies consists in enhancing the individual's deeper attitudes and values, in refining them, and giving them new meanings and dimensionalities. In large measure the religion teacher can do no more than this.

Finding #1 underscores the importance of the family as the primary agent of religious instruction. Parents are not to be involved as satellites to the work of the religion teacher; rather it is the work of the religion teacher which must be dependent on and ancillary to the work of the family.[40]

If primary responsibility for religious instruction cannot be delegated to religion teachers, neither can it be assigned to the church. It is the family, not the church, which exerts the principal and deepest influence. In this connection the conclusion of the empirical investigation conducted by Robert Peck and Robert Havighurst bears striking similarity to that of other related studies: no religious denomination stands out as being closely associated with high or low morality, but children who ranked high in morality tended to come from families which are actively religious.[41]

Nor can primary emphasis for teaching religion be palmed off on the church-sponsored school, whether this be an all-day school or a part-time institution such as CCD or Sunday School. In their well-executed study of Catholic elementary and secondary schools, Andrew Greeley and Peter Rossi noted, among other things, that every major religious effect of these schools could be explained by family variables.[42] Ronald Johnstone came to a similar conclusion in his comprehensive investigation of Lutheran elementary and secondary schools.[43] Donald Erickson found the same thing in his study of a selected group of Fundamentalist day schools.[44]

It would appear that even the learning and active retention of religious rituals are etched more deeply in the family context than in church settings, school milieux, and so forth. Thus Sarah Frances Anders concluded from her investigation that family patterns of religious rituals (for example, saying grace at meals) tend to persist throughout the individual's life. Once established in the home, they tend to be long retained even if church participation later declines.[45] Further, religious practices tend to be passed on within families from one generation to the next. Thus in a midwest survey, David Moberg discovered that there were no significant differences between the family religious practices of 211 contemporary families and those of their parents' childhood homes.[46] These and other parallel data suggest that nonparental religion teaching should be done within the broader context of reinforcing, expanding, and if necessary, deflecting the manifest or latent religious education given in the home. But even when deflection is required, the research suggests that this can be typically done only within the basic parameters of the deeper attitude and value structure developed in early childhood in the home. Apropos of this, it is well to recall the conclusion of the carefully-conducted inquiry into character development made by Robert Peck and Robert Havighurst. Their data support the basic finding that moral character is formed in the family milieu; the peer group, the school, and the church serve to reinforce and expand rather than to establish the individual's moral value system.[47] In short, the more that religion teaching is radicated in direct or indirect family milieux, the more effective it is likely to be. Further the data quite possibly suggest that in the area of religious education of children and youth, education by parents might well prove more effective than that offered by the usual institutionally-centered religious education programs which operate without close parent involvement.

Finding #2: The particular environment in which an individual develops, matures, and interacts exerts an extraordinarily powerful influence on his learning.

Scientific analysis reveals unsuspected causative if not at times controlling relations between an individual's behavior and his environment.[48] Indeed the extent of an individual's learning is typically dependent on the power of his environment. In Paul Maves's words, "the power of the environment is a function of its ability to offer an abundance of resources or to withhold them, to deprive, provide, or inundate."[49]

By environment is meant that aggregate of external physical, biological, cultural, and social conditions or stimuli to which an individual consciously or unconsciously responds. The seven environments of especial interest to religious educators are the overall cultural environment, the local environment, the school or institutional environment, the classroom or learning group environment, the peer group environment, the home environment, and the immediate physical environment. No one environment acts in isolation; rather, each environment interpenetrates the others in the actual learning process.

The overall cultural environment in which an individual lives exerts a powerful influence on his behavior. Adolescence, for example, is "a culture-bound process of maturing; it must be viewed as a cultural phenomenon whose meaning is unique to the special culture in which it occurs."[50] In and of itself adolescence is not a period of storm and stress, as comparative studies of other cultures bear out.[51] A review of the pertinent research by Robert Peck and

Herbert Richek indicates that adolescence is probably no more or less stressful than other periods of life for people in similar cultures.[52]

The local environment and the subculture in which an individual lives play a significant role in shaping his behavior. Benjamin Bloom's carefully conducted investigation revealed that the child's environment was one of the principal determinants of his school achievement.[53] Studies show that there is more political tolerance and less religious observance (especially in the form of church attendance by men) in cities as compared with rural areas.[54] An investigation by Hortense Doyle of Canadian, English, and American teenage pupils concluded that the students' self-concepts were significantly influenced by the subculture in which they lived.[55]

The school or other kind of educational institution in which an individual is situated exerts a powerful impact on his behavior. Schools and other educational institutions which supply rich cognitive, affective, and lifestyle environments provide different stimuli and exert a different influence from environments not so characterized. One review of the pertinent research goes so far as to suggest that in the case of maladjusted pupils, the school is often a major factor in contributing to the maladjustment.[56] James Coleman's investigations found that the school environment can stimulate or stifle student effectiveness and development.[57] Irvin Lehman discovered that in a large midwestern state university the incoming freshmen from parochial high schools (mostly Catholic) tended to be more authoritarian and dogmatic in their thinking than those from public or independent private schools. (However, this characteristic might also stem from the home environment of the student).[58] A study by Alice Wessel and Rita Flaherty disclosed that after one year in a Catholic women's college, the girls were significantly less feminine than when they entered, as measured by a standard masculinity-femininity index.[59] In an important longitudinal study, Marie Francis Kenoyer compared two groups of matched Catholic girls, one of which had entered the religious life (Group A) and the other which had remained in the lay life (Group B). After a number of years had elapsed, Kenoyer compared the two groups of females. The comparison showed that the females in religious life perceived themselves as more submissive, more oriented to self-abasement, more in need of being dominated, and more shy than the originally matched group of lay women. Kenoyer concluded that this difference in personality traits was due to the effect of the convent environment on group A.[60] Robert Brooks's study of the influence of seminary environments on candidates for the Catholic priesthood found that these milieux tended to heighten the candidates' submissiveness, indecisiveness, docility, and conformity.[61] (Parenthetically, it is interesting to note that in an effort to develop a new and more relevant priest and nun, many seminary and convent officials have begun to drastically change the nature and thrust of seminary and convent environments.)

The composition and texture of the classroom or learning group environment exerts a significant impact on learning. The size of the learning group, for example, has been shown to affect both the quantity and quality of interaction among group members.[62] Edwin Thomas and Clifford Fink conclude from their review of the research that group size is related to (1) group and individual performance, (2) distribution of participation, (3) the nature of the members' interaction, (4) group organization, and (5) satisfaction of members with the group experience.[63] Robert Bales and his associates report that as group size increases, there emerges less sensitive exploration of the point of view of other members and more direct attempts to control others. Apparently there is greater anonymity of fellow members in a large group resulting in less identification with the self. As the group grows larger, the individual still retains his desire to participate.[64] A study by Jack Gibb revealed that as the size of a task-oriented group increased, a greater proportion of members reported feelings of threat or inhibition of impulses to participate.[65] A review of the relevant research by Bernard Berelson and Gary Steiner concludes that the larger the informal group (from two or three up to fifteen or twenty), the greater become the demands made on the leader and the more he becomes differentiated from the membership at large. Further, the larger the group, the more the activists dominate interaction within the group and the more the ordinary members inhibit their participation; consequently the larger the group, the less exploratory, less imaginative, and less adventuresome the group decisions tend to be.[66] Everything considered, the studies seem to indicate that four to six persons constitute the ideal number of participants in committee or task-oriented groups. D. W. Taylor and W. L. Faust found that groups of four solve abstract problems faster than did groups of two.[67] A study by Philip Slater revealed that member satisfaction for groups of five was higher than for larger or smaller groups.[68] Research by R. C. Ziller concluded that "the accuracy in decision making is superior in groups of six than in groups of two or three."[69] Class size has been studied experimentally by Gwendolyn Cannon who found that large groups in kindergarten (34-39 children) result in more aggressive pupil behavior and longer intervals awaiting turns for a favorite activity, both of which result in learner frustration and less teacher attention.[70] William Kvaraceus's review of the pertinent research concludes that larger classes are more likely to produce juvenile delinquents than are smaller classes.[71]

The peer group to which one belongs also is a potent force in shaping the direction and contours of an individual's learning. James Coleman's researches highlight the significance of the influence of the peer group within a school on a student's motivational level and direction as well as on his performance.[72] Morton Deutsch conducted an experimental investigation utilizing two groups of matched students. One group was structured so as to solve tasks in a highly competitive setting; the other group was arranged in small cooperative subgroups. Deutsch reported that in the cooperative group there was more work output per unit of time, more pressure to achieve, more friendliness, and a more favorable evaluation of the situation and its effects on group members.[73] Merrill Roff's investigation demonstrated that peer rejection in early school years is a strong predictor of young adult maladjustment.[74] Noteworthy in this connection are studies by Samuel Cox,[75] and S. B. Sells and Merrill Roff[76] which found that peer acceptance or rejection tended to result from aspects in the individual's personality makeup which could be traced to his early childhood upbringing in the home environment. A review of the research by A. Morrison and D. McIntyre concludes that group structures and processes not only help or hinder pupils' responses in the instructional dynamic, but also affect pupils' or teachers' attempts to establish and implement standards of behavior.[77] An experimental study by Solomon Asch demonstrated the operation of pressures toward agreement with the opinions, attitudes, and judgments of the majority of one's peer group. In Asch's experiment the subject was placed among confederates of the experimenter. These confederates made a deliberately distorted judgment of a physical stimulus. Under these conditions it was common to find the subject moving in the direction of group judgment despite the contrary evidence of his own senses.[78] Monroe Lefkowitz and his associates showed in their study that certain kinds of moral behavior can be influenced by group pressures. The Lefkowitz experiment discovered that the incidence of pedestrian violations of a traffic signal was increased when one of the experimenters disobeyed the signal. The higher the social status of the experimenter, the greater were the breaches by individuals. Where only about one percent of the pedestrians ordinarily crossed the street against the traffic light, this figure rose to four percent when the experimenter who disregarded the signal was dressed in low-status fashion and increased to fourteen percent when his attire suggested that he came from one of the higher social levels.[79] A study by Herman Turk and his associates suggested that common group membership and high group cohesion vary with social influence and social influenceability. The more an individual perceives commonality between himself and another member of the group, the more receptive he becomes to social influence and the more he anticipates influencing the other person.[80] It should be underscored, however, that peer group or other group pressure seems to have little if any effect on altering those behaviors which constitute part of the individual's complex of deepest attitude and value commitments.

The socioeconomic status of the home and the neighborhood environments in which an individual grows up constitutes a highly significant variable affecting learning. Lloyd Warner's classic study concluded that the values held by children from families in lower socioeconomic localities are frequently different from those held by children in more prosperous circumstances. For example, the former often regard school attendance as a waste of time while the latter view it as crucial to social and economic success. Street fighting and boisterousness are considered signs of strength in underprivileged neighborhoods whereas in wealthy areas the same behaviors are considered manifestations of weakness, barbarity, and low intelligence.[81] A comprehensive study by Refia Uğurel-Semin of Turkish youths revealed that poor children were the least selfish and ranked high in generosity; rich children tended to be generous rather than equalitarian; and middle-class children were the least generous and the most selfish.[82] Bernard Spilka concludes from his review of the pertinent research that church attendance and church membership generally appear to be correlated with socioeconomic status.[83] The research data typically indicate that church members come from somewhat higher socioeconomic levels than nonmembers and that lay leaders in congregations rank higher than other members.[84] Clement Cosgrove's study revealed that the socioeconomic status of the Catholic elementary school children investigated had a significant influence on the extent of their theoretical and practical knowledge of religious and moral truths.[85] In a study of 200 English compositions written by children in elementary schools representing three different grade levels, Jack McClellan discovered that skill in organization and length of sentences varies directly with socioeconomic level. Further, middle-class children wrote more words at all grade levels than did children of lower and higher income classes.[86] A celebrated investigation by Jerome Bruner and Cecile Goodman disclosed that poor children visually overestimated the size of coins (ranging from a penny through a half-dollar) significantly more than did wealthy children.[87] This study is highly important since it demonstrates how socioeconomic status can affect even so basic and primary a human characteristic as visual perception. A review of the research by Bernard Berelson and Gary Steiner indicates that at least in the United States, mental illness is more prevalent and more severe in the lower socioeconomic classes than in the upper.[88]

Finally, the immediate physical environment in which learning takes place exerts a powerful impact on that learning. Color, for example, is a significant variable in learning. R. Srivastava and T. Peel conducted an experiment in which they varied the color of a contrived art gallery. They discovered that subjects in a dark brown room took more footsteps at a faster pace than subjects who were placed in a light beige room. Further, subjects in the brown gallery covered nearly twice as much area, exhibited a less dense movement pattern, and spent less time in the room than did those in the beige gallery.[89] Faber Birren has cited empirical evidence which indicates that human reactions are twelve percent faster than average under red lighting conditions. Green and blue lights, on the other hand, seem to generate reactions which are slower than normal.[90] Kurt Goldstein's experimental research showed that colored lighting also seems to influence judgments of time, length, and weight. Under red lighting these judgments tend to be overestimated, whereas green or blue lighting seems to elicit the opposite effect.[91] D. B. Harmon's research suggests that humanistic responses to mental and visual tasks may be facilitated by soft and deep colors in the environment.[92] A study by Robert Gerard found that hues such as red and blue aroused different feelings and emotions in the individuals investigated. Red was somewhat disturbing to more anxious persons while blue had a soothing effect.[93] John Black conducted an experimental study on the effects of room size and acoustical qualities on verbal behavior. He found that the individuals in his experiment read aloud more rapidly in small rooms than in large rooms. Within the large rooms themselves, the individuals read aloud at a more rapid rate in acoustically "dead" rooms than in "live" rooms. The acoustically "dead" rooms seemed also to generate a greater intensity in oral reading.[94] The aesthetic quality of a room also appears to elicit distinctive kinds of behavior. Abraham Maslow and Norbett Mintz placed their subjects in three rooms; one room was pleasantly decorated and furnished, the second was in an unsightly and sloppy state, and the third in an average neutral decor. After spending ten to fifteen minutes in rating a series of face photographs, the individuals in the "beautiful" room rated the faces as having significantly more energy and well-being than did subjects tested in either an "average" or an "ugly" room.[95] Along a similar line Norbett Mintz investigated the effect on examiner performance over a long term in "beautiful" and "ugly" rooms. The results indicated that the examiners working in the "ugly" environment typically completed their testing performance in a shorter period of time than those in the "beautiful" environment. Moreover, the reactions of the examiners in the less attractive environments were fatigue, discomfort, monotony, and irritability. Examiners conducting tests in the "beautiful" room, on the other hand, expressed feelings of enjoyment, pleasure, comfort, and energy.[96] Of especial interest to religious educators is the research which indicates that interaction among members of a group is significantly affected by the design and arrangement of the physical environment in which the group activity is carried on. This holds true for groups of rather diverse kinds. R. F. Srivastava and L. R. Good studied patterns of group interaction in a psychiatric treatment ward over a five-week period. Their investigation showed that group interaction was significantly different in ward environments which were dissimilar in architectural design. Further, group interaction was not significantly different in ward environments of similar architectural design.[97] Robert Sommer and Hugo Ross conducted an experiment with patients in a geriatric ward who were behaviorally apathetic despite their being in a "bright" and "cheerful" environment. By experimental arrangement of furniture to encourage interaction, the researchers were able to double the frequency of patient conversations.[98] A study by Robert Sommer found that seats at corner table spaces generated more interaction among people than did seats either facing each other or alongside each other. The results also indicated that the subjects displayed a preference for face-to-face seating arrangements as compared to seats next to each other; however, this did not obtain when distance became a factor. When the distance between the chairs in the face-to-face configuration exceeded five feet, and when the distance between the face-to-face chairs markedly exceeded that in the alongside arrangement, the latter arrangement was selected. An interesting sidenote is that the schizophrenic subjects' in Sommer's investigation chose distant seating arrangements while non-schizophrenics preferred close positioning for discussion purposes.[99] This supports the principle that personality variables are meshed with environmental variables in the shaping of behavior.

Significance of finding #2 for the teaching of religion. The major import of finding #2 is that if religion teaching is to be effective, it must concentrate much of its attention not only on working with existing environments (for example, the local environment) but even more crucially on endeavoring to do everything possible to optimally structure the classroom or other specific environment in which religious instruction takes place. Certainly the learning situation must be one attuned to the sociocultural environments from which the students come. Even in its indispensable prophetic and reconstructionist aspects, religious instruction must take the learner where he is, as a product of a particular set of "outside" environments, all of which have an enormous influence on the way in which he can and will learn. The imaginative and creative religion teacher can capitalize on such "outside" environmental variables as peer-group values and socioeconomic status in order to accelerate learning and make it more goal-directed than if these "outside" environmental variables were neglected or ignored. In short, the teacher's primary function qua teacher is to so structure all the environmental variables (including teacher-student interaction) that the power of these variables is released, thereby maximizing the opportunities for learning. In instances in which the students come from culturally-, socially-, or religiously-deprived environments, the religion teacher must compensate for the deprivation by providing an exceptionally enriched learning environment. The teacher should be keenly aware of the contrasting effects which disparate environmental climates have on learning outcomes. The investigations of Marie Francis Kenoyer and Robert Brooks on the effects of convent and seminary life bear eloquent testimony that different environmental climates do produce significantly different learning outcomes. The research I cite in connection with finding #2 as well as Clifford Drew's more extensive review of the relevant research[100] clearly demonstrate that modification of the immediate physical environment represents a highly significant variable in the facilitation of desired learning outcomes. It may well be that furniture arrangements, architectural design, and other features of the learning environment are selected on the basis of convenience and ease of housekeeping, with little, if any, concern for enhancement of learning.[101]

Finding #3: The directness, immediacy, quality, and texture of an individual's experience have a great deal to do with the richness, impact, and perdurability of his learning.

Experience is both action and interaction. "Learning involves interaction between the learner and his environment, and its effectiveness relates to the frequency, variety and intensity of the interaction."[102] Experience is not a *superadditum;* it is at the very heart of learning. Experience of all kinds is necessary for growth and learning. One research experiment has demonstrated that if the channels of sensory communication are cut off or even muffled, abnormal reactions resembling psychoses ensue.[103] Placing an individual in an environment in which he experiences either distorted stimuli or no stimuli at all has been shown to drastically disorient his psychological equilibrium. Indeed, stimulus deprivation and stimulus distortion are standard interrogation procedures by secret police in totalitarian states. A review of the relevant research by Benjamin Bloom and his associates concludes that perceptual development is stimulated by environments plenteous in their range of available experiences.[104] The converse also obtains. Thus environments which provide relatively little in the way of rich or varied experiences, such as total institutions (for example, orphanages)[105] and socially or culturally impoverished homes,[106] often result in a physical, emotional, and intellectual malfunctioning in the children involved.[107] Direct experiences in environments pullulating with tactile and social stimulation are necessary for the normal growth and development of young children. Indeed, Leon Yarrow's study showed that the severity of personality disturbance and the degree of developmental retardation are in proportion to experientially-deprived environments during childhood.[108]

Norman Wallen and Robert Travers conclude from their review of the research that an individual learns more efficiently "if he makes the responses to be learned than if he learns by observing another make the response or makes some related response."[109] Thus a direct, immediate, firsthand experience tends to produce more effective learning than one which is indirect, mediate, or vicarious. From very different vantage points, the researches of B. F. Skinner,[110] Carl Rogers,[111] and Hans Eysenck[112] all concur that the more full and more complete the experiential response of the learner, the more effective his learning.

Synthesizing the relevant research, Edgar Dale has devised his celebrated "cone of experience" model. This model places learning experiences on a conical continuum from the base (the most concrete, direct, and immediate experiences) to the tip (the most abstract, most indirect, and most remote). From the base upward, these experiences are: direct, purposeful experiences (for example, going to the store to buy food); contrived experiences (for example, role-playing, in which the individual takes on a role which is so arranged as to focus and heighten certain variables present in the fabric of everyday experience—or another example, learning to drive an automobile in a mechanical device having many of the salient features of an automobile); simulated experiences (for example, a miniature working model of Eli Whitney's cotton gin or a model of the Jewish temple); dramatized experiences (for example, acting out a particular part in a religious play); demonstrations (for example, demonstration by the teacher of the use of certain liturgical altar vessels); field trips (for example, an excursion to an ecumenical religious education center); exhibits (for example, ancient realia such as coins from the time of Jesus, or specimens such as plants or a piece of mica); television; motion pictures; visual symbols (for example, flat maps of the Holy Land, diagrams, charts, and chalkboards); and verbal symbols.[113]

Significance of finding #3 for the teaching of religion. If religion teaching is to be effective, it must be not only rooted in but also saturated with experience. This experience must be as direct, as immediate, and as rich as possible—in other words, as close as possible to the base of Dale's cone. The more direct and firsthand the experience and the less indirect or symbolic, the more effective the learning tends to be. A key function of the religion teacher, then, is to so structure the learning situation that it becomes an environment characterized by stimulus richness rather than by stimulus deprivation. Where students come from homes or communities lacking in the availability of rich and varied experiences, the religion teacher must make sure that his class is conspicuously rich in experiential stimuli. In this connection a research study by Yvonne

Sayegh and Wayne Dennis concluded that appropriate supplementary experiences can result in rapid increases in behavioral development among children coming from impoverished environmental conditions.[114]

The value of learning by direct experience and by the response of one's total self does not minimize either the fact or the importance of indirect learning or learning by vicarious experience (such as watching another person make the response). Actually, the religion teacher is often faced with structuring learning situations in which direct experiences and total learner response are not possible. In such circumstances—and they are frequent—finding #3 suggests that the religion teacher orient the elements within the indirect experience toward approximating as closely as possible the kinds of experiences and responses found toward the base of Dale's cone. Thus, for example, pedagogically speaking a liturgical celebration is a contrived experience. But it has elements in it ranging from verbal symbolization, visual symbols, dramatized experiences, and even some direct purposeful experience. The religion teacher who wishes to enhance the learning outcomes accruing from a liturgical celebration might do well to downplay the visual and especially the verbal symbolizations, while accentuating the direct experiences and other elements more toward the base of Dale's cone.

Experiences are not all of the same quality, either objectively or from a pedagogical standpoint. As John Dewey observes, effective education depends not on experience simply considered but rather on those kinds of experiences which are educationally of high quality.[115] In this connection, Michael Lawler comments that the learner's own experience represents, for him at least, experience of a very high subjective quality.[116] What all this suggests is that the religion teacher should utilize the learner's experience as he creatively fashions high quality pedagogical experiences in the educational setting.

Finding #4: The meaningfulness of the learning task constitutes a very important factor in the attainment of a desired learning outcome.

Lee Cronbach's quite comprehensive review of the pertinent research concludes that if the learning task is meaningful to the learner, he will be able to accurately judge what he should do in order to succeed at this task. Consequently, meaningfulness heightens the probability of success in learning what is to be learned. More than that the learner will thereby be able to evaluate his progress in attaining the learning goal early enough to forestall errors. Cronbach concludes that the individual who learns without understanding will make errors because he is unable to adapt his learning to a new or changing situation.[117]

Berelson and Steiner conclude from their review of the research that things which are important to remember are remembered better than things which do not make any difference to the individual.[118] By "important" here is meant personally meaningful. Importance in this context is defined subjectively. This point is decisive. Perhaps the major thread running through the research on meaningfulness is that while the objective meaningfulness of the learning task does play a role, nonetheless the primary factor encouraging heightened learning is the subjective meaningfulness of the task. Thus the research suggests that learning is most likely to occur when experiences "are perceived by the learner as pertinent to his needs and purposes, are consistent with his personality organization, and are associated with self-directive behavior."[119]

Benton Underwood's review of the research indicates that for all kinds of verbal learning tasks, the higher the meaningfulness, the more rapid the learning.[120] Another review of the research concludes that "meaningful material is easier to memorize than non-meaningful material; and once learned, it is retained easier."[121] From a strictly cognitive perspective, the power and effects of meaningfulness are significantly related to the way in which the learning takes place. Thus David Ausubel's summary of the research concludes that "whereas *rote* learning and retention are influenced primarily by the interfering effects of similar rote materials learned immediately before or after the learning task, *meaningful* learning and retention are influenced primarily by the properties of the relevant subsuming ideas in the cognitive structure with which they interact."[122]

In one sense meaningfulness is a function of the individual's age and personality organization. Two studies made by Glenn Terrell and his associates found that young children and many lower-class children, regardless of age, learn faster when rewarded with something material than when rewarded with praise.[123]

The research suggests that goal-relatedness constitutes one of the most important variables in arousing, heightening, and sustaining an individual's motivation to learn or to perform a specified task.[124] Since meaningfulness is in one respect the degree to which a thing furthers the attainment of one's goals, meaningfulness and motivation appear to be positively correlated.

Relevant empirical investigations indicate that meaningfulness is also associated with both the individual's needs and problems.[125] A need is that which a person must have in order to fulfil himself in some way. Needs can be classified in at least three ways: by source, direction, and perception. Considerable research has gone into identifying and classifying human needs. Adolescent needs seem to be a favorite for such investigation and classification. From an intensive survey of the literature, Charles Lucas and John Horrocks extracted approximately 70 stated needs of adolescents. They then constructed and administered a research instrument and located a cluster of five major adolescent needs.[126] Professional associations such as the National Association of Secondary-School Principals have scrutinized the research and developed their own list of "imperative needs of youth."[127] Perhaps the most famous classification of human needs is that made by Robert Havighurst, who recast these into ten developmental tasks which every individual must accomplish to achieve maturity and self-actualization.[128] Closely associated with needs are problems. A problem arises when for some reason a need is not being met. The research suggests that meaningfulness is highly correlated with problems; the more a particular learning task will enable the learner to solve a particular personal problem confronting him, the more rapidly a task or material will be learned and the longer this learning will be retained.[129]

The research also suggests that the greater the personal involvement, the greater the meaningfulness. Thus in a study made during World War II, the investigators initially hypothesized that persons who had relatives or loved ones in the armed forces would be more affected by Kate Smith's war bond drive than would other Americans. Generally speaking this held true. Yet the researchers were surprised to discover that there was a significant number of individuals with relatives or loved ones in the armed services who did not respond to Kate Smith's appeal. Further analysis of the data revealed that the nonrespondents had relatives or loved ones who were either at bases in the United States or at stations removed from the active war zone.[130]

Significance of finding #4 for the teaching of religion. Effective religious instruction is that which is rich in personal meaning for the learner. Meaningfulness is inherent in the learning task. But meaningfulness is also a subjective affair, something of a personal relevance and significance to the learner. It is this second form of meaningfulness which is so essential in religious learning. In a sense all meaningfulness resides in the learner and is subjective, because humanistically speaking, no nonpersonal reality such as "objective content" has any meaningfulness outside the person interacting with it.[131] Meaningfulness is logical (objective content), but even more it is psychological (subjective personal introception and interpretation). The research suggests that in terms of meaningfulness the teaching of religion ought to be primarily psychologically-oriented and only secondarily logically-oriented. Subjective meaningfulness to the learner is a key to effective religious instruction. In teaching the bible, for example, the teacher and the curriculum builder might well start with and work through what is meaningful to the learners. Appropriate biblical passages or themes (not necessarily in any sort of logical or chronological order) are then selected and brought into the lesson in a psychologically developmental fashion. This educational practice is in contrast with the usual procedure of teaching the bible in an objectively meaningful manner, that is, what is meaningful in terms of historical discipline (for example, the account of Paul's missionary journeys) or in terms of theological science (for example, prophets as types).

Another way of looking at the same point is to introduce the distinction between meaningful learning and the learning of meaningful material. Meaningful learning is that which has subjective import to the learner. Meaningful learning connotes the significance of the learning task to the learner's life and goals. The learning of meaningful material, on the other hand, connotes only the objective worth of the learning task; it says nothing of the subjective worth of the task, its potential place in the learner's life, or even how the task is to be accomplished. Indeed, meaningful materials can be learned by rote.

In one sense all living and therefore all learning are goal-directed. To say that a particular learning task is meaningful is to say that it fits into the overall framework of the individual's overall goal-directedness. The more the learning task fits into this overall goal-directedness, the more meaningful it is. If the learning task is such that it thwarts the immediate or long-range goals of the individual, he will be thwarted in his goal-seeking. In such instances he will tend to erect substitute goals or deflect the learning task toward goals other than those circumscribed by the original task itself. As a consequence the objectives of the religion lesson or class are not attained.

Personal involvement is typically a prerequisite for subjective meaningfulness. Moreover, personal involvement heightens the meaningfulness present in the learning task itself. Therefore the pedagogical strategy which the religion teacher employs must be one that allows for maximum personal involvement on the part of each and every learner. Pedagogical strategies vary in the degree to which they feature personal student involvement. The transmission strategy, for example, permits little or no personal student involvement while the structured learning situation strategy of its very nature incorporates the widest possible personal involvement of each learner in the learning task.[132]

Teaching methods and techniques ought to be highly differentiated and personalized since meaningfulness varies according to the family background, social class, level of religiosity, local milieu, individual needs, and personal problems of each learner.

If the learner's present and future religiosity is to have meaningfulness, then the religion class must perforce bristle with personal meaning and significance for him. One review of the research suggests that man needs meaningfulness in his life if he is to attain and maintain personality equilibrium and adjustment, to say nothing of personality fulfillment.[133] Surely then, a prime responsibility of the religion teacher is to heighten personality adjustment and fulfillment by providing the learner with religious experiences which are highly meaningful to him.

Finding #5: The kind of reinforcement given to a particular experience exercises a powerful influence as to whether this experience will be learned or forgotten.

A reinforcer is an event, stimulus, or state of affairs which changes a subsequent behavior when it follows the original learned behavior.[134] Reinforcement describes the process by which some entity serves to strengthen, weaken, or eliminate a behavior which preceded that entity in time. The significance of reinforcement in the teaching of religion is that reinforcement increases the probability that a given response or set of responses will recur.

In general, the occurrence of a reinforcer strengthens the initial behavior, while omission of the reinforcer weakens or eliminates that behavior. The contradictory of reinforcement is extinction. Extinction refers to the elimination of a behavior by removing that which reinforces it. Relatively speaking the research indicates that acquisition of behavior occurs rapidly while extinction takes place slowly.[135]

There are at least five general categories of reinforcement: (1) type of reinforcement (positive, negative, or nonreinforcing); (2) level of reinforcement (primary or secondary); (3) sequence of reinforcement (immediate or delayed); (4) diversity of reinforcement (similar or varied); and (5) schedule of reinforcement (continuous or intermittent).

Positive reinforcement consists of a pleasant consequence resulting directly from a particular behavioral response. Typically these pleasant consequences are in the form of some kind of reward to the individual for his response. Rewards are of many types: primary and secondary, direct and indirect, and so on. A positive reinforcer enhances the possibility of the recurrence of the initial behavior. Praise, for example, acts as a positive reinforcer to a student; anything the student does which is followed by praise from teacher or peer is more likely to be repeated. The research has found that of all three kinds of reinforcers, positive reinforcers are the most effective in bringing about a desired learning outcome. Negative reinforcement consists of unpleasant consequences resulting from a particular behavioral response. As a general rule these unpleasant consequences are in the form of a punishment to the individual for his response. Like rewards, punishments are of many types: primary and secondary, direct and indirect, and so on. A negative reinforcer reduces the probability of the recurrence of the initial behavior. Reproof, for example, serves as a negative reinforcer to a student; anything the student does which is followed by reproof from teacher or peer is less likely to be repeated. Negative reinforcers can be either aversive stimuli or punitive stimuli. Aversive stimuli consist of those which are so arranged as to punish the individual for making a particular response while at the same time structuring the contingencies so as to enhance the probability that he will make some other desired response. Punitive stimuli consist of those which are arranged so as to punish the individual for making a response and therefore to extinguish the response. It does sometimes happen that when learning occurs under relatively aversive or punitive conditions, such as a response's requiring much effort, or punishment at the goal, or delayed reward and so on, a greater resistance to extinction is manifested.[136] Nonreinforcement consists of no linked stimulus-response pleasant or unpleasant consequence accruing to an individual for making a particular behavioral response. In short, nonreinforcement means that nothing happens as a result of an individual's initial response. When the teacher ignores a student's response, for example, he is using a nonreinforcer. The research evidence indicates that while negative reinforcers do indeed tend to extinguish the probability of the recurrence of given behaviors, nonreinforcement is even more powerful in this regard.[137]

A primary reinforcer is one which derives its power from an innate and elemental need of an individual, for example, food, water, sleep. A secondary reinforcer is one which does not derive from such a need, but rather owes its power either to the level of its exchange rate for goods, services, and privileges (for example, money) or to its symbolic value as representing an accomplishment (for example, praise).[138] Though admitting of many exceptions, primary reinforcers are more powerful in bringing about desired learning outcomes (responses, in this case) than are secondary reinforcers. Because of the nature of the classroom or other learning site, the religion teacher typically is restricted in the number of primary reinforcers at his disposal. Hence the research on secondary reinforcers assumes an even greater importance for the effectiveness of his instructional activities. The relevant research suggests that a secondary reinforcer can strengthen responses other than the one used during its original establishment, and can do so with motives other than the motive prevailing during the original learning.[139] Consequently, secondary reinforcement greatly increases the range of possible reinforcement and learning. A verbal promise of food to a young child, for example, can reinforce a behavior which would otherwise require the food itself. Or again, mere praise without the promise of a primary reinforcer itself becomes reinforcing. Dewey Lipe and Steven Jung conclude from their review of the research that the teacher can keep the value of secondary reinforcers high by means of judicious and appropriate diversification of the exchange incentives.[140] It should be noted that personality variables and also concrete changing circumstances in everyday living can alter the pleasantness (and hence the reinforceability) of primary and secondary reinforcers. For example, reading a particularly interesting book (secondary reinforcer) might have more power than sleep (primary reinforcer) for one person but not for another. Parents are typically attuned to the relativistic power of reinforcers: for example, if at a given moment playing is a higher-strength behavior for a child than eating is, the parent uses play as a reinforcer for eating by allowing the child to play for a certain length of time if he eats his lunch.

Sequentially speaking, the research clearly indicates that immediate reinforcement is more effective than delayed reinforcement in producing a desired learning outcome.[141] Summing up the research, Ernest Hilgard and his associates observe that in general, responses temporally close to reinforcement are learned more quickly than responses remote from reinforcement.[142] The emphasis of programed instruction (teaching machines and the like) centers on the necessity for decreasing the delay of reinforcement in the instructional process. One significant aspect of delayed reinforcement is that during the delay period other behaviors intervene which may be unrelated and possibly even detrimental to the ongoing learning. Sometimes the intervening behavior is stronger than the intended reinforcer; when this occurs, the learner is distracted from his original task.

For human subjects at least, the research seems to indicate that varied reinforcers tend to be more effective than identical or similar reinforcers in producing a desired learning outcome.[143] Robert Packard's study found that an array of attractive response-type incentives served as a reinforcement device to heighten the attention of students to the learning task.[144] A varied menu of reinforcers appears to be necessary in some instances to counteract the fatigue factor which results from a constant diet of similar or identical reinforcers. Assessing the research, Harry Nelson suggests that a certain deviation, either upward or downward from the typical level of stimulation for a particular individual, is maximally reinforcing to that individual.[145]

A schedule of reinforcement is the programatic plan setting forth when and how often desired responses are to be reinforced. There are two basic forms of reinforcement schedules, continuous and intermittent. In a continuous reinforcement schedule there is constant, uninterrupted, and consistent reinforcement of the desired response. An intermittent reinforcement schedule, on the other hand, is one in which the desired response is reinforced only a fraction of the times it occurs. Intermittent reinforcers are always provided or administered according to some sort of schedule. There are two basic kinds of intermittent reinforcement schedules, time-oriented and response-oriented. The time-oriented schedule is itself subdivided into two types, the fixed interval schedule and the variable interval schedule. A fixed interval schedule is one in which the time interval remains constant and regular from reinforcement to reinforcement while a variable interval schedule is one in which the time interval is allowed to be haphazard or irregular. There are also two forms of the response-oriented schedule, the fixed ratio schedule and the variable ratio schedule. The fixed ratio schedule is one in which reinforcement occurs regularly after a previously-determined number of responses, for example, after every tenth response, while a variable ratio schedule is one in which the reinforcement occurs on a more irregular plan.[146] In teaching as in most other life activities, it is rare that reinforcements can be given or are given on a continuous basis. Reinforcement, therefore, is usually only intermittent. The research indicates that the schedule of reinforcement is more important in bringing about desired learning outcomes than is the amount of reinforcement which the learner receives.[147] Certain schedules generate a great deal of behavior in return for very little reinforcement—this is the basic principle underlying slot machines in Las Vegas. Moreover, a reinforcer which is inherently weak becomes powerful when properly scheduled.[148] Significantly one of the most important effects of intermittent reinforcement is that it appears to produce great resistance to the extinction of a learned behavior.[149]

Verbal reinforcement constitutes one of the behaviors most frequently used by teachers, hence the research on verbal reinforcement is particularly germane here. A comprehensive review of forty-six different studies reveals that a learner's behavior can be changed in a desired direction by skillful use of verbal reinforcers.[150] The research suggests that subjects who "typically" comply, that is, in whom compliance has become a personality pattern, respond more readily to verbal reinforcers.[151] On occasion the teacher uses verbal reinforcers to get the learner to alter his verbal behavior, for example, to give a correct answer. Other times the teacher uses the same kind of reinforcers to alter the learner's nonverbal behaviors, for example, to stop misbehaving. A review of the research suggests that the social prestige of the communicator significantly affects the amount and kind of verbal production in another individual. A person's psychological, social, or other kind of dependence on the communicator accelerates the shaping of certain classes of that person's verbal content. Simple participatory comments by the communicator (for example, mm-hmm) appear to be as effective as his complex verbalizations in accelerating the communication of emotionally-laden verbal content.[152] A study by William Verplanck concluded that positive verbal reinforcement (word-for-word agreement or paraphrased agreement) accelerated an individual's opinion statements, while negative verbal reinforcement (disagreement) and nonreinforcement (silence) had an extinguishing effect.[153] An investigation by Don Thomas and his associates found that when the teacher tripled the number of disapproving remarks, the frequency of disruptive behavior by primary school students increased.[154]

Praise and reproof are the most typical forms of teacher verbal positive and negative reinforcement, respectively. Elizabeth Hurlock's celebrated study found that pupil achievement improved most by praise, next under reproof, and least of all when the student was neither praised nor reproved but ignored. Praise was more effective with girls than with boys; the latter achieved more under reproof than did girls.[155] A review of the pertinent research by Harold Stevenson and Leila Snyder confirms this conclusion.[156] Some studies suggest that praise facilitates learning in some instances and inhibits it in others; different studies reach the same conclusion with respect to reproof; and still other investigations show that a combination of praise and reproof constitutes the most effective motivational force.[157] This divergence of results can perhaps be partially explained by G. G. Thompson and C. W. Hunnicutt's study which indicated that the effects of praise or blame as motivational factors bear a functional relationship to the personality of the learner, for example, extroverts respond less negatively to reproof than do introverts.[158] Additional support for the Thompson and Hunnicutt conclusion comes from data in a study made by Gerald Levin and John Simmons. Investigating the effects of praise given to emotionally disturbed boys, Levin and Simmons discovered that praise did not function as a positive reinforcer for the group as a whole or even for a majority of the boys.[159]

Reward and punishment constitute, in the teacher's perception at least, the most clearcut form of positive and negative reinforcement. Since reward serves as a positive reinforcer and punishment as a negative reinforcer, it is not surprising that the overwhelming mass of research concludes that in general rewards tend to augment the probability of attainment of a desired learning outcome while punishment tends to diminish the probability of such attainment. It should be noted that a particular reward might include several reinforcers, some of them competing with one another. By and large, the more complex and meaningful the learning task is, the more numerous and varied will be the reinforcers present within the specific reward given for successful completion of that task. Put another way, the more complex and meaningful the task, the more will various contingencies of reinforcement be operative. This accounts for the varying degrees of success which rewards have in the enhancement of different kinds of learning outcomes in different circumstances. Material rewards seem to encourage learning more with younger and lower-class children than with older and middle- or upper-class children.[160] The research further suggests that rewards appear to affect the learning of unappealing tasks; in such cases rewards can have a detrimental effect.[161] There is, then, a built-in connection between reward and punishment and what is being learned.[162] Punishment can be operationally defined as the presentation of a punitive or aversive stimulus following a response—a punitive or aversive stimulus being defined as a stimulus that increases the probability of responses which terminate that stimulus.[163] A considerable body of research exists on the effects of punishment on learning.[164] Punishment can be considered as a kind of negative instance. Indeed, punishment by the teacher may elicit heightened pupil misbehavior rather than lead him to engage in proper and appropriate classroom conduct.[165] An investigation by Jacob Kounin and Paul Gump revealed that pupils who have punitive teachers "manifest more aggression in their misconducts, are more unsettled and conflicted about their misconduct in school, and are less concerned with learning and school-unique values" than are pupils who have nonpunitive teachers.[166] Sheldon and Eleanor Glueck discovered from their research that the less parents used physical punishment and the more they used reasoning with the child, the less likely was the child to later engage in delinquent behavior or to become a delinquent.[167] An investigation by John Whiting and Irvin Child found that guilt is more likely to occur in societies employing severe techniques of socialization such as frequent punishment or the enforcement of rapid changes in habit patterns.[168] It should be noted that punishment illustrates the difference between learning and performance. The performance of an undesired behavior might be extinguished by punishment but this is different from saying that the habit itself is broken or that the performance will not be repeated once the punishment ceases to be present. Apropos of this, the research suggests that "punished behavior is likely to reappear after the punitive contingencies are withdrawn."[169] Finally, punishment might include several reinforcers, not all of them negative. Personality variables, for example, play a key role here. In general, punishment seems more effective with young and lower-class children than with older and middle- or upper-class children.[170]

Knowledge of progress is the information supplied to the individual at various intervals in the total learning situation concerning his achievement level in terms of the desired educational goal to be attained. Independent reviews of the research by Francis Harmon[171] and by William Kelly[172] conclude that knowledge of progress during the learning situation significantly enhances the attainment of the desired outcome. A study by Marion Panyan and associates of hospital attendants' use of operant techniques with patients found that the amount of attendant task performance increased sharply when knowledge of their results was made public.[173] Of particular interest to religion teachers is the study made by Vance Hall and his associates. In this investigation the teachers were informed about their students' progress by showing them charts of the observed student behaviors. The researchers discovered that these daily contacts, together with the weekly conferences in which the procedures were discussed and the teacher was praised for bringing about desired behavioral change, appeared to be the cause of improved teacher performance.[174] Synthesizing one aspect of the research, David Ausubel observes that an individual's awareness that he is successfully learning serves to energize subsequent learning efforts by enhancing his self-confidence, encouraging him to persevere, and increasing the subjective attractiveness of the learning task. Further, it motivates him to practice what he has already learned.[175]

Several times in this section I have noted that personality variables are quite significant in the effect which a particular reinforcer has on the learner involved. For example, studies by Hani Van De Riet[176] and by Hershel Berkowitz[177] report that positive social reinforcement in the form of praise seemed to produce negative affect and actually retard the performance of certain individuals. One plausible explanation of this phenomenon is that a person's tendency to perform through the use of social reinforcement depends significantly on his own social reinforcement history. If, for example, praise has led to undesirable or neutral consequences, then subsequent praise will either be blunted as an effective reinforcer or will have no reinforcement effect at all. The implications of this for learners coming from underprivileged neighborhoods is somewhat discouraging as far as the effectiveness of the school environment on learning is concerned.[178] Interactions between and among the personalities of individuals in the reinforcement situation also play a role in the effect of a particular reinforcer. Thus one study found that second-, sixth-, and tenth-grade black students improved their performance when they were subject to blame and reproof by black examiners; when the examiners were white, however, the same kind of blame and reproof served to decrease the performance of the black students.[179] A study by G. M. Della Piana and N. L. Gage found that some learners in the classroom setting are mostly concerned about feelings and personal relationships, while others are primarily achievement-oriented.[180] Consequently, the effect of praise or blame or other kinds of social reinforcers will have differential effects depending on the personality of the learner.

   Significance of finding #5 for the teaching of religion. Reinforcement is a necessary, effective, and helpful tool in enhancing learning. Indeed, reinforcement is ever present in the teaching-learning dynamic. If teaching is truly teaching, then the direction (and often the very existence) of the student's learning flows from what happens to him after he has produced a particular behavior. If, for example, the learner states that there are eleven commandments, the religion teacher typically gives him negative verbal and nonverbal reinforcements, with the result that the learner tends to extinguish his original behavior. Conversely, when the learner indicates that social justice is a duty of every Christian, the religion teacher positively reinforces this behavior, thus encouraging the learner both to fix this learning in his mind and possibly also to explore this learning in greater depth. The important thing for the religion teacher to do is to heighten his own awareness that virtually all his pedagogical behaviors act as reinforcers in one way or another. When the teacher smiles, this is not just an isolated or irrelevant bit of behavior; rather it is a bit of behavior which acts as or can act as a reinforcer to that teacher or learner behavior which preceded that smile. With this heightened awareness of the reinforcing nature of his pedagogical behaviors, the religion teacher can further augment the effectiveness of his teaching.

   Whenever possible, teacher reinforcement should follow as closely as possible the particular learner behavior which is to be reinforced. Immediate reinforcement is typically more effective than delayed reinforcement. Moreover, the teacher should utilize primary reinforcers whenever possible. This highlights the pedagogical advantage of the learner's being enmeshed in concrete firsthand experiences. Life and pedagogy being what they are, most of the reinforcers the teacher uses are secondary rather than primary. But this is no reason for discouragement since the research indicates that even the weakest of reinforcers can be rendered powerful when placed in an appropriate schedule. This in turn suggests careful teacher planning in setting up a schedule which will maximize the potency of the reinforcers. Reinforcers should also be as diverse and varied as possible. A rich and protean menu provides the best nourishment for learning. In this regard the religion teacher should avoid excessive or even heavy reliance on spiritual or "supernatural" reinforcers. Too much manna makes for an unbalanced diet.

The religion teacher should use reward and punishment judiciously, appropriately, and always in a way which will enhance learning. In general, reward is a more effective reinforcer than punishment. When in doubt, the teacher is well advised to prefer reward over punishment. Lee Cronbach observes that rewards given to a student during the learning process provide him with an incentive to undertake a task which otherwise would have little or no appeal. To achieve this function, it is necessary for the reward to outweigh the rewards from competing activities and to offset the possible unpleasantness of the effort itself.[181] Reward is a tool, and like any other tool it is effective only when used skillfully. In this regard Ernest Hilgard and David Russell caution that "because rewards are regulated by authority, too much emphasis on rewards encourages docility and deference to authority rather than originality and spontaneous endeavor."[182] Where this obtains, pupils will more readily strive to please the teacher than to seek the truth.

When punishment must be used as a reinforcement device, it should never be used by itself. Rather, effective management of learning dictates that along with the punishment the teacher offer the student a concomitant positive alternative so that the punishment will propel him to seek these realities more avidly than he otherwise would. Punishment is a negative and blind means of control. It simply says to the student "stop this particular behavior"; it gives no indication at all of which behavior he should turn to. Further, as Leonard Berkowitz observes, punishment often engenders hostility in the individual punished with the result that he may reject the very learnings the teacher is attempting to facilitate.[183] To extinguish a particular learned behavior, the teacher might keep in mind that nonreinforcement is more effective than negative reinforcement. Also, there are typically less harmful side-effects from nonreinforcement than from negative reinforcement.

Finally, as B. F. Skinner remarks, "a person is least free or dignified when he is under threat of punishment."[184]

Above all, the religion teacher ought to adapt his reinforcement procedures to the nature, background, and circumstances of the learner. The effective teacher, therefore, is one who is keenly attuned to the particular reinforcers which are of high-strength for a particular learner. Yet all too frequently, teachers seem unaware of which reinforcers are of high- and which of low-strength in their effect on learners. One study, for example, compared the views of teachers and their students on the relative effects of reinforcers used in the classroom. The teachers ranked, in descending order, quiet appreciation, election to posts of responsibility, and public praise as the three most potent reinforcers of learner behavior. The students, on the other hand, ranked reports to parents, referral to higher authority, and loss of privileges in one-two-three order.[185]

A sidenote seems appropriate before concluding this section. Some religious educators might contend that positively reinforcing desired learner outcomes and either negatively reinforcing or non-reinforcing undesired ones represent an unjustified control of the learner's freedom. This argument is specious: it ignores the nature of teaching and the nature of learning. An individual learns by being properly reinforced—a fact grasped by any parent or teacher who reflects on his pedagogical behavior. Virtually everything the teacher does in the pedagogical dynamic is done within the contingencies of reinforcement. Whether the teacher realizes it or not, every stimulus he furnishes the learner and every response he makes to the learner constitute a reinforcement of one kind or another. Every unit of teacher behavior is a reinforcer or at very least has reinforcement potential. The issue is not whether the religion teacher should or should not use reinforcers; to teach is to constantly structure reinforcements so that learning will be optimally facilitated. The issue basically is the wise and effective use of reinforcers to enhance the attainment of desired learning outcomes. A knowledge of the relevant research on how reinforcement affects learning, coupled with his constant awareness during the teaching-learning dynamic of the consequences of his pedagogical behavior will enable the religion teacher to more wisely and more sensitively utilize reinforcement procedures to enhance learning.

Finding #6. An individual's achievement need constitutes an important factor in the amount, the quality, and the thrust of what he learns.

The research suggests that achievement need or aspiration level not only emanates from one's inner personality structure but also is an integral part of one's total frame of reference.[186] One's personality structure is in part inherited and in part shaped by home, societal, peer, and educational environments.

Family variables appear to affect both the offspring's need to achieve and indeed his actual achievement of educational goals. One review of the research concludes that the earlier the parental expectations and demands for achievement, the stronger will be the individual's subsequent achievement motivation.[187] Leonard Berkowitz's summary of the research indicates that mothers and fathers with strong needs for achievement typically set higher standards of excellence for their *sons* than did other parents. Conversely, parental indulgence or carelessness apparently produces weak achievement needs in boys.[188] A survey of the research studies by David McClelland and his associates together with their own investigations concludes that the greatest source of achievement motivation is parental emphasis on their child's independence and self-reliance.[189] A review of the relevant research in Britain as well as in the United States similarly shows that children who achieve the highest in school tend "to come from families where the mothers lay stress on independent mastery—leading other children, self-assertion, making one's own friends and attempting difficult tasks without help—and where parents typically set high standards for the child's work, coupled with expression of warmth and emotional involvement." Low motivation appears to be correlated with parents who make strong demands for routine compliance, who are indulgent and pampering, and who accept low standards of performance.[190] The research also suggests that parental attitudes toward learning and education constitute powerful variables affecting the child's motivation to both learning in general and school-related learning in particular.[191] Achievement motivation in the school setting seems to be related to certain family characteristics. Bernard Rosen's investigation found that family size, birth order, and mother's age, all interacting with the family's socioeconomic status, are related to the development of achievement motivation in boys from eight to fourteen years of age.[192] The research also indicates that strong control by the father over his son seems to be especially inhibiting as far as the boy's achievement motivation is concerned.[193] Apropos of this, father-dominance is said to be the reason for the relatively weak need for achievement in the American and Turkish upper class.[194]

The socioeconomic status of a child's family appears to exercise a significant influence over his achievement. A review of the research by Robert Peck and Herbert Richek suggests that social class is consistently associated with achievement motivation.[195] Charles McArthur's investigation indicated that the upper-class youths in his sample tended to be past-oriented, while the middle-class youths were more future-oriented. This might partially account for the higher achievement motivation typically found in individuals coming from middle-class families as compared with persons coming from upper-class families.[196] In turn, empirical comparisons of middle- and lower-class groups have usually shown stronger needs for achievement in the former.[197]

Religious affiliation seems to constitute a significant variable affecting achievement motivation. It will be recalled that the research cited earlier in this section indicated a positive correlation between childhood independence and achievement. Leonard Berkowitz's review of the relevant research suggests that Catholics in general do not value intellectual independence as much as Protestants or Jews do; consequently, Catholics as a group tend to place less importance on independence for children than do Protestants or Jews.[198] This finding refers to Catholics as a group and hence is not applicable in every specific instance. Gerhard Lenski's study disclosed that eighty-one percent of the Catholic clergy investigated ranked obedience as far more important than intellectual autonomy as a key learning outcome in the church-related school.[199] Nathaniel Pallone's interesting investigation found that an unknown confederate dressed in clerical garb was able to get students in an Eastern Catholic college to conform to his obviously erroneous judgments about grossly distorted visual stimuli whereas a neutral confederate dressed in secular garb was unable to get the same students to conform in like manner.[200] A subsequent investigation by Francis Yeandel utilized an experimental procedure similar to the one employed in the Pallone study, except that his subjects came from an ROTC group in a midwestern Catholic university, and that in addition to the one neutral confederate dressed in secular clothing was added a confederate dressed in a military uniform. In Yeandel's investigation the unknown confederate attired in clerical garb was able to induce the students to conform to his obviously erroneous judgments about grossly distorted visual stimuli, while both the confederate dressed in military uniform and the confederate wearing secular clothing were unable to do so. Yeandel's study concluded that here was a clear triumph of religious authority over military authority in inducing conformity.[201] A summary of the pertinent research by Annette Walters and Ritamary Bradley concludes that an individual's motivation toward intellectual achievement tends to vary according to his denominational membership.[202] John Tracy Ellis's[203] celebrated review of the research, later updated by Seymour Warkov and Andrew Greeley,[204] has found that American Catholicism produces a much lower percentage of intellectuals, social scientists, and natural scientists than its proportion of the total population. John Donovan's investigation showed that Catholic college and university professors have a relatively poor record of professional achievement measured in terms of scholarly publication; professors who did not publish generally came from more religious families than those who did publish. Professors holding a doctorate from a non-Catholic university published more frequently than those with a doctorate from a Catholic university.[205] It should be noted that all these data cannot be considered in isolation but must be regarded in the total achievement context. Religious variables do not constitute the sole influence regulating achievement motivation; indeed, in certain instances they might not even be the most important ones in such an influence cluster. The impact of family variables and socioeconomic variables in some or many cases might well be more important than religious variables in building and shaping achievement motivation. To be sure, as a study by Albert Mayer and Harry Sharp indicated "religious performances appear to have meaningful consequences for economic achievement, quite apart from other factors associated with religion."[206] Yet there are other data which suggest that economic success itself generates different kinds and levels of achievement motivation.[207]

The ability of an individual to delay gratification is an important benchmark of the level of his achievement motivation. Delayed gratification may be defined as the willingness to defer immediate, less valued rewards for the sake of more valuable but temporarily deferred ones.[208] Indeed, the research evidence indicates that strong needs for achievement accompany the ability to postpone pleasures in the interest of greater future rewards.[209] Walter Mischel's investigation found that Trinidadian Negro children scoring high on the Thematic Apperception Test (TAT) of achievement motivation were more willing than children with low achievement scores to put off getting a present reward in order to obtain a larger reward in the future.[210] Mischel also conducted another investigation in which a large group of Trinidadian adolescents were asked whether they preferred to receive a small piece of candy right away or a bigger piece sometime in the future. The results of this study showed that juvenile delinquents were the most likely to insist on the immediate reward, even though the piece of candy involved was smaller.[211] Roy Fairchild's review of the relevant research shows that middle-class children generally possess more ability to delay gratification than do lower-class children. The older the child or youth becomes, the more the effect of class difference manifests itself in this regard.[212] A study by Jeanne Block and Barclay Martin of nursery school children found that those children who were able to delay gratification also exhibited more constructive-type play and showed less hostile outward aggression following a frustrating experience than those with low levels of ability to delay gratification.[213] It is well to note that the research suggests that an individual seems more willing to delay gratification if he has previously learned both to expect and to receive the rewards at a future time. A history of frequent and/or severe frustrations in this regard might well teach the person to take his pleasures here and now, lest he be thwarted once again and not receive the sought-after but delayed pleasure.[214]

The research indicates that a teacher's expectation of how well his students will achieve in class decidedly affects their achievement.[215] There is perhaps no attitude of the teacher which more influences pupil achievement than his expectation of what the pupil will or will not achieve. A well-publicized study by Robert Rosenthal and Lenore Jacobson investigated the effect of teacher expectation on student achievement. The students in this study were enrolled in five different grades in a West Coast elementary school. A test was administered to all these students. The teachers in the school were told in advance that the test was a special new instrument designed at Harvard to predict potential intellectual gains in children. Actually, however, the test was a regular, often used I.Q. test. At the beginning of the new semester four months later, when the children had advanced to the next grade level, the teachers were told that the test had identified certain children as "spurters" who would soon manifest unusual intellectual gain. The names of these children were mentioned to the teachers in a casual and informal manner during a staff meeting held before the opening of the new school year. In point of fact, the names mentioned constituted twenty percent of the children chosen at random. Other than their names, no additional data concerning the children were supplied to the teachers. For the next year and a half all the children in the five classes were retested at regular intervals. Gains in I.Q. test performance for the alleged "spurters" exceeded those of the other learners, the most dramatic results being with the youngest children. Further, at the end of the year and a half, when the teachers were asked to describe the classroom behavior of all the children in their classes, the alleged "spurters" were described as being happier, more intellectually curious, and more interesting as persons than the others. Moreover, teachers tended to perceive the alleged "spurters" as more affectionate, less in need of social approval, and having a better chance of success in later life. Some of the children in the "nonspurter" group also made significant I.Q. gains, but the more they gained the less favorably the teachers rated them on behavior. It should be underscored that the basic pedagogical methods used by the teachers remained unchanged, nor were there any special enrichment programs given either to the "spurters" or the "nonspurters." The researchers concluded that the gains recorded by the so-called "spurters" resulted primarily from elevated teacher expectancy.[216] A review of the pertinent research by Philip Baker and Janet Crist concludes that teacher expectancy appears to affect both pupil scholastic achievement as well as pupil classroom deportment.[217] A review of the research in Britain concludes that teacher attitudes and expectancies significantly affect the deportment and attitudes of the pupils.[218] There also seems to be some evidence that low teacher expectations have in the past hindered the achievement levels of black ghetto children.[219]

Recognition, that is, the acknowledgment by others of one's worth or achievement in some activity, appears to constitute a potent motivator in enhancing learning achievement.[220] The now-classic Hawthorne experiment dramatically demonstrated the importance of recognition as a stimulant to performance. The management of the Western Electric plant in Hawthorne, Illinois, wished to improve production. Researchers conducted an experiment in which they isolated a group of workers and began first to have the management improve lighting conditions, and then successively to increase the number of rest periods, reduce working hours, and provide certain added economic incentives. As the management did each of these things, the researchers continually sought the workers' opinions and encouraged them to make suggestions. With each successive improvement in working conditions, production increased. To test the validity of their data, the researchers systematically removed all the newly introduced benefits, leaving the workers with the same conditions as prevailed before the experiment. The result was unexpected—an all-time high in production. After considerable analysis and interpretation of the data, the researchers concluded that it was not the improvement in physical or other conditions which motivated the workers to steadily increase production, rather, it was the recognition and attention which management and researchers were according them by seeking their opinions, implementing their suggestions, and involving them in the total situation.[221] F. J. Ryan and James Davie's study showed that a small, positive correlation exists between social acceptance and the academic marks a learner receives in school.[222]

It would appear that the level of the learner's anxiety has effects in terms of his achievement or performance. Ned Flanders conducted an investigation in which he experimentally produced two classroom climates. In the first climate the teacher was acceptant and supportive of the student and used a problem-centered approach. In the second climate the teacher was directive and demanding, often disparaging in his behavior toward the student. Flanders concluded that when a conflict arose, learner behavior oriented toward the handling of interpersonal anxiety took precedence over behavior oriented toward achievement and performance goals. Further, in the first climate the learners manifested a decrease in interpersonal anxiety and became more oriented toward achieving a solution to the problem-task at hand. By contrast, in the second climate they became hostile toward themselves or toward the teacher, aggressive or apathetic, and failed to target themselves efficiently toward the achievement of the learning goal.[223]

Significance of finding #6 for the teaching of religion. The research indicates that an individual's achievement need, as conventionally assessed, has not proved to be an especially good predictor of scholastic achievement.[224] One possible explanation of this phenomenon is that the school or other kind of learning environment is structured in such a manner that a student's achievement potential is not released by the kind and form of the learning tasks given to him. The implication here is that the teacher might do well to give careful attention to so structuring the learning situation that when the learner interacts with this environment it will bring forth his full achievement potential. That this can and indeed should be done in a humanistic way is demonstrated by the Flanders's study I have already mentioned which revealed that students manifest less anxiety and learn more in humanistic, achievement-oriented environments than in achievement-oriented environments which are nonhumanistic. A humanistic setting is a necessary but not a sufficient condition for the optimal release of a learner's achievement potential.

Learner behavior which represents the achievement or the partial achievement of a desired learning outcome should be reinforced. Reinforcements can be of divers kinds, including social reinforcements such as praise and recognition.

Teacher expectancy, as we have seen, exercises a significant impact on learner achievement. The teacher communicates his expectancy in countless ways, some of which he is aware and others of which he is unaware—but from all, or almost all, the learner gets the message. The research evidence suggests that it might be quite possible that in the past religion teachers—notably Catholic religion teachers—have stressed otherworldly achievements to the neglect and detriment of worldly achievements. It seems plausible that this emphasis has resulted largely from a faulty theological conception of the relationship between the natural and the supernatural. It may well be that this faulty conception has been caused by a certain residual Jansenism which still seems to flow through much of American Catholicism. Elements of this residual Jansenism include a severe undervaluing of the positive functions of man's knowing and willing powers, a minimization if not an outright denial of the important role of the layman in ecclesiastical and civil affairs, an overemphasis on obedience to the clergy and religious who in turn are regarded as the proper leaders and lawgivers, and an interpretation of faith as a kind of blind obedience. The pedagogical fruit of such a theological mentality is that the teacher holding it entertains expectancies for his students which are otherworldly-pointed rather than oriented toward achievement in this world. But to be otherworldly-pointed is not to be "supernatural"; it is to be literally out of this world and hence unreal and irrelevant. To be otherworldly-pointed is, theologically speaking, to be neglectful of one of the aspects of the message of the parable of the ten talents (Luke 19:11-27). Interest in and involvement with social action programs are only part of an orientation to this world, and only the superficial would regard such interest and involvement as constituting the total orientation of an individual to this world. The religion teacher's expectancy colors and at times even creates, as it were, the learner's performance. Hence the religion teacher should devise learning activities which emphasize individual initiative, independent judgment, and self-directed behavior. Moreover, learner behavior which represents an achievement or partial achievement of these educational objectives should be reinforced and rewarded. It appears that independent and creative learners are typically unwelcome by teachers in general. Thus a study by Paul Torrance revealed that teachers regarded highly creative individuals to be less desirable as pupils than conforming individuals whom the teachers judged to be of higher mental ability, despite the fact that the two groups of students did not differ on standardized achievement tests.[225] Religion teachers in general, and clerical and religious teachers in particular, should bend every effort to promote independence and creativity in the learner rather than dependence and conformity. The research cited earlier in this section suggests that there might possibly exist a tendency on the part of clerical and religious teachers to put an undue premium on dependence and conformity in the learner. This has unfortunate pedagogical and theological implications. Pedagogically this kind of emphasis blunts the learner's achievement potential. Theologically it results in a diminution of optimally individualized responding behavior, a type of behavior which is crucial if the learner's response to God is to be as authentic and as totally representative as possible of his uniqueness.

Maximizing the learner's achievement potential implies that the teacher provide a learning environment which contains sufficiently differentiated stimuli so that each learner or at least the different kinds of learners can be motivated to learn in terms of their own relative achievement potential. Thus, for example, students who have strong achievement needs should be provided with learning tasks which are moderately difficult since the research suggests that this type person works hardest on a moderately difficult and risky task.[226]

Inasmuch as parent expectations and demands are so crucial in the genesis and actualization of a child's achievement level, it behooves the religion teacher to work closely with the parents. The significance of home and family variables in the personal and religious success of an individual can never be overemphasized.

Finally, it should be stressed that not only is the individual's achievement ceiling affected by his level of aspiration, but so also are often his method, procedure, and manner of learning. Bonnie Tyler's investigation identified two groups of students confronted with a similar problem-solving situation, namely, those who had little expectancy of solving the problem and those who had a high expectancy. "Significantly, more pupils in the low expectancy group attempted to memorize a solution to the problem in contrast to working out a logical solution."[227] Expectancy, then, constitutes a process- as well as a product-self-fulfilling prophecy.

Finding #7: Both as a discrete content and as a factor in a learner's total interaction with all the persons, objects, and symbols in the learning environment, affect is a highly significant variable in producing broadened, deepened, and personalized learning outcomes.

In three companion research investigations of enormous significance for religious instruction, David Elkind studied religious identity conceptions of Jewish, Catholic, and Protestant children aged five to twelve. These studies found that the child is most like the adult in his affects and least like him in his cognitions. Thus the child is able to experience religious affects before he can entertain religious thoughts. Indeed, the religious cognitions which he does employ will typically be of a confused and garbled nature, especially with regard to symbolic materials.[228]

Ronald Hyman's overview of some of the relevant research indicates that a warm affective climate pervading the teaching-learning dynamic significantly elevates the probability that learning will occur. Further, a favorable interpersonal relationship between teacher and pupil also increases the chance that learning will occur.[229] Morton Trippe Kelsey's examination of some of the relevant research suggests that even cognitive learning is facilitated by an affective learning environment and by the teacher's warm interpersonal relationships with his students.[230] Mary Agnita Spurgeon concludes from her review of the research that the teacher's personality characteristics, especially the degree of warmth and kindness and consideration toward his students, tend to be a more adequate predictor of teacher effectiveness than his academic learning in the area or subject he is teaching.[231] After an extensive study of elementary school teachers with contrasting success records, Herbert Olander and Helen Kleyle concluded that emotional maturity on the part of the teacher ranked first among the four best predictive measures of teacher effectiveness.[232]

The research indicates that a concerted deliberative effort on the teacher's part to employ affective pedagogical behaviors does indeed have a significant effect on enhancing learning in desired directions. In other words, the kind and amount of affective pedagogical behavior is within the teacher's power to control and utilize. Anna Burrell attempted to assess the effectiveness of a deliberate effort on the part of teachers to meet the emotional needs of students who were evincing learning problems and blocks. Two groups of teachers in two different schools were asked to identify five students in each of their classes who exhibited learning difficulties. One group of teachers employed their regular instructional practices with these students; the second group were told to deliberatively try to meet the emotional needs of these particular students. The results of the investigation indicated that the students having the second group of teachers manifested improved learning, improved social relationships, diminished deviant behavior, and improved work habits. In addition the attitudes of group two teachers toward these students improved.[233]

The research suggests that the teacher's choice of instructional process and strategy also significantly influences the affective climate and hence the kind of learning which ensues. The studies of Harold Anderson and his associates found that the teacher's use of dominative pedagogical behaviors tended to produce in their pupils aggressive and antagonistic behaviors. Conversely, the teacher's use of integrative pedagogical behaviors resulted in friendly, cooperative, and self-directive behaviors.[234] Hugh Perkins investigated the effects of teacher-centered versus learner-centered classroom climate on in-service teachers. His study concluded that the degree of affective climate makes a remarkable difference in problem-orientation, in the learning of factual material, in attitudes toward other persons, and in human relations skills. Perkins found that as contrasted with the in-service teachers in leader-centered study groups, those in learner-centered study groups made markedly superior use of evidence to substantiate their concepts and interpretations of child behavior, gave more evidence of useful insights and sound reasoning, revealed greater objectivity and warmth in their attitudes toward children, and expressed more child-development concepts.[235] A classic study by Kurt Lewin and his associates found that when adult leaders in children's play groups utilized autocratic leadership which was cold, impersonal, and generally low in positive affect, the children showed significantly less self-directed behavior and exhibited more extremely high or extremely low aggression than the children in groups characterized by democratic leadership or by laissez-faire leadership.[236]

Despite the relatively substantial amount of evidence that warm, affective behavior on the part of the teacher significantly enhances student learning, the available research data seem to suggest that teachers typically make little use of this kind of pedagogical behavior. A notable research study undertaken by Ned Flanders on junior high school mathematics and social studies classes indicated that less than one percent of the teacher's verbal behavior was directly affective, while an additional six percent was indirectly affective. In Flanders's category system directly affective verbal behavior occurs when the teacher accepts and clarifies the feeling tone of his students in a nonthreatening manner. Indirect affective verbal behavior includes teacher praise and encouragement and also acceptance and utilization of ideas expressed by the student. Flanders hypothesized that the teacher's verbal behavior was representative of his other kinds of pedagogical behaviors.[237] In one of the rare empirical investigations featuring high school religion teachers as the population studied, Raymond Whiteman found that the directly affective verbal behavior of these teachers as measured by the above-mentioned Flanders categories was less than one percent of all teacher talk while the indirectly affective verbal behavior amounted to ten percent.[238] A study of the questioning pattern employed by student teachers in social studies classes at the junior and senior high school levels revealed that no student teachers in the senior high school classes and very few student teachers in the junior high school classes asked questions which could be classified as affective. It is not surprising, then, that the pupils in most classes at both levels failed to raise questions requiring the teacher to make either affective responses or responses having affective content.[239]

Many more investigations have been conducted on the effects of positive affective behavior of counselors toward their clients than on the effects of such behavior of teachers toward their students. A summary of the pertinent empirical research by Carl Rogers concludes that if the counselor provides a relationship in which he displays considerable positive affect such as acceptance of the client, praising him as a person of worth, and manifesting empathic understanding of the client's world of feelings and attitudes, then positive changes occur in the client. Some of these positive behavioral changes include the client's becoming more realistic in his self-perceptions; more self-directing and confident; more mature, socialized, and adaptive in his behavior; less upset by stress and quicker to recover from it; and more likely to be a healthy, integrated, well-functioning individual in his personality structure.[240] James Dittes's investigation revealed that the degree of a client's registered physiological changes, as measured by a psychogalvanometer, depended on the warmness and permissiveness of the counselor.[241]

The research indicates that both the degree and the pattern of parental affectivity exercise an enormous influence on the personality, behavior, and achievement of the offspring. This influence is felt not only during childhood but throughout the life of the offspring. A review of the research by Jeffrey Keefe concludes that love and consistency as demonstrated by parental affectivity seem to be the two crucial factors in the internalization of socialized value systems as the child grows toward adulthood.[242] Martin Hoffman's review of the pertinent research concludes that an individual's internalized moral standards appear to be fostered by an affectionate relationship between parent and child in combination with the use of discipline techniques which are oriented around and which utilize this relationship by appealing to the child's personal and social motives.[243] A comprehensive survey of the research by Bernard Berelson and Gary Steiner reveals that severe socialization practices by parents seem to make for generalized anxiety in later life. The more the control of the child is love-oriented rather than based on bald physical punishment, the more effective are the parent's attempts to get the child to act in a desired manner and the stronger will be the development of the child's healthy guilt feelings toward improper behavior. The less affection and less warmth the child receives (that is, the more reserve, neglect, rejection, and other negative affects) the less likely he is to develop strength of character and a sense of self-identity. In general the unloved child tends to become an unloving adult—unloving of himself, of others, and of society.[244] A study by Albert Bandura and R. H. Walters discovered that parents with law-abiding teenage sons typically were more affectionate toward their boys than were the parents of teenage sons who were in trouble with the law for aggressively antisocial offenses.[245] Research by David McClelland found that in addition to setting high standards, the parents (especially the mothers) of boys with elevated achievement scores indicated that they expressed their approval of good performance by hugging and kissing their sons when they did well. They were also more likely to exhibit warmth toward their sons while the boys were working.[246]

A brief summary of two famous investigations might place in a somewhat dramatic context the data thus far reported in this section. In an adult follow-up study of a prior investigation, Harold Skeels demonstrated quite clearly the significance of early affective experience on later cognitive development. The subjects of this study were orphaned children who manifested such unmistakable signs of acute mental retardation that they constituted poor adoptive risks and consequently could not be placed. A radical change was tested; thirteen of the twenty-five children living in the affective-deprived orphanage were transferred to a mental institution where the inmates provided them with constant mothering experiences. The progress of these thirteen orphans in their new affective-rich environment was so great that they soon became adoptable and home placement was made. After a lapse of twenty-four years, the children in both groups typically maintained their divergent patterns of cognitive competency. The children who remained in the original affective-deprived orphanage reached an average of less than third-grade level while those who were removed to the affective-rich mental institution had accomplished a median of twelfth grade. All thirteen children in the transferred group were self-supporting while among those kept at the orphanage only four were self-supporting.[247] The second study, a classic investigation by Harry Harlow and Robert Zimmerman of affectional interaction, reinforces the conclusions of the Skeels investigation but from a different vantage point. Infant monkeys removed from their mothers almost immediately after birth were presented with two objects. One, called the "hard mother," consisted of a sloping cylinder with a nipple from which the neonate might feed. The other, termed the "soft mother," consisted of a cylinder made from foam rubber and terry cloth. Even when the neonatal monkey received all its food from the hard mother, he clearly and increasingly preferred the soft mother. The data strongly suggest that intimate warm physical contact is a variable of "overwhelming importance" in the development of affectional responses, overshadowing rather completely the variable of nursing. Thus it seems that a warm affectional relationship mediated through physical stimuli is more significant, at least to monkeys, than is the primary reinforcing stimulus of food.[248]

Significance of finding #7 for the teaching of religion. The major thrust of finding #7 is that affective behavior is at once a pedagogical means and a desired learning end of religious instruction. Pedagogically and axiologically the affective domain represents a key and indispensable factor in every aspect of religious instruction. If, as Morton Trippe Kelsey aptly remarks, the Christian notion that God is love is correct, then it is hardly possible to learn God or even to learn of God primarily on an intellectual basis. It is difficult and perhaps impossible to teach love except through love, and this is affect as well as lifestyle.[249]

Yet throughout recent centuries in both religious education and "secular" education, there seems to run a strong and pervasive current of antiaffectivity and contraaffectivity. Kelsey's well-documented overview of modern history shows how the yeast of rationalism has leavened so much of modern culture.[250] Similarly James Hillman's comprehensive review of the literature concludes that the divorce of affect from cognition is now so long-standing and has worked so to the benefit of reason that affect (usually called "emotion") has become a pejorative concept, a sort of dark side of rationality.[251] The neglect, devaluation, and indeed the outright denigration of affect by religious educators is well exemplified by Michael Warren's statement that affect is simply a cognitive device for mentally investigating and clarifying man's rationality. Warren clearly implies that affect does not have its own ontology and reality. In fact, Warren holds that affectivity is at bottom only a mode of knowing.[252]

The data reviewed in this section point up the fact that teachers in general and religion teachers in particular neither make adequate or sufficient use of affective pedagogical strategies, nor target their instruction to affective goals. One encouraging bit of data, though, is Raymond Whiteman's discovery that religion teachers in the Catholic high schools he investigated utilized more indirectly affective verbal behaviors than did mathematics or social studies teachers in a secular secondary school. Yet even in this study, the religion teachers' use of indirectly affective verbal behaviors totalled only ten percent while their use of directly affective verbal behaviors constituted less than one percent.[253] Clearly, then, augmented use of directly and indirectly affective pedagogical strategies is called for. It should be underscored again that affective teaching practices do not constitute a by-product of religious instruction. Rather, affect as practice and as outcome is one of the essential ingredients of adequate religious instruction. Religious instruction with a head (cognition) but without a heart (affect) is generative of religious practice with a head but without a heart. Robert O'Gorman perspicaciously illumines the deep unsunderable interconnection of affect as pedagogical practice and as outcome when he shows how the religion teacher's formulation of affective instructional objectives will perforce lead him to develop and utilize affective pedagogical practices while his deployment of affective pedagogical practices will facilitate the acquisition of affective outcomes.[254]

The research data in this section highlight the fact that the teacher's pedagogical behavior can and indeed does influence the affective responses of the learner as well as the more generalized affective outcomes in him. The ingredients of the religion teacher's pedagogical behavior are not mysterious or unfathomable as the blow theorists suggest; nor are the results of his repertoire of behaviors explained only by God's unknowable working in the human spirit. The data plainly indicate, for example, that pedagogical strategies based on a learner-centered process tend to yield more affective responses and outcomes on the part of the pupil than those strategies based on a teacher-centered process. Similarly, methods and techniques which are affective in orientation typically produce more affective outcomes than do nonaffective methods and techniques. What all this underscores is that teaching religion is not simply letting the teacher's Christian personality and witness flow through. Teaching religion is far more complex and behaviorally chained than merely being an authentic person. There is a mass of research data which indicate that the teacher's awareness of the ingredients, contours, and outcomes of his pedagogical behaviors leads to a changed and improved teaching style.[255] Raymond Whiteman reported that when he and another graduate student in the Notre Dame religious education program used clinical supervision procedures (including videotape feedback) with religion teachers in a nearby Catholic high school, these teachers developed a fresh new awareness of and sensitivity to their own pedagogical behaviors. This led not only to more effective religion teaching, but also to an expressed desire on the part of the religion teachers for Whiteman and his associate to continue working with them.[256]

The Elkind investigation, reinforced by the Ronald Goldman data reported earlier in this chapter, suggests that religious instruction given to children before the age of ten or twelve must of necessity be done with an affective rather than a cognitive orientation. These data have enormous ramifications for the entire structure of childhood religious education programs, ranging from the very way the program is organized, to the curriculum materials employed, and the pedagogical practices utilized. Placing religious instruction for children on a cognitive base seems to insure only that they will misunderstand and misinterpret what is taught them. It well might be that many of the so-called "crises of faith" which adolescent and young adults experience actually represent their attempts to wrestle with and rectify the false interpretations of Christianity which they unwittingly received from the cognitively-based religion program they underwent in their childhood years, a program which *eo ipso* so easily lent itself to misinterpretation.

The research cited in this section shows that the level of affect present in the home environment exercises a tremendous and in many ways an almost irreversible influence on the offspring's later affective life and indeed on his entire personality development. Consequently, it behooves religion teachers, in concert with religious counselors and other professional staff in the overall religious education program, to work closely with those families which are characterized by either negative affect or low positive affect. Parent education which revolves around an affective axis is probably one of the most productive tasks of the religious educator interested in enhancing the religiosity of children as well as of adults. Of relevance here are the data given by the Spurgeon study and by the Olander and Kleyle study, both of which suggest that one aspect of the screening process involved in the selection of persons to become religious educators should be a personality test. Candidates who score low on a scale or scales measuring affectivity or warmth should not be admitted to the ranks of religious educators since such persons tend to be ineffective in working with learners and parents.

The religion teacher's creation of an affective climate and his deployment of affective pedagogical practices in no way imply that the religion class is or should be a counseling session. Instruction has its unique goals which are essentially distinct from the objectives of counseling. Further, the religion teacher fails as a teacher when he tries to psychologically seduce learners into gratifying his own affiliation needs by employing affective strategies so as to manipulate the learners into liking him as a person. Religion teaching of this sort is at the service of the teacher's needs rather than of the learners' religious development. Nor should the religion teacher, in the name of affect, hand-hold or be ultrasupportive of the learners. Such practices debilitate the student and make him dependent upon the teacher—which is often what the affiliative-hungry teacher unconsciously desires. In the end affective extortion tactics on the part of the teacher result in both the teacher psychologically seducing the learner and the learner psychologically seducing the teacher—all of which makes for psychological pain for all concerned.

Finding #8: The corpus of attitudes which an individual holds conditions what he will and will not learn.

An attitude is a relatively permanent disposition or mind-set toward a physical or mental object. Gordon Allport's classic definition states that an attitude is "a mental and neural state of readiness, organized through experience, exerting a directive and dynamic influence upon the individual's responses to all objects or situations with which it is related."[257] Another famous definition of attitude is that of David Krech and Richard Crutchfield: "an enduring organization of motivational, emotional, perceptual and cognitive processes with respect to some aspect of the individual's world."[258] George Stern's review of the research concludes that definitions of attitudes typically agree on four fundamental characteristics: (1) attitudes are socially formed, that is, they are based on cultural experience and education; (2) attitudes are orientations toward others and toward objects; (3) attitudes are selective in that they provide a basis for discriminating between alternative courses of action and thereby introduce consistency of response in social situations of an otherwise diverse nature; and finally (4) attitudes reflect a disposition to an activity, rather than either a verbalization or the activity itself.[259] Elsewhere[260] I observe that an attitude always involves a preconceived judgment about the object together with a feeling tone about that object and a prepared reaction toward it. Thus through attitude the learner is already conditioned on both how to evaluate and how to respond to a particular person or object before he ever actually encounters that person or object. For example, a Christian clergyman will usually react with interest, pleasure, and affectivity when the term "the Lord's supper" is mentioned.

Following the lead of Gordon Allport, Dale Harris discerns four psychological sources of attitudes. First, attitudes may develop through the integration of numerous specific responses of a similar kind. Thus a number of unpleasant experiences with members of a particular religious group may generate the attitude that all members of that group are unpleasant. Second, attitudes may arise from general approach or withdrawal tendencies. Consequently, specific attitudes of hate may develop out of more diffuse patterns of hostile antisocial aggression. Third, attitudes may result from a single highly-charged experience. Cruelty received from a group of consecrated religious personages may quickly crystallize a strong negative attitude toward all members of that group. Finally, attitudes may be taken over "ready-made" from others, such as parents, teachers, or marriage partners.[261]

Jeffrey Keefe's review of the literature indicates that values are regarded as being more general than attitudes. Attitudes are limited to a fairly specific class of objects or persons (such as clergymen or schools or black people) or to an abstraction (such as foreign aid) whereas values encompass generalities.[262] A belief is an attitude which incorporates a large amount of cognitive structuring. Operationally, one has an attitude *toward* and a belief *in* or *about* an object or person.[263]

Attitudes largely account for a person's approach and subsequent response to values and indeed to most of reality. It is almost impossible to exaggerate the importance of attitudes in an individual's life as he actually lives it. Consequently, teaching attitudes toward realities constitutes one of the most important tasks of religious instruction. Attitudes condition virtually all learning. As Gordon Allport observes, "attitudes will determine for each individual what he will see and hear, what he will think and what he will do."[264] The differences in what individual students learn, as well as the rate and amount they learn are often due as much to their individual attitudes as to variations in their intelligence. A celebrated investigation by Jerome Levine and Gardner Murphy in which students read controversial material showed that if the opinion expressed in the material is in agreement with the opinion of the reader, the reader will remember it better and longer than if the opinion of the material disagrees with that of the reader.[265] Frequently learners remember what they are attitudinally conditioned to remember and forget what they are attitudinally conditioned to forget. It is also very important to note that attitudes are usually more permanent than specific bodies of information. Students forget in a relatively short time much of the facts, concepts, and theories which they acquire in religion class. The attitudes they learn, however, are perdurable.

A vital function of attitudes can be discerned in their interaction with facts. Facts are facts and hence possess a kind of objective certainty. When an individual's attitudes clash with facts, either the facts are rejected outright or they are interpreted so as to be consistent with the attitudes. The second reaction is typically the case.[266] This may be done in any one of at least three ways. First, a fact may be segregated on the ground that it is not relevant or that it is outdated.[267] Second, the meaning of the fact may be limited.[268] In the extreme instance the fact is taken to be an exception. Finally, a particular meaning which will fit into the attitude is selected for the fact. It should be mentioned that there is ample research evidence to indicate that persons tend to seek out facts which support preexisting attitudes while avoiding data which contradict these attitudes.[269] For example, it has been discovered that self-exposure to literature on the smoking-health issue was much greater among nonsmokers than among smokers.[270] A study by Shirley Star and Helen Hughes found that pro-United Nations literature was read principally by those whose attitudes favored the United Nations.[271]

The research seems to suggest that the three critical periods of attitude formation are early childhood (birth to six), adolescence (twelve to eighteen or so), and early adulthood (age of school leaving until thirty-five or so).

An individual's deeper attitudes are formed primarily (and some of the data imply almost exclusively) in early childhood in the home environment. One review of the research concludes that attitudes are "inherited," so to speak, from one's parents. An individual learns them early in life, and this learning persists throughout his life. Indeed, the early incorporation of parental attitude-orientation itself makes for the stability which one's attitudes manifest during later life.[272] The degree of the stability of one's attitudes tends to depend on their original intensity, the valence of the affective elements integrated into the attitude, and the ego-service which the attitude provides him.[273] Jeffrey Keefe's review of the research suggests that Sigmund Freud's clinical research indicated that a person's basic attitude structure is shaped by the age of three. Alfred Adler's clinical data suggested that at age four or five the individual's attitude configuration is permanently established.[274] A carefully-conducted longitudinal study of midwestern youths came to the conclusion that an individual's pattern of basic motivating attitudes is set by the age of ten.[275] Psychoanalysts tend to place the age of the relatively permanent establishment of attitudes at around six. Jeffrey Keefe implies that these data are not conflicting but rather suggest that it is from birth to six years that an individual's deeper attitudes are formed, and during latency (six to ten years) are consolidated cohesively into his personality structure.[276] These data are not surprising. After all, attitudes do contain substantial affective components, and it therefore makes sense that the broad configuration of an individual's attitude orientation would occur in preintellectual life since emotional life precedes intellectual life in human development.

Adolescence represents the second life period during which an individual's attitudes undergo significant change. At least three basic factors explain why this is so. First, during adolescence a person's cognitive processes begin to ripen. Second, at this time he begins to deeply explore the matter of his own personal identity. Finally, the whole realm of interpersonal relationships starts to take on heightened meaning and significance. It should be emphasized, however, that the deeper attitudes acquired in childhood can rarely if ever be reversed or extinguished. Rather, during postchildhood and later life, these attitudes can only be reinforced, given new significance, or expanded on the one hand, or regrouped to take on different colorations on the other hand. Take, for example, a boy who in early childhood acquires a pattern of aggressively antisocial attitudes. During that time in his life, he may manifest these attitudes by beating up other little boys in the neighborhood. During adolescence these same attitudes might assume a new configuration, that of dating many girls and subtly belittling them when they are out together for the evening. During young adulthood these very same deep attitudes might motivate him to march on a picket line to protest the actions of a particular majority or to become a clergyman condemning most people to hellfire and damnation.

Attitudes have a strong cognitive component; consequently, the significantly new dimensions of knowing and understanding which develop during adolescence manifest themselves in the shaping of attitudes. In general, the research has found that during adolescence, the individual becomes deeply concerned with the meaning of religion and what he should do with and about the religious attitudes and beliefs he learned during childhood.[277] Not infrequently the realization of the theoretical and practical consequences of his attitudinal structure leads to a religious conversion. The classic investigation by Edwin Starbuck found that religious conversion among American Protestants reaches a peak at about age fifteen or sixteen, after which it rapidly declines, becoming asymptotic at about age twenty-five.[278] Michael Argyle's review of the relevant research concludes that between ten and thirty percent of Americans experience so-called religious "crisis conversions," the modal age for such conversions being about fifteen years.[279] Another major factor causing significant attitude modification in adolescence is the onset of the individual's deeper exploration into his personal identity. From one perspective adolescence is a search for self. Because growth in cognitivity, affectivity, and in physique erupts dramatically in this period of life, the quest for self-identity is particularly acute during adolescence.[280] This search for "Who am I?" leads the adolescent to examine the content of his personal experiences, including his religious experiences, with considerable attention. Thus a study by David Elkind and Sally Elkind of adolescents thirteen to fourteen years old found that most of these young people were able to describe in vivid detail what they perceived to be immediate personal experiences of God.[281] From his existential analysis of his identity as a unique self and from his growing realization of where his own past and present religious experiences fit into his self-identity, the adolescent works on reinforcing, shifting, or expanding —as appropriate—his attitude configuration. The third major factor in enabling an attitude regrouping during adolescence is the youth's heightened sensitivity to interpersonal relationships. A review of the research by Robert Havighurst and Barry Keating concludes that the most pressing concerns of adolescents tend to be those of their own personal-social relationships.[282] On the basis of previous investigations plus their own studies, two groups of researchers conclude that the onset of adolescence is characterized by a new note in the individual's notion of God, namely that of a sense of personal relationship between himself and God.[283] P. J. Lawrence made a study of the content of the questions directed to their parents and Sunday School teachers by New Zealand Presbyterian children aged seven to twelve. The investigation revealed, among other things, that there was an almost total lack of questions on both ethics and moral theology.[284] During adolescence questions on these subjects become a staple, thereby manifesting a search for awareness of one's proper relation to God.

Early adulthood constitutes the third and probably final life period during which an individual's attitudes can or do undergo marked change—all within the very general contours of the attitude structure acquired during childhood. Early adulthood represents a critical period in an individual's life and hence is amenable to significant attitude deepening and/or change. It is in this period of time that an individual can make or does make his last radical change in lifestyle. During this time he typically acquires a spouse and a family, tries out and consolidates a career in the world of work, assumes economic power and responsibility, and begins to take on a prestige role in reference to significant others. Reviews of the research on the impact of entry into marriage[285] and into the world of work[286] suggest that the power of these variables to effect personality change in an individual is considerable. A review of the relevant research by Paul Maves suggests that the amount of attitude change occurring in early adulthood is dependent on the power of this new personal, social, cultural, and economic environment.[287] Naturally, the power of this new environment takes effect according to the mode and inner valence of each individual's attitude structure. If the concerns of one's adjustment to spouse, to children, and to career are more potent than one's religious attitudes, then the manifestation of those religious attitudes acquired in childhood might take on a different form. In the whole domain of religious attitudes of adults, only meager data exist because of the scant number of empirical investigations undertaken in this area thus far. Much more empirical research needs to be done before a clear picture can emerge on the development of religious attitudes in adult life.

It is commonly assumed by religious educators that peer-group influences constitute a potent and effective force in shaping and substantially altering an individual's attitudes. Yet Leonard Berkowitz's review of the relevant research shows unmistakably that people do not automatically introject whatever attitudes their peers happen to hold.[288] Some attitudes are accepted while others are rejected. The research demonstrates that at bottom the basis of attitude acceptance or rejection is the degree to which these new attitudes are consistent with an individual's own initial and foundational attitude configuration. It may well happen that under certain circumstances a peer group can exert tremendously powerful psychological pressures toward conformity, virtually forcing the person to come over to some new attitude at variance with his basic configuration.[289] But in such circumstances the individual does not really introject the attitude but rather feigns accepting it until the group pressure ceases and he can safely and without threat revert to his old attitude. It should be noted that manifestations of deeper attitudes, as well as opinions not deeply rooted in attitudes, can be changed by peer group members; but this is quite a different matter from asserting that peer group influences can substantially alter an individual's basic attitude. Elizabeth Douvan's study exemplifies this point. In her investigation midteen boys were asked to rank the relevance and legitimacy of influence on their behavior by certain individuals or groups. Parents were typically regarded as having a legitimate say about the hour their offspring should be in at night, even if these offspring disagreed with the time proposed. However, peer influence was more readily accepted in judgments of what to wear or which particular friends to select.[290] Stephen Withey's review of the research concludes that effective functioning of the family can weaken the disruptive pressures of peers in zones in which such pressures can have an influence on the offspring.[291] To be sure, the research shows that people tend to hold those attitudes and beliefs which are congruent with their group memberships. But this same research also indicates that people tend to become members of groups which are congenial with their already-existing attitudes. Hence the attitudes of the group serve not only to support already existing attitudes but also to clarify and crystallize these attitudes.[292] Much—if not most—of the empirical research done on acceptance or rejection of peer attitudes has been made with adolescents who, at least according to popular folk wisdom, are supposed to constitute the age group most susceptible to pressures from peers. In their review of some highly representative research, Robert Bealer and Fern Willets conclude that the adolescent tends strongly to accept rather than reject parental attitudes and values.[293] As Jeffrey Keefe suggests, in the last analysis it is the parents who control or allow membership in peer groups.[294] One of the few longitudinal studies in which children were followed intimately from latency to midteen-age demonstrated that peer-group influence seldom if ever changes the basic attitudinal and value system which the boy or girl acquired in the family. The researchers found that the peer group tends to be less an originator than a reinforcer of moral attitudes and behavior patterns originally developed in the family. The strength of peer-group influence depends on the present and particularly on the prior family history of the individual.[295] A national study of teenage youths found that in the matter of personal problems or troubles fully three-quarters of these adolescents believed that the advice of their parents and other significant adults was more important than that of their peers. Sex, age, community, and family income were found to have no significant effect on this attitude.[296] In short, adolescence is a time when deeper attitudes previously imposed by the family become accepted attitudes. Peer-group influence—as was indicated earlier in this chapter—is most potent on opinions or on surface attitudes. Deeper values and attitudes appear to be very little affected by peer-group influences.

The research suggests somewhat of a positive correlation between attitudes and membership in a religious group. Michael Argyle's review of the research concludes that religious people tend to be more conservative in politics than other people. Catholics typically seem to have the most conservative attitudes, but in Britain and America at least they tend to support left-wing political parties (this is partly due to class differences). Jews support the left and have politically "radical" attitudes. Catholics tend to be the most prejudiced. The Catholic-Protestant difference here is slight as compared with the Jews, and "it has occasionally been found that Catholics are less prejudiced" than Protestants. Regular and devout churchgoers tend to be somewhat less prejudiced than nonattending religionists, although religious people in general seem to be more prejudiced than nonreligionists. The more conservative a religionist is, the more he tends to be subject to suggestions from individuals or groups perceived to have prestige. Authoritarianism is higher for religionists than for nonreligionists. This is particularly true of Catholics, fundamentalist Protestants, and probably of orthodox Jews.[297] John Fox's investigation concluded that students attending a midwestern Catholic college appeared to display a greater degree of authoritarian attitudes than matched students at a government-operated university in the same state.[298] However, as James Dittes has cautioned, more research is needed to be able to distinguish with greater certainty the effect of gross attitudinal differences between and among various denominational groups.[299] As a final note, "the preponderance of the data suggests that it is persons least mature in personality and social outlook who are more likely to participate in religious activities of the kind measured in these studies."[300]

There is some research on the effect of various persuasive strategies on facilitating or hindering attitude change. Two areas of particular interest to the religious educator in this regard are the effect of one-sided versus two-sided communication, and the effect of fear-oriented communications. In their summary of the research, Paul Secord and Carl Backman indicate that the effect of one-sided versus two-sided communication in changing attitudes varies with the original attitudes and level of knowledge of the learner. One-sided communications (that is, arguments solely in favor of the content of the message) appear to be more effective than two-sided communications if the learner's attitude, beliefs, or opinions are already in accord with the content, or if the learner lacks previous information about the content.[301] E. J. Faison's study of the effect of one-sided versus two-sided commercials for automobiles found that the two-sided commercials proved more effective.[302] The research also suggests that two-sided communications appear to innoculate the individual against later counterarguments to which he may be exposed. A famous experiment by Irving Janis and Seymour Feshbach examined the effects of various threat-laden and fear-inducing appeals on attitude and behavior change. A fifteen-minute illustrated lecture was prepared in three forms, all identical in their objective product content of the causes of tooth decay and in their recommendations of an oral hygiene program. Each of the three forms differed in the nature and amount of threat material woven into its message. In the strong appeal form, decay, pain, and disease were stressed verbally, reinforced by photographs vividly portraying tooth decay and mouth infections. In the moderate appeal form fewer and less dramatic references were made to the deleterious consequences of neglecting oral hygiene. Photographs of less serious cases of tooth decay and oral infection were used. In the minimum appeal form still fewer references were made to the consequences of poor oral hygiene. Instead of photographs of mouth infection, X-ray prints were used. The photographs employed in this form were of healthy mouths only. The results of this experiment showed that while the strong appeal produced the greatest amount of worry and anxiety, the minimum appeal proved to be the most effective in bringing about conformity to the message.[303] Similarly, a study by Jum Nunnally and Howard Bobren discovered that individuals were less likely to pay attention to mental health messages arousing high anxiety and presented in a highly personal manner ("this could happen to you") than they were to less anxiety-arousing, more impersonally presented statements.[304]

Significance of finding #8 for the teaching of religion. The major import of finding #8 is that teaching for wholesome attitude development constitutes one of the two or three principal pedagogical tasks of the religious educator. The importance of teaching for attitudinal outcomes cannot be overstressed. This is borne out by the research which strongly suggests that an individual's attitudes condition what he learns and what he does not learn. Moreover, attitudes shape the individual's interpretation of what he does learn.

The research reviewed in this section clearly indicates that an individual's deeper attitudes are formed by the age of six. This fact should not be cause for despair among religious educators. Rather, it should motivate these educators to devote the major share of their religion teaching at those pivot points in the individual's life when the acquisition of deeper attitudes is possible.[305] These pivot points, it will be recalled, are early childhood (when the individual's basic attitudinal configuration is fairly well established), adolescence, and young adulthood (when the basic attitude configuration can be modified within the parameters of that configuration). In terms of bringing about attitude change, religious education programs will be most fruitful when they concentrate on these three periods. This has far-reaching consequences for the allotment of budget, personnel, and energy in parochial, diocesan, and national religious education programs. It suggests less attention to religious education in the elementary school, and increased efforts at the preschool, high school, and young adult levels. Following the hard data rather than clinging to one's personal biases favoring retention of the present system with its extraordinarily disproportionate heavy effort and expense (of manpower, money, and material) in the elementary sector will doubtless lead to the development of enriched religious outcomes in all the people of God.

Strong emphasis on early childhood education can return very high dividends to religious instruction in terms of shaping the basic contours of an individual's religious attitude structure. The research indicates that cultural, socioeconomic, educational, and religious conditions frequently operate in partially shaping parental attitudes —the same attitudes which they pass on to their children. By closely cooperating with parents in the home situation, the religious educator can work toward modifying and bringing to salience the attitudes of parents. This modification of parental attitudes (done within their own basic attitude configuration) not only affects the attitudes which their children will "inherit" from them, but also heightens their own religious attitudes. Hence a double gain is achieved by very heavy attention to a home-oriented program of religious education for children. Indeed, such a program is probably the most effective way of helping to influence the attitudes of young adults. (It will be recalled that young adulthood represents the third of the pivot points highly amenable to attitude change.) In any event, religious educators would do well to heed the research data which strongly indicate that agencies such as the church or the school can match no more than one-tenth of parental influence on an individual's basic attitude structure.[306] Teaching religious attitudes to adolescents is not only possible, but indeed quite probable if teachers deliberatively structure their pedagogical activities so as to achieve this outcome. The teacher seems to be much more influential than the peer group in enhancing or redirecting a youth's basic attitudes. The ineffective religion teacher should not attempt to mask his weak or unscientific or unimaginative teaching by claiming that peer-group influences render his pedagogical efforts fruitless.

It should be emphasized and reemphasized that attitudes can be taught and in fact are taught. The religion teacher who believes that attitudes cannot be taught but can only be "caught" very likely is either unaware of the research on attitude formation or has an unduly restricted notion of the nature of teaching.[307]

The research on the teaching and the learning of attitudes suggests at least four pedagogical practices which the religion teacher can employ to bring about attitudinal outcomes in his learners. *First,* the teacher should consciously and deliberatively teach for attitudes. Studies by Abraham Kroll, as well as other investigations, show that the teacher can and does effect an attitudinal change in his students, especially if he desires to do so.[308] A famous investigation by Austin Bond on the use of rational, factual material shows how pupils' attitudes can be changed. A science class was divided into two groups, the experimental and the control. The students in the experimental group learned the concepts of genetics and were given a few indications by the instructor on how these concepts might apply to racial problems such as miscegenation. The control group, on the other hand, studied genetic concepts without any hint as to their applications. The results of the test administered to both groups after the completion of the instruction indicated that those in the experimental group were more favorable to Orientals, Jews, and Italians and less favorable to imperialism than were those in the control group.[309] The use of noncognitive and situational pedagogical practices has proven quite effective in achieving attitude and value outcomes in learners.[310] *Second,* the teacher should put the student in a learning situation which is concrete and which contains many firsthand experiential variables. Situations which are concrete rather than symbolic (for example, purely verbal) have been found to be generative of attitude change. A study by Ira Brophy of merchant seamen concluded that the greater the number of times a sailor had shipped with a Negro seaman, the less prejudiced he became. Thus forty-three percent of those who had shipped two or less times with a Negro were prejudiced as compared with only eleven percent of those who had shipped three or more times. In the latter group eighty-four percent had favorable attitudes toward Negro sailors as compared with only forty-three percent of those sailors who had shipped two times or less.[311] Other studies show that the majority of white persons who lived in housing projects which subsequently became racially integrated,[312] who had to work with black persons,[313] or who attended schools which became racially integrated[314] developed more favorable attitudes toward blacks than they previously had held. In Jack Brehm's experiment young adolescents were induced to eat vegetables they disliked intensely. A follow-up assessment revealed that the negative valence of their attitude toward the vegetables decreased considerably.[315] An interesting study by Melvin DeFleur and Frank Westie showed that it is in concrete overt behavior (as contrasted to symbolic abstract behavior such as verbalizations) that an individual's true attitudes typically come to the fore. After being shown a number of photographs of attractive, cultured-looking blacks, a group of whites were asked to verbally express their attitudes toward black people. Following this the whites were asked to sign a standard photograph release agreement allowing them to be photographed with Negroes. As expected, persons who had verbally expressed a prejudiced attitude toward blacks typically refused to sign the agreement; however, some of the individuals who had verbally expressed favorable attitudes toward blacks declined to sign the agreement. The investigators concluded that overt acts bring attitudes more truly to the fore than do symbolic acts.[316] The investigations of Milton Rokeach on attitude formation and change similarly concluded that it is in concrete "overt" situations that an individual's deeper attitudes are manifested.[317] All this suggests to the religion teacher that it is in a learning situation characterized by concreteness and firsthand experiences that the student's attitudes can be most effectively revealed and then modified appropriately. *Third,* the teacher should so structure the concrete learning situation that it features considerable interpersonal interaction among the members of the learning group. One review of the research concludes that attitudes are not developed by some sort of straight transfusion from parent or teacher, but rather are learned in a meaningful concrete situation characterized by interpersonal interaction.[318] This indicates that it would be pedagogically profitable for the religion teacher to make use of those educational practices which accentuate interpersonal experiences. While direct experiences are the most fruitful here, high-level contrived experiences which are pedagogically-pointed have been shown to be particularly effective in bringing about attitude change. For example, the research suggests that role-playing is an effective pedagogical tool in the modification of attitudes.[319] *Fourth and finally,* all the variables in the total educational environment must be deliberatively targeted toward the learning of values. Studies on behavioral change in both loose and tight organizations show that no one single element within the organization is generally potent enough to effect a change unless the rest of the organization is also targeted toward producing that change.[320] In a church-related school, for example, if the religion class is structured toward the teaching of certain attitudes while the other aspects of the school milieu are not so structured, the effectiveness of that class will be severely blunted if not rendered altogether nil.[321] An investigation by Antonina Quinn of 4,000 Catholic secondary school students found that the religion class of itself was not sufficient for changing the students' attitudes. Other variables such as the courses offered, the way in which the courses were taught, the goals of the courses, the activities program, and even the physical plant were all found to be factors of high importance in effecting desired attitude learnings.[322] Quite a few studies have been made on the influence of college in changing student attitudes. The bulk of the research seems to show that the effect of the college courses themselves upon deeper attitudes and values is negligible, especially when compared to the pervasive college climate.[323] Perhaps one cause of this finding is that these courses are typically not consciously and deliberatively thrusted toward attitude development and change. An investigation by Marie Edmund Harvey concluded that in the Eastern Catholic girls' college studied, there was no significant change in the religious attitude of students from freshman to senior year.[324] Robert Hassenger's study of students in a midwestern girls' college revealed that the seniors were minimally different from the freshmen in terms of fundamental attitudes and values, moving only slightly away from a preoccupation with both doctrinal and ethical orthodoxy and ritual performance. Indeed, a later longitudinal study by Hassenger of these same freshmen found a considerable decrease in the moralistic religious orientations of these freshmen as they progressed through college.[325] Philip Jacob's celebrated study indicated that college experiences by and large have a limited effect on the attitudes and values of the students. Further, Jacob discovered that students tended to graduate from college mostly unchanged in their basic attitudes, or at best, only a little less rigid or conservative than when they entered. With a few college students attitude change does come; however, such change does not derive primarily from the formal educational process.[326] In what is probably the most comprehensive review of the relevant research to date, Robert Hassenger concludes that Catholic colleges, like all other levels of the Catholic educational system, appear to be having their greatest impact in precisely those areas where individuals can be expected to adhere to attitudes and values even without such education.[327] What all these data point up is that in order to promote change and deepening in attitudes, the teacher must deliberatively structure the learning experiences in his lesson so that the probability of such change and deepening are enhanced. Further, if attitude change is to result from the total school environment, then all the variables within the institutional situation should be consciously shaped in such a manner as to be able to produce attitude change. Attitudinal learning is not a matter of luck or happenstance; it must be worked for.

The data also appear to indicate that children, adolescents, and young adults have deeper and more pervasive attitudes than the older generation seems willing to admit. Older adults are often fooled on this score because the younger generation's outward manifestations, forms, and expressions of religion do not usually coincide with what they have been accustomed to associate with religious signs.

If religion teaching is to be effective, it should include attitudinal learning as one central outcome. This means two things: (1) teaching for attitude development, and (2) employing evaluation devices to ascertain the nature and depth of this development. Religion teachers speak much about their classes being attitude-soaked. Yet their evaluation instruments tend to be primarily verbal and cognitive; consequently they have little, if any, valid evidence that their students do learn attitudes or even that their classes are in fact attitude-soaked. Religion teachers might do well to develop evaluation procedures for attitude development along the lines suggested by Benjamin Bloom, Thomas Hastings, and George Madaus in their highly significant volume *Handbook on Formative and Summative Evaluation of Student Learning.*[328]

Finding #9: Religious and moral development are deeply and intricately intertwined with the entire process of human learning and development.

Less seems to be known about religious learning and development than about any other kind. Quite possibly this represents a fallout from a theological worldview of many religionists and churchmen that religious and moral development is something "special," "supernatural," or "otherworldly" and hence not amenable to social-science investigation except in a superficial way. In turn, all too many social scientists (perhaps adversely affected by the expressed negative attitudes of these religionists and churchmen) never bothered until recently to conduct empirical studies of the same range, intensity, and frequency as they did in other areas of human learning and development. Consequently the conclusions of the research presented in this section should be interpreted more strictly and more parsimoniously than in the cases of the first eight findings.

One of the aspects of religious growth and development which is of most interest to religious educators is that of a person's conscience. At the outset it must be observed that "conscience" is basically a conceptual construct used to tentatively explain specific attitudinal or value responses, whether these responses be of a judgmental, regulatory, or motivational sort. Conscience, then, is an inference from moral behavior, and only confusion results when the two are identified. Moral behavior can be tested and is empirically testable; the interpretation of the structure of the "conscience" which allegedly gives rise to moral behavior in a kind of cause-effect relationship falls within the domain of theory rather than of an empirically-verified finding. Thus while the research suggests that religious behaviors are decidedly multidimensional rather than unitary,[329] there is nonetheless some dispute on whether the conscience itself is unitary or multidimensional.[330] On the latter point Freudians call conscience the superego and contend it is a unitary process while the learning theorists typically regard conscience as multidimensional. Whatever the theoretical interpretations religious behavior is certainly multidimensional. The classic study by Hugh Hartshorne and Mark May concluded that many of the children studied exhibited little consistency in their moral behavior from one occasion to another.[331] An investigation by Wesley Allinsmith found that the amount of guilt a person feels following one type of transgression does not relate to the amount of guilt he feels following another.[332] A similar study conducted by Martin

Hoffman reached a similar conclusion.[333] It is these and other investigations which have led the vast majority of social scientists to draw the inference that "conscience" is multidimensional rather than unitary. Leonard Berkowitz sums up this position most forcefully when he states that "the conscience is not a unitary entity ever on watch against immoral temptations. Rather it is an abstraction referring to various ideals and behaviors, and these components may not form a consistent, ever-active whole. . . . All in all, we have little reason to picture the conscience as a constantly alert, unitary law-enforcing agency."[334] Still, as noted previously it is important to separate the empirically-demonstrated multidimensionality of religious behavior from hypotheses about the nature, potency, and influence of the construct we call "conscience."

Considerable controversy rages among developmental psychologists as to whether human growth is primarily maturational or is primarily affected by one's learning experiences. This is a form of the old familiar nature-nurture debate. On the maturational side of this nature-nurture continuum, the investigations of many developmental psychologists, particularly in Europe, suggest that all human development including religious and moral development occurs progressively during certain times or stages of an individual's life. It must be emphasized that this notion of relatively fixed developmental stages refers to maturational levels and should not be confused with specific age ranges. There is a positive correlation between age level and maturational stage, but correlation is not cause. Perhaps the most famous of all the research along this line are the investigations of Jean Piaget in Geneva.[335] While Piaget tended to concentrate his investigations around cognitive development in children, nonetheless he also researched the development of moral judgment in children. Piaget investigated moral judgments rather than overt religious behavior. To test the moral judgment of children, he presented them with a series of brief stories. Some of these were arranged in pairs while others consisted in a single narrative in which three possible solutions were presented from which the child was to choose one. In all cases the children were told to make their choice on the basis of what they believed to be right and good. A paraphrase of one of the paired stories illustrates this. In the first story a little boy whose name is John is called to dinner. Unknown to John, behind the door to the dining room is a chair on which is resting a tray holding fifteen cups. As John enters the dining room, the door knocks against the tray and all the cups are broken. In the second story of this pair, a little boy, Henry by name, tries to get some jam from a cupboard while his mother is away from the house. He climbs on a chair to reach the cupboard. In his attempt he knocks over a cup which breaks. Whose action, John's or Henry's, is the worse offense? On the basis of their responses to the problematic presented in each story, Piaget was able to identify two major and discrete stages of moral judgment. The first stage, which lasts until seven or eight years of age, can be termed the "morality of constraint" and is based on an ethic of authority. Moral rules and restraints are viewed by children as being laid down by adults. These rules must be interpreted literally; they are eternal and unchanging, cannot be altered, and are to be accepted automatically and without question. At this stage children judge behavior according to its objective consequences. For example, in the paired stories mentioned above, John is naughtier than Henry because he broke fifteen cups whereas Henry broke only one. Hence Piaget called this first stage "heteronomy." Sometimes it is also referred to as the period of "moral realism." Further, this stage is characterized by the principle of "immanent justice." By this is meant that punishment flows inevitably from a moral violation, and the severity of the punishment is directly proportionate to the seriousness of the consequences of the misdeed—regardless of the motive which inspired it. At this stage moral rules are not internalized but are adhered to solely through fear of external punishment by superior authority. The second stage which begins at about the age of eight can be called "autonomy." Often it is termed "the morality of cooperation" because it is based on an ethic of mutual respect. The child's unilateral respect for the all-knowing and dominant adult by this time has yielded to a progressive awareness of his (the child's) autonomy as a person. Moral rules can be altered and are not intrinsically coercive. Punishment for wrongdoing is now guided by the principle of reciprocity; that is to say, punishment should set things right again rather than being merely retributional. The motive underlying a person's act is now regarded as more important than the objective act in determining guilt or innocence, as well as degree of guilt. For example, in the paired stories Henry's misdeed is now regarded as being more serious because unlike John he intended to commit a bad act (taking the jam without permission). Moral principles begin to be increasingly internalized so that the child now believes that a person should act morally regardless of the presence or absence of external sanctions. Piaget's investigation led him to identify what some observers[336] label a third stage, and what other commentators[337] regard as an advanced level of the second stage.[338] At this level which sets in toward eleven or twelve years of age, the morality of an action is not only circumscribed by the objective nature of the deed and the individual's motive, but also by the circumstances surrounding the act. Taking circumstances into account, the child now might either judge the seriousness of a misdeed as lessened, or forgive the offender outright for having fallen prey to the circumstances impinging upon him. Moral rules are now viewed as compacts between people which are formulated and maintained in the common interest. The principle of equity in judging moral behavior now assumes great importance.

Though proponents of the maturational theory of religious development often cite Piaget's conclusions as supporting their view, the fact of the matter is that Piaget himself inferred from his investigations that an individual's maturational sequence is affected by his environment and the contours of his interaction with this environment. But because of a lack of methodological rigor in Piaget's early works (including the investigation reported above),[339] many other researchers have directly or indirectly replicated Piaget's studies utilizing more sophisticated controls. Some of these investigators, for example, David Elkind in the United States and Ronald Goldman in England, are Piagetians, while others such as Lawrence Kohlberg and Arnold Gesell and his associates in the United States, André Godin and his students in Belgium, and Jean-Pierre Deconchy in France pursue a more globally developmental tack in their research. David Elkind's investigations of the religious identity conceptions of children from Jewish, Catholic, and Congregationalist Protestant denominations supported much of Piaget's findings that concepts (in this case religious concepts) develop in a necessary sequence of maturational stages which are age-related. In stage one (usually ages five to seven), the child has a global, undifferentiated conception of his religious identity. He knows only that the denominational terms refer to persons in general, with no particularized referent. Although the child could identify his denominational affiliation, he often confused this with race or nationality. For example, "Are all boys and girls in the world Catholic?" "No." "Why not?" "Some are Irish and some are Russian." In stage two (usually ages seven to nine), religious identity is particularized. The child has abstracted certain concrete observable referent properties, primarily actions, which are characteristic of different denominational groups. For example, "What is a Catholic?" "He goes to Mass every Sunday and goes to a Catholic school." In stage three (usually ages ten to twelve), children no longer look for manifestations of denominational identity solely in a person's outward behavior; they seek it also in evidence of his innermost beliefs and convictions. For example, "Can a dog or cat be Jewish?" "No." "Why not?" "Because they are not human and would not understand religion." Elkind's research confirmed Piaget's conclusions that at each developmental stage the form of thought is determined by endogenous factors whereas the content of the thought is determined by one's experiences.[340]

Ronald Goldman's highly significant investigation of the development of religious thinking in children and youth made use of Jean Piaget's stages of cognitive development as a research scaffolding. Goldman concluded that the maturity of religious thinking is related to maturation and to age. In investigating children's understanding of bible stories, his study found the following concerning the narrative of the temptation of Jesus. In stage one (up to nine years), the children hold trivial, irrelevant, or rudely literal conceptions, typically involving authoritarian obedience or Jesus' nature or his vast powers. In stage two (up to twelve years), the essentials of the narrative are seen in terms of a more personalized context but are still grossly misrepresentative, for example, the command of Satan or Jesus explains everything. In stage three (after twelve years), there is a growing awareness (dimly at first, but growing clearer later) that evil and conflict are woven into the very fabric of the human condition. Goldman referred to the three stages as preconceptual, concrete, and symbolic (or insightful) respectively. In his examination of children's conception of the effectiveness of prayer, Goldman discerned three and in some cases four stages. In stage one (up to nine years), children believe that prayer is efficacious because it automatically guarantees an answer from God, usually in terms of a magically produced materialistic result. In stage two (up to twelve years), the children believe that prayer is efficacious not only because of God's power, but also because of the power of semimagical intermediaries, for example, a prayer of petition to cure a sick person is effective because God helped the physician to "make better medicine." In stage three (beginning at about twelve years), there is a growing awareness that the efficaciousness of prayer is not magical but is due to the active relationship of the petitioner with God. Some adolescents reach a fourth stage in which they believe the efficaciousness of prayer depends on the submissive faith of the supplicant, a faith which shows that even when the outcome to what one petitions in prayer is different from his hopes, the prayer has been answered since the result indicates God's will and helps make man's reaction more closely aligned with that will.[341]

Lawrence Kohlberg's research on the moral judgment (as contrasted with moral conduct) of children ten to sixteen resulted in his identification of discrete stages and substages in this domain.[342] Like Piaget and similar researchers, Kohlberg studied moral judgment in terms of the child's use and interpretation of rules in conflict situations together with his reasons for moral action, rather than either as correct knowledge of rules or as conventional beliefs in these rules. Kohlberg distinguishes as does Piaget also between moral structure and moral product content in the whole affair of moral judgment. Moral structure is the organizing form or whole that makes up the moral judgment, while moral content consists in the actual rules and commands contained in each morality.[343] Piaget's research found that heteronomy and autonomy explained or determined a child's moral judgment, while Kohlberg's investigation concluded that the child's moral judgment is based on a hedonistic view of right and wrong. The research approach of both Jean Piaget and Lawrence Kohlberg situates moral judgment in a framework of overall cognitive development. Consequently neither investigator is able to adequately relate the connection between cognitive development and moral development. The most either researcher will say in this respect is that cognitive development is a necessary but not a sufficient condition for moral development. The stages (Kohlberg prefers to call them levels and types) of moral judgment in children as found by Kohlberg's empirical research are as follows: Level I is the preconventional or premoral level. There are two subdivisions or types of Level I: Type 1 is a punishment and obedience orientation; Type 2 is a naive instrumental relativistic hedonism. Level II is the conventional or the morality of conventional role-conformity. There are two subdivisions or types of Level II: Type 3 is the good-boy morality of maintaining good relations with and approval of others; Type 4 is an authority-maintaining morality. Level III is the postconventional or the morality of self-accepted moral principles. There are two subdivisions or types of Level III: Type 5 is the morality of contract and democratically-accepted law; Type 6 is the morality of individual principles of conscience. Kohlberg's investigation also identified the motivational aspects of each stage. In Level I children, material rewards and punishments are the critical variables; in Level II children, nonmaterial rewards such as praise and blame assume the ascendancy. In Level III youths, reference to an ideal becomes paramount. Kohlberg's investigations were also able to isolate thirty-two different "aspects" of moral judgments on which persons in each of the six general types of orientation respond differently. One of these "aspects," designated by the investigator as "Aspect 10," is "motivation for rule obedience and moral action." Persons in the different types conceptualized or judged "Aspect 10" as follows: Type 1: obey rules to avoid punishment; Type 2: conform to obtain rewards, to have favors returned, and so on; Type 3: conform to avoid disapproval or dislike by others; Type 4: conform to avoid censure by legitimate authorities and resultant guilt; Type 5: conform to maintain the respect of the impartial spectator who is judging one's morality in terms of overall community welfare. Type 6: conform to avoid internal self-condemnation. Kohlberg's research concluded that moral judgments of the Type 1 and 2 variety decrease with age. Those of Types 3 and 4 increase until age thirteen and then stabilize, while those of Types 5 and 6 increase from age thirteen to sixteen.

André Godin[344] and his students have conducted numerous investigations on the genetic development of religious ideas, affects, and attitudes in children and adolescents. A study by S. Marthe made under Godin's supervision found a steady decrease in the magical approach to religion by Roman Catholic children eight years of age to fourteen. Marthe found that children of eight years of age quite uniformly give answers which reflect a magical mentality vis-à-vis religion. The age of eleven to twelve seems to mark a transition from the magical mentality to a more mature religious conception. By age fourteen about half the children investigated had reached this mature level. For purposes of her study, Marthe conceptualized magical mentality in terms of automatic causality between the reception of a sacrament and a spiritual effect, the causal efficacy between the reception of a sacrament and extraordinary material benefits, and a general confusion between the sacramental sign and its signification.[345] Bernadette Van Roey, also working under André Godin's supervision, found an age-related change in Belgian children's conceptions of the efficacy of prayer regarding immanent sanction and divine protection.[346]

Making use of the problem-story method employed by Piaget and by Godin and Van Roey, R. H. Thouless and L. B. Brown studied the notions of petitionary prayer in Australian adolescent girls aged twelve to seventeen. Their investigation concluded that the older the adolescent girls become, the more constantly they move away from notions of high causal efficacy (magical mentality) of petitionary prayer. This age-related trend appears to be quite independent of the denominational affiliation of the girls. Belief in the appropriateness and the causal efficacy of petitionary prayer appears to depend upon a moral evaluation of the situation in which the prayer is offered as well as on an assessment of the moral object of the prayer. Finally, belief in the appropriateness or rightness of petitionary prayer seems to depend upon the kind of religious instruction the girls received. The thrust of this religious instruction varies from one denomination to another and is largely independent of belief in the degree or kind of causal efficacy of such prayer.[347]

Diane Long and her associates conducted a study on the conceptions of prayer among elementary school children. The investigators found that the prayer concept seems to develop in three discrete age-related stages. At the first stage (ages five to seven), the children had an undifferentiated conception of prayer in the sense that their notion of prayer was both vague and fragmentary. At the second stage (ages seven to nine), the children had a concrete and differentiated conception of prayer, recognizing that it involves some sort of verbal activity. At this stage, however, prayer was still regarded as an external activity, a routine form, instead of a personal and internal activity. At the third stage (ages nine to twelve), the children had developed an abstract prayer conception in the sense that they regarded it as a personal activity deriving from personal conviction and belief. Only at the third stage did prayer develop as true personal communication between the child and what he considered divine. With increasing age the product content of prayer also changed from egocentric and materialistic wish-fulfillment (candy, toys, and so on) to altruistic moral desires (peace on earth, for example). At the same time affects associated with prayer activity became less impulsive and more modulated among the older children. Concomitantly, prayer came to be a deeper and more satisfying experience.[348]

Christian Van Bunnen studied the conceptions of the biblical story of the burning bush on two groups of Belgian children, aged five to six and eleven to twelve. The children aged five to six conceived the burning bush in terms of physical or magical danger of fire rather than as a symbol; they saw the bush affectively through their imaginative perceptions of fire and judged Moses's actions in terms of one's normal reactions to fire. By contrast the conceptions of the children aged eleven to twelve began to grasp the symbolic value of the story (the oldest of the children appreciated the sense of man's distance from God and reverence for what is sacred), to widen in their sense of God, and to judge the actions of Moses as quite possibly being an offense against God.[349]

Godelieve de Valensart studied the spontaneous reactions to religious pictures of five-year-olds, seven-year olds, ten-year olds, and twelve-year olds in Belgian schools. The pictures were in four series. Each series contained three pictures of the same gospel scenes depicted in a different artistic style. The first style was identified as the "realistic-sentimental" style which through its technique and colors creates a sentimental atmosphere and attempts primarily to document the gospel scene by presenting it objectively. (In Europe this style is frequently called the "St. Sulpice style," while in America it is commonly referred to as "Barclay Street art.") The second style was labelled "hieratic-emotional." Here the pictures are executed in a more stylized mode and are intended to produce a certain feeling of happy peace, a childlike atmosphere in the manner of the Italian primitives, while still remaining realistic. The third series was designated "schematic-symbolic." Its technique is to portray through the use of general feeling and atmosphere the outering of the symbolic nature or essential religious content of the scene. This style is somewhat realistic, but less so than the other two. Copies of all the pictures used in de Valensart's study came from missals or religious textbooks commonly used in France or Belgium at the time. The results of this study indicated that the youngest children preferred the "schematic-symbolic" style while the older children overwhelmingly favored the "realistic-sentimental" style. The older children criticized the figures and objects in the other two styles as not being true to life in the sense that they did not accurately depict the people and things they themselves encountered in daily living.[350]

Jean-Pierre Deconchy made use of a semantic free-association test as a methodological base in his study of the genetic structure of the idea of God in French children attending Roman Catholic schools. Deconchy's data allowed him to identify three stages. Children between eight and ten stressed "attributive themes" about God. These themes clustered around three axes: objective attributes (for example, omniscience, omnipresence), subjective attributes (for example, goodness, justice), and affective attributes (for example, strength, beauty). Children in the eleven to thirteen age range emphasized personalization themes such as sovereignty, redeemer, and fatherhood. At the third stage from fourteen to sixteen years, there develop interiorization themes of God which revolve around the subjective such as love, prayer, fear, trust-dialogue. At the second and third stages, girls seem to develop later than boys.[351]

A study by Arnold Gesell and his associates based on longitudinal and cross-sectional samples examined adolescent attitudes toward God, the church, and death. Gesell found that the preadolescent years tended to be a time during which the individual's ideas about God gradually deconcretized. Fifteen-year olds displayed an oscillation between faith and scepticism while sixteen-year olds displayed a conception of God which strongly resembled adult ideas of the deity.[352]

Earlier in this section, it was noted that there is considerable controversy on the part of some developmental psychologists on whether human growth (and hence religious growth also) is primarily affected by maturation or by learning. There have been some psychologists and religious educators who have interpreted the developmental stage findings detailed above as supporting the maturational point of view as against the learning point of view. However, the bulk of the research evidence would seem to suggest that human (and religious) growth is affected by both maturation and learning. The growth changes which take place in an individual are not necessarily products of an automatic maturational process. Indeed, Merton Strommen declares that the vast majority of American cognitive psychologists reject the stage theory as the necessary and sufficient explanation of human growth. For them the important element is not the age level but the experiences which usually accompany these levels.[353] This is a cardinal point. Further, it should be underscored that maturation or stage is not the same as age. Persons who make a particular age coincide perfectly with a given stage are unjustifiedly overextending the findings of the stage psychologists.

Jean Piaget's researches, while pioneering, nonetheless were marred by a certain lack of empirical rigor in methodology.[354] Further research has led to acceptance of many of his conclusions, modification of others, and rejection of still others. Apropos of the last point, whereas Piaget regarded moral judgments as forming a unitary pattern in a given maturational stage, subsequent research suggests that there are different and independent forms of judgment even at the same age level.[355] Indeed, the various components of moral thinking which Piaget contends go together to form a stage pattern have been discovered to be not always together at a particular stage.[356] To be sure, Urie Bronfenbrenner's review of the research concludes that an impressive number of studies over a quarter century in two continents report age differences consistent with Piaget's data of a shift from moral realism toward reciprocity and equity.[357] Yet these studies all point out that sociocultural differences significantly modify both the ages at which the stages take place and also the relative importance of each of the factors within a particular stage. Piaget's studies were done with poor children in Geneva; the farther one moves away from this milieu in culture and distance, the more frequently can be found departures from or even contradictions of certain of Piaget's conclusions. For example, replicating Piaget's methodology, M. R. Harrower investigated the moral judgments of socioculturally advantaged and disadvantaged children in London. Her data supported Piaget's with respect to the moral judgments of the socioculturally disadvantaged children but not with the socioculturally advantaged. Harrower concluded that Piaget's stages of moral development are not universal characteristics of maturation per se, but vary according to the texture of one's broader sociocultural environment.[358] Confirmatory evidence for Harrower's data and conclusion comes from a series of investigations conducted in the United States and also crossculturally concerning the effect of class differences in moral development.[359] It is possible, of course, as Urie Bronfenbrenner suggests that Piaget (and I might add the other stage theorists) unduly minimizes the highly potent roles of environmental influences and learning experiences on the development of a child's moral judgment and conscience. But it must be borne in mind that Piaget himself believes that the stage sequence he describes resulted from an interactive combination of maturational events and learning experiences.

An important study by Albert Bandura and Frederick McDonald found that external nonmaturational variables such as social reinforcement and modeling caused children at one stage level to develop the moral orientation of children at a different stage level.[360] If a child's moral judgment at any given stage can be modified by the application of external experiences, then the notion of a necessary, fixed, and maturation-bound process of human growth represents an overly restrictive explanation. The results of this study are easily integrated into Edith Dowley's review of the research which indicates that early childhood experiences do have a significant effect on an individual's later growth and behavior. Indeed, the data seem to indicate that nursery school experiences appear to also play a measurable role in helping to shape human growth.[361] The research suggests that experiences in differentiated sociocultural milieux do exert a significant impact on an individual's moral judgment independent of fixed maturational development.[362]

In short, the data would seem to imply that stages in moral judgment are not simply a direct unfolding of biological or neurological structures. Rather, moral stages appear to represent the influence of interactive learning experiences on one's natural maturational development. In other words, learning experiences in differing environmental contexts accelerate, retard, or otherwise modify the age trends of development. Thus the combination of (1) maturation influenced to a particular degree (depending on the quality and nature of the experience) by (2) external learning experiences produces the age shifts and trends. It is especially important to note that within the stage levels, the coloration of the child's moral judgment is radically affected by his home experiences and also to a lesser but nonetheless highly significant degree by other environmental variables with which he interacts.

According to the research data there appear to be at least three major nonmaturational factors or forces which significantly affect the development of one's conscience: parental influence, socioeconomic class influence, and religious influence. As the investigations cited throughout this entire chapter strongly suggest, parental influence is by far the most powerful of the three. Even if the child does not introject his parents' moral judgments in every detail, nonetheless the research does indicate that the manner (process content) in which parents treat their offspring is the critical factor.[363] Two aspects of parental treatment stand out as being especially critical variables: the kind of disciplinary techniques used and the degree of affectivity displayed.

The research data indicate that harsh, highly assertive, and physically punitive disciplinary techniques on the part of parents tend to have the effect of producing weak consciences and weak moral standards in their children.[364] A study by Donald MacKinnon cited quite early in this chapter found that college students who cheated on examinations tended to have parents who exercised physical discipline, whereas those college students who did not cheat typically had parents who used rational, affective, or psychological disciplinary procedures. The investigator concluded that the use of differential disciplinary procedures plays a significant role in the development of a strong or weak conscience.[365] Justin Aronfreed's investigation of the effects of disciplinary techniques found that those parents who employed physical punishment and assaultive verbal attacks tended to have children with "external consciences." When these children committed what they regarded as a violation of a moral rule, they tended to feel remorseful, anxious, and willing to confess and make amends principally because they were afraid their actions would be detected and they would thereby be subject to punishment. Parents who resorted to psychological rather than physical forms of discipline, who reasoned with their children, and who left them a relatively large amount of room to make their own moral decisions tended to have children with "internal consciences." When these children committed what they believed to be a moral infraction, they displayed a relatively autonomous need to make restitution regardless of detection by others of their misdeed; moreover these children seemed to exhibit characteristics of true guilt.[366] An investigation by Wesley Allinsmith found that when parents are arbitrary in their demands and fail to supply reasons and explanations for their rules, their children are likely to be less able to resist temptations and more prone to violate moral canons than is the case when parents discuss with them at some length the basis of moral regulations and encourage them to make their own moral judgments to some degree. Of particular interest are Allinsmith's data which suggest that children whose parents are authoritarian and use strong disciplinary measures tend to rely heavily on external cues as indicators of right and wrong. On the other hand, children whose parents use more rational, self-actualizing disciplinary procedures tended to look more to internal cues for indicators of right and wrong.[367] In this entire consideration of the effect of parental disciplinary measures, however, one further factor has been shown by the research, namely the contextual variables. In Leonard Berkowitz's words, "psychological disciplinary methods may foster the growth of moral values (assuming that the parents also possess such values), but whether these moral values are operative and controlling depends on other factors in the situation."[368]

It should be underscored that the research clearly indicates that it is not the parents' disciplinary or controlling behavior in itself which plays such a powerful role in forming the strength and texture of the child's conscience; rather, the most significant variable is the degree and coloration of the feeling-tone and affective context in which these parental disciplinary or controlling behaviors are embedded.[369] It is the affective structure in which these parental behaviors are situated that gives the child the basic inner meaning and existential reference point of the parental disciplinary measures. This is why the research indicates quite positively that love-oriented techniques are usually associated with strong moral values in children.[370] Thus an investigation by Robert Sears and his associates concluded that the love-oriented disciplinary pattern was found to relate to development of a strong conscience in the child only in conjunction with frequent parental expressions of love and affection.[371] Far more than any other social group, the home promotes identification of the child's conscience with his parents' consciences. It is this identification which fosters internalization of values. Affective parental behaviors, or perhaps more accurately parental behaviors that are affectively-oriented and situated in an overall warm caring affective context, are the ones which so effectively facilitate identification by the child.[372] If a child has grown up in a love-deprived family environment, affectively-valenced disciplinary techniques will take on a different hue. For example, a parent's threat to withdraw love is not overly upsetting to a child who has learned not to need or to want this love.[373] By way of summation of the differential effects of disciplinary techniques and affective context, the research appears to indicate that the general affective context and relationship foster the development of the overall kind of moral value structure, whereas the variations and types of disciplinary and controlling techniques account for the particular thrust, coloration, and direction which this moral value structure takes.

The socioeconomic status of the family in which the child grows up constitutes a second major nonmaturational factor or force significantly affecting the development of one's conscience. Urie Bronfenbrenner's digest of the research shows that the child's cognitive resources for moral judgment are more closely correlated with socioeconomic status than with any other cultural variable.[374] This is a very significant fact because it implies the availability of highly differentiated factors and forces which are not necessary accompaniments of advancing age. The previously cited Harrower study indicated that Piaget's data held true with London children from the poorer classes but did not obtain for London children from the higher socioeconomic levels. In fact, the children from the more prosperous families in Harrower's sample tended to exhibit relatively mature moral judgment even at the youngest ages, and the percentage of such evaluations remained fairly constant over the age range. Clement Cosgrove's study conducted in the United States revealed that the socioeconomic status of the Catholic elementary school children investigated exerted a significant influence on the extent of their theoretical and practical knowledge of moral and religious truths.[375] The studies show that differences in parental disciplinary techniques tend to be reflective of social class. Middle-class parents tend to use psychological and moderate techniques while parents from the lower classes are more inclined to employ physical and severe procedures. Justin Aronfreed's investigation concluded that middle-class mothers are prone to rely heavily on disciplinary techniques which are focused on inducing stable moral standards in their children whereas mothers from the lower classes incline toward physical procedures such as spanking which do nothing more than sensitize their offspring to the painful external consequences of the misdeed.[376] These data are plainly related to those presented in the previous paragraph concerning the effect of differentiated parental disciplinary techniques on the child's moral value system. One investigation concluded that in response to another child's moral transgression, a lower-class child tends to prescribe direct punishment while the middle-class child often will first examine the facts to ascertain whether the young culprit's environment perhaps was a prominent factor giving rise to the misdeed. If the middle-class child does advocate some form of punishment, he is less likely than the lower-class child to prescribe personal punishment of the offender.[377] One researcher has hypothesized that Piaget's data can be more adequately explained by the arbitrary and authoritarian disciplinary procedures practiced by Swiss European lower-class parents than by age-related causality.[378]

The influence of an individual's belonging both to a denominational group in particular and to some religious group in general possibly constitutes a third nonmaturational force affecting the development of his conscience. Bernard Spilka indicates in his review of the research that hard data are very sparse and often lacking about the influence of specific denominational groups on the moral development and moral judgments of their members.[379] The review of the research by Michael Argyle cited previously in this section suggests that racial prejudice seems correlated with the broad denominational group (Catholic, Protestant, Jewish) with which a person is affiliated. Leonore Boehm found that Catholic parochial children tended to make more mature moral judgments on Piaget-type stories at an earlier age than did public school children, regardless of the intelligence level or socioeconomic class of the children. Quite possibly these data can be explained by the emphasis which Catholicism has traditionally placed on preparation for the reception of the sacraments of confession and the eucharist, a preparation which is typically presumed to necessitate critical reflection by the child on the more mature aspects of moral judgment such as the object, end, and circumstances of moral transgression.[380] The studies by Alfred Kinsey and his associates indicated that there is a correlation between one's religious denomination and one's sexual behavior. Catholics, for example, tended to engage less in certain sexual practices forbidden by their religion than did members of other denominations whose moral code system was either less emphatic or nonexistent on the specific sexual practices in question.[381] Yet these fragmentary data must be counterbalanced by other data of a more global sort. A study by Terry Prothro compared several "philosophies of life" held by two samples of Arab students. One group was Moslem, the other, Christian. The investigator found that in general there was no basic difference in value orientation between the two groups.[382] One review of the research has discovered that religionism—membership in a particular religion—has no pivotal relationship with humanitarianism, altruism, nondelinquency, or ethical behavior (except in the latter case for sexual mores).[383] Leonard Berkowitz's review of the research leads him to conclude that "religion, as it is currently practiced, may promote asceticism, at least in some cases, but it does not in itself reduce the incidence of stealing, cheating, or aggression."[384] More data are required to determine the extent of the influence on value system and conscience development which a specific religious denomination exerts on its members. It well might be that religious affiliation is a crucial nonmaturational variable primarily to the extent to which the beliefs and code-system of the denomination are both interpreted and lived out by parents as modified by the sociocultural milieu in which the parents live.

Significance of finding #9 for the teaching of religion. The principal and overarching significance of finding #9 is that religious and moral development takes place according to the normal interactive growth patterns of human maturation and learning. Religious and moral development does not take place in some magical, otherworldly, or supernaturally unfathomable manner. The data presented in connection with finding #9 should therefore go a long way in helping to "demythologize"—and even "despookify"—religious instruction.

The impressive data drawn from the studies by Piaget, Goldman, and Kohlberg abundantly indicate the necessity of architecting both the individual lesson and the entire curriculum around the developmental growth pattern of the learner. An individual can be taught religion only to the extent, degree, and manner that he can learn it. As David Elkind observes, there now exists an empirical basis for systematically building lessons and curricula in an optimal fashion, that is, around the contours of the learner's growth.[385] For example, the studies by Elkind suggest that it is not until the age of eleven or twelve that children can accurately understand religious concepts. When confronted with religious concepts before this developmental level, children spontaneously give meanings to these concepts which betray their lack of comprehension.[386] The investigations by Goldman, Van Bunnen, and others show plainly that the deeper cognitive symbolism which undergirds and suffuses so much of the bible is grossly misunderstood by children under the age of around ten. In this connection one pilot study of children's religious ideas (as reflected in their early drawings of God and later expanded upon in interviews with the researcher) found that children have a magical convoluted "bible story orientation" rather than an understanding of God. For example, a seven-year-old child was convinced that God always travels on a little donkey.[387] Despite the readily available empirical data, there does not appear to be a single American Roman Catholic curriculum plan or textbook series at the elementary school level which is based *primarily* on the growth, development, and learning patterns of children. This is certainly a shocking state of affairs. To take one example, a curriculum series developed in the late 1960's entitled *Life, Love, Joy*[388] takes the concept of life as its theme for Grade One elementary school children (six-year olds). This concept is rather abstract, to say the least. If one is to place credence in the empirical research, it is highly problematic that a six-year-old child can understand, even minimally, the concept running throughout the very first unit of Grade One, namely "the gift of life." The research cited in this chapter shows that early childhood curricula should revolve around an affective rather than a cognitive axis. Yet the emphasis of the *Life, Love, Joy* series for six-year olds is decidedly cognitive. Even when pictures and graphics are presented in the textbook, the teacher is instructed to "make certain that each child sees and understands the picture, or part of the picture, under discussion."[389] The great potential of art as a heavily affective medium is thereby minimized in the *Life, Love, Joy* curriculum. The research summarized under the ten findings in this chapter also implies that richness in various environmental stimuli, together with a well-structured and varied reinforcement menu of these stimuli, is crucial for enriched learning. Yet the activities suggested for the teacher to do with his or her class in the *Life, Love, Joy* curriculum are so few, and so unvaried, and so typically unidimensional as to provide learners with an environment characterized by stimulus deprivation rather than by stimulus enrichment. The research also indicates the critical importance of the home in the genesis and strengthening of attitudinal and value learning. Yet in the *Life, Love, Joy* curriculum there are hardly any pupil activities which involve parents. Finally, the authors of the *Life, Love, Joy* curriculum emphasize that this curriculum is architected around the scriptures. But if the research cited under finding #9 means anything, it is that an effective curriculum must be architected around the learner, the way he matures and learns.

The studies by Piaget, Goldman, Kohlberg, Elkind, and others suggest that moral and religious development is maturational. Does this mean that the teaching of religion is a hopeless or impossible task, since the individual develops according to internal maturational forces outside the control of the teacher? The question must be emphatically answered in the negative. Maturation is indeed an important constituent in an individual's growth pattern; however, it should not be forgotten that the research indicates that individuals grow not by maturational processes alone, but by an interactive combination of internal maturational forces and external learning experiences. Since the essence of religious instruction is the deliberative structuring of learning experiences to facilitate religious growth, it is eminently clear that the religion teacher can exert a significant influence on the course and direction of an individual's religious learning. Further, the hard data show that the religion teacher's pedagogical behaviors can influence the coloration and thrust of a person's unfolding maturational forces. Both Piaget and Kohlberg emphasize that maturation is a process related to the overall structure of moral development. But the kinds, the salience, the focus, and the specific composition of the contents within that overall structure are strongly conditioned by the dynamic inter-action between the inner maturational forces and the external environment within which the individual is in contact. Studies by MacRae, Harrower, Bandura and McDonald, Peck and Havighurst, and so on show that the nature and texture of an individual's environment exert a powerful influence on his moral and religious growth. Since it is within the capability of the teacher to structure the learning environment, then clearly the teacher can influence the course of an individual's moral growth. Consequently the effective religion teacher is one who structures the learning environment in such a way that it capitalizes on the research findings concerning both the maturational level of the learner and the factors most highly correlated with the enhancement of learning.

Religion teachers can significantly affect the student's religious and moral learning, but do they? Lawrence Kohlberg's observation on this point still is cogent: "recent research provides little reason to revise the conclusions of Hartshorne and May and others that formal or conventional character education classes or programs in the school or church have little or no effect upon the children's moral character."[390] But as I have shown previously, the fact that religion classes appear to be ineffective does not mean that the teacher or curriculum builder is unable to exert a very considerable impact on the learner's moral and religious growth. Urie Bronfenbrenner's review of the research indicates that in the Soviet Union, where all the activities in the classroom are deliberatively geared to producing "character education," that is, making good socialist citizens, the teacher appears to have a very strong influence on shaping the learners' moral standards and conduct.[391] Soviet teachers and curriculum builders typically utilize the empirical research to a high degree when architecting their pedagogical strategies or building their curricula. The Soviet data strongly suggest that conscious, deliberative, research-based pedagogical behaviors directed toward stimulating and enhancing religious development can produce the desired effect in learners. Summarizing and interpreting the pertinent research, Leonard Berkowitz even goes so far as to maintain that an individual's learning experiences play a more important role than do his internal maturational processes in forming his moral judgments.[392] One of the conclusions drawn by Justin Aronfreed from his research study was that the role of the cognitive equipment in a child's moral behavior tends to be dependent on the kinds of experience provided by the environment with which he interacts.[393]

What can the teacher do to enhance religious behavior in the pedagogical setting? Certainly the teacher might well concentrate on modifying specific learner behaviors rather than attempting to develop his global conscience or moral structure. After all, "conscience" is a construct, a hypothetical and tentative device to facilitate explanation of and research into phenomena. To reify a construct is to deflect attention from what is known to be real toward something which is real only as an hypothesis or an inference. Hence the teacher should teach for specific, observable, verifiable religious behaviors rather than focus his attention on a construct. Just as the construct "learning" should not be confused with "performance," so too the construct "conscience" must not be confused with specific "religious behaviors." To facilitate religious behavior, the teacher ought to provide the student with a rich and varied menu of learning experiences. These experiences should be of a cognitive, affective, and lifestyle kind.

The research cited in support of finding #9 indicates that the affective context in which behavioral modification is done strongly conditions the effectiveness of whatever specific pedagogical techniques are employed. These data are consonant with finding #7 which shows that affectivity is both an indispensable educational practice and educational outcome in the work of religious instruction. It is probably true that religion teachers pay insufficient attention to affectivity both as a practice and as a process content. Commenting on the Van Roey study, André Godin poignantly remarks that "a number of children of 12 and even of 14 years of age have yet to find out, on the psychological level of their deepest affectivity, what characterizes truly religious and adult souls: that God's justice is none other than the victory of his ever-enduring love."[394] Creating a love-oriented teaching atmosphere and employing love-oriented pedagogical practices are, of course, quite different from transforming the learning environment into an ultrapermissive or hand-holding affair. To have a love-oriented learning environment is not the same as having an atmosphere which is oriented primarily around gratifying the learner's every whim or desire. One review of the pertinent research concludes by noting that need-gratification in itself tends to blunt or even destroy some of the strongest religious and moral behaviors associated with the notion of conscience.[395]

Healthy affect is not self-indulgence. Indeed, as part of its basic fiber, healthy affect has built-in cognitive and affective controls. A learning environment permeated by warm affect is not an orgy in self-indulgence; rather, it is a warm socioemotional climate in which there are built-in limits. These limits are determined by the nature and type of the learner as well as the nature and type of the learning task. Affect in service of the learner is that which incorporates those other forces and experiences which acting in concert produce the finished man of character, the man who can say "yes" to some things and "no" to other things while feeling secure and comfortable in doing so.

The teacher who wishes to be optimally effective in facilitating religious behaviors in learners should utilize research data as much as possible when planning and executing the lesson. For example, one study found that girls are significantly more likely than boys to give unstructured morally-oriented story endings in which the blame is placed on others. Girls, then, rely more than boys on external definition of moral consequences; their focus is more on external responsibilities. Further, this same study discovered also that as compared with boys, girls respond more to corrective practices of their moral behavior when initiated at the behest of someone else and that they tend more to exhibit their moral responses before someone else.[396] By making use of such data, the teacher can fashion differential pedagogical practices in facilitating desired religious outcomes in boys and girls. Or to use another example, the data cited under finding #9 suggest that process content is a critical factor in facilitating moral development. Thus the manner (process content) in which parents treat their child represents the critical factor in the child's introjection of the moral and religious value-system of its parents. Armed with such data the teacher can structure learning experiences which are rich in process contents. Again, to offer one final illustration, the data from the Piaget, Goldman, Kohlberg, and Elkind studies indicate that there is a generalized age-related internal maturational flow of moral and religious development. When used imaginatively and pedagogically, these data can form a springboard for accelerating the learner's religious growth. For example, Lawrence Kohlberg and his associates have worked out a series of pedagogical "match situations" between an individual and a moral situation which tend to have the effect of hastening his moral growth. These "match situations" are derived from Kohlberg's research data on maturational stages. The "match situation" consists of a proper coupling of the individual and a moral situation. This is done by presenting a "stage two person," for example, with a dilemma that can be resolved only by "stage three thinking" (a +1 match). This coupling or matching can actually induce enough creative tension, structural conflict, and direction to cause moral judgment to take place at the next higher stage over a period of continuous interaction situations. This is usually brought about by structuring the learning situation so that the individual engages in "active coping" with the environment together with opportunities for role-taking.

But even heavy utilization of the research data on how learning takes place does not directly yield effective pedagogical practices. As I emphasize in Chapter 5, learning is not teaching. Teaching is not just the converse of learning; it is much more. Further, the facts of teaching are far more inclusive, and to some extent are of a different ontological order than are the facts of learning. Teaching and learning are reciprocal activities with reciprocal task descriptions. But in accomplishing its task successfully, teaching must be constantly nourished in the soil of learning facts. More specifically teaching for religious learning must not act either in ignorance of or at crosspurposes with the facts of religious learning. Knowledge and utilization of the facts of learning will do much to convince the religion teacher that in the religion lesson the Spirit does not blow willy-nilly but rather blows according to the laws and realities of the nature which the Triune God made from eternity and continues to make until the end of time.

Finding #10: Transfer of learning constitutes the most important intermediate- and long-range outcome of instruction in formal and informal sites.

Transfer of learning is the influence of a previously established learning outcome on the acquisition, performance, or relearning of a second learning outcome. The term "transfer" is used because it implies that what is learned with respect to one task is transferred to the learning of future tasks. Transfer, then, refers to the influence of prior learning upon later learning. Transfer of learning may take three different forms: (1) positive transfer, when the learning of one task aids or facilitates the learning of some second or subsequent task; (2) negative transfer, when the learning of one task inhibits or impedes the learning of some second or subsequent task; (3) zero transfer, when there is no influence of the prior task on the subsequent task.[397]

From another vantage point transfer can be classified as horizontal or vertical depending on the level of influence involved. Horizontal transfer is that which refers to the influence of a prior task on a subsequent task of the same level of competency. Vertical transfer has to do with the influence of a prior task on a subsequent task of a higher or lower level of complexity.

During the first few decades of this century there was considerable controversy about whether transfer of learning existed or not. By World War II the evidence was so overwhelming that virtually no serious social scientist denied its existence.[398] The present concern is with ascertaining the precise variables together with their interactive patterns which influence transfer.

Perhaps there is no learning finding more important than transfer. It lies at the base of every pedagogical activity conducted in any kind of formal or informal site. At bottom, the basic goal of teaching is to enable the learner to apply the behaviors he learns in the teaching-learning environment to all aspects of his life—in other words, to transfer what he learns in the teaching-learning environment to every other relevant situation in his life. Hence religion teachers and curriculum builders are deeply concerned with ascertaining which educational practices most effectively facilitate transfer.

As one would expect, the research indicates that the greater the similarity between the various features of the prior learning task and the subsequent task, the more readily will transfer be facilitated. Three of these features have been investigated, namely task similarity, stimulus similarity, and response similarity. In terms of the gross characteristics of the overall task itself, the more the similarity between the prior and subsequent task, the greater the positive transfer.[399] With regard to stimulus similarity, two complementary facts seem to obtain. First, as the similarity among stimulus components increases, corresponding increases in positive transfer occur when the response components are functionally identical. Second, as the similarity among stimulus components increases, negative transfer increases when both stimulus and response components are simultaneously varied. With regard to response similarity, as the similarity among response components increases, corresponding decreases in negative transfer occur when the stimulus components are functionally identical.[400]

Because positive transfer is more relevant and more useful to religion teachers than is either negative transfer or zero transfer, the research presented in the remainder of this section will concentrate on data dealing with the heightening of positive transfer.

The research indicates that concepts or generalizations are more transferrable than facts or specific bits of information.[401] Further, those concepts which are abstracted from a relatively large number of facts have been found to be more amenable to positive transfer than are concepts drawn from a small sample of information.[402] Also concepts based on inherently meaningful associations are more transferrable than those based on associations which are either arbitrary or externally meaningful.[403] A study by Jack Kittel concluded by observing that "evidence from this experiment in conjunction with that of similar experiments indicates that furnishing learners with information in the form of underlying principles promotes transfer and retention of learned principles and may provide the background enabling future discovery of new principles."[404] (Principles are different from concepts. Both are abstractions. However, a concept is simply an abstract generalization about a certain class of reality, while a principle is a concept which explains the fundamental operation of that class of reality.) A celebrated study by G. M. Haslerud and Shirley Meyers came to the conclusion that "independently derived principles are more transferrable than those given" by the teacher or some other individual.[405] Finally, abilities including strategies and "learning to learn" skills facilitate positive transfer not only to subsequent tasks of the same class but also to other classes of tasks.[406]

The research evidence suggests that extensive practice on the original task increases the likelihood of positive transfer to a subsequent task, whereas more limited practice may result in zero transfer or even negative transfer.[407] This practice should be varied and multifaceted if transfer possibilities are to be maximized. In this connection a review of the research by Robert Travers indicates that there are considerable data to support the generalization that a wide range of similar or related experiences which differ somewhat from one another promotes transfer more effectively than do baldly unidimensional experiences. Strictly speaking this may be termed "training for flexibility"; however, such training represents one of the keys to transfer of learning.[408] The data suggest also that "insight," defined behaviorally as the rapid solution to problems, appears to develop as a result of extensive practice in solving similar or related classes of problems.[409] The probability of transfer is heightened when both principles and practice in their application are learned together.

Robert Craig's study concluded that the amount of transfer tends to increase as more and more clues are provided to aid the learner's discovery of the bases for correct responses. Further, the transfer effects of increasing the extent of teacher help in proferring clues become greater as the difficulty of the situation to which the learning is to be transferred increases.[410] Of course, as the previously mentioned Haslerud and Meyers investigation showed, the more the teacher's helps and clues are along the line of enabling the learner to derive for himself the underlying principles, the more readily will transfer ensue.

The probability of transfer is also enhanced when the teacher or student labels or otherwise identifies the important features of the original learning task.[411] A study by D. H. Holding discovered that with a simple task optimum transfer occurred when the learner progressed from the easier to the more difficult problem. However, in the case of more complex tasks, optimum transfer occurred when the learner progressed from the more difficult to the less difficult problems. Holding's data indicate that there is a complex relationship between task difficulty and the amount of transfer.[412]

Transfer of learning can be minimized and even eliminated when other experiences intervene between the original task and the subsequent task. In such cases the degree to which transfer is minimized or eliminated depends on the nature and valence of the intervening experience. Here the research suggests that the more similar in meaning and in structure are the interposed experiences (short of identical), the more pronounced are the inhibiting effects of this experience on transfer.[413]

Significance of finding #10 for the teaching of religion. Quite possibly the greatest significance of finding #10 is that it clearly indicates that the kind and quality of educational practice can and do exert an enormous impact on the amount of positive transfer effected. By "educational practice" in this context I mean not only the direct teacher-student encounter, but also the pedagogical arrangement of all the variables within the structured learning situation. Indeed, it has been shown in the research that the amount of transfer can be multiplied five or six times if the teacher's pedagogical practices are changed.[414] Now all this suggests that the skills of Christian living (the objective of religious instruction) should be taught in class not with the vague hope that they will be transferred later on to out-of-class or postclass life, but rather that these skills be deliberatively taught in such a way as to enhance the probability of their transfer to out-of-class and postclass life. Teaching for transfer is not a matter of hope; it is a matter of deliberative and conscious structuring of the learning situation so as to effect desired outcomes. Nor is the transfer process itself an esoteric thing which depends on some mysterious superadditum by the Holy Spirit after the religion lesson has ended. If the doctrines of divine creation and the incarnation mean anything, it is that the Holy Spirit works in and through nature instead of by means of external and extrinsic magic. The work of the Holy Spirit is enfleshed and made operable to the degree that the teacher's pedagogical behaviors are themselves effective. Human activity is a two-way cooperative venture between God and man. If man fails to do his part, it is sinfully presumptuous to expect God to do everything. To be sure, man's actions in this regard are prompted and quickened in their every aspect by God's power; yet man's action is still fully man's action.

The religion teacher quite frequently centers his pedagogical activity primarily or even exclusively around effecting religious knowledge outcomes, hoping that in some mysterious way the learners will transfer these outcomes to their own religious lifestyle. In this connection the teacher (and curriculum builder) might well keep in mind that the research has repeatedly shown that religious knowledge does not insure religious conduct. Thus one study found that penitentiary inmates and college students when asked to rank the ten commandments in order of importance to themselves came to a high degree of similarity in their conclusions.[415] Carmen Diaz's investigation of a matched group of Catholic girls in Catholic and public high schools showed no differences in their ability to apply selected principles of moral law to actual and hypothetical life situations. Indeed their religious education seemed to have had no significant effect on the performance of these students.[416] The celebrated study by Hugh Hartshorne and Mark May discovered that moral knowledge and moral behavior are separate and distinct. These researchers also found that church attendance in itself did not seem to lead to increased honesty on the part of the children investigated. Nor did the frequency of Sunday School attendance show any correlation with the amount of honesty displayed by the children.[417] These findings should come as no surprise to the religious educator; after all, it seems quite obvious that religious knowledge is not coextensive with religiosity but rather constitutes only one strand within the total fabric of religious behavior. From his review of the relevant research, as well as from his own studies, Charles Glock is able to identify five dimensions of religiosity which when all together incarnated as a unit at the human existential level, comprise lived religion. Religious knowledge constitutes only one of these dimensions.[418] The research on transfer cited under finding #10 indicates that both religious knowledge and religious practice will each be better transferred from in-class to out-of-class situations when both are taught together as a meshed unit. Such a meshing will transform the religion class into a laboratory for Christian living.[419] The greater the similarity between the meshed knowledge-affect-lifestyle activities in the class and those which take place outside the religion class, the more probable it is that these learnings will be transferred. The use of behavioral objectives as target performances in religion class is of great help in keeping the lesson continuously geared to that ongoing meshing of principles and practice which facilitates transfer.[420]

In general, the most effective pedagogical practice to enhance the probability of transfer is to maximize the similarity between what is taught and the ultimate specific situations. In terms of religious instruction, this general rule means that the teacher should make the contents and the conditions of the lesson resemble as far as possible those of ordinary life. Such similarity should extend to all the contents of the class: process as well as product, affective as well as cognitive, nonverbal as well as verbal. The conditions also should be similar; thus, for example, the research suggests that there is no evidence that there is automatic transfer of problem-solving skills from a group situation to an individual situation.[421]

There are, moreover, many specific things which the religion teacher can do to maximize the probability of transfer of learning. Transfer takes place more readily when the learners want to transfer. Hence the teacher should impress upon the students the value of transferring learning and should encourage transfer by structuring transfer-oriented activities right in the lesson itself. Practice in transfer increases the facility to transfer. The religion teacher should consequently provide the students with as many opportunities as possible to transfer learning, especially in the application of transferable principles to action-oriented situations. Persons transfer better when they know which learnings can and should be transferred. Accordingly the teacher should strive to make salient the feature or features to be transferred. The length of the interval between what has been learned and the new situation affects the quality and degree of transfer. Therefore the religion teacher desiring to promote transfer should endeavor to structure the two situations as close together in time as possible. Furthermore, the religion teacher should not get bogged down in too many facts if he wishes to enhance transfer, since broad concepts are easier to transfer than facts. Students transfer better when they understand the relationship between what is to be transferred and the new situation or new material. Consequently in his organization of the lesson, the teacher should so structure the learning environment that the relationship between the two situations is readily grasped. Independently derived principles are more transferable than those given. For this reason the religion teacher should not directly or indirectly tell the learners the principles, as is done in the transmission strategy or the lecture technique, but rather through the fostering of their maximum self-activity the religion teacher should assist the students to derive these principles by themselves. This can be done, for example, by the use of the strategy of structuring the learning situation or by the technique of role-playing. Finally, overlearning of the original task facilitates transfer just as it facilitates retention. Indeed, David Ausubel's review of the studies concludes that prior learnings are not transferable to new learning tasks until they are overlearned.[422] Overlearning in turn requires an adequate amount of and diversification in practicing the original learning. Further, frequent provision for various types of feedback, especially where learnings demand fine discrimination among alternatives, is an essential ingredient in overlearning. Such feedback enhances consolidation of the elements involved in the original learning by confirming, clarifying, and if necessary correcting the original learning.

Persons do not transfer automatically what they have learned. Therefore teaching for transfer must be a conscious and deliberate activity of the teacher, one which is incarnated in all phases of educational practice. In short transfer must be worked for.

In one sense the transfer of learning underlies everything the religion teacher does. If the student cannot use or apply in real life that which he has learned in real life, then what he has learned is of little enduring worth. Transfer of learning, therefore, is a vital and indispensable process outcome of all religious instruction.

CONCLUSION

A wide variety of data touching on many aspects of the learning process has been given in this chapter. What is the overall conclusion one can draw from this mass of facts and their interrelationships? Simply speaking, the overall conclusion is nothing more than this: learning is an event brought about and shaped by other events; it is not a willy-nilly, mysterious, capricious, and unexplainable phenomenon. The data in this chapter indicate that specific learning outcomes flow from the development of specific teacher behaviors. The Holy Spirit blows where he wills in the sense that he wills what he has made. What the Spirit has made is the regular cause-effect relationship governing human events. What the Spirit has not made is magical, continuous, external interventions in the ongoing flow of nature. To allege, as many religious educators have done, that religion teaching is somehow an affair basically distinct and apart from the regular cause-effect relationships present in "other" kinds of teaching is therefore un-Spirit-ual. It is a negation of continuous creation. It is a negation of God's omnipresence in reality according to the aptness of that reality. It is a negation of the structure of religious experience. It is a negation of the facts of learning.

This rather lengthy chapter on the facts of learning should in no way be construed as a minimizing of the basic distinction between teaching theory and learning theory. The teacher starts with the facts of learning. Using these facts both as his point of departure and his continual reference point, he then devises and deploys pedagogical practices most conducive to effecting desired learning outcomes. There are facts of learning and facts of teaching, much as there is a theory of learning and a theory of teaching.

THEORETICAL APPROACHES TO TEACHING RELIGION

*"You resigned yourself," he said, "to celebrate [Mass]
archeologically because it brought you esteem. Good God, čan it
have been that public opinion did so much to ... pin us down
to a dead ritualism?"*

—Daniel Pezeril[1]

Introduction

A theory of teaching religion is one of the most important determinants of both the kind and the quality of the practice of teaching religion. This is so because a theory, among other things, generates pedagogical practice and pedagogical invention. Indeed, in one respect pedagogical practice is basically a function of the particular pedagogical theory from which it necessarily flows. Theory is the soil in which practice is rooted and nurtured. Consequently the particular theory of religious instruction which a religion teacher holds makes a great deal of difference in the actual moment-to-moment way he teaches.

A theory both explains and predicts pedagogical practice. It enables a religion teacher to discover why this particular pedagogical practice produces one kind of learning rather than another. Also a theory enables the religion teacher to predict that one pedagogical practice is superior to another in bringing about a desired learning outcome in a particular situation. From theory the teacher can thus forecast the differential effects of various pedagogical practices.

A theory of religious instruction represents a model or set of guidelines for the pedagogical behavior of the religion teacher in his professional relationship with his students. Therefore it is crucial for the religion teacher to select from among the many existing theories of religious instruction that particular theory which is most positively correlated with teaching effectiveness. In other words, the religion teacher should adopt that theory which is most generative of optimum pedagogical practice. Usefulness is the criterion for the selection of one theory over another; all other considerations are secondary.

Debates among adherents of various theories of religious instruction have often been carried on with none of the protagonists apparently sensing any need for scientific study of the religious instruction act. Conclusions concerning the superiority of one theory over another are typically drawn from scientifically untested assumptions rather than from the hard data. Few hypotheses are submitted for verification before the court of research evidence, that is before the tribunal of actual reality. Such research evidence can be drawn primarily from two sources, namely the facts of behavioral facilitation and the facts of learning. From these two data sources a theory of religious teaching (as distinct from a theory of religious learning) is fashioned. Only by utilizing these two data bases can one theory of religious instruction be demonstrated to be more useful than another to the religion teacher. Appeals to the Holy Spirit, to the mysterious workings of divine providence, or to the unfathomability of the human person as the basic foundation of religious instruction miss the mark pedagogically and theologically. If the Holy Spirit is truly the Holy Spirit, then he works through that which the Triune God created and and continues to keep in being; he does not work in some strange, enigmatic, extrinsicist *deus ex caelo* manner. Indeed, the surest way to bring a theory of religious instruction to those heights of humanity and divinity of which it is capable is to make it as scientific as possible. One task of a contemporary and viable theory of religious teaching is the stripping away of those elements of sham mystery and eerie spookiness which obscure its human and divine countenance. What a scientific foundation for religious instruction theory can do is to give us a more precise and illuminative understanding of the dynamics of the religious instruction act. It is this kind of understanding, rather than an envelopment in the misty fogbank of man-made mystery and phony mythological constructs, that will enhance the effectiveness of religious instruction.

In this chapter I will briefly discuss some of the major "theories" of religious instruction which have been historically or are presently proposed. These theories include the personality theory, the authenticity theory, the witness theory, the blow theory, the dialogue theory, the proclamation theory, the dedication theory, and the teaching theory. It should be noted at the outset, however, that the research evidence seems to indicate that the teaching theory is the most appropriate form for the task of religious instruction. This is not to suggest that the other "theories" do not have some merit; they do. However, in terms of a theory which is of prime utility and benefit to religious instruction in general and to religion teachers in particular, there seems little doubt that the teaching theory is far and away the most adequate.

It should be noted that only the teaching theory merits the term "theory" in the strict sense of the term. Other so-called "theories" are more properly designated as theoretical approaches. By its nature a theory includes all the relevant variables in a given situation together with a specification of the interaction among these variables. Only in this way can a theory have that sweeping explanatory and predictive power essential to its nature.

Since Chapters 8, 9, and 10 elaborate on the teaching theory in some detail, I am deferring the discussion of the teaching theory until the latter part of this chapter where it can better serve as a link between this chapter and final three chapters.

In examining the theoretical approaches (which for convenience, not accuracy, I label "theories"), it might be well for the reader to test for himself the degree of adequacy to which each of the "theories" explains and predicts successful teaching practices. The reader might also wish to test the degree to which each of the "theories": (1) includes all four major components of the teaching act (teacher, learner, environment, and subject matter content), and (2) specifies how all four components interact with one another so as to most effectively produce a desired learning outcome or goal.

The Personality Theory

The personality theory of religious instruction holds that the teacher's personality represents the sole basic variable involved in the modification of the learner's behavior along religious lines. The personality theory is derived from an examination of the exercise of the teacher's personality structure as it manifests itself in the religious instruction act. "Show me a teacher with an exciting, dynamic personality and I'll show you an effective religion class" is the popular way of phrasing the personality theory of religious instruction.[2]

The term "personality" is used in several different ways. Some use it to refer to a summary description of an individual's total ways of behaving. Others employ the term "personality" to refer to an internal frame of reference consisting of self-evaluative feelings and attitudes regarding one's adequacy, worth, capacities, and so forth. Still others make use of this term to designate constitutional characteristics such as being withdrawn or outgoing, enthusiastic or apathetic, thoughtful or unreflective. It is by no means clear which of these three meanings is attached to the term by advocates of the personality theory of religious instruction. One often suspects that it is the third sense which is typically meant, although it might well be that the first sense comes into play to a certain extent.

Sometimes the personality theory of religious instruction is referred to as the charismatic teaching theory. Charism appears to have always had a special appeal for Christians. What was regarded in the primitive Christian community as the charismatic activity of the Spirit seems to have been everywhere palpably present, as is seen, for example, in connection with the event in the Cenacle. Charism was identified with the *pneuma* or the Spirit and hence has always held a singular attraction for the devout.[3] Indeed, in the long history of the Church, when the ecclesiastical role assumed by a churchman was so powerful as to crush or at least blunt the personality of the role incumbent, charism was regarded by theologian and layman alike as that special grace or power by which the churchman could break out of his role and truly become the person and prophet he was destined to be. Thus charism came to be identified with vigor, enthusiasm, apostolicity, and forward-lookingness.

There is much to be said in favor of the personality theory of religious instruction. The empirical research indicates that the teacher's personality is one of the most significant variables related to the facilitation of desired learning outcomes.[4] Some, including theologically-oriented religious educationists, even argue that it is the most significant natural variable.[5] Certainly the personal characteristics of the teacher represent major factors in shaping the social relationships, activities, and achievements of learners.[6] Further, the data suggest that there is no such thing as the presentation of textbook or curricular materials as they are in themselves. Each teacher filters the materials through his own perceptions and personality structure so that what the learners receive is not exactly the same as the contents of the materials themselves.[7] This is particularly true when the religion teacher employs teacher-centered instructional practices. Teacher personality variables are potent because, among other things, they act as social reinforcers on learner behavior.[8] Data from the counseling process suggest that certain personality characteristics of the counselor are positively related to engendering openness and transparency in the client.[9]

Despite its strong points the personality theory has so many deficiencies that it constitutes an inadequate theory upon which to build an entire practice of religious instruction. An adequate theory of religious instruction is one which of necessity is not heavily dependent upon a particular teacher's personality. An adequate theory of religious instruction has as one of its essential characteristics the capability of generating effective teaching practices regardless of the personality of the religion teacher—assuming, of course, that the religion teacher has a psychologically normal personality.

While it is true that the data indicate that teacher personality is a highly significant variable related to the facilitation of desired learning outcomes, nonetheless it is not valid to therefore assume that one can automatically jump from the personal characteristics of the teacher to the achievements of the learner. A host of other variables, including the personality characteristics of the learner, the quality and texture of class interaction, the teaching-learning environment, and so forth, operate as mediate variables even in a situation characterized by the most delightful and enthusiastic teacher personality traits. It might well be that the high power of the teacher's personality in facilitating learning is due to his failure to make heavy or integral use of instructional devices (for example, environment, materials) other than his personality. In such instances —probably more numerous than is commonly suspected—it stands to reason that the teacher's personality is the most significant variable in facilitating learning, since no other pedagogical variables are employed to any appreciable extent in the class. Indeed, it can be legitimately hypothesized that the more the teacher's personality comes into active and overt play in the teaching-learning situation, the more teacher-dominated and teacher-centered is that particular class.

Teacher personality variables do not have an effect on the facilitation of learning solely or even primarily in terms of that personality variable itself. Teacher personality characteristics do not produce identical automatic effects on all learners. Rather, the potency of teacher personality characteristics varies in direct ratio to the personality characteristics of the students with whom they are interacting. Thus learner achievement is not so much a function simply of the teacher's personality characteristics but of how the learner interacts with these characteristics. This capital point again draws attention to the inadequacy of the personality theory as the overarching macrotheory explaining and predicting religious instruction.

In terms of the preceding paragraph, some empirical data might be relevant. One study involving eight years of research classified teachers as "spontaneous," "orderly," and "fearful," further subdividing them into "superior" or "inferior" according to their warmth and responsiveness to the learners. Pupils were classified as "strivers," "docile conformers," and "opposers." All possible combinations of teachers and pupils were then examined in relation to pupil achievement. Not taking into account pupil differences in personality, the study showed that teachers ranged in effectiveness from the "superior orderly" (warm, relatively dominant, and businesslike) through the "superior spontaneous" (warm, exuberant, highly independent, with a strong liking for expression of ideas) and down to the "superior fearful" (warm, dependent, severely conscientious, and fearful of a threatening environment). The least effective teachers were found to be of the "inferior spontaneous" type. However, when pupil differences were scrutinized, then the strivers typically did well regardless of the personality characteristics of the teacher. Docile conformers did exceptionally well with superior spontaneous teachers, while the opposers (who as a whole performed at relatively low levels for all teachers) tended to be the most responsive to the superior orderly teachers.[10] A study by Wilbert McKeachie and his associates found that male students high in the need for affiliation tend to make relatively superior academic scores in classes where the teacher manifests a high level of affiliation whereas men with a low need for affiliation perform relatively better in classes where the teacher exhibits few affiliation cues.[11] Studies by Solomon Asch,[12] Jerome Kagan and Paul Mussen,[13] and by Norman Livson and Paul Mussen[14] concluded that dependent-prone individuals are more likely to comply with authority figures and conform to group pressures than the less dependent-prone. The obvious implications of these data for teacher-student interaction in the learning situation was investigated by Edmund Amidon and Ned Flanders. These researchers interpreted their data to mean that dependent-prone students are more sensitive than are other kinds of students to the directive aspects of the teacher's behavior. With more directive teachers this type of student finds increased personal satisfaction in more compliance, often, however, with less understanding of the subject matter studied. When the teacher is indirect in his behavior, these students also comply with the teacher's lead; but in terms of learning they perform better under the indirect teacher because they are encouraged to ask questions, think through problems, and develop deeper understanding, all with the reinforcement of the teacher qua authority figure.[15] Finally, a study by Norman Chansky showed that student ratings of teacher attitudes are influenced to a significant degree by the attitudes which the rating students themselves hold, for example, the attitude of an authoritarian student toward a freedom-loving teacher.[16]

An examination of teacher personality characteristics per se adds further weight to the argument that the personality theory of religious instruction is an inadequate one. Teachers like members of other kinds of helping professions (such as clergymen, social workers, and particularly guidance counselors and psychologists) have been revealed by the research to be individuals who seek out a career which affords them the opportunity to exercise dominance over others as a vehicle for countering or alleviating their own perceived and actual needs for submissiveness to peers or to superiors. The teaching career provides just such an opportunity. One review of the research indicates that those who pursue teaching as a career are "essentially cooperative, restrained, lacking in social boldness, friendly, and anxious to please."[17] The data also suggest that those who are preparing to enter teaching tend to be typically less intellectually endowed than the other students in the same undergraduate college. This particularly holds true for individuals seeking teaching careers at the elementary school level.[18] Research on teacher personality characteristics using the Minnesota Multiphasic Inventory (MMPI) has failed to discover that in terms of abnormal personality qualities, public school teachers deviate significantly from any other segment of the population. However, teachers did score higher than others on the K scale of the MMPI suggesting that they do manifest some degree of social anxiety overlaid with a reaction formation directed toward control of inner impulses combined with a thrust toward adaptation to the demands and needs of other persons. Hence teachers in general seem more inclined than other segments of the population to behave in conformity with the social pressures which they experience.[19] Such social pressures may, of course, come from the very students whom they are trying to influence. In contrast to the data from the MMPI on the psychological abnormality of teachers and teacher candidates as compared to other segments of the population, a study by Robert Peck found that over fifty percent of a sample of university women majoring in elementary education suffered from personality disturbances sufficiently acute to make guidance or therapy advisable.[20] Peck's finding possibly suggests also that the MMPI, which was standardized on patients in a Minnesota mental institution and hence geared toward identification of psychoses and other severe personality aberrations, might not be the appropriate instrument for investigating teacher personality characteristics.

Since a goodly percentage of religion teachers, especially in church-related day schools, are clergymen or religious, it might be helpful to briefly summarize the research on the personality characteristics of these individuals. Inasmuch as clergymen and religious are members of a helping profession, it is not at all surprising that the findings relative to their personality characteristics are similar in many respects to those of other kinds of teachers. This is certainly true in terms of the submissiveness factor. Thomas McCarthy's investigation concluded that Catholic seminarians scored higher than the norm on a psychological scale of submissiveness.[21] A study by Rayner Van Vurst found that seminarians from a religious institute had more deference needs than did lay students. Deference was here defined as the tendency to receive suggestions from others, to find out what others think, to follow instructions, to do what is expected, to conform to custom, and to avoid the unconventional.[22] An investigation by George Stern and his associates discovered that both theology and education students showed more conflict over impulse control than did physics students.[23] In what is perhaps the most comprehensive review of the research in this area, James Dittes reports that the research evidence suggests that religious professionals of both genders and of all denominations tend to be relatively introverted, distant from others, and not confident about personal relationships.[24] A review of the research by George Hagmaier and Eugene Kennedy indicates that at least for Catholic religious professionals, the seminary, novitiate, and convent experiences seem to reinforce rather than extinguish these introverted, submissive tendencies.[25] Of interest also is the research which suggests that religious professionals of all denominations tend to have stronger family ties during childhood than did laymen. These professionals were likely to have been the favorite child in the family. They were more strongly attached to their mothers than is usual. In turn their mothers tended to be more strict and their fathers less influential. Indeed, their families appeared to be stricter than the average in terms of discipline. All in all, the data show that in early life religious professionals manifest a strong dependence on their parents, particularly on their mothers, for basic emotional gratification; however, concomitantly there seems to have been an unevenness or inadequacy with which these gratifications are forthcoming.[26] James Dittes undertakes to explain and interpret these data on religious professionals in terms of the "little adult theory." By this he means that as children and youths persons who enter religion tend to be more comfortable in the adult world, to seek after adult values and adult lifestyle, and to either neutralize or reject their peer world and peer values.[27]

These data on the personality characteristics of teachers and particularly of religious professionals as teachers highlight from yet another vantage point the inadequacy of the personality theory as providing the overarching macrotheory for religious instruction.

More often than not, then, the religion teacher is a person who has a strong need to be liked and psychologically supported. Probably he becomes a teacher at least partially to receive this warmth and support from his students. Hence the teacher frequently tends to unconsciously orient his pedagogical practices in such a way that his students will come to like and psychologically support him. At the unconscious level, therefore, the teacher strives to please his students, not only because pleasing his students will of itself facilitate learning more effectively, but perhaps more importantly because pleasing his students represents one of the most successful ways of insuring that these students will in turn give the teacher the love and psychological support he needs. Yet ironically the teacher who covertly (or even overtly) strives to be popular and to be psychologically supported is being controlled and manipulated by the very students he himself seeks to control and manipulate. The students in this case act as the reinforcer of teacher behavior, and indeed these contingencies of reinforcement condition and control the teacher's pedagogical behavior. The teacher, then, is being controlled by the very people he is seeking to control. The following actual dialogue between two teachers can be illustrative here.

First Teacher: But I haven't moved him away from his friends. I told him to find a place where he thought he could do his work. If he sat on the chandelier, I'd just love it if he would pay attention. He says, "Why are you always picking on me?" I said, "You're the one I see talking. But you contribute so much when you do contribute." I told him it's constant turmoil and I just can't have it.

Second Teacher: Maybe he knows you are fond of him and he can get away with a little bit.

First Teacher: (sighs) It would be so easy if I didn't like him. So easy to tell him to sit down and shut up, but I'm afraid I'm going to hurt his feelings and squander the little initiative he has.

Second Teacher: Maybe it's not *his* feelings so much. . . .[28]

Commenting on this dialogue, Othanel Smith writes: "The teacher apparently is afraid to exercise control over the pupil for fear of driving him to show dislike for her, an action which would fly in the face of her need of him."[29] The religion teacher might attempt to refute all this by maintaining staunchly that his pedagogical behaviors flow out of a genuine love for his students. Gregory Baum offers a penetrating comment which might be of some use here: "Human love is always marked by some destructive tendencies. It is always tempted by some self-seeking. It is possible that love may become a screen for the desire to possess another person. We use love as an extension of our own power: we want other people because we need them so desperately for the building up of ourselves."[30]

An enthusiastic, charismatic, dynamically attractive teacher personality might in fact be a psychological cover-up for a subtle but forceful teacher-centered and teacher-dominated lesson. Marshall McLuhan's distinction between the effect of a cool medium (low definition) and a hot medium (high definition) is instructive here. McLuhan contends that if the medium is hot, then active participation by the audience is low. If the medium is cool, that is, of low intensity, audience participation is high.[31] Charismatic teachers are, of course, hot media.

Emphasis on the personality theory as the macrotheory underlying the work of religious instruction can lead to all sorts of abuses. It can be used to justify the teacher's building for himself a cult of personality among the students. It can exalt the value of personality far beyond what really matters, namely the teacher's pedagogical behaviors. Apropos of this, Josef Goldbrunner remarks that a statement such as "personality is really all that matters in religious instruction" not only results in a total discarding of pedagogical practice, but would probably lead to what he terms "textbook exegesis" by the religion teacher.[32] Or is it possible that undue emphasis on personality characteristics might lead to the return of that type of mentality which regards a cleric as the ideal kind of religion teacher precisely because he is a cleric? Finally, it might well be that there is a subtle form of demagoguery in the religion teacher who "turns on the personality" for its own sake.

From the viewpoint of charism the personality theory again proves inadequate to serve as the overarching theory out of which religious instruction flows. Inasmuch as the charismatic teacher rules by a kind of "pizzaz" or "presence" or "revelation," he must continually prove his worth to his followers. This pattern of teaching is therefore inherently unstable. Charismatic teaching comes and goes depending on the appearance of teacher heroes and teacher prophets on the scene. Because it is built around flaming manifestations of personality characteristics, charismatic religion teaching is usually rudimentary in both product content and method.[33] From the theological perspective it is being increasingly recognized that charism is not restricted to personality variables; rather, charism is now being regarded as an amalgam of an ecclesially-commissioned office and personal holiness.[34]

One of the unhappy fallouts of the past reliance on the personality theory by both Protestant and Catholic religious educationists has been that personality characteristics were thought to be sufficient criteria for the selection of religion teachers. Personality thus became a substitute for training and an excuse for lack of professional preparation. As Othanel Smith observes, the tendency to reduce teaching to a craft and thus to require only a knowledge of product content and on-the-job experience stems from a belief in the mystical power of personality as well as from a lack of information about teaching behavior and what is required to develop it.[35]

To summarize this section, it can be said that the personality theory of religious instruction is simultaneously so specific and so global that it is unable to generate useful prescriptions for an across-the-board educational practice. An adequate theory of religious instruction delineates the effects of personality characteristic x or personality characteristic y for different kinds of situations and purposes which occur in the teaching-learning dynamic. We have seen that the personality theory is unable to so indicate these effects since its emphasis lies elsewhere. The key to an adequate theory of religious instruction is not that it is based on personality characteristics of the teacher, but that it radicates these personality characteristics in a broader framework of purposive, deliberatively controlled teacher behavior which is productive of designated learning outcomes.

To suggest that teacher personality characteristics cannot serve as the basic theory explaining and predicting teaching effectiveness in no way minimizes the pivotal importance of the teacher's personality in effecting learning. Indeed, pedagogical practice flows through the person of the teacher in the teaching-learning process. This is nicely summarized in Beryl Orris's celebrated apothegm, "you can't teach anything you're not." A shy teacher cannot, even if he tries, use pedagogical practices appropriate for a highly-extroverted individual. It is teacher personality which gives special coloration and individuality to instructional practice; but this personality does not change the basic structure of the practice.

The teaching theory of religious instruction suggests that teacher personality characteristics do not constitute their own norm and end. Rather, these characteristics are to be controlled and utilized by the teacher solely to facilitate desired learning outcomes in the students. In the religious instruction act the teacher's personality exists for one purpose only: to facilitate learning. It is in this way that the religion teacher achieves what is the loftiest level of his profession, namely service without vanity. The religion teacher's role is to light up, not to shine. Theologically speaking the gift of charism is granted by God to the person not for his own benefit but for the sake of others. Religion teaching is not the proper career for an individual who consciously or unconsciously is primarily attempting to meet his own needs. It is entirely possible that some or even many persons currently teaching religion are utilizing the teaching-learning dynamic to satisfy their own emotional needs. This indicates the need for screening devices to insure that only emotionally mature individuals are entrusted with the task of religious instruction. But in any event the key to effective religion teaching is not so much the teacher's personality, but how the teacher puts his personality to work in order to bring about desired behavioral changes in the learner. This in turn suggests that the key to optimum religion teaching is (1) the teacher's awareness of his own pedagogical behavior; (2) his awareness of the consequences which this pedagogical behavior has on the learner; and (3) his skill in controlling and managing his pedagogical behavior so that he can deploy it in such a way and to such an extent as to bring about the desired learning outcomes.

The Authenticity Theory

The authenticity theory of religious instruction holds that the authentic manifestation of the religion teacher's personality as it is here-and-now in a particular moment in the teaching-learning dynamic represents the basic and most widespread variable involved in the modification of the learner's behavior along religious lines. The authenticity theory is derived from two sources: an examination of the way grace or Jesus or the Holy Spirit most clearly shines through the behavior of the religion teacher, and second that special form or thrust of the teacher's personality which is believed to have the greatest effect on allowing for a grace-full synapse with the learner as he is living and experiencing in the here-and-now moment. The authentic religion teacher, according to this theory, is one who is a living celebration of the God living and working in him.[36]

The authenticity theory has considerable merit. Empirical support for the effectiveness of authenticity or genuineness as a facilitational device comes from the counseling and therapeutic area where this variable has been researched in some detail. Summarizing the pertinent studies which his students and his associates have made over the years, Carl Rogers is able to conclude that "when the facilitator is a real person, being what he really is and entering into a relationship with the learner without presenting a front or a facade, he is likely to be effective."[37] To Rogers and therapists of his orientation, being genuine or authentic means to be "transparent," that is, to interact with the learner not from behind a psychological mask but rather openly and in such a way that one's outer personality characteristics act as a window instead of a barrier to the real person. To be authentic and transparent one must be "congruent," that is, the "inner" and "outer" aspects of one's personality coincide so that there is a perfect melding of the two.

Notwithstanding its strong points, the deficiencies of the authenticity theory are so great as to render it inadequate as a macrotheory upon which to build an entire practice of religious instruction. At bottom the authenticity theory is based merely on the teacher's psychological or existential state at the moment rather than on the teacher's conscious control of his behavior so as to facilitate desired outcomes in the learner. If it is to serve as an adequate basis for instructional practice, a theory of religious instruction must be totally pointed toward the facilitation of desired learning behavior rather than exclusively to the teacher's manifestation of personal genuineness. The authenticity theory in effect makes the teacher a prisoner of his own self as he experiences reality at a particular moment. What if at this particular moment a religion teacher is angry or tired? If he is authentic, then he will scream at a learner or go to sleep in the class. Thus authenticity looks to what is genuine in the teacher instead of at what will help the learner. This, of course, runs counter to the very nature and meaning of the teaching process and of pedagogical effectiveness. In the facilitation of learning, the teacher's authenticity is significant only to the extent that it enhances the attainment of a specified learning outcome. Hence teacher authenticity is a relative and not an absolute condition for effective instruction. It is relative in the sense that it comes into play only in so far as it facilitates learning. What is absolute in the teaching-learning process is that the teacher deliberatively control and utilize his repertoire of behaviors for the sole purpose of facilitating desired learning outcomes. It is for this reason that the authenticity theory is an inadequate macrotheory for religious instruction and why teaching theory is the proper and useful one.

If the authenticity theory imprisons the teacher in the web of his own presently-experienced feelings, the teaching theory serves to emancipate him from these pressures. The teaching theory of religious instruction suggests that the religion teacher continuously examine his own feelings so as to control and harness them for the sole purpose of facilitating desired learning outcomes. This serves as a great liberating source for the teacher. No longer are the religion teacher's pedagogical behaviors controlled or thwarted by his own present existential state. Rather, consciously examining the effects of his present feelings and behavior on the quality of his ongoing pedagogical activities, he can now block, blunt, or release these authentic feelings according to how they facilitate learning. By knowing the antecedents and consequences of his behavior, the teacher is free to be effective. This freedom is purchased with the coin of knowledge of and control over his present pedagogical behavior, a fact which has great practical ramifications in the form which the professional preservice and inservice preparation of religion teachers takes.

The religion teacher's authentic feelings about himself or his authentic religious convictions ought not interfere with a student's learning. The teacher's authenticity is at the service of whatever will be most effective in helping the learner develop religiously. The successful religion teacher is one who varies his behavior according to the purpose of the lesson. Pedagogical practice is governed by educational purpose; yet when the practice deviates, the purpose changes. This is particularly true because the religious instruction act is a mediational new reality in which content and method are no longer separate entities, but are now one; hence to change one aspect of this united reality is to change all its other aspects.[38] Making authentic teacher behavior the foundation of religious instruction theory is to change the focus of teaching religion from learner-centered to teacher-centered.

It might well be that emphasis on authenticity is really a psychological coverup for the teacher's unconscious (or conscious) need for self-gratification. Being authentic will always by its very nature be personally satisfying to the teacher and hence go far in meeting his needs for self-expression and affiliation. But the key question is how satisfying or effective is teacher authenticity in terms of facilitating learning? In this connection a study comparing teacher qualities liked and those disliked by children vis-à-vis adults is informative. According to the data children tend to be more concerned with the qualities of teachers in terms of their facilitational skills and abilities, while the adults judge teachers more in terms of personal attributes.[39] Hence it would appear that learners regard facilitation as the key variable.

It is useful to examine the conditions of which authentic teacher behavior is a function. No one is ever simply authentic. One is authentic because certain things one experienced in the immediate or remote past operate to evoke certain feelings in him now—feelings which are authentic. By being authentic, therefore, the teacher is directly under the domination of those past and present conditions which cause a particular behavior to become at this moment "authentic."[40] Viewed from this perspective, teacher authenticity is really being conditioned operantly in the most unfree sense of the term. But to be effective, what the religion teacher really needs is the exercise of behavior which liberates him from the contingencies of the past and the present so that he can effectively facilitate learning. It is this kind of teacher freedom—which is the foundation of pedagogical effectiveness—that undergirds the teaching theory of religious instruction.

What I have written in the last few paragraphs in no way implies that the teacher should be inauthentic or artificial or phony. What I am saying is twofold. First, authenticity is simply a pedagogical tool to enhance facilitation; it is not an end in itself much less a foundation stone for teaching. In this connection Carl Rogers himself observes that to be authentic means that the facilitator has at his command the feelings which he is currently experiencing so that he might be able to tap this resource if, and only if, these feelings will facilitate learning. To be authentic for Rogers and those of his persuasion means the ability to live fully one's present existence in all its modalities and to communicate these modalities to the learner *if* they will be appropriate to helping the learner.[41] Second and more importantly, if the religion teacher is truly a professional, then he is authentic only when he is facilitating learning in an optimal fashion. Therefore when, for the sake of facilitating learning, the teacher deliberately chooses not to express or otherwise manifest his feelings or his psychological state, he is in fact being truly authentic; he is not at such a time being inauthentic or phony. This is a capital point. For the religion teacher as professional, personality is subsumed by role and function. When exercising his teaching role professionally, the religion teacher is therefore authentic only to the extent that he is optimally facilitating learning.

To summarize this section, it can be said that the authenticity theory of religious instruction is inadequate as the overarching theory explaining the teaching of religion. Authentic teacher behavior comprises a part, often an important part, of the religion teacher's pedagogical repertoire. But this is quite a different thing from asserting that from this one chunk of pedagogical behavior we can derive an entire theory capable of generating a whole host of prescriptive pedagogical practices. Teaching is a complex of acts which comprise enriched and controlled experience in contrast to nonpedagogical behaviors. This implies that authenticity should be used as a pedagogical tool, a tool which varies in its effectiveness depending on all the conditions present at any given moment in a particular instructional setting. Both the psychological state and needs of the religion teacher must be brought to a condition of congruence if his authenticity is to be at the service of the facilitational process. By congruence is generally meant a matching of experience with awareness. The religion teacher is congruent when he is fully and accurately aware of what he is experiencing at this moment in the teaching-learning situation. When the teacher is congruent, he can control and husband his behavior solely for the purpose of facilitation. Authenticity in the final analysis is a pedagogical tool; it is not a theory of religious instruction.

The Witness Theory

The witness theory of religious instruction holds that the witnessing of the Christian message through the words, deeds, and lifestyle of the religion teacher represents the basic and most widespread variable involved in the modification of the learner's behavior along religious lines. The witness theory is derived from an examination of the way the teacher's overt behavior most clearly testifies to the Christian truths which he is proclaiming.

The witness theory is one of the most popular of all among both Catholic and Protestant religious educationists. Gabriel Moran, for example, writes: "The catechist [i.e., the religion teacher] testifies to the presence of the Spirit by showing that his whole life has been grasped by the Spirit of God. Without desiring to minimize the importance of educational apparatus and organization, we may still assert that the focal point of catechetical improvements ought to be the teacher and the apostolate of witness."[42] Wayne Rood remarks: "Horace Bushnell said that 'the most effective edition of the Gospel is bound in human hide'. This principle explains, of course, the effectiveness of Jesus as teacher: he was his message."[43] Often the witness theory is expounded in passionate terms. Thus William Reedy writes: "For it is not a mere body of truth with which we are concerned, but a message of light. The 'viva voce' of the teacher, the heart inflamed with a realization of what it is to be sharing divine life by grace so that he communicates his message by his very presence, is truly the method with which to be concerned."[44] One of the strongest statements in behalf of the witness theory was made by Augustin Gruber of Salzburg and was later supported by Josef Jungmann:

> Consequently, in the form of his instruction, in the tone of his voice, in the attitude of his body the catechist [i.e., religion teacher] must give the impression that he speaks as the ambassador of God. Any carelessness in his demeanor, any frivolity in his voice, any facetiousness in his expression must be avoided. In order to convey to the children the dignity of being an ambassador of God the catechist himself must be fully imbued by the greatness of divine revelation. When he proceeds to give an instruction he should recall as vividly as possible the sublimity of Him whose ambassador he is, the greatness of the message which he as ambassador must impart, and the love of our Lord for those to whom he as ambassador must speak. In this way he will acquire that spiritual disposition which befits the ambassador of God among men.[45]

There is much of worth in the witness theory. At bottom the

witness theory is a sort of baptized version of the identification or modeling theory and hence partakes of the natural merit of this unbaptized version. A model is a leader who deliberately or inadvertently demonstrates to the learner how he might behave. There is, then, a lifestyle orientation in the modeling process, a fact which makes it highly useful to the work of religious instruction. Definitions of identification posit a relationship between a self and a model, commonly including any one or more of at least three aspects: (1) a patterning of the behavior of the self after the model; (2) a belief by the self that he is similar in some way to the model; (3) a vicarious sharing by the self of the model's attitudes, values, emotions, and sometimes worldview.[46] Most of the theoretical formulations of and researches into the identification process center on the first of these aspects, often subsuming the second and third into it. Thus Albert Bandura and Richard Walters define identification as "the tendency for a person to reproduce the actions, attitudes, or emotional responses" of the model.[47] Percival Symonds's definition is "the modeling of oneself in thought, feeling, or action after another person."[48] Carter Good defines it as "the appropriation into the self of the characteristics of an admired group or person."[49] Lawrence Kohlberg describes identification as the "tendency to model one's own behavior after another's."[50] Urie Bronfenbrenner's concept of identification is that the individual tries to model himself after another person as a whole rather than merely to select specific traits for imitation.[51]

Identification can be regarded in any one or more of three ways: as a behavioral pattern in which the individual actually behaves like the model; as a motive in which the individual is internally or externally stimulated to act like the model; and as a process by and through which the individual is impelled to act like the model.[52] The first of these three is of particular interest to learning theorists, especially those of the classical-conditioning and operant-conditioning schools. Identification as behavioral imitation has been classified by Neal Miller and John Dollard into three different categories: same behavior, matched-dependent behavior, and copying.[53] The developmental psychologists are intrigued by identification as motive; the psychoanalytic school, on the other hand, conceives of identification largely as process.

Just as there are three basic vantage points from which to view identification, so too there are three basic theoretical formulations explaining how identification does in fact take place. The learning theory predicts that it is the contingencies of reinforcement especially secondary reinforcers which most effectively cause an individual to imitate the model's behavior. For its part the developmental theory predicts that it is the behavioral pattern of the model which is perceived by the individual as helpful or necessary for his self-growth that causes this individual to imitate the model's behavior. Developmental theory in this instance is divided into two major schools, differing primarily over the motivational source of identification. The anaclitic school sees identification as a function of the individual acting to maintain the love and esteem of the parent or significant other who serves as a model. From his dependency drive the individual derives nurturance from the model. The social-power school maintains that an individual identifies with a model who has the power to control goals or rewards which are important and significant to that individual. Finally, psychoanalytic theory hypothesizes that an individual identifies most strongly with a rivalrous person who is receiving many rewards desired by the individual. The individual envies the other person and as a result identifies with him. Psychoanalytic theory has received the most attention because psychoanalysts are typically more interested in identification than are other kinds of social scientists. Yet the research data as reviewed by Kenneth Wodtke and Bobby Brown seem to support the learning theory as the adequate explanation for identification.[54] Indeed, Albert Bandura and his associates conducted a study to assess the predictability (and hence the adequacy) of these basic theories in terms of producing imitative behavior. The results indicated that the learning theory was the most predictive.[55] Nonetheless it should be also noted that the other two theories have likewise received empirical support, albeit of a less potent nature, from other noncomparative studies. It would appear that these seemingly conflicting data can be easily reconciled on three grounds. First, each theory is dealing with a different aspect of identification (behavior, motivation, or process); hence it is unwarranted to generalize data from one theory to that of another theory explaining a different phenomenon or different aspect of that phenomenon. Second, there are many forms and levels within identification—for example, modeling, copying, imitating, and so forth; often the data gathered from research on one level are not correctly matched with the theory explaining that level. Finally and very importantly, data supporting each of these theories do in one sense support an overarching reinforcement theory since each of the theories or their subdivisions, for example, social power theory, depend on reinforcement of one kind or another.

But regardless of how one explains identification, it remains a proven fact that individuals do imitate the behaviors of significant others including teachers. Modeling works in at least three areas: (1) qualities, such as mannerisms, temperamental characteristics, motivations; (2) roles, that is the systematized pattern of duties, attitudes, and actions which typify such persons as father, woman, Christian, teacher; and (3) demands, that is, adherence to specified rules of conduct.[56] Further, there are data to suggest that in terms of facilitating a desired learning outcome with kindergarten children, the presence of a teacher employing identification-inducing behaviors is more effective than the absence of such a teacher.[57] To be sure, there has been relatively little research done on modeling in the teaching-learning situation; however, extensive work has been done on modeling in parental and familial contexts, and it would not appear entirely unwarranted to somewhat cautiously extrapolate these data to that of the learning site. Pursuing this tack, the research data suggest that there are several factors which seem to develop or enhance an individual's identification with a model. The amount of affective nurturance which a significant other gives to an individual is highly correlated with the selection of that significant other as a model.[58] This effective nurturance is a very important component of that largely unconscious emotional relationship between "identifier" and the "identificand."[59] The degree to which the significant other meets the needs of an individual tends to determine the amount of behavior modeled.[60] The capacity of the individual to be similar to the significant other has also been shown to positively influence the development of modeling behavior.[61] Sex-role matching of the individual with the significant other also facilitates modeling but in a complex way depending on age and sex. Sex-role matching is particularly significant in early childhood and appears to play a goodly function in the development of moral conscience.[62] The more closely acquainted or related is the individual to the significant other, the greater is the likelihood of identification. Parents and elementary school teachers thus have greater potency for being modeled after, other things being equal.[63] Finally, the nature, kind, menu, and schedule of reinforcement which the significant other provides are highly productive of modeling behavior. One study, for example, showed that children's moral judgments could be modified by exposure to models who used

selected patterns of social reinforcement.[64] Even sex-role identification seems heavily influenced by the contingencies of reinforcement;
thus, for example, boys who strongly identified with a male role,
presumably as a consequence of identification with their fathers, are
inclined to view their fathers as powerful sources of both reward and
punishment.[65] There are other data which indicate that identification with a model depends on the model's ability to reward or
punish the individual: the child, for instance, copies a parent because
the parent controls the goals which the child desires.[66]

Despite its many strengths the witness theory has so many
deficiencies that it constitutes an inadequate macrotheory upon
which to build an entire practice of religious instruction. Witnessing
is to a certain extent and under certain conditions an effective
pedagogical method. It is in this specific zone, rather than in the
extremely broad arena of macrotheory, that witnessing can make its
contribution to religion teaching praxis. Witnessing is a unidimensional affair, and a theory of religious instruction must of its very
nature be multidimensional.

To possess adequate explanatory and predictive power, a theory
of religious instruction cannot be based on either the teacher's total
personality pattern or on any single cluster of characteristics (for
example, witnessing) of that pattern. This is because an adequate
theory of religious instruction must explain and predict pedagogical
effectiveness regardless of who the teacher is. It is precisely at this
point that the witness theory is too limited to qualify as a
macrotheory of religious instruction.

Implicit in the witness theory is that the supreme criterion for
hiring a religion teacher is his personal holiness rather than his skill
in facilitating desired learning outcomes. This mentality, much too
prevalent in the history of Protestant and Catholic religious instruction, leads to a total disregard and devaluation of the teaching-
learning process itself. Exemplifying this denigration of teaching
effectiveness criterion Michael Warren writes that "religious education is more about the teacher's revealing himself and his own free
response than it is about leading students through structured
situations to produce predetermined behavioral objectives."[67] One
practical consequence of this mentality is the neglect of professional
preparation for religion teachers, a situation which has contributed
more than anything else to the ineffectualness of religious instruction throughout the centuries. The emphasis by the witness theory
on the personal holiness of the teacher has not infrequently led to

the notion that the religion teacher must become depersonalized and dehumanized if he is to be successful. It is from this perspective that M. Virgine comments: "The teacher must be Christ to the students."[68] To become Christ while remaining oneself is not only existentially impossible but is also psychologically damaging. One mirrors Christ to the extent that one fully self-actualizes. To put on the Lord Jesus Christ (Romans 13:14) possibly suggests that Jesus is part and parcel of this actualization rather than of the dissolution of self. One wonders where a religion teacher can be found who is so audacious and so puffed up as to imagine himself so holy as to serve as a model of Christian witnessing.

There does not appear to be any corpus of data demonstrating that in and of itself a teacher's personal holiness is the characteristic most positively correlated with his teaching effectiveness. As a matter of fact, there have been instances in which highly effective religion teachers and religious leaders seemed to be "living in sin," as judged by the generally-accepted criteria of holiness and sin.[69] Further if Christian witness is the all-important criterion for a religion teacher, then it follows that a non-Christian or a Christian from another denomination would not be permitted to teach religion in a church-related learning situation sponsored by a particular denomination.[70] It would appear, too, that there is a tinge of certain elements of Donatism in the witness theory. Donatism, it will be recalled, was a schismatic movement of the fourth and fifth centuries which stemmed from an exaggerated insistence on the displayed holiness of the minister in the confection of the sacraments.

The witness theory is too vague and too general in delineating antecedent-consequent relationships in the teaching act; consequently it does not possess the level of explanatory or predictive power required of a theory of religious instruction. Identification, or witnessing if you will, is far more complex than monkey see, monkey do. It does not specify or control which elements of the witnessing teacher the learner will imitate. One thing is sure: the learner does not imitate everything in the witness's behavior. True, the learner can imitate meaningful and appropriate witness behavior, but he can also imitate behaviors of the witness which are irrelevant or inappropriate for him. Imitation is selective. Nevitt Sanford relates the story of a two-year old child, initially terrified by a puppy dog, was within a few hours crawling about, barking, and threatening to bite people.[71] What all this suggests is that the learning outcome of witnessing in and of itself is chancy. In witnessing there is no built-in check against the acquisition by the pupil of insignificant learning. Only when the elements in the antecedent-consequent behaviorial chain of teaching are specified can witnessing be an effective pedagogical practice. But to conceive and implement such a specification is to at once embrace the teaching theory of religious instruction and leave the witness theory behind. The teaching theory appropriates witnessing or identification as a pedagogical tool to be judiciously used; the witness theory overgeneralizes these tools into a macrotheory.

Witness theorists tend to oversimplify in that they imply that the religion teacher is merely witnessing lived Christianity. The teacher is witnessing Christianity as it operates in his life, a life which also reflects many other personality variables such as age, socioeconomic class, sex, canonical status, and so on. Consequently the kind of Christian witness which a particular religion teacher gives might well be unsuitable for the learner. Often the teacher and learner are widely separated in age; on this score, the religion teacher is not an adequate role model for the learner. The predominantly lower middle-class background of religion teachers has a variety of repercussions in their witnessing behavior, a number of which are singularly inappropriate for the learner. The sex of the witness also tends to make for frequent unsuitable identification by the learner. There is ample evidence that the feminization of schooling due to the heavy percentage of women at the elementary level has had particularly adverse effects on boys. For instance, studies show that many more boys than girls of elementary school age are brought to mental health clinics. A high percentage of the religion teachers in Catholic church-related schools are clergy and religious. Such persons, because of the lifestyle demands made on them by virtue of their profession, are unsuitable models for many learners. One only has to think of celibacy and the vow of poverty in this regard. Finally, the religious lifestyle (or faith-life as it is sometimes called) of the witness might be ideal for his personality configuration but terribly inappropriate for the learner whose personality characteristics are dissimilar from those of the witness. No single witness is appropriate for all learners. It is here that the witness theory as a broad macrotheory collapses.

The witness theory implemented on a global scale tends to foster inaction on the part of the learner. Imitation is, after all, primarily a reproductive rather than a productive activity. It is quite possible that a heavy emphasis on witnessing as an instructional method encourages learner dependency on the model. Yet there is scarcely an educational philosopher or educational psychologist who advocates passive learning as against active learning, or dependent-oriented learning as against independent-oriented learning.

The witness theory represents a direct assault on the learner's freedom to learn and live Christianity in a manner most appropriate and most comfortable to him. At bottom witnessing in and of itself constitutes an unjustifiable imposition of the religion teacher's religious lifestyle on the learner. To set an example, to witness, is a very powerful way of controlling the learner.[72] The witness paradigm holds that the teacher gets results by being prestigious or positively cathected. Indeed, the witness theory implies that prestigious and significant models can succeed in teaching even basically inconsistent, invalid, or inappropriate behaviors.[73] Fortunately the learner has built-in defenses against an assault of this kind by the witness; it often happens, therefore, that the witness cannot get the student to learn what he (the student) clearly regards as behavior inappropriate or invalid for him. Yet the assault on learner freedom remains, especially for dependent-prone learners. A review of some pertinent research investigations concludes that dependent-prone individuals are more likely to comply with authority figures (which the teacher as model is) than are the less dependent-prone.[74] These data suggest that the dependent-prone learner might well become overly concerned with imitating the behavioral patterns of the model. George Stern's review of the relevant research has found that a teacher's attitude-scale scores are consistent with his classroom behaviors. Thus, for example, a teacher who scores high on authoritarianism will subtly or overtly demand conformity not only in thought but in outward behavior patterns as well.[75] The implications of these reviews of the research for the witness theory are evident. Further as the data I cite earlier in this chapter indicate, the religion teacher typically has strong needs for affiliation and nurturance; hence he can very easily utilize the witness theory to unconsciously justify his unwarranted controlling of the learner.

Finally, the witness theory tends to be teacher-oriented rather than learner-pointed. Thus Michael Warren, a witness theorist, regards religious education as more concerned with the teacher witnessing to his own religion than in structuring the situation so that learning is facilitated.[76] The teaching theory by contrast would view such witnessing as appropriate only to the extent that it is directed toward learner outcomes and is inserted into that kind of pedagogical structure which insures as far as possible that it is so pointed. Pierre Babin puts it nicely when he remarks that the religion teacher should avoid jumping to the conclusion that what he sees through his own faith is relevant for others. "To teach," continues Babin, "is to help another in a progressive working out of things, and thus the teacher cannot presume that his students will spontaneously see things in the way he does."[77]

To summarize this section, it can be said that the witness theory of religious instruction is inadequate as the overarching macrotheory explaining the teaching of religion. Witnessing is an important part of the religion teacher's repertoire of pedagogical behaviors, but it is only a part. No part is capable of adequately explaining the whole. By definition the task of teaching is the optimal arrangement of conditions so that the pupil directs his energies toward the attainment of worthwhile goals. There are four major classes of these conditions, all of which must be present and dynamically interactive in the teaching-learning situation: teacher behavior, learner behavior, the course or subject matter content, and the environment (physical, socioemotional, and others). Hence teacher behavior comprises only one variable in the total pedagogical act, and witnessing constitutes only one kind of teacher behavior. Viewed in this light, the limitations of witnessing both as a teaching method and as a would-be macrotheory are evident. In this vein it would be well to recall the celebrated Teacher Characteristics Study, an eight-year empirical investigation consisting of over one hundred separate but integrated research tasks. One of the conclusions which emerged from this major research effort is the great number and complexity of teacher behaviors, to say nothing of the coloration which these behaviors take when they interact with other variables such as the learner and the environment.[78]

Witnessing is a helpful teacher behavior but it is also a blind one. It takes on the tint and hue of both the personality of the witness and the way the teacher chooses to husband his personality in the teaching-learning situation. In studies of self-controlling, fearful, and turbulent teachers, the best results, by achievement measures, were obtained by the teachers who were themselves self-controlled.[79] What is pedagogically significant is not the sheer witnessing but how the religion teacher structures his behavior so that this witnessing is placed at the service of facilitating desired learning outcomes. The research data indicate that the witness method (I do not here say witness theory) as modeling does indeed produce desired learner behaviors but only or at least principally when this witnessing is placed within those contingencies which reinforce the learner.[80] It is the religion teacher's professional task to so structure the learning situation that the proper contingencies are selected and made operable. Thus witnessing is a useful pedagogical method when it is a tool consciously and deliberatively deployed by the teacher; as such witnessing is a part of the teaching theory of religious instruction. In the final analysis the religion teacher is the most effective witness when he is the most effective teacher. He witnesses best by teaching best.

The Blow Theory

The blow theory of religious instruction holds that the invisible and incomprehensible action of the Holy Spirit represents the basic and at bottom the sole causal variable involved in the modification of the learner's behavior along religious lines. The blow theory is derived primarily from an interpretation and extension of John 3:8, "the Spirit blows where he wills." The blow theory is derived secondarily from a theological conception of the supernatural dimension as "beyond," "outside of," "higher than," and "over against" the natural component of terrestrial existence.

The blow theory enjoys much support from both Protestant and Catholic religious educators. Sara Little, for instance, maintains that religious learning characterized by a transformational awareness of the meaning of God's self-communication cannot be structured or facilitated by the teacher; such religious learning is the work of the Holy Spirit.[81] Wayne Rood for his part declares that religious outcomes cannot be facilitated by careful preplanning and execution of the religion lesson. For Rood the Spirit cannot be controlled or manipulated; religious instruction is always free, like the Spirit who blows where he wills.[82] From the Catholic standpoint Gabriel Moran likewise contends that the outcomes of religious instruction, particularly lifestyle outcomes, are not the prerogative of the religion teacher to facilitate. Such outcomes belong entirely to the province of the Spirit. "The Spirit works where He wills and how He wills and it is not for man to control Him. The religion teacher, like the apostle, invites men to respond to God, but when, where, and under what conditions is not for the religion teacher to decide."[83]

The blow theory is not without merit, although I must say in all candor that of all the major theories I discuss in this chapter, it is probably the one which has the least to commend it.[84] Perhaps the blow theory's strongest feature is its emphasis on the continual presence of the Spirit in religious instruction—a presence which ever renews, makes fresh, and enables.[85]

However, as a macrotheory upon which to build an entire practice of religious instruction, the blow theory is riddled if not suffused with deficiencies which render it inadequate. The blow theory is in no way productive of instructional practice. Quite the contrary; it is destructive of all pedagogical practice. Since according to this theory the Spirit blows where he wills, pedagogical practice does not and indeed cannot make any difference in the long run (or even, perhaps, in the short run). Nor is the blow theory able to generate predictions on the relative effectiveness of various pedagogical strategies, methods, or techniques. In this vein Gabriel Moran, an advocate of the blow theory, writes that "the task of the adult [parent or religion teacher] is to listen to the Spirit and to guide the child by awakening his consciousness in the Spirit."[86] This is all well and good in the domain of pure speculation, but it tells the religion teacher nothing about what to do to help "guide the child by awakening his consciousness in the Spirit." About the only possible pedagogical practice which can be derived from the blow theory is the seed-sowing strategy. According to this strategy the task of the religion teacher is to simply sow the seeds of truth and the Spirit will blow these seeds where he wills. The teacher's task in this situation is to listen to the Spirit and to study theology and on the basis of these twin criteria select the seeds which are hypothesized to yield the most fruit. (The seed-sowing strategy, like the proclamation strategy, is basically a variant of the transmission strategy.) At bottom the blow theory serves to destroy the causal connection between teaching and learning. Thus T. W. Dean, another blow theorist, remarks: "Strictly speaking, we do not and cannot teach people to pray; the art of prayer is learnt rather than taught, for in this matter the one who instructs is none other than the Holy Ghost himself."[87] Such assertions, of course, go counter to all the research data we have about teaching and learning. Indeed, such assertions posit but in no way demonstrate or prove that some other and totally potent variable intervenes in the teaching-learning act. If the Spirit is the teacher as Dean suggests, then what is the role of the religion teacher? If the real teacher is "none other than the Holy Ghost himself," is not the terrestrial religion teacher superfluous? Does it really matter which pedagogical strategy or method he uses? Is preplanning the lesson either a waste of time or even deleterious since it might get in the way of the blowing Spirit? Thus Michael Warren, a blow theorist, remarks "and in any case after all our [pedagogical] planning, the 'Spirit blows where he wills'."[88] This manner and course of the Spirit's intervention in the teaching-learning act is terribly opaque and unclear and mysterious, as the proponents of the blow theory readily admit. This being the case, it would appear futile to construct a theory of religious instruction around such a posited reality. Surely if the macrotheory is unclear and opaque, how can it then explain and generate pedagogical practices which perforce are specific and often precise? In short the blow theory is not really a theory in the proper sense of this term since it ex professo disclaims any explanatory or predictive role. Nor is it a pedagogical practice; in fact it is the abdication of pedagogical practice. All this implies that the blow theory—and the blow practice—are pedagogically useless.

The blow theory seriously denigrates the role of the religion teacher, particularly with respect to his effectiveness. This is clearly exemplified by Gabriel Moran who writes: "The human teacher is always subordinate to the Holy Spirit in the catechizing of the child." Quoting Franz Arnold with approval, Moran continues: "Religious instruction is not an event between the religion teacher and the child, but between God and the child."[89] The mass of research I cite in the rather lengthy Chapter 6 of this book certainly indicates that the teacher's behaviors do have a distinct and observable effect on the facilitation of desired learning outcomes. The data suggest beyond doubt that pupil learning is a function of teacher behavior. Use of reinforcement contingencies by the teacher produces specified and predictable learner outcomes. Deployment of selected affective teaching practices yields behaviorally-chained learner outcomes. An investigation by Morris Cogan found that teachers who exhibit warm and considerate behaviors get an unusually high amount of original poetry and art from their high-school students.[90] Ronald Lippitt's study concluded that different leadership styles produce different socioemotional climates and bring about different group and individual behaviors.[91] The research data show that the teacher's behavior affects the cohesiveness of the class.[92] An investigation by Everett Bovard discloses that the more talking the teacher encourages and allows pupils to have among themselves, the greater their tendency toward mutual liking and the greater the class cohesiveness.[93]

The preceding paragraph in no way implies that all aspects of the influence of teacher behavior on learner response are known in a precise one-to-one fashion. The scientific study of the dynamics of the teaching-learning process is still in its infancy, and we are far from identifying all the conditions which interact to bring about a particular behavior in the learner. But this lack of complete data on the effects of the teaching-learning process no more warrants the positing of the Holy Spirit as the proximate causal variable than does the lack of a complete corpus of data on the healing process warrant the positing of the Holy Spirit as the proximate causal variable in medical or dental practice. A retreat into the amorphous clouds of mystery is patently less productive of improving religious instruction than continuing to explore the interactive behavioral relationships we already know exist in the teaching-learning act.

Nor is there somehow implied in the rejection of the blow theory that there are not unobservables operating in the teaching-learning dynamic. An adequate theory (and practice) of religious instruction must have the power to discriminate between the observables and the unobservables in the behavior of both teacher and learner. Making such a distinction spells the destruction of the commonly untested assumption that certain internal changes have occurred in the learner even though there are no observable manifestations of the change. In other words, unobservables can legitimately be said to exist in the teaching-learning act only if these unobservables are operationally defined in terms of observable antecedents and consequences. Lacking this condition, it is impossible to say with even the slightest bit of assurance whether the hypothesized unobservables are objective realities or simply figments of the imagination.

Rejection of the blow theory of religious instruction in favor of the teaching theory does not imply any attempt at "controlling" or "manipulating" the Spirit. As I observe in *The Shape of Religious Instruction,* "the pedagogical problem is not controlling the actions of the Spirit, but rather shaping the learning conditions in such a way that the Spirit will be enabled to most fruitfully operate."[94] Religious instruction heightens the work of the Spirit precisely to the extent that it is effective. The work of the Spirit is augmented through the teacher's purposive behaviors to enhance the conditions optimally promotive of learning. The Spirit works in and through life's conditions, not outside them or at odds with them. The teaching theory of religious instruction clarifies from a pedagogical vantage point what Jean Le Du and Marcel van Caster aptly term "the question of the relationship between human experience and God's speaking."[95] In accomplishing this task the teaching theory of religious instruction together with the pedagogical practice it generates helps in its own way to illumine theological investigation of the divine-human encounter.

Perhaps at this juncture it might not be too tangential to suggest that the blow theory is not only inadequate and defective from a pedagogical point of view but from a theological standpoint as well. A person's stance on the relationship between the "natural" and the "supernatural" is encapsulated in his judgment of the blow theory. Advocates of the blow theory implicitly or explicitly conceive of an ontological cleft between "natural" and "supernatural." They view the "supernatural" as something over against and outside of the natural, entering the natural only to elevate and redeem it. It is this mentality which attempts to drag the Holy Spirit in from "outside," as it were, to enable, to vivify, and to mysteriously produce effects in the "natural" order—an order in which the Spirit is already present according to the mode of that order. Gerard Sloyan remarks in this connection that "we are almost totally disarmed for the current secular-sacred conflict because we have plumped so vigorously for the religious or the sacred as more or better— 'supernatural'—hence, by definition, an extra, an addendum."[96] Behind the blow theory lie the theological assumptions of an extrinsicist God and the supernatural as an over-against super-additum. Thus, for example, Roger Shinn, who seems to agree with the blow theory, claims that while religious instruction is a significant work because it offers the person an opportunity for a transforming relationship with God, nevertheless it is a somewhat impotent activity because "God continues to act outside our plans and arrangements."[97] Such an attitude neglects the basic theological position that it is in the affairs of men that the affairs of God are enacted according to the mode of the affairs of men. God created man and the world according to certain specifications and with certain properties, and in his relationships with men down through the centuries, he works within these specifications and properties. God does not disclaim or disavow his once and continuous creation by acting in ways other than those he created and continues in creation. Curiously, when Shinn describes how an individual is transformed by being adopted into the family of the church, he delineates certain contingencies of social reinforcement which have as their natural effects the modification of behavior along specified lines. I contend that the Spirit works in the world to bring the new; but he works in the world according to the manner of the world, and what he brings new is new within (rather than outside) the parameters of the world. Blow theorists seem to conceive of the action of the Spirit as a sort of magic. It would indeed be interesting to conduct a research investigation to find out if there is any correlation between possession of a magical mentality and advocacy of the blow theory. In any event it is not unreasonable to suggest that while earnest secular leaders wear themselves out searching for answers to particular problems in the modern world, Christians tend to wait apathetically for a movement of the Spirit to solve the entire dilemma. God's power over the world, as Gregory Baum reminds us, is not the miraculous or magical action by which he makes things happen as he pleases, but the redemptive action by which he enables man to actualize the potentialities he already possesses.[98] Religious people today, as in the days of Jesus, still seem to have a proclivity for looking for magical signs and miraculous wonders, all of an extrinsicist kind.

To summarize this section, the blow theory is inadequate as a macrotheory for religious instruction. Its power of prediction is little or nothing, and its explanatory capability is shrouded in opacity and mystery. The great significance of the blow theory, it seems to me, is that it represents a pervasive substrate out of which virtually all religious educators operate. This is especially true of religious educators and educationists who cling to the theological rather than the social-science approach. One can only speculate whether this apparent fondness for the blow theory on the part of theologically-oriented religious educators is a result of a theological worldview. In any case the issue for the religious educator remains: What are the criteria for deciding whether behavioral changes in learners can be attributed directly to God rather than directly to man? André Godin cogently addresses himself to this question: "A pious interpretation of the situation might be given in this way: the Holy Spirit, rather than the scientific efforts of men, is at work in the catechetical renewal. Without raising an objection to this interpretation, one can share the conviction of [Leonard Sibley] who wrote: 'If the Holy Spirit can guide a group of people who try to formulate objectives by argument and discussion, why can the Spirit not also guide a group who uses scientific technique to set objectives and evaluate programs?' "[99] In this respect the blow theory posits so many untested assumptions about the nature and causes of learning as to make it not only inadequate as a pedagogical macrotheory but also highly suspect as a theological viewpoint. Concerning the former, a major weakness in religious instruction is the absence of an adequate conceptual analysis of the teaching act. The availability of such an analysis could allow educational practice to be more systematically planned and implemented, thus leading to enhanced pedagogical effectiveness. Improvement of religious instruction will come from the teacher's awareness and control of his pedagogical behaviors, both of which in turn will generate heightened learner awareness of teacher-learner instructional interactions. Charles Melchert perceptively remarks in this connection that "the educational process should finally turn the student as well as the teacher to looking at his own educational process, so that he can become intimately aware of the 'moves' he is making and why, and thus begin to free himself from the total subjective dependence upon those who teach no matter in whose name."[100] Belief in the activity of the Spirit should in no way stymie the teacher from transforming and enriching his own pedagogical behaviors. This seems so obvious, yet it is a notion so typically resisted in religious education circles. The roots of this resistance go deep, right down to a theological worldview and a defective understanding of the "natural-supernatural" relationship. Emanating as it does from a theological worldview, the blow theory is difficult for many religious educators to shuck, despite the weight of the evidence against it. This is illustrated in Anita Stauffer's carefully-researched article which, after indicating the empirically proven effects of identification and modeling in facilitating desired behaviorial change and after outlining the value of identification and modeling for religious instruction, concludes by reverting to the blow theory. The final words of the article are: "At the heart of growth in faith is the mysterious work of the Holy Spirit. Teachers can seek only to be instruments of the Spirit."[101]

The Dialogue Theory

The dialogue theory of religious instruction holds that the basic causal variable involved in the modification of the learner's behavior along religious lines is that kind of interactive teacher-pupil relationship which represents the deepest personal sort of encounter. Much, if not most of contemporary dialogue theory is derived from Martin Buber's philosophical analysis of the encounter which man makes with reality. Buber was a philosopher and often philosophized on both theological reflection and religious experience. He was not a religious educationist. Nonetheless, the fruits of his rich speculative efforts have served as the source and model for the dialogue theory of religious instruction, especially in Protestant circles.

For Buber the world is basically relational. There is no such thing as man in and of himself; rather man is either an I in dialogue with a Thou, or an I in relationship with an It. Man, then, is basically man-in-relation; this describes his humanity. An I-Thou relationship is a true dialogue since both the I and the Thou are giving forth of their total selves interrelationally in a personal encounter. An I-It, on the other hand, exists when a person interacts with an It but there is no relational initiation or feedback from the It representing the total personal being of the It. An It can be a nonhuman being (animal, plant, stone, and so on), or a person whom the I has not permitted to initiate or give feedback totally on the Thou's terms as a unique, unbounded person. When man meets another person and places that other person in bounds, he reduces the Thou to an It. Man needs to have both I-Thou and I-It relationships; he is a twofold being. But the I-Thou represents a more fulfilling relationship, one which is more self-actualizing. I-Thou is dialogue, while I-It is a nondialogical form of interaction.[102]

Reuel Howe follows Buber's dialogue model in building a theory of religious instruction. For Howe dialogue is that address and response between persons which enables and deepens their relationship. In dialogue each person gives himself as totally as possible to the other. Without dialogue there can be no real communication and no true learning. Howe believes that every man is a potential adversary, even those whom one loves; it is only through dialogue that one is saved from this enmity toward one another. Dialogue staunches monologue and in so doing saves man from himself. Dialogue as relationship determines the form of teaching. In dialogue the student becomes the teacher's teacher; in dialogue the teacher also remains the teacher.[103]

Another dialogical theory of religious instruction which owes its inspiration and form to Buber's model is the engagement theory propounded by David Hunter. For Hunter engagement is "meeting, knowing (not knowing about), responding to or ignoring, loving, hating." Engagement is thus an encounter—an encounter with the world, with other persons, and with God. In the religious instruction act, learners and teachers encounter each other in a deeply human transaction in which they give of themselves to the other in an open and unrestricted manner. Engagement has its theological as well as its instructional form. As a theological act engagement refers to the synaptical moment when God acts in or upon the life of a person and the person responds in a fully existential total fashion. As a theological immanentist, Hunter believes that God is always in engagement with man and that the instructional act enables this engagement to be heightened by and through a thoroughgoing engagement pedagogy. The opposite of engagement is detachment, which consists in the separating, fragmenting action of man by which he resists the encounter with God in or outside the religious instruction act. Engagement, by contrast, is the existentially reconciling and uniting dialogue of God with man in which man can be caught up with his whole being and thus become self-actualized.

Perhaps the clearest and pedagogically the most highly developed form of the dialogue theory of religious instruction is that of Wayne Rood. Rood attempts to clarify the distinctive features of his dialogue theory by contrasting it with three other theories of religious instruction. Serving as the axis of his distinction is the teacher-learner-content triad. In theory A (Rood never designates any of these theories by name, so I can only label them by letter) the teacher carries the product content to the learner. The teacher is the active person in this relationship, and his activity is the ground of the process. This theory generates the lecture technique. In theory B the teacher and the learner meet in the product content. The product content is inert. Both the teacher and the learner are active and approach the product content together. This theory generates the debate technique. In theory C there is a direct meeting between teacher and learner without regard to objective product content. Here the content is wider than product content; indeed content becomes the very selves of the teacher and the learners. This theory generates the discussion technique or the therapeutic technique. Finally there is the dialogue theory in which the ground of the process is not content of any sort but rather the teacher's active concern (love) for both learner and content. This theory gives rise to what can be termed the passover technique because the teacher steps across or passes over to the learner's side of the relationship to see or experience the content from the learner's point of view. What happens, claims Rood, is that in this passover practice the response of the teacher is to both the learner and to the content and the response of the learner is to both teacher and content. In this way both the teacher and learner become learners in relation to a shared content which is no longer objective but has become personalized by love and the passover act. This is Buberian, of course, but Rood sees religious instruction as going beyond Buber because of the nature of its content. Since the content of religious instruction is God, the content is active rather than passive and therefore does not need to be acted upon as in the case of secular content. As content God is both active and meaningful. Thus the content (God) addresses both teacher and learner; in their joint response, made the more joint by the teacher's passover to the learner's side of experience, the teacher and the learner are drawn closer to each other through God and closer to God through each other. Consequently the dialogue theory enables the religious instruction act to be a perfect amalgam of content-centeredness and person-centeredness.[104]

The dialogue theory of religious instruction has at least four commendable features. First of all, it emphasizes teacher-learner interaction. Rood highlights the dynamism of the pedagogical act when he describes religious instruction as "the art of enabling dialogue."[105] David Hunter further delineates the nature of this interaction when he notes that at every moment in the teaching-learning act, the religion teacher serves as a change agent. "Either he is contributing to the further watering down of the Christian way of life (which goes far beyond morals) or he is enabling the power of God through his life to affect and change an essentially godless culture."[106]

Second, the dialogue theory stresses the deeply interpersonal character of the teacher-learner interaction. Above all, teaching embodies an interpersonal relationship between teacher and learner, and between the learner and other learners.[107] For Wayne Rood the main focus in teaching is on persons and their relationships because a prime goal of religious instruction is the establishment of that kind of relationship between teacher and learner which models the possibilities of divine-human interaction. As both Rood and Pierre Babin observe, a true interpersonal encounter presents a double problem for both teacher and learner: (1) a restriction on each individual's freedom is introduced because the very nature of interpersonal relationships is to limit the freedom of each of the individuals, and (2) the psychological difficulty of jumping into the perceptual skin of the other person.[108] With reference to the latter, one task of the teacher is to perceptualize, empathize, and localize—that is to see reality as the learner perceives it, to feel the world as he feels it, and to experience the world as he experiences it as far as he is able.[109]

In one respect the perceptualize-empathize-localize triad of "crossing over to the learner's side" entails a personal sacrifice on the part of the teacher since he is letting himself be invaded by the other person in a certain manner. Yet this triad is necessary for effective facilitation of desired learning outcomes. A review of the pertinent research by A. Morrison and D. McIntyre concludes that teachers are often very poor judges of the actual social, personal, and existential conditions of their students. They not only tend to make errors about their students but often fail to recognize even the most general patterns of preference. Two main sources of teacher misjudgments about their students can be identified. First, teachers seem to misinterpret the limited interpersonal cues which the learner provides during the learning environment. They frequently make erroneous judgments of the level of a student's popularity with his peers. For example, a student who mixes with many others on apparently good terms may be judged to be popular even though the observed activity may in fact represent unsuccessful attempts to establish a peer relationship of any sort, especially with a high-prestige individual who tolerates or possibly even cultivates many minions. Second, teachers seem to overgeneralize the effects of one known student trait. For example, a teacher who believes a student is popular and cheerful predicts a parallel high level of self-confidence.[110] By using both the triad and scientific assessment inventories the religion teacher can derive a more accurate picture of the inner perceptual and existential framework of the learner.

A third strong point of the dialogue theory is its esteem for the learner. Indeed, the learner is valued so highly that the religion teacher at considerable sacrifice to his own freedom and his own personal feelings crosses over to the side of the learner totally on the learner's own terms. Further the dialogue theory insists that the learner himself perceive that the religion teacher has in fact crossed over to his side of experience. In this connection Carl Rogers observes that it is not enough for the facilitator to cross over to the learner's side of experience. It is also necessary for the learner himself to experience or perceive something of the facilitator's crossing over, of his empathy, of his unconditional positive regard. These must to some degree have been successfully communicated to the learner.[111]

Finally, the dialogue theory is centered more on process content than on product content in the sense that product content is viewed as being something which is inserted into process content rather than vice versa. David Hunter remarks that the problem with religious instruction lies in the fact that it is almost solely based on transmitting the heritage and the culture of Christian fellowship. Thus its focus is immediate detachment; the best it can ever produce is future engagement.[112] The content of which Wayne Rood speaks is the interpersonal relationship that transmutes distance into immediate contact and estrangement into Christian fellowship. This kind of content is one of the forms of overall content, the Word of God.[113]

Despite its praiseworthy aspects the dialogue theory nonetheless has too many fundamental deficiencies to be acceptable as an adequate macrotheory for explaining and predicting effective religious instruction. The dialogue theory fails to generate an interconnected series of pedagogical practices and facilitate the divine-human dialogue. Indeed, it seems to generate inconsistent pedagogical practices, though this might be due less to the inadequacy of the dialogue theory than to the inadequacy of the theorists in expounding the theory. For example, Wayne Rood is one of the stoutest of all the defenders of the lecture technique in religious instruction,[114] yet the lecture technique is hardly a pedagogical practice for enabling the teacher to operationally pass over to the learner's side.

Dialogue theorists quite frequently deny the very basis which makes a theory of religious instruction possible, namely a pedagogical practice based on scientifically-verified facts of learning and facts of teaching. Wayne Rood, for example, specifically states that dialogue does not come about by design so much as the Spirit blowing where he wills.[115] There is a decided penchant on the part of dialogue theorists to completely adhere to the blow theory or at least to strongly favor it. One practical consequence of all this is to destroy religious instruction both as a profession and as an art-science. Thus Wayne Rood contends that "given the common talent possessed by everyone to be human beings, anyone who cares to try can learn to practice [effective religion teaching] ."[116]

Dialogue appears to be not only a theory of religious instruction, but its goal as well.[117] From the standpoint of explaining and predicting teaching effectiveness, this total identification of teacher and pupil activities with learner goals presents many of the same difficulties found in the witness theory. Hence David Hunter asserts that effective engagement teaching is that in which the teacher through his mode of living enables the power of God to be rendered operable in the religious instruction act.[118] For Wayne Rood religious instruction becomes a function and a law when the teacher influences the lives of others by his own life which is "otherwise to be found only as grace, inlaid in the folds of life." In this way by intentionally bringing the learner to his own unity, the teacher helps put the learner again face to face with God.[119] The obvious weakness of such a position is that it makes all learning a function of the teacher's personality and the teacher's sanctity. The corpus of data on the personality of teachers and clergymen (which I present in the section on the witness theory) forcefully underscores the gross inadequacy of any theory of religious instruction based on teacher personality and teacher holiness.

Another major shortcoming of the dialogue theory is the strong tendency to regard teaching solely as communication between persons.[120] As the review of the research presented in the preceding chapter clearly demonstrates, teacher-pupil relationships, and even pupil-pupil relationships comprise only one of many variables present within the total environment in which the religious instruction act takes place. The exclusive, tunnel conception of learning is effected solely through interpersonal media has tended to insulate many religious educators against the skillful use of the very powerful effects of other elements within the instructional environment. For example, the deliberative structuring of the physical environment so outstandingly successful in Montessori instructional practice has seldom if ever gained a firm foothold among religious educationists. It may well be that the blind opposition and resistance manifested by many religious educationists to the structured learning situation strategy stem from a failure or an unwillingness (or both) to see the religious instruction environment as involving many powerful variables other than interpersonal communication between teacher and learner.[121]

The dialogue theory rarely if ever admits of a distinction between teaching and learning. Each partner in the dialogue becomes teacher to the other; further each partner becomes a learner from the other. All this is going on at the same time. This is all well and good, but the problem is that as the posited explanatory reality, the dialogue theory fails to specify which particular behaviors the teacher is employing during the engagement or dialogical moment. Dialogue is a form of social interaction and we know that social interaction is that kind of relation between persons where "the behavior of either one is a stimulus to the behavior of the other."[122] The dialogue theory does not seem to have generated any corpus of empirical research on the interactive behaviors of the participants in the engagement process. Yet such research is one of the hallmark criteria of the utility—and by inference of the validity—of any theory of instruction. By way of contrast, the teaching theory has given rise to many empirical investigations of the teaching-learning act, including the interpersonal interaction occurring between teacher and student. To be sure instruments to empirically describe this interaction have been developed.[123]

Vagueness and a kind of eerie spookiness hang over the dialogue theory. This appears partly due to the winds of the blow theory which swirl through it. Thus David Hunter writes: "The focus [in religious instruction] must be on what God is doing, not on what we are doing, except as what we are doing is a response to what He has done and is doing. It must be on what God is doing now, not primarily on what He has already accomplished in the past or on what He will most certainly bring to pass in the future."[124] Now all this says absolutely nothing about which pedagogical behaviors the religion teacher should employ to effect desired learning outcomes. Nor does such a statement generate any kind of educational practice. As a matter of fact Hunter's statement veritably tolls the death knell to any sort of explanation or prediction, both of which are essential characteristics of any theory. The effect of not focusing on what God (and man) have done is the rejection of all empirical data on what has proved effective in the teaching-learning act.[125] By not focusing on what God and man will probably do in the future is totally to discount prediction. Yet without making predictive hypotheses on which pedagogical practice will work, the religion teacher becomes powerless and unable to perform. At bottom Hunter's assertion is wrapped in unnecessary veils of amorphous mystery. The effective religion teacher is one who concentrates not so much on God's past, present, or future actions but rather on the past, present, and future behaviors of the learners and himself. God by definition is directly unknowable by man; he is knowable only in and through the actions of man and other terrestrial creatures—all of which underscores from a different vantage point the necessity of the religion teacher to concentrate primarily on his own pedagogical behavior and the effects of that behavior on facilitating learning.

Perhaps a remark or two on the theological underpinnings of some of the dialogue theorists might not be amiss at this point. The blow theorists seem to posit an extrinsicist God who works in mysterious fashion over against reality rather than from the withinness of reality. Thus Wayne Rood seems to distinguish between a content which is God and some sort of hypothesized content in which God is not vitally present. The theological weakness in this dichotomy is twofold. First, no person can experience God directly but only as he is in some reality. Second, in a world created by God and kept in continuous creation by him, in a world in which God's redeeming action constantly suffuses, there can be no such thing as a content which is not thoroughly God-soaked according to the manner of that content. For his part David Hunter writes that the religion teacher "must be willing to wait on the action of the Holy Spirit, withholding the authority of his own views until such time as the group is yearning for assistance and ready to use it."[126] But theologically it would seem that the action of the Holy Spirit is encapsulated by whatever teacher behaviors most effectively produce the desired religious learnings in students.

To summarize this section, it can be concluded that the dialogue theory of religious instruction is inadequate as the overarching macrotheory explaining the teaching of religion. Dialogue is a condition present in much of effective religion teaching; it is not a macrotheory explaining and predicting instructional practice. The dialogue theory does not seem to have generated a wide variety of mutually interconnected and hierarchically separated pedagogical practices. About all the dialogue theory seems to have given rise to is the empathy technique. The dialogue theory would appear to be more appropriate for counseling and therapeutic encounters in which the content is totally the client, nothing more and nothing less.

The Proclamation Theory

The proclamation theory of religious instruction holds that the announcing or heralding of the good news of salvation represents the primary and basic variable involved in the modification of the learner's behavior along religious lines. The proclamation theory is derived chiefly from two sources, namely a homespun exegesis of several key texts in the bible and the radication of religious instruction within the overall structure of the Church's preaching mission.

Roman Catholics seem to have a much greater affinity for the proclamation theory than do liberal Protestants; indeed, it is difficult to find many religious educationists from mainline American

Protestant confessions who embrace the proclamation theory. And Europeans on the whole espouse the proclamation theory more than do the Americans. Quite possibly the almost childish dependence which American Catholic religious education has had on Europe partially accounts for the strong appeal the proclamation theory has had on this side of the Atlantic.

The image often used by the proclamation theorists is that of the king's herald. According to history and especially to historical imagination, the herald would precede the entry of the king, and with fanfare and flourish on his golden trumpet announce the monarch's arrival to the populace. Or the herald would stand before assembled gatherings of the people of the realm and read aloud the king's message of good tidings or his commands.[127] In Catholic religious instruction terminology, the first heralding image is commonly referred to as "pre-evangelization," while the second is subdivided into the stages called "evangelization" and "catechesis."[128]

Advocates of the proclamation theory are typically very clear in their enunciation of teacher behaviors and learning outcomes. Thus Johannes Hofinger, a proclamation theorist, writes that "the presentation is by far the most important part of a good [religion] lesson."[129] Marcel van Caster, another proclamation theorist, announces that "catechesis [i.e., religious instruction], as the ministry of the word of God, consists in proclaiming and interpreting the word of God."[130] Josef Goldbrunner is even stronger: "Man cannot discover the message of salvation, which is divine revelation, on his own. It must be announced, proclaimed, transmitted as the Word of God, under his mandate."[131] Alfred McBride, an American proclamation theorist, states that the religion teacher "reports godly deeds to the community of believers" in the hope that they will thereby believe the message and the Jesus in the message.[132] In a 1966 publication Gabriel Moran seems to have espoused the proclamation theory,[133] while in a book published four years later he appears to have eschewed adherence to the proclamation theory.[134]

The proclamation theory is not without its strong points. First, there is strong emphasis on solid product content and worthwhile cognitive content. Proclamation theorists usually devise well thought-out product and cognitive objectives which they intend the learner to acquire. Typically, scripture and liturgy form the foundation of the message to be proclaimed, thus promoting the learner's acquisition of what some persons like to term "the basics of the faith." If skillfully executed, curricula are tightly organized on a well-delineated hierarchical order of theological learnings, proceeding from what is logically most simple up through various stages of logical complexity. Second, the instructional practice advocated by proclamation theorists is a highly structured one. There is little or no fuzziness or vagueness: the teacher proclaims and transmits a particular message almost exclusively through the lecture technique or its derivatives. It is unusual for a proclamation theorist to advocate a "happening" as a religion lesson, since "happenings" are formless affairs characterized by no logical or psychological structure and hence by no deliberative teaching and goal-directed learning. Third, the pedagogical practice generated by the proclamation theory, that is, lecture and its derivatives, form the easiest and simplest pedagogical technique for the religion teacher to use. Hence the proclamation theory is useful not only for professionally trained religion teachers but also for those who have never received any formal professional preparation. Finally, there are times when the lecture technique can be effectively employed to facilitate the acquisition of desired learning outcomes.

Despite its advantages the proclamation theory has too many drawbacks to allow it to constitute an adequate macrotheory upon which to build an entire religious instruction practice. The proclamation theory is not multidimensional; it focuses on only two of the conditions present in the learning situation, namely teacher behavior and course (subject matter) content. It pays little or no attention to the other two indispensable elements contained in the pedagogical act, namely learner behavior and environmental variables. Further, it ignores and negates the wide variety of available and empirically demonstrated effective teacher behaviors, confining teacher activity to deployment of the transmission strategy and the lecture technique. The power of the proclamation theory to explain and to predict, therefore, is seriously limited. Indeed it has generated only one strategy (transmission) and only one basic form of technique (lecture).

The proclamation theory mirrors the "radio model" of teaching, consisting of the sender, the message to be sent, and the receiver. When the three of these form one integrated unit, the outcome in Josef Goldbrunner's view is what religious instruction is meant to achieve.[135] But this radio model of religious instruction practice is based on a highly mechanistic conception of human communication. Studies in modern communication have shown that a paradigm for human interactive communication is far more complex than the simplistic radio model. For example, the radio model assumes there is no change in the sender, the message, or the receiver during the various phases or stages of the communication process. At the human level this is patently impossible. During the course of the teacher-learner interaction, both the teacher and the learner are constantly being changed as a result of the feedback being received from both the other person and from other stimuli present in the situation. To a certain extent the message itself is changed and colored during the interactive process. Also the teacher and the learner are not *tabulae rasae* as posited in the radio model; rather the teacher and learner interact with each other from the framework of previous attitude, value, and perceptual sets, so that the messages sent by either teacher or learner are not and cannot be received by the other on blank sets, as it were. The proclamation theory in short is not based on a model of human communication.

A major weakness in the proclamation theory is its stipulation that the learner should remain inactive during the religion lesson. Josef Goldbrunner spells this out: "whatever the form [of the religion lesson], it is essential to the method that the message be transmitted with authority. It cannot be found by itself, it cannot be grasped through the 'learning by doing' principle. It must be proclaimed and heard."[136] In the Munich Method, which is founded on the proclamation theory, the learner must sit absolutely quiet and at strict attention while the herald proclaims the message during the presentation phase of the lesson. Josef Jungmann, another proclamation theorist, has this to say on the discussion technique: "The catechist [religion teacher] will to some extent remain skeptical toward pupil discussion. If he should be assigned to a school in which certain periods are devoted to such discussions, he would for the sake of prudence not forbid them entirely."[137] Yet as the mass of research data which I adduce in Chapter 6 clearly demonstrates, meaningful, experiential student involvement in as many phases of the learning situation as possible is necessary for learning.

Three reasons can be advanced to explain this stress by the proclamation theorists on total teacher control and student passivity. First, these theorists are wont to place extremely heavy emphasis on the religion teacher's absolute fidelity to the message.[138] Total teacher control eliminates as far as possible the intrusion into the religion lesson of any elements which might contaminate the fidelity of the lesson to the message to be proclaimed. Since students *eis ipsis* do not yet have a sufficient grasp of doctrine and are not yet mature enough in their comprehension of the person of Jesus, their active participation is regarded as a threat to preserving total fidelity. Second, proclamation theorists heavily accentuate the religious, intellectual, and social authority of the teacher. Reinforcing this is the emphasis which these theorists accord to the maintenance of a proper and respectful distance between teacher and student. One can readily appreciate, therefore, why European religious educationists, notably the Germans and Central Europeans, lean to the proclamation theory. Finally, proclamation theorists are typically theologians and hence concentrate their attention on theological content rather than on the dynamics of the teaching-learning process.

What few educational practices do flow from the proclamation theory seem to be excessively verbal in nature. Teaching is perceived to reside entirely in the verbal transmission of the message. Pupil commitment and consequent pupil activity are regarded as somehow issuing from the teacher's transmission of the message. Never does the proclamation theory suggest how this happens or how the teacher can facilitate its occurrence. Yet it is impossible that verbal behaviors will of themselves generate nonverbal and lifestyle behaviors.

There seems to be a positive correlation between verbal behavior and cognition. By this I mean that emphasis on the teacher's verbal behavior seems to be accompanied by emphasis on cognitive content and outcomes and a deemphasis on affective and lifestyle content and outcomes. Hence the proclamation theory appears to leave in its wake a deprivation of affective and lifestyle learnings. Of course it is true that proclamation theorists talk about the person of Jesus as the message, and "faith-commitment" or "faith life" as the objective. But these outcomes are not meshed with the educational practice side of the proclamation theory; the practice is not geared to noncognitive outcomes. The consequence is a decidedly cognitive, verbal cast to the religion lesson.

The proclamation theory makes an inappropriate if not an incorrect use of scripture as its foundation. Proclamation theorists frequently assert that the instructional practice which they espouse is drawn from the bible itself. Thus, for example, Alfred McBride states: "I opt, then, for a catechesis [religious instruction] which is a theology of proclamation. Such a catechesis assimilates the literary and pedagogical categories of the Bible. The pedagogy of Scripture is simple. Some religious message is stated, and then followed by a series of stories or parables or poetic apparatus to illustrate the meaning and quality of the message."[139] The conclusion reached by the participants in the Eichstätt Conference was along the same lines: "Catechesis [religious instruction] follows God's method of proclaiming the Glad Tidings of salvation."[140] But it is a commonly accepted hermeneutical principle that the bible is not a textbook for natural science or for engineering or for instructional practice. Hence to indicate that Jesus or one of the old testament prophets used such-and-such an instructional practice does not mean that this practice has the force of revelation, or even the force of optimum pedagogy. Even if the instructional practices used by Jesus were optimum pedagogy, still the arguments of the proclamation theorists on behalf of the lecture or other heralding techniques are very weak. As I note at length elsewhere,[141] the instructional practices of Jesus as narrated in the new testament unmistakably indicate that Jesus made use of the structured learning situation strategy as a matter of course. Jesus did not frequently lecture except when circumstances forced him to, such as when addressing a very large crowd. In such cases Jesus often used the parable, which is a verbal representation of a structured learning situation. Whenever possible Jesus placed what lecturing and proclaiming he did within the context of a structured learning situation, for example, the Last Supper (John 13-17).

Proclamation theorists typically cite two favorite biblical texts in an attempt to justify their position. In Second Isaiah (sometimes called Deutero-Isaiah) 53:1 we find the text "Who has believed our report?" A text employed even more extensively than this is the one from Romans 10:17: "faith comes from listening." But the context of these verses strongly suggests that it is faulty exegesis to employ them as linchpins for the proclamation theory of teaching. Suffice it to say that there is a difference between preaching mission and preaching style, a difference frequently blurred or eradicated by the proclamation theorists.

To summarize this section, the proclamation theory of religious instruction is inadequate as the macrotheory explaining the teaching of religion. Generating as it does the transmission strategy and the lecture technique almost exclusively, it fails to meet the criterion of multidimensionality which an adequate theory of religious instruction must possess. In many if not in most ways, the proclamation theory is not a genuine theory but rather a strategy at widest or a technique at narrowest. As a strategy or technique it has its limited place in the broader spectrum of all the religion teacher's arsenal of pedagogical strategies and techniques. The proclamation theory yields a pedagogical situation which is almost totally teacher-dominated and subject-centered; the research adduced in Chapter 6 strongly indicates that both of these characteristics are not productive of optimum attitude, affective, and lifestyle learnings. Elements of the blow theory are frequently incorporated into the proclamation theory. Presumably the rationale for this is that the Spirit blows what the herald proclaims. In a nutshell the proclamation theory generates a preaching model rather than a teaching model and so is inappropriate as a theory of the whole of religion teaching. Elsewhere I remark: "Teaching religion is far more complex than standing in front of the class 'presenting' or 'imparting' the Good News. The sooner religious instruction sheds the simplistic mantle of 'presenting' and 'imparting,' the sooner it will mature and come of age."[142]

The Dedication Theory

The dedication theory of religious instruction claims that the level of the teacher's dedication represents the primary and basic variable involved in the modification of the learner's behavior along religious lines. The dedication theory is derived from an examination of the personality characteristics of those who choose to become religion teachers and those who continue in this career despite hardships and vicissitudes. This theory enjoys considerable support, particularly from the hierarchy and other ecclesiastical officials in both the Protestant and Catholic churches. Indeed, the totally volunteer character of CCD and Sunday School teachers represents an enactment of the dedication theory.

Although the dedication theory is not totally devoid of merit, nonetheless there is very little which can be said in its behalf. Perhaps its strongest suit is that a high level of affective and attitudinal commitment on the part of religion teachers has enabled them to persevere in their career despite the scandalous lack of financial and professional support from ecclesiastical officials.

Shortcomings in the dedication theory abound. The dedication theory fails totally to yield any explicit teacher behaviors. Nor does it specify in any way the relationship between particular pedagogical behaviors and optimum teaching effectiveness. Both of these constitute hallmark criteria of any adequate theory of religious instruction.

The dedication theory appears to be based on the assumption that a good man can do anything. But dedication and good will are no substitutes for pedagogical skill and knowledge. Pedagogical skill is that without which even the most lively dedication is incapable of using nature for God. Dedication without pedagogical skill is dangerous to the learners since it can lead to many pedagogical errors and actually harm the students. Teaching is a profession; hence professional competence and the skillful exercise of this competence are the chief requisites of a religion teacher. As I observe elsewhere, a person in the street may have a deep dedication to humanity and to medicine but this does not make him qualified to perform a brain operation.[143]

Indeed, proponents of the dedication theory frequently downplay if not completely deny the necessity of professional training and skill in religious instruction. Professional training and professional skill are deemed unnecessary; all that is required is a high level of dedication. Thus Wayne Rood, who subscribes to the dedication theory as well as to the dialogue theory, states flatly that dialogue cannot be taught professionally. The essence of Christianity, he maintains, can be taught only by the amateur, that is by the person who does it for love, as the root word *amare* suggests. Professionalism, he concludes, is not the cure-all for religious instruction; dedication is.[144] In the end such an outlook erodes the religion teacher's authority and leads to inept teaching. It erodes the teacher's authority because this authority derives from his expert knowledge of religious behavior combined with his pedagogical skill in facilitating religious outcomes in others.[145] It leads to inept teaching because effective pedagogy is largely a function of (1) the teacher's awareness of the consequences on learning of his antecedent pedagogical behaviors, and (2) his skill in so structuring his antecedent pedagogical behaviors that the desired consequent learner outcomes are optimally facilitated.

To summarize this section, the dedication theory of religious instruction is inadequate as an overarching macrotheory explaining the teaching of religion. It fails to either generate any educational practices or to specify the consequent-antecedent relationships between particular instructional practices and desired learning outcomes. It is destructive of emphasis on professional pedagogical knowledge and skills, both of which are absolutely requisite for effective religious instruction. At best dedication is a helpful—and sometimes a very helpful—ingredient in the religion teacher's personality structure. Basically the test of dedication is the degree to which it enhances learning. Put another way, the worth of dedication is the degree to which it contributes to the effectiveness of the already existing repertoire of the teacher's professional behaviors. A religion teacher who is truly professional will in the exercise of his instructional activities manifest whatever favorable features accrue from dedication. Conversely, however, the religion teacher who has dedication but nothing more, most likely will not and in fact cannot display those pedagogical attributes which are the fruits of professionalism.

The Teaching Theory

The teaching theory of religious instruction holds that the significant variables explaining and predicting the process of teaching religion are those involved in the effective modification of the learner's behavior along religious lines. The teaching theory is derived from descriptive statements of the empirically demonstrated causal relationship between the teacher's antecedent pedagogical behaviors and the student's consequent performance behaviors. From teaching theory it is possible to devise and design prescriptive and predictive statements about effective educational practice. The content and contours of the teaching theory are derived from hard empirical research data on the dynamics of the facilitational act and the learning process.

According to the teaching theory, the distinctive characteristic of religious instruction is that it is the purposeful and deliberative modification of learner behavior along religious lines. Thus, for this theory the goal of religious instruction is to bring about some kind of change in the learner, a change called learning. At time t it is observed that the learner cannot perform task X. A period of religion teaching is then put into operation. Then at time t+1 it is observed that the learner now performs task X and further that he is still able to perform task X after an additional interval, for example at time $t+2$. As a result of these measured observations, we can infer that learning has taken place since a change in performance has occurred and recurs.[146] The learner's performance is a consequent behavior produced by the teacher's antecedent behavior(s). By this is meant that if the learner's consequent behavior is not brought about by the teacher's antecedent behavior, then no teaching has taken place even though the learner's behavior did change. Teaching consists only in those deliberative and conscious variables which the teacher structures to bring about a change in learner behavior. Thus teaching does not include the factors by which an individual learns on the basis either of his own maturation or from experiences which were not planned for generally or specifically by the religion teacher.

The teaching theory suggests that the religious instruction act can be analyzed from two reciprocal human vantage points, namely the teacher's pedagogical activities and the learner's performance of desired outcomes. First, the religion teacher engages in a wide variety of activities such as the deployment of different pedagogical practices, record-keeping, curriculum planning, testing and assessment, and so on. All these diverse activities are done with one purpose in mind, namely, to facilitate behavioral change in the learner. Second, the learner's behavior is modified both in terms of broad educational objectives (for example, cognitive, affective, psychomotor) and of specific educational outcomes (for example, knowledge of the ten commandments, feeling compassion for a fellow student, threading film in a motion picture projector). The behavioral chain which is the teaching-learning process suggests that the teacher must vary his repertoire of pedagogical behaviors in accordance with the learning outcome(s) to be facilitated. The teaching theory adequately explains the cause-effect connections between all the sailent disparate variables involved in the network of antecedent teacher behaviors and consequent learner responses.

To make a theory optimally parsimonious, understandable, and useful, it is necessary to organize its constituent components into the fewest possible number of cluster variables. To this end four major classes of independent or causative variables can be identified: namely the teacher, the learner, the course, and the environment. The teaching theory of religious instruction seeks to delineate the causative connection among all these interacting variables on the learner's performance of the desired learning outcome. Teacher variables include the pedagogical behaviors he utilizes in the instructional situation. These behaviors comprise all those contained in the taxonomy of the instructional act listed and discussed in Chapter 4, namely, approach, style, strategy, method, technique, and step. Learner variables embrace a constellation of characteristics such as intelligence, affective level, attitude structure, creativity, values, motivation, and so on. Course variables include subject-matter area (religion, theology), level (elementary, intermediate, advanced), type (compulsory, optional), and orientation (learner-pointed or academic-pointed). Environmental variables include the characteristics of the physical setting in which the teaching is carried out, the number and kinds of learners and teachers involved, and so forth.[147] It is the function of the teaching theory of religious instruction to weave all these variables into one fabric which explains their dynamic interactions in terms of how they account for and predict teaching effectiveness. Such an explanation sharpens the religion teacher's understanding of the consequential effects of the interaction of specific variables, thus enabling him to structure these variables in such a way as to enhance the effectiveness of his pedagogy. The teaching theory of religious instruction thus raises to the highest level of intelligibility and usefulness the basic multidimensionality of the religious instruction act.

The fact that the teaching theory of religious instruction is multidimensional is reflective of the multidimensional character of the religious instruction act itself. To be sure, "teaching" is possibly a misleading generic term since it might suggest to some people a single unitary phenomenon. But as I indicate above, teaching covers a wide variety of processes; it is a highly complex human activity. Religion teaching involves an intricate network of interactions among variables. Hence it requires an intricate web of communication with the learner in a manner which is deliberative and calculated rather than accidental. Thus Othanel Smith aptly remarks that teaching is a highly complex activity, although to the uninformed it appears so simple that anyone can do it.[148] Its complexity is traceable to the fact that the religion teacher must so structure the learning situation that all the salient variables interact in concert with one another so as to bring about the desired learning outcome. Few if any other occupations involve so much complexity in theory and in implementation—a fact which has profound implications for the entire issue of professionalization of religious instruction. Unfortunately all too many religious educationists and educators fail to recognize the complexity and multidimensionality of religion teaching and mistakenly assume they have tapped its essence when they locate one dimension or even perhaps a subcategory of a dimension. Thus some of these individuals identify religious instruction with the single dimension of witnessing, others with teacher authenticity, and still others with the action of the Holy Spirit. Indeed, such emphasis on a supposed unidimensionality of religion teaching has led quite a few religious educationists to believe that the one dimension they single out is a sort of "philosopher's stone" of teacher effectiveness. The fact of the matter is, of course, that there is abundant research evidence suggesting that there are multiple criteria rather than a single criterion of teacher effectiveness. In other words teacher effectiveness must be assessed both on the grounds of the differentiated outcomes the religion teacher wishes to bring about and on the basis of the multifaceted variables which he pedagogically architects in the production of these outcomes. Ted Ward and John Ivey delineate eleven major factors from among the host of variables with which the teacher must work in his exercise of the instructional act. These variables, all of which fall under one of the four major variable clusters I have previously mentioned, are: outcomes desired; characteristics and needs of the learners; hypotheses about the means to achieve these outcomes; experiences regarded as necessary or helpful to produce the outcomes; characteristics of the learning environment selected to supply the experiences; tools and materials required to provide the experiences; teacher roles in managing the learning environment; other human roles (such as students) in operating and heightening the learning environment; evaluation systems to determine outcomes achieved; instrumentation to measure the relationship between the outcome and the pedagogical means; and the systematic development of instrumentation to assess the effectiveness, efficiency, and costs of the means in securing the outcomes desired.[149] The function of the teaching theory of religious instruction thus becomes one of situating all of these and other impinging variables into a broad framework which will enable the teacher to orchestrate all the variables so that each will play its proper interconnective and reinforcing role in the harmonious symphony which is the teaching act. It is for this reason that I sometimes refer to the teaching theory of religious instruction as the orchestration theory to distinguish it from the single-note theories such as the blow theory or the witness theory.

A critical function performed by the teaching theory of religious instruction is that it both allows for and delineates a closed-loop system of religion teaching. If religion teaching is to be effective, it must approximate as closely as possible a closed-loop system. By closed-loop here I mean that each of the variables involved in the instructional act interacts with the other variables in a closed-loop fashion so that the effects which any single variable has on the next linked variable in the behavioral chain eventually return to the original variable to modify, reinforce, or enhance it. Closed-loop teaching is another way of describing the feedback system so essential to the communication model of social interaction. Feedback is a technical term to describe the return to the input of a part of the output of a particular system, in this case the social system called religion teaching. This return of the output to the original input serves to modify, strengthen, or augment the input and thereby make it more effective. Feedback leads to the self-correction of the input of a social system such as teaching. A classic example of the usances of feedback is the household thermostat. In this closed-loop feedback system the room temperature acts upon the thermostat which in turn acts upon the furnace which in turn acts upon the room temperature which in turn acts upon the thermostat, and so on.[150]

Teaching (as distinct from maturation) is the deliberative "arrangement of the external conditions of learning in ways which will optimally interact with the internal capabilities of the learner, so as to bring about a change in these capabilities."[151] Therefore teaching deals with the structuring of the conditions of the learning situation itself. Indeed, the environment in which teaching-learning takes place is precisely one which is under the teacher's control. Hence the major emphasis in the design of effective religion teaching is on so structuring the learning environment that the desired learning outcomes are attained. The teacher does this by carefully arranging all the learning stimuli in such a way that they operate as mutually reinforcing vectors to bring about the desired change in learner behavior. These stimuli may be arranged in a variety of ways depending on the pedagogical approach, process, strategy, method, technique, and step the teacher decides to employ. The burden of the teaching theory of religious instruction thus is to discover and illumine the combinations of learner, teacher, environmental, and course variables maximizing the attainment of desired educational outcomes.

It is immediately apparent, then, that the teaching theory of religious instruction clearly points to the structured learning strategy as the most effective pedagogical strategy for religion teaching and also for any other kind of teaching. To be sure, the structured learning situation strategy flows naturally from the teaching theory of religious instruction.[152] One of the strengths of the structured learning strategy is that it allows for the productive interplay of the multidimensional factors inherent in the religious instruction act. It accentuates the primary function of the religion teacher as the professional specialist who implements his capability of so arranging conditions that the learner has the optimal opportunity for attaining the desired learning outcomes according to the psychodynamics of his own personality in the here-and-now. In the final analysis all the conditions which the teacher ever structures in order to facilitate the learning process are situational variables in the sense of factors extrinsic to the learner.[153] Indeed, teacher behaviors as well as course content and all the other elements of the instructional environment are conditions extrinsic to the learner—conditions, however, which do exercise a definite influence and direction on the learner's response, as has been amply demonstrated in the preceding chapter. Thus building a religion lesson or an entire instructional program for that matter is, as David Hunter suggests, basically like the process of conducting a political campaign or planning a large-scale military operation. In each of these operations, certain basic procedural steps must be systematically followed, else little will come of the operation.[154] The steps can be mapped out as follows. First, a task is examined to ascertain both its properties and the criteria determining its accomplishment. Second, a theory hypothesized to correlate highly with this task is tapped. The task specifies the requirements of the theory to be selected. This theory in turn generates the general directions of the enterprise. Next, the successive steps of pedagogical approach, processes, strategies, methods, techniques, and steps are devised which the original theory, undergirded by the pertinent empirical data, indicates as the most effective pedagogical campaign to bring about the desired learning outcomes in a given situation. These educational practices are then allowed full play in a closed-loop kind of behavioral chain with adjustments being made by the teacher as the instructional act takes place. These adjustments are made according as how the relevant data, interpreted by the original and pervading theory, disclose the learner is progressing toward the attainment of the desired learning outcome.

What the teaching theory of religious instruction suggests is that effective teaching is effective teaching regardless of whether it is the teaching of literature or of history or of science or of religion. I know of no corpus of research data which indicates that teaching religion is basically a different kind of teaching process than the teaching of literature or history or science. Similarly I know of no corpus of research data which demonstrates that the learning of religion is fundamentally different from the learning of any other content area. Teaching is teaching, and learning is learning. To be sure, the subject matter of what is taught does condition the way in which the teaching process is carried on. However, such conditioning influences the teaching process in much the same way as theology works within the overall structure of social science in the paradigm I outline in *The Shape of Religious Instruction.*[155] The basic point is that the processes involved in facilitating behavioral change remain the same; only their tint and hue are altered by the kind of learning being facilitated. But this is true of any relation of process to product. The research data I cite in Chapter 6 clearly indicate that there is a direct, known relationship between teacher behaviors and student learnings. These data also indicate quite clearly that factors such as the learning environment, parental influences, socioeconomic class play a known and measurable influence on student performance. The data also show that when the teacher shapes the learning conditions in X way, then student performance Y will result; or again if the teacher shapes the learning conditions in L manner, then M student performance will ensue. There are no data to suggest that if the teacher shapes the learning conditions for religion class in X way, then student performance Q or V rather than performance Y will result. David Hunter cogently writes on this point that "we do not learn secular truth one way and religious truth another. Truth is truth, and when it is comprehended and assimilated and understood and used, the distinction between the sacred and the secular falls away."[156] Now all this in no way denies God's action in religion teaching, but it does deny that God's action is restricted to religion teaching and is somehow excluded or diminished or obscured in other kinds of teaching. At bottom God is the source of every type of teaching and learning. It is only the rankest sort of theological imperialism which would restrict God's activity in the pedagogical process to the teaching of religion. One can only wonder whether it would necessarily follow that a person has to leave the realm of human affairs in order to teach religion. Is it necessary to abandon men and life and the natural order of reality in order to teach religion?[157] Men of religion should think twice before they utter the word "can't" in relation to the deliberatively structured pedagogical processes involved in producing a desired learning outcome in the religious dimension.

Cloaking religious instruction in the mantle of pseudomystery results only in impeding the development and advancement of this art-science. Moreover it also tends to have a dampening and discouraging effect on men and women—clerics and laymen alike—who are engaged in teaching religion. There is nothing more effective than being told that he is operating in an unknown, mysterious terrain to scare a person off. Yet all too often it is emphasized that the religious instruction act is a mystery. Thus, for example, Wayne Rood flatly calls both teaching and learning "mysterious acts."[158] Despite all the empirical evidence to the contrary, Rood dismisses the findings (laws) of learning on the grounds that each individual is different.[159] In one sense, of course, all of life is mysterious; in another sense, however, all of life is governed by laws which can be known and discovered. Were this not so, human activity would be impossible. It is a crass form of theological reductionism to make all reality an unknown mystery. Such reductionism can work only toward giving ready ammunition to the secularists and antireligionists. It would appear that the reduction of the teaching act and the learning process to the realm of the unknowable and the darkly mysterious is a natural outgrowth of one kind of theological worldview.[160] But as Chapter 6 clearly demonstrates, we do know that certain teacher behaviors produce certain learner performances. We do know that certain environmental factors generate certain learner outcomes. We can also measure that so-called "mysterious" socioemotional, affective atmosphere in which the teaching-learning act is being conducted. We can even predict what type atmosphere the teacher will create by analyzing his pattern of verbal statements.[161] One of the first and most important steps involved in the improvement of the quality of religious instruction is to demythologize and demystify it. Wrapping religious instruction in a veil of mystery makes it a vague and terribly fuzzy affair. Indeed, such a procedure gives no practical help whatever to the religion teacher who wishes to improve the quality of his instruction. Actually transmuting religious instruction into a mystery merely serves to confuse and demoralize him. The mystification of religious instruction is not only bad pedagogy, it is bad theology as well. In the latter vein, Gregory Baum remarks:

> We are often told that it is difficult to believe, and by this is meant that the truths revealed by God are beyond the understanding, that they demand the sacrifice of the intellect, and that the more opaque they are to human understanding, the greater the merit in believing them. When Christians have difficulty with certain doctrines, for instance with the dogmatic statements on the Trinity or the eucharist, they are sometimes told by ecclesias-

tical authorities that there is a special merit in not understanding, in being baffled by a teaching that sounds unlikely, and in obediently accepting a position that has no other link with the human mind than that God has revealed it to men.[162]

To be precise in predicting and explaining which teacher behaviors produce which learner outcomes is in no way inhuman. As a matter of fact, such prediction and explanation are far more human than operating in the dense fog and eerie shadows of mystery since it is of the essence of man that he use his cognitive powers to divine reality and direct his actions. To remain in the opaque shadowland of mystery when one has easy access to the brightly-lit terrain of understanding is not being human; it is being stupid.

The history of religious instruction over the centuries suggests that the theory of religion teaching evolved either out of a theological model or from a preaching model (or a combination of both)—not from a teaching model.[163] Largely as a result of this, religious instruction has been characterized by no special theory; its theory was essentially derived in some sort of fuzzy way from theological theory. One fallout of this is that religion textbooks and curricular materials typically give inadequate attention to the facts of the teaching-learning process and fail to relate their product and process contents to any theory which is meaningful to effective teacher behavior. It is my hope that this book in general and this chapter in particular will serve to inaugurate serious efforts to develop and build an adequate theory of religious instruction. As I indicate elsewhere,[164] such a theory must be radicated in a social-science approach since it is this approach which is *eo ipso* geared to an exploration and an improvement of that process of behavioral facilitation we call religious instruction. Now this further implies that the theory of religious instruction must perforce be the teaching theory rather than the personality theory or the authenticity theory or any other theory. I have tried to briefly sketch the broad outlines of the teaching theory of religious instruction. In the years to come, when such a theory is more fully developed by others, it will relate the two areas of teaching and learning in such a way as to generate principles and practices of instruction which have definite functional value to religion teachers and curriculum builders.

CONCLUSION

In this chapter I have briefly outlined the salient features of some of the more popular and prevalent contemporary "theories" of religious instruction, highlighting their strong points and drawing attention to their defects. Each of these so-called theories seizes a certain truth about the teaching-learning process. Yet their one common weakness is that unlike the teaching theory which represents a multidimensional paradigm, each of the other "theories" concentrates its entire focus and energy on the one truth it did manage to capture. The result is that in contrast to the teaching theory, the others all tend to be quite unidimensional and hence seriously limited in character. The teaching theory, then, incorporates virtually all the favorable elements of the other "theories" in addition to those inherent in this theory itself; this flows from its multidimensional nature. If religious instruction is to be truly effective, it must simultaneously work toward and work out of a teaching theory.

THE NATURE OF TEACHING

SECOND PRIEST: *Do you, too, want to fight for the love of wisdom?*

PAPAGENO: *Fighting is not my bag. And, to be perfectly honest, I really don't need wisdom. I'm basically a child of nature, content with sleep, food, and drink. And if I could, I'd like to catch a pretty little wife.*

SECOND PRIEST: *That you shall never do unless you undergo our trials.*

PAPAGENO: *What do these trials consist of?*

SECOND PRIEST: *You must submit yourself to all our laws, and show no fear of death.*

PAPAGENO: *I'll stay single.*

—Wolfgang Amadeus Mozart[1]

Introduction

Toward the beginning of the previous chapter I indicated that there are four major classes of independent (causative) cluster variables present in the instructional situation. These four are the learner, the course or subject matter, the environment, and the teacher. Any adequate examination of the teaching-learning process must take in all four independent variables interacting in a dynamic relationship. This chapter will explore the nature of the religious instruction act from a vantage point which incorporates these four variables, namely, from a teaching perspective.

A Definition of Teaching

Teaching is that orchestrated process whereby one person deliberatively, purposively, and efficaciously structures the learning situation in such a manner that specified desired learning outcomes are thereby acquired by another person.

If this definition is complex and contains many elements, it is precisely because the teaching act itself is complex and contains many elements. Indeed, fifteen discrete elements are incorporated into this definition of teaching. Each element further delineates and specifies the particular nature of that human endeavor we call teaching.

Teaching is an *orchestrated* process in that all the relevant constituent aspects present within each of the four major independent (causative) variables in the instructional situation are brought together by the teacher in such a harmonious manner as to produce a unified pedagogical symphony. It is here that the teacher as artist works to fashion from a host of variables and subvariables a pedagogical process in which the richness of each variable and subvariable is so blended with all the others as to at once bring a new dimension to the process and serve as a reinforcer as well to all the other constituent variables and subvariables. This kind of coalescence results in a process which heightens the richness of each component element while at the same time directly contributing to the attainment of the specified desired learning outcome.

As an orchestrated *process* teaching is a continuous multifaceted activity through which learning is facilitated. As such it represents an onward movement and ongoing flow of enablement in which those variables productive of learning are structured and brought into play. Teaching, then, is a dynamic and not a static activity.

Teaching is enacted by and through a *person* called the teacher. Sometimes the teacher encounters the learner directly in a face-to-face exchange of one sort or other. At other times this encounter is an indirect one, as when the learner interacts directly with aspects of the consciously-prepared learning environment (for example, materials, other learners) rather than with the teacher. Indirect encounter of the learner with the teacher is no less teaching than is direct encounter, since in both cases the teacher has so structured the variables of the learning situation (including himself) as to optimally facilitate the acquisition of the desired learning outcomes.

Teaching as *deliberatively* structuring the learning situation means that throughout each and every phase of the instructional process the teacher is deeply aware of what he is doing. This awareness is typically focused on the antecedent-consequent relationship. In other words the teacher consciously makes and operationally tries out a data-based hypothesis that such-and-such an antecedent pedagogical behavior will be productive of a particular consequent learning outcome. As a deliberative and intentional process, teaching is the very antithesis of a "happening."

To state that teaching is *purposively* structuring the learning situation unmistakably implies that it is a goal-directed activity. To teach is to attentively target one's pedagogical behaviors toward the attainment by the learner of a previously specified learning outcome.

As a goal-directed activity, "to teach" is at the opposite end of the spectrum from "to let happen by chance."

As an *efficacious* structuring of the learning situation, teaching is contingent upon the presumed efficacy of a particular pedagogical practice to bring a specified learning outcome to pass. This presumption is constructed by the teacher on the basis of hard research data on both learning and the facilitation process. The teacher then fashions the presumption into a working hypothesis which in turn serves to predict the degree of efficacy of the pedagogical practice he subsequently employs to produce the desired learning outcome. To teach, then, is to predict.

Teaching is *structuring* the learning situation. It is the process of consciously and deliberatively arranging those variables and conditions which are most productive of facilitating the desired learning outcome. These variables as we have seen fall into four broad classes: namely the learner, the course or subject matter, the environment, and also the teacher. To teach, then, is to create situations in which students learn what is intended they learn. Pedagogy is making educational provision; it is managing the process of change by so architecting the learning situation that desired performance outcomes are enabled to be realized.[2] Teaching is an activity of professional intervention in both natural life processes in general and in learner growth in particular. The purpose of professional intervention is to heighten, focus, or bring to salience those aspects of natural life processes and growth which otherwise would not of themselves be targeted toward producing at this moment and in the most efficacious way possible the desired learning outcome. Professional intervention is done at two different levels: in shaping and architecting the learning situation itself, and then in readjusting or realigning particular elements of the learning situation during the ongoing pedagogical process.

To say that teaching consists in structuring the *learning situation* indicates that it is the creation or utilization of those settings, circumstances, activities, or experiences designed to facilitate the attainment of a desired learning outcome. A learning situation is one which by its very character and composition establishes or fortifies the conditions of learning.

Teaching is the arrangement of pedagogical conditions *in such a manner* that specified learning outcomes are thereby induced. The way in which the elements comprising the learning situation are put together is such that in and of themselves they have the potency of bringing to pass the intended learning outcome.

Teaching as facilitating the acquisition of *desired* learning outcomes means that teaching consists in effecting a predetermined behavioral change in an individual. Indeed, the ultimate criterion of teaching is the successful bringing to pass of a desired learning outcome; any intermediate criteria must be shown to be correlated with this ultimate criterion. The source of the decision on what constitutes the predetermined desired learning outcome is irrelevant for the teaching act considered purely in itself. Who should make such determination is a philosophical, theological, and typically a political question. But whoever makes the ultimate or penultimate decisions, the nature of the course or subject area studied has a definite bearing on the determination and composition of the desired learning outcome. The contours and flow of the pedagogical process vary according to the kind of learning outcome desired. Consequently, there can be no such thing as *the* teaching method or technique; method or technique vary according to the learning outcome sought.

Teaching as facilitating the acquisition of *specified* learning outcomes means that teaching is directed toward producing readily identifiable, clearly distinguishable performance outcomes. It is necessary but by no means sufficient that teaching be targeted toward specified yet highly generalized outcomes such as product learnings or process learnings, cognitive behaviors or affective behaviors, and so on. Teaching as facilitating the acquisition of "specified" learning outcomes also suggests that the desired behavioral outcomes can be precisely delineated in terms of concrete particularized bits of behavior which will actually be performed by the learner. This suggests three conditions for the specificity of the desired learning outcome: (1) identification and description of the desired outcome; (2) indication of the principal conditions under which the outcome is to occur; (3) criterion of acceptable performance.

Teaching is always and in every way targeted toward the attainment of desired *learning outcomes.* There is no teaching apart from learning outcomes. Indeed, the facilitation of learning outcomes constitutes the very *raison d'être* of every phase of teaching.

To state that teaching is a process in which a learning situation is so structured that specified desired learning outcomes are *thereby* facilitated clearly implies that it is the teaching act which brings the learning outcomes to pass. If a particular learning outcome is a result of something other than the teaching act, then in such a case there was no teaching.

Crucial to the definition of teaching is that the pedagogical process causes desired learning outcomes to be *acquired* by the learner. Teaching, then, is defined in terms of how successful the act is in inducing the learning outcomes sought. Teaching does not consist in the intention of the teacher to induce desired learning outcomes; it is the degree and extent to which these outcomes are in fact learned. To teach is to be effective; by definition, there is no such thing as totally ineffective teaching, for such an activity would not be teaching but something else.

Finally, teaching is the process through which desired learning outcomes are acquired by *another person*. Teaching is a two-party contractual relationship in which each party expects something of the other to be delivered over a specified period of time. The learner is central in the teaching act—central as the point of departure, central as the constant focus of pedagogical activity, central as the one in whom the learning outcome is acquired. The student, not the teacher, is the primary proximate internal agent in effecting the desired learning outcomes. This in no way minimizes the key and indispensable role of the teacher; rather it stresses that the learner is an integral partner and active coparticipant in the pedagogical process. Teaching is an activity which is based on the needs, capabilities, goals, and histories of the individual learners.

The definition of teaching, together with my brief elaboration of each of the fifteen elements comprising this definition, plainly shows that teaching is at bottom a process of facilitation. Teaching is enabling. It is the readying of activities and experiences so as to empower the learner to acquire desired learning outcomes. Teaching is therefore a helping activity.

It should be noted that the definition of teaching which I offer is stated in behavioral terms. The reason for this is that teaching can only be adequately defined and conceptualized in terms of teacher behaviors and learner behaviors. What has hindered the development of religious instruction for so many centuries have been definitions of teaching which sound lofty, sublime, and majestic, but which in reality are amorphous, pseudo-mystical, and fuzzy precisely because they fail to delineate which behaviors are included in the teaching act. Wayne Rood, for example, defines the teaching of Christianity as "a common activity, raised to intentionality, conducted in sensitivity, and completed in action of any kind."[3] A definition of this type is virtually useless in pinpointing those specific kinds of behaviors which characterize the pedagogical act. Indeed, Rood's definition could hold true for group prayer, for attending a church service, and even for dancing with one's favorite partner. If the teaching of religion is to develop and grow, then its definition and conceptualization must be operationally based. Planning and implementation of educational practice require that the religion teacher make choices from among a variety of identifiable operations.

Teaching, therefore, consists of constant behavioral analysis and behaviorial control on the part of the teacher. Such behavioral analysis and behavioral control are targeted toward producing the specified desired learning outcomes in the student. Thus the key to optimum teaching is threefold: (1) the religion teacher's awareness of his own pedagogical behaviors; (2) his awareness of the consequences which his pedagogical behaviors have on the learner; (3) his skill in controlling his pedagogical behaviors so as to deploy them in such a way as to lead the learner to acquire the desired learning outcomes.

The essential characteristic of the religion teacher is that he is a competent specialist in the modification of learner behavior along religious lines. The religion teacher can be called a teacher only because he has the technical competence or process expertness to facilitate these behaviors in learners.[4] To illustrate by way of analogy, the physiologist possesses expert knowledge of the nature and functioning of the material aspects of the human organism, but it is the physician-surgeon who has the technical competence or process expertness necessary to perform an appendectomy. This technical competence or process expertness of the physician-surgeon does not deny the fact or the importance of his possessing a high-level knowledge of physiology. In the words of Walter Doyle, "his primary concern as physician in learning physiology is not necessarily to advance the frontiers of knowledge in this science. Rather, as physician, he is charged with the application of the findings of physiology to promote human physical development. Hence competence in physiology as such constitutes only a part of the defining competence of a professional physician. His essential competence lies in the process involved in the application of the knowledge of physiology to promote health in the patient."[5] (Parenthetically I might add that the principle underlying the analogy of the physiologist and physician can be applied to the distinction between the theologian and the teacher of religion. The theologian is one who is competent in the content of the science or study of God. His task is to inquire into the nature and workings of God and if possible to advance knowledge and deeper understanding in this field. The religion teacher, on the other hand, besides possessing a knowledge of the science of theology, must also have the technical competence or process expertness to so structure the learning situation that the learner's behavior is modified along religious lines, which is to say that the student learn religion.)

Teaching as Prediction and Hypothesis-Making

Crucial to both the nature and the effectiveness of religion teaching is the art of prediction. To teach is to predict. A teacher opts to use pedagogical practice X rather than pedagogical practice Y to produce the desired learning outcome precisely because he predicts practice X will be more effective than practice Y. To predict is not to decide; rather it forms the basis for instructional decision. And the religious instruction act is one of continual decisions which all revolve around the antecedent-consequent axis.[6]

"Prediction represents an effort to describe what will be found concerning an event or outcome not yet observed on the basis of data or information considered to be relevant to this unobserved event."[7] Implicit, then, in the religion teacher's selection of pedagogical practice X is a statement about a future and hence unobserved learning outcome. This statement is made by the teacher with some confidence because of his awareness of the existence of data or information which he considers relevant to the relationship of pedagogical practice X and the desired learning outcome. For example, the teacher had previously used pedagogical practice X with this same learner, and it produced the same kind of learning outcome as the teacher now wishes to produce. Or again, the teacher knows that the pertinent empirical data on attitude learning suggest that technique X is particularly effective in bringing about a specific kind of attitudinal outcome in a learner having such-and-such personality characteristics. Prediction highlights the antecedent-consequent chaining that is teaching. Data (observed events) which yield information for forecasting a desired learning outcome (observed event) is the antecedent—commonly called the "independent variable" in social-science literature or the "cause" in theological terminology. The desired learning outcome which is forecast (and hence cannot be initially observed) is the consequent—typically referred to as the "dependent variable" in social science or as "effect" in theology.

The efficacy of religious instruction varies directly with the skill with which the religion teacher can predict that the independent variable (for example, pedagogical practice) he selects will yield the sought-for dependent variable (desired learning outcome). The specification of the predictive interrelationships between antecedent (independent) variables and the consequent (dependent) variables is therefore crucial to effective religion teaching. Using the term "attributes" to represent discrete or qualitative variables, and the word "measurements" to describe a continuous variable on which scores are available, J. P. Guilford makes four permutations of independent and dependent variables from which he postulates four basic kinds of prediction: (1) attributes from attributes, as, for example, the presence or absence of religiosity from socioeconomic status; (2) attributes from measurements, as illustrated in the prediction of religiosity from scores on a religiosity inventory instrument; (3) measurements from attributes, as when probable scores on a religiosity inventory instrument are predicted by one's membership in the clerical or lay state; (4) measurements from measurements, as in the case of predicting job ratings from scores on personality tests. Guilford also describes statistical procedures for carrying out such predictions and for furnishing indications of the margin of tolerable error involved.[8]

The effective religion teacher is always seeking the most successful way to produce desired learning outcomes. To this end he places within the learning situation those variables he predicts will prove most efficacious in bringing about this desired learning outcome. In the past he has done this with the help of personal experience and folk wisdom. It is now time for the religion teacher to utilize the scientifically-verified facts of learning and facts of teaching to sharpen the potency of his prediction and so render his instructional activities more fruitful. This is one of the many significant benefits which the social-science approach to religious instruction has for both the workaday religion teacher and the curriculum builder.

Some theologically-oriented religious educationists have argued that attempts by the religion teacher to inject the predictive element into the mainstream of his instructional activities represents blasphemy against God and a frontal assault on the learner's freedom.[9] Such contentions reveal a woeful lack of awareness of what really takes place in the instructional act. If one were to analyze the pedagogical behavior of a religion teacher, one would soon find that the basic reason why the teacher selects pedagogical practice X in preference to pedagogical practice Y is precisely because the teacher, at least implicitly, predicts that practice X will be more effective than practice Y in bringing about the desired learning outcome. Further the teacher works assiduously to arrange conditions so that this prediction will be even more likely to come true—indeed, from another angle the arrangement of these conditions itself represents an integral aspect of the predictive act since the teacher predicts that one set of conditions will be more effective than another set in producing the desired outcome. There is nothing blasphemous in making use of the data of God's world to bring about a godly learning outcome; in fact I maintain that in a certain sense it is blasphemous not to use predictive data since such deliberate nonuse represents a rejection or at least a lack of cooperation with God as he is in the world. Nor does the use of prediction represent an assault on the learner's freedom. The teacher can predict with a considerable degree of accuracy the conditions which will bring about a desired learning outcome. But the arrangement of these conditions of itself does not compel the learner to learn. Inducement is not coercion. Probability is not certainty.

There tend to be serious inconsistencies in the writings of many theologically-oriented religious educationists on this matter of prediction. These men, notably the advocates of the blow theory and the witness theory, strongly denounce prediction as a threat to the learner's freedom. Yet an examination of their statements unmistakably indicates that their own suggestions for a more effective religious pedagogy are based on what they perceive—usually without the necessary supporting empirical data—to adequately predict desired learning outcomes. For example, Wayne Rood who espouses both the blow theory and the dialogue theory declares that since not everything can be learned, the religion teacher must make a selection of the effective world to present to his students.[10] But the very basis for this selection is the religion teacher's predictive judgment about which aspects of the world are the most relevant and most efficacious for this particular group of learners. Gabriel Moran, another blow theorist, proposes religion lessons which are community-centered because he "presupposes that the individual becomes a person only in and through community."[11] Moran's decision to advocate a community-centered religious pedagogic stems from his prediction that such a pedagogic is more effective than another in bringing about the desired learning outcomes.

Michael Warren, who champions the witness theory, similarly bases his own religious instructional activity on the predictive element even though elsewhere he takes pains to vigorously denounce prediction as an assault on learner freedom. In describing the high school religion program in which he was personally involved, Warren writes that "a second characteristic of these [modern Christian experience] programs is that more learning is expected to take place through interaction and through group activities than through one-way verbal presentations."[12] It would be difficult to find a statement on teaching as prediction which is stronger than this quotation from Warren.

Teaching then is predicting. Surely much remains to be done about which learning conditions most effectively predict ·desired outcomes. Nonetheless, social science has made impressive strides in this direction. The facts of learning and the facts of teaching reviewed throughout this book provide the religion teacher with a solid though by no means a perfect base for selecting those conditions which have been empirically demonstrated to predict specified performance outcomes. Enhancement of the potency of prediction represents one of the firstfruits of the social-science approach to religious instruction.

If teaching were not prediction, it would be blind. It would be unable to look confidently toward the effecting of desired future learning outcomes. Moreover if teaching were not prediction, it would be reduced to a chance "hit or miss" activitiy yielding desired results only by "happenstance." But because teaching is prediction, it can be deliberative in structure and fruitful in results, rather than haphazard in structure and potluck in results.

To say that teaching is predicting is to agree that the religion teacher is an hypothesis maker. He hypothesizes that pedagogical practice X is more productive of desired learning outcomes than is practice Y. Consequently, to teach is to make tentative generalizations about the efficacy of various pedagogical practices. As I point out earlier in this book, it is the role of instructional theory to provide the base and the ground for generating usable and fecund hypotheses as well as providing the framework for verifying the results of the teacher's testing of these hypotheses in pedagogical practice.

Teaching as an Art-Science

The often presumed dichotomization of teaching into either an art or a science is an erroneous one. Indeed, this presumed dichotomization has done much to hinder the development of teaching in general and religion teaching in particular. Teaching is neither an art alone nor a science alone; it is an art-science. Teaching is an art-science since it is the practice or enactment of a science. In one sense teaching is more of an art than a science; to be precise, teaching is an art generated by a theory (science) and regulated by both the facts of learning (science) and the facts of facilitating (science). But teaching is also very much a science; the teacher's knowledge of the scientific basis and process of teaching provides him with continuous cues as to which pedagogical behavior to employ in the instructional act at any given moment.

As an art teaching is the appropriate application of science to the exigencies of a particular situation.[13] To be fruitful, this application calls for the exercise of the teacher's judgment about how and when to apply the science. This kind of judgment concerning which pedagogical behaviors to employ depends not only on his ability to know which scientific aspects of teaching and learning are germane to a particular learning situation, but also on the teacher's own personal artistic skill to fashion from these scientific data that kind of pedagogical experience which will be productive of the desired learning outcomes. Like all other artists, the teacher must be sensitive—sensitive to the learner, sensitive to the consequences of his own pedagogical behavior, and sensitive to those conditions which at a given moment will most efficaciously work toward bringing about the desired learning outcome. The teacher as artist is constantly engaged in two activities: (1) analyzing his own pedagogical behavior in terms of its effectiveness in the here-and-now instructional act, and (2) playing and experimenting with new means of arranging experiences.[14] Because teaching is an art, cookbook formulas for pedagogical practice are of little or no real help to the religion teacher. Teaching as an art always involves a constantly changing series of readjustments in pedagogical practice, and hence precludes that kind of automatic application which the cookbook approach implies.

Teaching is the enfleshment and exercise of a science. Teaching is, from one vantage point, an empirical process. In other words it is a scientific process based on scientifically-derived and verified data, rather than a matter of teacher opinion rooted in sources other than data concerning the teaching-learning process. As a science teaching is a matter of explaining classroom phenomena and predicting the efficacy of a particular pedagogical practice. Teaching in the scientific sense is the bringing into existence of the complex of teacher, learner, subject matter content, and environmental variables in such an integrated pattern of purposive pedagogical behavior that these variables all interact productively with each other to bring about the desired learning outcomes.

Teaching viewed solely as an art makes pedagogy deteriorate into a process devoid of valid foundation or criteria. Teaching regarded simply as a science causes pedagogy to degenerate into a bald technical exercise. The artistic and scientific elements of teaching act as a control and corrective on each other so as to preserve both the creativity (art) and the validity (science) of the pedagogical act. Just as technical facility alone does not create art, neither does aesthetic experience cause science. A learning situation in the hands of the teacher as artist-scientist offers a controlled environment in which with the infusion of science the teacher can arrange the conditions so as to bring about the desired outcomes effectively rather than leave the matter to chance. Teaching as an art-science demonstrates that the facts of learning and the facts of teaching are both indispensable in the instructional act. Teaching viewed as an art-science suggests that effective pedagogy derives from an analysis of the facilitatory behaviors of teachers shown to be effective (facts of teaching) and from those data about the learning process which are relevant to enhancing the success of this particular learning situation (facts of learning). Teaching considered as an art-science also has by this very fact a built-in generator for pedagogical improvement since it is the function of an artist-scientist to observe the consequences of his own instructional behavior and to adjust this behavior in accordance with the scientific evaluation he makes about the degree to which these consequences have met his stated performance objectives.[15]

Theologically-oriented religious educationists typically regard the teaching of religion as either solely an art or as neither an art nor a science. I have already demonstrated the inadequacy and lopsidedness of the first of these views. The second view usually is radicated in a fuzzy, hypermystical, and spooky notion of religious instruction. Thus Wayne Rood, a proponent of this position, argues that since Christianity brings into education an entirely new dimension, neither the scientific nor the artistic approach is adequate.[16] If teaching religion is neither an art nor a science, what is it? Rood never really says except to hint that an intensification of humanity is by itself not productive of Christian blessedness. But this fails to address the point. More significantly by skirting the issue entirely and taking refuge in the mists of opacity, theologically-oriented religious educationists of Wayne Rood's persuasion fail to offer any concrete analysis of the act of religious pedagogy. As a consequence they provide no help in the improvement of the teaching of religion.

Teaching as a Cooperative Art-Science

An operative art is one which is exercised on passive matter such as sculpting. A cooperative art, on the other hand, is one which is exercised together with an interactive agent. Teaching is a cooperative art-science rather than an operative one.[17] Teaching is a single social activity in which the four elements of the learning situation (teacher, learner, subject matter content, and environment) interact with each other in such a way that the desired learning outcome is thereby facilitated. As a social activity involving persons, teaching is perforce a cooperative rather than an operative art-science. From the viewpoint of pedagogical dynamics, the classroom represents a constantly shifting pattern of interaction of the four basic constituents in the teaching-learning situation. Were teaching simply an operative art-science, the richness and diversity brought about by this kind of multifaceted interaction would be inoperable.

Enactment of teaching as an operative art-science is destructive of many of the goals of religious instruction. Surely one of the prime objectives of religious instruction is the development of a deeper self-understanding and self-actualization of the learner. Yet as Thomas Aquinas notes, a person can have no knowledge of himself except through his acts.[18] Ellis Nelson perceptively observes that a person comes to an understanding of himself only in dynamic relationship with others in his environmental framework.[19] It follows logically, therefore, that the student in the learning situation has a pressing need to relate and to interact with all the significant elements in that learning situation, for this is how he finds himself and God as well. Because teaching is a cooperative and interactive process, both teacher and learner are artists in the pedagogical dynamic—artists in the sense that they both exercise the artistic quality of "making."[20] In their interactive behaviors both the learner and the teacher assume many roles. The teacher's main role in that cooperative art-science which is teaching is to orchestrate the patterns of interaction to effect the desired learning objective.

Teaching as a cooperative rather than an operative art-science nicely meshes with the Christian doctrine of revelation. Thus Randolph Crump Miller points out that learning is typically a social process, and "the Gospel of redemption is learned by sharing the redeeming relationships within a community."[21] To be sure, God reveals himself to man at every moment and in every place. But the receptibility and yeastability of God's revelation seem to be heightened in that kind of situation which is Christianly social, that is, one which features cooperative interrelationships in a climate of fellowship. Concerning this Lewis Sherrill comments that Christian fellowship can best be described as *koinonia,* a communion, an interaction, a sharing, and a participation in that which binds together believers and God.[22] For Sherrill *koinonia* is a particularly fruitful setting for God's revelatory activity not because of some special superadded attribute of the *koinonia* experience, but because it is an activity featuring open cooperative interaction. This kind of human activity enables man to contact God in a zone the nature of which allows for the presence of God to be more manifest.

Down through the centuries, religious educationists have tended to regard teaching as an operative art instead of a cooperative activity. Hence they typically advocated the preaching model rather than the teaching model and the transmission strategy instead of the structured learning situation strategy. The result quite naturally was and still often is a teacher-centered pattern of religion teaching. Thus, for example, Marcel van Caster can write that teaching is the attempt of the teacher to convey by words and witness the truth which he himself possesses to the minds and hearts of his students.[23] In van Caster's conception teaching is an operative art: the learners are worked on rather than worked with. Even when the learner is taken into consideration by theologically-oriented religious educationists, it is typically in isolation from the dynamic and interactive relationships he has with the other variables in the ongoing learning situation.

The conceptualization of teaching as a cooperative art-science will cause religious pedagogy to become more learner-centered and less teacher-centered. Maria Montessori, for example, derived her pedagogy as well as her instructional materials from working directly with learners and finding out from observing them what worked most effectively.[24] Since teaching is a cooperative endeavor, feedback to the teacher from the learner is absolutely indispensable for the improvement of the pedagogical act. Curiously this is true also in an operative activity such as, for example, dart-throwing.[25] A blindfolded person throwing darts at a target will get no closer to the bullseye with continued throwing. Once the blindfold is removed, however, his aim improves. This improvement is due to both a knowledge of the results and the corrective effect which this knowledge brings—feedback, in other words. In a sense it is possible to regard the religion teacher as "throwing" his behaviors at his students. How "close" he gets to the students—that is, how well they learn from him—depends in large measure on the amount and kind of feedback he gets and is willing to receive from the students. But teaching is a cooperative and interactive process, and hence another look at the dart-throwing analogy is necessary. Learners are not inanimate, standardized, motionless, passive targets. Nor are the pedagogical behaviors of religion teachers vis-à-vis learners the same from one learner to another. After each effort at hitting the mark, both the "dart" (instructional behavior) and the "target" (learner) may and often do change. Even if we disregard the fact that the teacher is also changing, this formulation helps us to understand why effective teaching is dependent upon feedback from learners and the correctives in teacher behavior which such feedback generates. What this clearly implies is that teaching is a cooperative rather than an operative art-science.

Teaching as a cooperative activity suggests that teaching is directed toward persons-as-persons; teaching as an operative activity indicates that teaching is directed toward persons-as-objects. On this point the research has found that the cooperative or interactive stance toward teaching facilitates the desired learning outcomes more effectively than the operative stance. Thus, for example, a study by John Whitehorn and Barbara Betz of young resident physicians working with schizophrenic patients in a psychiatric ward revealed that the patients who improved the most had as their physicians men who regarded them as human beings and whose treatment was oriented around an interactive behavior pattern, while those who improved the least had as their physicians men who treated them as "objects" to be worked on.[26] Although these investigators emphasized that their findings strictly applied only to the treatment of schizophrenics, Carl Rogers has hypothesized that similar results would be found in almost any kind of helping relationship (for example, teaching).[27] Indeed, prior and particularly subsequent research has supported Rogers's hypothesis. In his summative overview of the pertinent research, B. Othanel Smith concludes that many classroom difficulties stem from the fact that the teacher's attitudes are often in conflict with those of his pupils and that the teacher works on rather than works with these pupil attitudes.[28] To say that teaching is a cooperative art-science is to say that it is a joint enterprise between the learner and the teacher. If this is so, then the student should be personally and actively involved in every phase of the religion class including the planning phase. Joint teacher-student planning is one manifestation of teaching as a cooperative art-science.[29]

The conceptualization of teaching as a cooperative art-science is not restricted to the area of intellectual interaction as some theologically-oriented religious educators like Michael Warren suggest. For Warren and those of his persuasion, the learner's religious life "is both formed by and is formative of a community of shared understandings."[30] But teaching-learning as a cooperative venture suggests that not only are intellectual aspects lived and shared in common, but even more importantly affective and lifestyle factors are lived out together. Warren's unduly narrow notion of religion teaching quite possibly has led him to excessively restrict the zones of teacher-pupil sharing which are generated by the cooperative nature of pedagogical art-science.

The Teacher as Catalyst

The religion teacher is typically described as a catalyst in the facilitation of learning.[31] The term catalyst derives from chemical usage. By definition a catalyst is a foreign substance which accelerates (and often initiates) a chemical reaction while itself remaining chemically unchanged.[32]

The notion of the religion teacher as catalyst fits in nicely with the traditional view of religious instruction as "proclaiming the message" or "transmitting the story of salvation." Thus, for example, Johannes Hofinger conceives religion teaching as "the art of transmitting a given doctrinal content to others."[33] Such a view of religious pedagogy regards the teacher as a "foreign substance" to the learning situation and more significantly perhaps as one who remains unchanged during the pedagogical dynamic.

The conceptualization of the religion teacher as a catalyst is sharply at variance with the notion of teaching as a cooperative endeavor. Teaching is by its very nature an activity characterized by reciprocal relationships. The catalyst viewpoint would deny the reciprocity of this relationship, transforming it into a one-way process. In any reciprocal relationship both parties involved undergo change as a result of their interaction. The religion teacher is not a paternal extrinsic ruler of individuals or of groups; rather he is an enabler who works to bring alive in persons and in groups desired behavioral changes and who in this very pedagogical process undergoes change. During the instructional act, the teacher himself undergoes growth and change as a result of his varied professional relationships in the learning situation. This is not to imply that teaching qua interaction process is simply a vague, overgeneralized instructional device; it is instead to indicate that the pattern and thrust of the interactive process which is religion teaching must be purposively and specifically fitted to each of the phases of learning and behaving in order to yield its real potential. To suggest that teaching is an interactive process is to assign important rights to each of the four major variables involved in the teaching-learning dynamic, namely the teacher, the learner, the subject matter content, and the environment. Every pedagogical experience is a dynamic interplay among these four factors in which each of these factors undergoes some change.[34]

The "teacher as catalyst" view is pitifully neglectful of the obvious fact that in human interaction the teacher is always undergoing change. Sometimes the pupils deliberatively work for such change, as for example when they set about getting the teacher to talk about his own pet interests so as to divert him from pursuing what they regard as an uninteresting lesson. At other times the pupils unintentionally produce this change, as for example, when some pupils pass sarcastic remarks to the teacher during the lesson and thereby cause him to become flustered or angry. The teacher as facilitator purposively varies his pedagogical behaviors on the basis of how the learner and the other variables in the environment behave toward him. For example, if a particular teacher behavior leads a student to make an incorrect response or causes him to be unduly embarrassed, the teacher then shifts away from those pedagogical behaviors which produced these undesired student outcomes to other pedagogical behaviors which he predicts will bring about desired learning outcomes. A student's response, therefore, causes the teacher to either continue the pedagogical behaviors he is using or to alter them. Because the pedagogical dynamic is an interactive process, teacher behaviors become cues for student responses, and student behaviors become cues for teacher responses. Both teacher and student are in the process together.[35] Since teaching is a cooperative activity, the effective religion teacher is the one who throughout the entire lesson continually remains open to experience and incorporates himself into the process of change.

In altering his pedagogical behaviors as a consequence of student behaviors, the teacher becomes in a sense a learner. By no means does this imply that the roles of teaching and learning are not essentially distinct; indeed, they must be kept distinct if the teacher is to perform his basic task of facilitation. Teacher behaviors are distinct from student behaviors and must be delineated and specified as such. It does imply, however, that through interaction and truly existential dialogue (as opposed to mere verbal or cognitive dialogue) that "the teacher-of-the-students and the students-of-the-teacher cease to exist and a new term emerges: teacher-student with students-teachers. The teacher is no longer the-one-who-teaches, but one who is himself taught in the [existential] dialogue with the students, who in turn while being taught also teach. They become jointly responsible for a process in which all grow."[36] This is teaching as a cooperative activity rather than as a catalytic process. The teacher is still the teacher with a distinct repertoire of behaviors which set him off from the learners. He is basically a facilitator who works in the interactive process to help people learn. It is by immersing himself in this interactive process and becoming a kind of learner thereby that he is better able to become a more effective facilitator.

As a cooperative activity in contradistinction to a catalytic one, teaching necessitates a "crossing over to the other side of the learning experience," to use Wayne Rood's felicitous and expressive phrase.[37] Such a passover can take place on three axes, namely the cognitive, the affective, and the lifestyle. The teacher can cross over to the learner's side by thinking with him and understanding him and the views he takes from his own (that is, the learner's) cognitive vantage point. On the affective axis the teacher can empathize with the learner, that is, feel the world from the learner's affective inner world. Finally, the teacher can make the passover by attempting to experience and live in the world just as the learner experiences and lives in the world. In the preceding chapter I term the cognitive passover as perceptualizing, the affective as empathizing, and the lifestyle as localizing. The teacher's crossover to the learner's side cannot be total, of course, since each person's self is unique and not totally sharable. But such a crossover can facilitate learning if the teacher does it consciously and deliberatively as a pedagogical behavior which is designed to enhance learning. For example, the aware teacher knows that such a crossover, especially of the affective and lifestyle types, communicates to the learner a sense of the teacher's unconditional positive regard for him. This sense of being prized by the teacher for what he is represents a kind of teacher expectancy—an expectancy that the learner will fully become what he can be and is. The research evidence adduced in Chapter 6 clearly indicated that positive teacher expectancy is highly correlated with subsequent pupil gains in learning.

Teaching is facilitating. The implication here is that it is the learner and not the teacher who is the center of the instructional act. Religion class exists primarily for the learner, not primarily for the teacher (or primarily for the church). Thomas Aquinas in his usual pithy style observes that the student is the primary proximate cause of learning, with the teacher being the secondary extrinsic proximate cause.[38] This suggests that the teacher best works for the learner when he works with him.

Since the instructional act is interactive rather than catalytic, each of the four basic cluster variables changes in some way during the lesson. This means that not only the teacher, the learner, and the environment undergo some change as a result of interaction, but the subject matter content also undergoes alteration. This is a cardinal point, one typically overlooked by religious educators in general and theologically-oriented religious educationists in particular. This change in subject matter content takes place in three spheres, namely the logical, the psychological, and the ontological. In the logical sphere the interaction which takes place in the religion lesson changes the content in the sense that its "objective" logical aspects are reworked by the learner and by the teacher in accordance with their own principles of logic and cognitive operations. In the psychological sphere the cognitive and affective contents are altered through the way in which the teacher and especially the learner respond to the content, what he remembers and what he forgets, how he feels about the content, and in general how he churns up and digests and incorporates the content into his self-system. But far more sweeping and far more radical is the ontological change which affects the very essence of the subject matter content considered in itself. By interacting with the content through the medium of the other variables in the learning situation, the teacher and the learner in some way change the content itself by adding to it (or in some cases subtracting from it) new dimensionalities. Interestingly enough this phenomenon of the interactive teaching dynamic which takes place in all kinds of pedagogy including religious pedagogy can also be explained by theology. God's continuing revelation, his ongoing suffusional activity in the world, constantly produces changes in all aspects of the world. Each Christian, each teacher, and each learner, too, are continually filling up the world.[39] In the context of the learning situation, this means affecting in some way and to some degree the essence of subject matter content. It is through an interactive teaching pattern that such a filling up of the world and of content can most fruitfully take place—which points up the pedagogical bankruptcy of the transmission strategy and the proclamation theory.

If the religion teacher is not a catalyst, then what is he? I would answer that he is a change agent. He deliberatively facilitates and consciously accelerates the desired behavioral change in the learner and in the process himself undergoes a certain change.

I have shown in this section that no element in the teaching-learning situation is a catalyst in the sense of remaining unchanged during the instructional dynamic. In the process of ongoing interaction which is teaching, the learner, the environment, the subject matter content, and the teacher himself all undergo change and alteration. Hence the sole theoretical model adequate to explain and improve religion teaching is the one which incorporates all four elements in an interactive system. Only by being incorporated into a system which is interactive can we be free to move into that behavioral analysis of the teaching act which is indispensable for the improvement of religious instruction. I will briefly outline and discuss such an interactive system in the next chapter.

The Teacher as Pure Function

The conceptualization and actualization of the religion teacher as pure function derive from the fact that teaching is pure function—nothing more and nothing less. Teaching as pure function suggests that pedagogy is not an entity in and for itself but rather is an activity organically related to something outside itself, namely learning, or more specifically the production of learning. As pure function the teacher as teacher exists totally for the other person, for the learner. The teacher as teacher exists for the purpose of aiding the learner to acquire an appropriate behavior repertoire. Now function connotes duty and responsibility; in the case of teaching, function implies that the person exercising this function is thereby charged with the duty and responsibility to see to it that the desired learning outcomes are effected. To be a function is to serve a purpose; it is to be socially (and in the case of religious instruction, religiously) useful.

To describe a religion teacher or any other kind of teacher is more to describe a function than to describe a person. To call an individual a teacher is to specify him in terms of the function he performs rather than the person he is. It matters not what kind of person he is; what matters is the kind of activity he performs. A function denotes that a particular kind of service is expected from the one performing that function. To say that an individual is a person is to indicate only in very broad global terms what generalized kinds of behaviors may be expected of him. But to state that an individual is a teacher is to point out or to delimit certain more or less specific kinds or classes of human behaviors. All human behaviors are not teaching behaviors, but all teaching behaviors are human behaviors either directly or by extension.

From the above analysis it can be clearly seen that to categorize the teacher as pure function is neither to impersonalize nor to depersonalize him. Instead it is to unmistakably call attention to the fact that teaching is the conscious harnessing and targeting of the teacher's personality toward the attainment of specified learning objectives. To say that the teacher is pure function is to assert that teaching is personality-neutral. By personality-neutral I mean that the teaching task does not of itself specify what kind of personality the teacher must have to engage in the profession of pedagogy. Because teaching is pure function and hence personality-neutral, any kind of person can become a teacher—as long as he is able to adequately deploy his personality toward achieving the function which is teaching, namely facilitating desired learning outcomes. Only because teaching is pure function can it be a task which can welcome into its ranks personalities of all types. What makes a teacher effective or ineffective is not the kind of personality he has, but rather the degree to which he effectively places his knowledges, his skills, and his behaviors at the service of the facilitation process.

Only because teaching is pure function and therefore personality-neutral is it possible to preserve and safeguard the personal element of teaching. This is so because as pure function the teaching task does not prescribe any one kind of person as being per se the best kind of teacher or the only kind of teacher. Since teaching is pure function, it prescribes only that the teacher's personality—whatever its hue or diversity—be marshalled in the pedagogical situation toward the facilitation of desired learning outcomes. An individual is teaching a particular religion lesson not because he is Mr. Smith but because he is a facilitator of learning. Indeed, it was precisely this denial of teacher-as-function together with the exclusive emphasis of teacher-as-personality which partially led to the opinion in Catholic circles well up to the 1960's that the priest or nun is a better religion teacher than a layman because he or she is a priest or a nun. In the teacher-as-function model it is immaterial whether the religion teacher is a priest or a nun or a layman or even a bishop—what counts is the effectiveness of his pedagogy.

Nor does the conceptualization of teacher as pure function imply that the teacher is somehow phony or inauthentic. A person as teacher is authentic only to the extent to which he is effectively facilitating learning. After all to be authentic is to be totally true to oneself as one is in a given situation. Authenticity is always localized and particularized; it is not some kind of free-floating genuineness. If the teacher is really a professional, he has so existentially meshed his personal and his pedagogical selves that in the instructional act he is actualizing as a person to the extent that he is actualizing as a teacher. The professional teacher is not acting out a role when he is facilitating learning; he has so become this function that he is genuine and authentic through performing the pedagogical function. To be authentic means to live fully one's present localized existence in all its modalities and to communicate these modalities to the learner if they are appropriate in helping to facilitate learning. Therefore if a teacher becomes angry or sad during a religion lesson, he is not being authentic if he communicates these feelings to the students; the teacher's behavior becomes authentic when he decides to reveal or withhold these feelings on the basis of their value in facilitating learning.

The teacher as pure function means that he will keep in constant sharp focus the goal-directedness of his pedagogical behaviors. Thus a study by Ned Flanders concluded that students who achieved the most had teachers who varied their pedagogical behaviors, presumably to facilitate learning.[40] Inasmuch as student behaviors are continually shifting during the lesson, the teacher must perforce keep on varying or adjusting his own pedagogical behaviors in order to be in continuous contact with the learners where they are existentially. This exemplifies the teacher as pure function, that is, a person who constantly alters his behavior on the basis of what will most effectively facilitate learning in the here-and-now. The previously-cited Whitehorn and Betz study revealed that it was not simply the fact that young resident physicians treated the schizophrenic patients personalistically which accounted for the improvement in their patients, but perhaps even more importantly that these physicians both selected personality-oriented goals and deliberatively targeted their functional activities toward the attainment of this objective. The investigators noted that these goals were operationally defined as "assisting the patient in definite modifications of personal adjustment patterns and toward more constructive use of assets rather than mere decrease of symptoms or vague 'better socialization'."[41] This last point is especially worthy of attention. Few things have hindered the growth of religious instruction more than the typical sloshing around in highsounding but gooey generalities of the teacher-as-person in alleged contradictoriness to the teacher-as-function. The teacher-as-person notion is of little use to the religion teacher in suggesting which pedagogical behaviors he should deploy under differing conditions. By contrast, the teacher-as-function conceptualization does offer the religion teacher an operational model from which he can intelligently deduce effective pedagogical behaviors. Further the teacher-as-function conceptualization in no way serves to diminish the intense personalism inherent in the teaching act but rather indicates how this personalism is to be incarnated and targeted in the teaching-learning situation. Indeed, the mature person is one who places his personality totally at the disposal of the task at hand. It is the immature person who either uses the task at hand primarily for his own ego needs or who lets his personality needs get in the way, so to speak, of the effective discharging of the task at hand.[42]

The conceptualization of teacher-as-function also assists the religion teacher to muster the courage to assess and criticize his own professional behaviors as objectively as possible and to seek critically constructive analysis from other professionally competent persons. This kind of assessment and criticism is particularly difficult to endure under the teacher-as-person scheme because it calls for a certain devaluation of the teacher's personality by himself and others. But in the teacher-as-function notion the teacher's personality as such is not what is being examined or criticized; rather the issue is the way he uses his personality in behalf of or at odds with the facilitating function. The religion teacher's knowledge of, attentiveness to, and subsequent control of his pedagogical behaviors are the key to effective and improved teaching. By reducing the anxiety of the teacher brought on by a critical assessment of these behaviors by himself or others, the teacher-as-function model serves as a paradigm which can contribute significantly to the improvement of religious instruction.

Function is the action for which a person (or thing) is specifically fitted or for which the person-as-function exists. Therefore to stress the teacher-as-function is to emphasize that the teacher does not exist for himself but to help another person. Teacher-as-function underscores the fact that pedagogy is a helping relationship, a transaction aimed at assisting another individual. Those who advocate the teacher as ego over against the teacher as function frequently end up, at least implicitly, by making teaching self-serving instead of other-serving. Apropos of this George Leonard has written eloquently:

> Retiring behind a psychic proscenium arch, the actor-teacher is forever safe from the perils of education. His performance flourishes. He plays for laughs and outraged looks. Phantom applause accompanies his trip home . . . and he cannot wait to go on stage again. Assured of a full house and a long run, he knows the critics will be kind. Those who give him a bad review will get a failing grade.[43]

Surely from the Christian perspective the religion teacher should be willing and eager to be used for God's sake—that is to be a tool or function for him. To be a religion teacher is to give service without vanity. The religion teacher ought not to be in the profession for what he can get out of it in terms of personal satisfaction but for what he can give, for what he can facilitate. Teaching is not an activity directly aimed at serving the teacher; it exists to serve the learner. Paradoxically perhaps, to the extent that the religion teacher unselfishly and totally serves the pupil as pure function, as pure facilitation, and as pure helping with no regard for himself, to that extent will his own needs and personality be optimally gratified and fulfilled. He who forgets himself for God's service may be sure that God will not forget him.

THE STRUCTURE OF TEACHING

"Of course you read Greek like a schoolmaster," he said. "I read it like a poet."
"And do you find it more poetic when you don't quite know what it means?"[1]

—W. Somerset Maugham

The Goals of Teaching

As I have indicated in the previous chapter, the teaching process can be conceptualized as the process by which four major clusters of independent variables (the teacher, the learner, the subject matter content, and the environment) interact in such a way as to produce a particular dependent variable (the learning outcome). This is to say that the learning outcome which is achieved in such-and-such a given situation is a result of or depends on the independent variables. The religion teacher (or curriculum builder) arranges these independent variables in such a manner that they will be most productive of the desired learning outcomes. The goals of the religion class or course, then, determine the way in which the teacher (or curriculum builder) arranges or structures the independent variables. Consequently a major function of the religion teacher is to be clear on which learning outcomes are desirable and within his scope and to be skilled in the use of those instructional practices which most fruitfully can bring about the attainment of these outcomes.

The attainment of the goals of teaching necessitates that the teacher (or curriculum builder) use the following sequential steps in architecting the overall structure of his lesson, unit, or course: (1) state the objective(s) sought; (2) arrange learning experiences in that kind of programatic form designed to most effectively produce the objective(s) sought; (3) try out and test the lesson or program where possible; (4) put the lesson or program into full-scale operation; (5)

evaluate the lesson or program to ascertain the extent to which it is achieving the objective(s) sought. These five steps should be integrated in such a way that they form a broad, unitary instructional system.

The first step in designing an instructional system is the specification of its purposes and the objectives to be achieved. In other words in building his lesson or unit, the religion teacher (or curriculum builder) starts with goals and works backwards. In this connection it is important to distinguish between instructional objectives and more general statements of aims or goals. Thus "the development of Christian awareness" is so broad an aim that in such a form it provides little direction for determining and sequencing appropriate learning experiences. This general statement or goal must be sharpened and made specific if it is to be useful. So, for example, it might be operationalized as "the ability to judge the civil rights movement by gospel criteria." Such an instructional objective is more specific and begins, but only begins, to give the religion teacher (or curriculum builder) some general direction with regard to the structuring of learning experiences designed to attain this objective.[2] Of course much more specification must take place if the original goal is to lend itself to effective instructional practice. To pursue our example, the goal can be further specified as "the ability to judge the civil rights movement by gospel criteria as evidenced by a successful student response in assessing a particular equality of opportunity law in the light of Matthew 22:36-40." Even this newly stated goal must be still further specified in terms of the minimum criteria a learner must demonstrate in order for the teacher to be able to adequately assess whether his response is successful or not. Now all this serves to indicate that the only acceptable and useful instructional goal is one which is stated in operational form, that is, one expressed in terms of a behavioral outcome which can be observed. Only in this way does an instructional goal have the capability of being rendered effective. Only in this way is the teacher able to evaluate whether or not the learner has indeed attained the desired learning objective.

The second step in designing an instructional system is the deliberative arrangement of learning experiences in that kind of programatic form which will most effectively produce the goal sought. This involves at the outset assigning different priority levels to each of the goals posited for the lesson or unit. Once this is done, the design and scope and sequence of the learning activities can be mapped out. Different kinds of learning objectives necessitate different kinds of instructional arrangements. Concept learning, for example, calls for certain prerequisite learnings of multiple discriminations, verbal associations, chaining, stimulus-response learnings, and the like.[3] In the here-and-now pedagogical moment the religion teacher acts as curriculum maker; the kind of curriculum or instructional program he fashions and implements will depend on the kinds of goals he wishes the learners to attain and the conditions of learning which optimally facilitate the attainment of these goals.

The third step in designing an instructional system is the testing out of the lesson or program. Sometimes this is not possible. However, when feasible such piloting of the system should be undertaken to insure its validity and reliability as well as to iron out any factors or "bugs" which might be operating to impede the full effectiveness of the lesson, unit, or curriculum. This step together with the first two steps is necessary for the successful achievement of the fourth step, that of putting the lesson or program into full-scale operation.

The fifth and final step in designing an instructional system is that of evaluating the system's effectiveness in achieving the goals sought. The most direct method for evaluating the functional effectiveness of a program is to measure the changes wrought in learners as a result of that program. At bottom the test of the effectiveness of an instructional program is the degree to which the learners have changed in the direction of the desired goals—assuming, of course, that the teacher has done his job adequately.[4] This evaluation is continuous and continual. Further it is both formative and summative, to use Michael Scriven's well-known distinction.[5] In formative evaluation, data are used to make judgments about what works when a teacher is attempting to achieve his goals. Summative evaluation is the purposive assessment of some whole.

I should emphasize that this five-step process in goal-setting and goal-achieving represents a closed-loop feedback system in the sense that I have defined this kind of system earlier in this book (recall, for example, my reference to the thermostat as a feedback system). In this feedback cycle of goaling, each step or stage provides feedback to the other stage(s) and in the process effects appropriate change or modification in the other stage(s). What feedback does among other things is to generate an in-system series of correctives which serve to make the system optimally effective in terms of the actualization of the desired goals. Assisting in the acceleration of that automatic feedback process which is a characteristic of any closed-loop system is the religion teacher who alters or continues, as appropriate, any and all elements within this system so as to make this system work more effectively in enabling the desired goals to be actualized.

A Teaching Model

In *The Shape of Religious Instruction*[6] I state that a model is a representational system of interrelated facts and laws subsumed in one theory which serves as a functional description of the reality being investigated. A model is closely related to a theory. It is a kind of embodiment of a structural analogy. The embodiment might take the form of a set of symbols or it might be presented in an isomorphic shape. A model acts as an approach to more fruitfully explore and evaluate the special interactive relationships existing among various connective elements within the theory from which it was generated. The purpose of reshaping a theory into a model is to extract from a theory significant inferences which might otherwise remain hidden from notice.

In this section I shall recast the teaching theory of religious instruction into a model. This should lead to the development of new pedagogical practices and the resolution of old problems within religious instruction. In this model I have placed all the major essential elements involved in the instructional act: the goal of the act and the four principal constituent cluster variables in this act (the learner, the teacher, the subject matter content, and the environment). The four cluster variables comprise the independent variables, and the goal is the dependent variable. If it is to serve its function of producing more effective instructional practice as well as more refined theory, a model must be thought of as the depiction of a system—for indeed it represents a system. For present purposes a system is defined as any identifiable assemblage of complexly organized elements or subsystems which are interdependent, united by a common feedback network, and function as an organized whole in order to attain some goal or produce some effect uniquely characteristic of the system operating as a unit.[7] This definition encapsulates several functions of a system which can be seen as highly useful for fructifying the work of religious instruction. A system postulates an observable end product or output of the system. This output embodies or fulfills some defined objective or goal; it is shown to be associated with certain necessary conditions or inputs to the system. Also the output is a function of the orderly interactive relationship and feedback among the elements or sub-systems comprising the system; this interaction is unique to the particular system and is controlled by identifiable and modifiable combinations and sequences of certain operating principles. These operating principles or controlling rules usually must be inferred. This entire conceptualization of a system is especially germane to religious instruction because from one vantage point the religious instruction act can be described as a system.

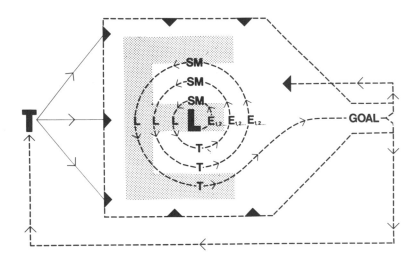

In this model T stands for the teacher, L for the Learner, E for environment, and SM for subject matter content. The large square circumscribed by dotted lines represents the learning situation. Notice that the learning situation converges toward a tight, open-ended funnel, suggesting that the dynamics of the learning situation are targeted toward a desired outcome or goal. Notice also that there is a large shaded-in E which covers the entire learning situation; this indicates that the learning situation is an environment, and therefore all four independent variables in the learning situation have their locus in an environment. Put another way it indicates that everything contained within the large dotted-line square comprises an aspect of the learning situation which is the instructional environment. Learning takes place within an environmental context and therefore is constantly being modified by all the relevant variables inside and outside it. The model indicates two functions of the teacher. The T outside the learning situation puts emphasis on the teacher as the initial and constant structurer of the learning situation. It is he who sets up the learning situation and continually adjusts it to promote the attainment of the desired learning outcomes. The T inside the dotted lines indicates that the teacher is also one aspect of the learning environment itself, a variable which dynamically interacts with the other variables in the ongoing instructional act. The environment is therefore one which is controlled by the teacher from both the outside and the inside, as it were. The model places the learner at the center of the pedagogical dynamic. This is where the cycle of learning (not teaching) begins. The cycle of teaching already began prior to this time when the teacher selected and structured a particular environment in which to situate the learner. This environment was selected and structured by the teacher on the basis of hypotheses he made on which kind of environment, subject matter content, and teacher variables are most predictive of success with this particular learner or group of learners.

In terms of learning the model indicates that it is the learner—his existential maturational and learned self, his perceptions, needs, and goals—that form the starting point. The circular lines indicate the path by which the learner modifies his behavior; this is the path that the teaching act, therefore, will follow. First the learner acts as a stimulus to the teacher, setting in motion the actual teaching-learning process. The teacher responds to this stimulus by modifying his pedagogical behavior according to the nature and kind of learner stimuli he receives. The teacher, as an aspect of the instructional environment, modifies his own behavior so as to facilitate the attainment of the desired outcomes; as a variable outside the instructional environment, he modifies the entire environmental situation, as needed, to facilitate learning. Then the learner, as is indicated by the circular dotted lines, interacts with various aspects of this teacher-prepared environment. E_1, E_2 ... are symbols designating particularized aspects of the environment, for example, differentiated learning materials, field trips, or the like. (These particular environmental aspects differ from the large shaded-in E; the large E suggests that the teacher, the learners, the subject matter content, and particularized environmental factors also constitute larger, more global chunks of the environment with which the learner interacts.) Next as suggested by the circular dotted lines, the learner interacts with various kinds of subject matter which the teacher has prepared or introduced; in our case this is religious subject matter. Proceeding along the circular dotted lines, we see the overall process being continued until it terminates in the attainment of the desired objective or goal. The circular dotted lines shooting into the funnel suggests that the instructional process is a task-oriented dynamic leading to the attainment of a desired goal. Each of the four independent variables acts and interacts within a structured learning situation to produce the goal. It will be observed that the goal is open-ended as depicted in the model. This suggests that once attained the goal acts as feedback both to increased or adjusted teacher behavior and to new learner activity; this feedback of the goal to the teacher and the learner is shown by the dotted lines emanating from the goal.

This teaching model suggests that in the dynamic circular interaction of teaching-learning, each of the variables involved is undergoing some change or alteration. As he interacts with the other elements in the learning situation, the learner undergoes change; so too do the teacher and the subject matter content and the particularized aspects of the environment. This model delineates and specifies relationships between the behaviors of the teacher and the learner, and the effects of the environment and the subject matter content on the goal. Such specification of relationships between the independent variables and the dependent variable is critical to any adequate theory of instruction. But it should be remembered that like the theory it pictorially illustrates, this model is perforce a general rather than a detailed explanation. Therefore it generates rather than finely specifies all the individual elements and behavioral components of each of the independent and dependent variables in the instructional process. It is not the work of this model qua model to specify finely the individual properties of the behavior or task to be learned or the characteristics of the learner or the environmental conditions which best promote learning in this particular set of circumstances. This model is thus value-neutral and variable-neutral in that it is the elaboration of a general process. As such it is optimally useful to the work of religious instruction because it can embrace instructional acts which involve every conceivable kind of learner or teacher or subject matter content or environment.

Perhaps a slightly more detailed treatment of some of the

independent and dependent variables will be helpful at this juncture. In terms of the teacher, this model clearly indicates that his behaviors are embedded with a common interactive framework rather than in isolation.[8] This clearly implies that the teacher's role is not one of transmitter or proclaimer or witness, but instead one of interaction orchestrator and supervisor. Our model shows that there are variables related to the learning process which the teacher is able to control and orchestrate. To teach is at once to be in the learning environment and to control it in such a way that the desired learning outcomes are attained. Naturally the teacher's personality, including his past history and present perceptions, represents the ground through which he predicts and structures learning experiences. Consequently any detailed elaboration of the model in terms of specifying the teacher variable in more detail must include teacher personality factors. It is the function of preservice and inservice training to enable the teacher to so control his behaviors that they are directed toward producing the desired objectives and goal.

The model highlights the crucial importance of the learning environment in the pedagogical act. It shows graphically that the learning situation consists of all the persons, objects, and symbols in the learner's environment. Therefore everything the learner encounters is in one sense an environmental variable which can be adjusted or structured to enhance the attainment of the desired outcome. The learning situation is not like a box occupied only by the learner and the teacher; rather it consists of a dynamic situation containing many stimuli, all of which interact and provide feedback to the learner. The effective learning environment is one in which stimuli are so structured that they will provide the learner with that kind of feedback optimally promotive of his attaining the goal at hand. The task of the teacher therefore becomes one of providing the learner with an environment rich in facilitatory stimuli. Optimal teaching is typically not a Mark Hopkins affair, with the teacher at one end of the log and the student at the other; rather the most effective teaching is usually done both within and through an environment.

In the pedagogical act the learner is at the center since all learning is according to the mode of the learner. All learning begins with and ends in the learner. Perhaps the most basic and elemental principle of teaching is this: "start with the learner where he is." All too often in religious instruction the subject matter content is erroneously made the center. But if teaching is to be effective, the subject matter content must be integrated into the learner as he is in the here-and-now. With respect to this point, Ellis Nelson emphasizes that "the learner at his stage of development—his needs, interests and capacities—should be the criteria by which the materials for religious instruction are selected."[9] The learner at his stage of development is a person who enfleshes characteristics resulting from both maturational and learning influences. Thus the learner as he is in the here-and-now is a person conditioned by his age, his needs, his problems, his perceptions, his socioeconomic milieu, his religiosity level, his family, and so forth. Chapter 6 highlights many of the salient characteristics of learners and how they learn; hence there is no need to dwell on this further. However, the student's patterns of interaction in the learning situation are worthy of brief mention. The learner interacts with other persons and objects in the learning situation. Precisely because they are members of a goal-directed or task-oriented group, students in the learning situation have a need to relate to one another in a way that will contribute to group maintenance and goal achievement. To meet this goal-directed need, students take on any one or more of the following roles when they function in a group: initiator-contributor; information seeker; opinion seeker; information giver; opinion giver; elaborator; coordinator; orientator; evaluator; energizer; procedural technician; recorder. Each group member must assume most and sometimes all of these roles if the group is to function smoothly and efficiently.[10] Learners integrate these roles into any one or more of seven dimensions by which they seek to relate to one another in a group situation: (1) the problem-solving dimension; (2) the authority-leadership dimension; (3) the power dimension; (4) the friendship dimension; (5) the personal prestige dimension; (6) the sex dimension; and (7) the privilege dimension.[11] Now all this indicates that the student's interactive behavior is dynamic and complex; it is not limited simply to interaction with the teacher (usually conceptualized as listening or answering questions) as is postulated by some religious educationists. In specifying the learner variable in our model of the teaching act, these interactive relationships must be delineated and otherwise taken into account. In any event the learner's here-and-now existential situation together with his interactive patterns of behavior in the learning situation clearly points out that the religion teacher's role must be defined in terms of starting with the learner where he is and working through the other variables in the learning environment so as to bring about the desired learning outcomes.

Subject matter content constitutes an important and indispensable variable in the instructional act. Earlier in this book I indicated that the subject matter content of religious instruction is religion and not theology. Religion, of course, contains theology but it is not the same as theology; it is wider than theology. The subject matter content variable is composed of many elements including product and process content, cognitive and affective and lifestyle contents, conscious and unconscious contents, verbal and nonverbal contents, theological content, and so forth. I will do no more than mention these contents since volume III of this trilogy (of which this book comprises volume II and *The Shape of Religious Instruction* comprises volume I) will be devoted entirely to a consideration of the contents of religious instruction. The only point I make here is that these contents must be so structured and orchestrated in terms of scope, sequence, design, and so on that they form a unified fabric of subject matter content which yields observable behaviors targeted toward the learning goal at hand. In this connection the distinction between component repertoire and content repertoire is germane. Content repertoire refers to a subject-matter oriented analysis while component repertoire has to do with behaviorial analysis.[12] In the teaching act the subject matter content is deliberatively arranged in such a way as to yield learner behaviors which admit of teacher analysis. Subject matter content, therefore, is neither a means nor an end in itself.

The dependent variable in the teaching act, namely the goal, is a valuable and potent factor. Indeed, the task of the teacher is to so structure the independent variables that they yield the desired dependent variable. Thus in a sense the tint and hue of each of the independent variables involved in the teaching act are determined by the desired goal. These four independent variables not only lead to the goal but are also led by it since teaching is a goal-directed activity. This is highlighted in the model I have given.

The model of the teaching act nicely encapsulates the teaching theory. It pictorially illustrates in representational form the multidemsional activity that is teaching. One inference which can be legitimately drawn from this model is that the only adequate pedagogical strategy for religious instruction is the structured learning situation. Unlike the transmission strategy or strategies derived from the witness or blow theories, the structured learning situation allows full play for the complex interaction of all the independent variables in the production of the desired goal. Aware of the predicted effects which various arrangements of the learning situation will have on bringing about the desired learning outcomes, the teacher is able to so structure the learning situation as to help insure the learner's attainment of these outcomes. To state this is to at once place the primacy in implementing educational practice on the teacher's pedagogical behaviors.

The Learning Environment

Because the environment in which learning takes place is so very important, I am spending a few pages on this crucial topic. By environment is meant that aggregate of external physical, biological, cultural, and social conditions or stimuli to which an individual consciously or unconsciously responds. In Chapter 6 I discuss the enormous impact made on the learner by all the environments in which he is situated. In this section I am restricting my attention to the highly significant impact which the immediate learning environment (in a classroom or other learning site) has on the student.

The classroom or other learning environment has many properties, including the physical, the social, the subject matter content, the teacher, other learners, the cultural, and the affective climate. From this we can see that it is simplistic to conceive of the learning environment as consisting of only the physical aspects of the pedagogical setting. The physical environment in which learning takes place does indeed play a potent role in enhancing or inhibiting the attainment of the desired learning outcomes, as the review of the pertinent research summarized in Chapter 6 indicates. The physical characteristics pervade the entire learning milieu, for example, temperature, humidity, light, and sound level. Most learning settings have doors, windows, and walls, as well as desks, chairs, and other physical things which do much to shape patterns of social inter-action in that setting. Learning milieux also have various forms of media equipment, such as textbooks and other printed materials, writing instruments, television sets, teaching machines, movie or slide projectors, and so forth. Also the presence (or absence) of these media, as well as the use to which they are put, is related to the facilitation of learning. The important thing about the physical environment is that with but a few exceptions such as the floor, it can be altered and shaped by the teacher to produce an environment optimally promotive of bringing about the desired learning objective.

The social environment consists of "the joint properties of social interaction that may be observed to take place at any given moment in time or characteristically over a period of time in the classroom" or other learning setting.[13] For instance, classrooms feature common patterns of traffic movement, rates of interaction among learners and teacher, physical and social groupings of learners and teacher. The teacher can structure the social environment to facilitate learning by deliberatively arranging those conditions within the learning setting which generate differential patterns of social interaction.

Subject matter content constitutes another aspect of the environment under the control of the teacher. He can shape the subject matter content so it will be cognitively-oriented, affectively-pointed, or lifestyle-directed, or a combination of these. Depending upon the kind of pedagogical practice he employs, he can make subject matter content something "out there" which is imparted or proclaimed externally by the herald, as for example in the Munich Method or in other forms of the transmission strategy. Or the teacher can make the subject matter content something learned by and through the internal interaction among members of the classroom group; in this case the intermember relations operating within the learning setting constitute significant environmental variables which the teacher must control and utilize so as to enhance the probability of attaining the desired learning outcome.

Fellow students constitute a significant aspect of the learner's environment. The characteristics of these fellow students—their family and socioeconomic backgrounds, levels of religiosity, needs and concerns, personality configurations—all interact with the learner in such a way as to markedly influence the direction and kind of outcomes he attains. The students are to some degree under the control of the teacher in that by the pedagogical behaviors he deploys he can either blunt or heighten the manifestations of these characteristics. The teacher's professional judgment as to which student behaviors enhance and which detract from the accomplishment of the desired learning goal determines the pedagogical practices he chooses.

The cultural peculiarities of the classroom also constitute an environmental variable. Students who are adults create a different classroom culture than students who are adolescents. Moreover adolescents from different socioeconomic backgrounds (for example, ghetto youth as contrasted to suburban youth) contribute to the making of differential cultural classroom environments. Also the fact that the learning setting is a goal-directed situation shapes the kind of culture the classroom is, as contrasted to a nongoal-directed situation such as sitting on a ghetto stoop "shooting the breeze." It should be underscored that it is within the teacher's capability to shape to a certain extent the culture of the classroom. The type of goal he sets for the learning group goes far in shaping a culture. Thus, for example, if the goal is lifestyle-oriented, the classroom culture will be significantly different than when the goal is simply cognitively-oriented. The grouping procedures the teacher uses, the way he structures the physical aspects of the learning environment, the amount of freedom he allows the learners, the types of materials and realia he inserts into the learning environment, all these help shape and color the classroom culture.

The affective climate is one of the most important aspects of the learning environment. Learning takes place in a particular socio-emotional atmosphere rather than in an affective vacuum. The research I cite in Chapter 6 clearly indicates that the socioemotional climate of the learning situation plays a significant role in facilitating or impeding the attainment of desired learning outcomes. Indeed, the research suggests that it is within the teacher's power to shape the form and thrust of the affective climate in the learning situation.

Without a doubt the teacher is the most significant aspect of the learning environment. The teacher as teacher, or more precisely the pedagogical behaviors he employs, more than anything else are correlated with successful learning. Indeed, it is the teacher who shapes and/or brings to salience all the other characteristics of the environment.

This brief consideration of some of the more important elements of the learning environment shows quite plainly that teaching is far from being a simple task or unidimensional activity. Further this short analysis indicates that the effective teacher is one who manages or orchestrates all the significant elements in the learning environment in such a way as to bring about the attainment of the desired learning outcome.

The model of the teaching act presented earlier in this chapter graphically illustrates the great significance and high potency of the environment with respect to facilitating the attainment of the desired learning outcome. Not only are specific environmental variables $(E_1, E_2 \ldots)$ present in the learning situation, but indeed the very learning situation itself is an environment. As Wayne Rood observes, the environment is the context of the learning experience.[14] Whatever the circumstances of learning, whatever goal is sought, the teaching-learning process deals basically with the inter-action of the learner with the instructional environment.[15] The research I review in Chapter 6 makes it very evident that the environment with which the student interacts has a powerful influence on the course, direction, and goals of learning. As the environment changes, learning changes.

The model of the teaching act also shows that the teacher is at once both inside and outside the instructional environment. As outside the environment the teacher is able to shape the environment. The environment, then, can be structured and manipulated by the teacher. To teach, therefore, is to shape the environment in such a way as to facilitate learning. Put another way to teach is to deliberatively and purposively structure the learning situation. The teacher's role vis-à-vis the environment is that of professional intervener. He sets up the learning environment to facilitate the acquisition of certain desired objectives. During the course of the ongoing instructional dynamic, the teacher makes adjustments in the environment; that is to say he periodically intervenes in the teaching-learning process to make sure that the lesson is most effectively proceeding on target. Instruction is the conscious shaping of the learner's environment in order to get him to engage in specified behaviors as functions of or responses to specified situations. All teaching, even the most teacher-centered lecture, is a structuring of the learning situation. The issue, then, is not pro or con the structured learning situation but rather how to most effectively structure the learning situation to bring about the desired goal.

The primary mark of a learning environment as structured learning situation is that it be facilitational. Teaching is the construc-tion and shaping and often the reconstitution of the pedagogical situation for more effective learning. Many and varied are the features of a learning environment which render it facilitational. Due to limitations of space, I shall discuss only a few of the more prominent of these features. A facilitational environment is one which is (1) purposively planned; (2) selective; (3) rich in stimuli; (4) evocative of a total response from the learner; (5) reinforcing; and (6) warm in climate. A facilitational environment is one which is so structured that it furthers the realization of the purpose for which it was created. Since an instructional environment is always purposive, it is always characterized by some sort of structure. In this sense there is no pedagogical environment which is not in some way structured. A facilitational environment is selective in that its shape, its coloration, and its constitutive elements are all deliberatively chosen because they all lead to the achievement of the goal in view. It is the business of the pedagogical environment to eliminate as far as possible those features which detract or lead the learner away from the attainment of the desired learning outcome. Selection, in John Dewey's words, "establishes a purified medium of action"; it "aims not only at simplifying but at weeding out what is undesirable" from the viewpoint of establishing the conditions optimally productive of learning.[16] A facilitational environment is one rich in stimuli. Learners of divers backgrounds, a subject matter content capable of myriad kinds of introjections into the learner's experience, a wealth of physical objects in a state of constant grouping and regrouping, a teacher whose experiential roots run wide and deep—such an environment provides that sort of learning situation optimally productive of rich and targeted learning experiences. A facilitational environment is one which evokes a total response from the learner. If religious instruction has been so largely ineffective down through the ages, it is because it has frequently evoked only a cognitive response. Responses which are total—cognitive, affective, and lifestyle—are the ones which most involve the total learner in the here-and-now pedagogical act and also which admit of being most effectively transferred to out-of-school life. A facilitational environment is one in which the situational contingencies are so arranged and structured that they act as continuous vectors converging on the target of the lesson. Finally, a facilitational environment is one in which the atmosphere and climate of the learning situation are open, warm, and therefore nurturant of student growth.

It may be argued that "a religion teacher—however skilled he may be—cannot create a truly authentic experience for the learner."[17] I believe that such a position is untenable precisely for the reason that it ignores the character and effect of the interaction of the learner with his environment. Teaching is shaping the form of human association. To assert that a learner interacts with his environment is to assert that the learner is being shaped and changed by this environment. As the mass of research evidence adduced in Chapter 6 underscores, persons do behave differently in different environments. Change the environment and the learner's behavior will change. Indeed, at the heart of communication theory is that there is active feedback between the learner and his environment—and as I indicated earlier, feedback by its nature changes and shapes the person or object receiving the feedback. Now every experience a person undergoes is an authentic one, by the very definition of experience as an individualized interaction between a person and his environment. Hence the issue is not whether the religion teacher can or cannot create an authentic experience for the learner, but rather which kinds of experiences will the teacher structure to be the most productive of the richest kinds of authentic experiences.

Many types and forms of differential environments have been developed to produce desired learning outcomes. I shall discuss only two major dyadic schemes, namely the consonant-disonant environment and the internal-external environment. The consonant-disonant dyad refers to learning environments which are characterized either by stimuli which are harmonious and closely related to each other (consonant stimuli), or those which feature stimuli which are discordant and not closely related to each other. B. F. Skinner's programed learning technique is representative of a learning environment in which the stimuli are consonant with each other. In this approach stimuli are presented to the learner in small, finely-graded steps which are very closely related to one another. Such arrangement and sequencing of environmental stimuli make it very difficult for the learner to make an error and deviate from the desired learning outcome.[18] An example of a learning approach in which the stimuli are disconsonant is the discovery or inquiry method advanced by Richard Suchman. In this method a puzzling problem or clusters of stimuli with no internal structure are placed in the environment and the learner is thereby motivated to discover for himself the missing unifying or essential element which ties together these disconsonant stimuli. These disconsonant stimuli are carefully arranged so as to provide the learner with that level of incongruous stimuli appropriate to his level of development.[19]

Illustrative of the external wing of the internal-external environment dyad is John Dewey. Dewey believed that a "real-life situation" represents that form of environment best suited to effectively produce desired learning outcomes. Therefore Dewey-style educational practice works with environments which are either outside the classroom situation (for example, field trips to the liturgical service of an Eastern Rite Liturgy) or transform the classroom situation into a real-life situation (for example, having an Eastern Rite Liturgy celebrated in the classroom itself).[20] The internal wing of the internal-external dyad is represented by Maria Montessori. This Italian educationist created her own environmental materials which were carefully designed to lead the learner step-by-step to the desired learning outcome. The Montessori design consists of prepared materials which specify that the learner carry out a long series of discrete discrimination tasks with a set of structurally-arranged stimulus objects.[21]

It has been argued that the classroom is an artificial learning environment and therefore is educationally inferior because it does not perfectly mirror real life. Such an argument tends to be specious inasmuch as it ignores the basic fact that the classroom environment is real life. There are not two disparate divisions of life, one real and the other somehow nonreal. It is more to the point to say that the classroom environment represents a different kind of life than nonclassroom life. To be sure, the whole thrust of religious instruction in formal settings is to provide learners with an environment which is so structured that it is more effective than ordinary life experiences in bringing about the desired learning outcomes. Religious instruction programs, then, are attempts to sharpen, enhance, and codify the educational process in an optimally efficient manner. Such sharpening and enhancing are done primarily by providing the learners with a special environment together with a person (the teacher) who is skilled in shaping and adjusting this environment in a way that will augment learning. The structured learning environment, then, represents an enriched form of real life, and in no way constitutes artificial life. The real issue, therefore, is not artificial life versus real life, but a rich and meaningful learning environment versus one which is stimulus-deprived and without meaning to the learner. When John Dewey pleaded for learning environments to be real-life situations, he was pleading for stimulus-rich and meaningful environments rather than the bookish, overly verbal, and cognitive environments which typified classrooms of his day.

It also has been argued that structuring the learning situation represents an unwarranted control over and manipulation of the learner. This argument is quite superficial in that it ignores both the object of the structuring and the contingent nature of terrestrial freedom. What is being structured is the learning environment, not the learner. Setting temperature controls, moving furniture, and the like are adjustments in the environment. Indeed, the very definition of the learning environment specifies it as a manipulable milieu, that is, one which can and should be arranged and shaped and adjusted by the teacher in such a way as to facilitate learning. Even the teacher's decision to call on one pupil rather than on another, to group the learners in one way rather than another, and so forth represents a structuring of an environment rather than a direct manipulation of persons. At a deeper level, all human activities here on earth are contingent. No one is ever completely free. Apropos of this Michael Warren perceptively observes that "structuring a lesson does not in itself limit freedom. Every situation has a structure which is somehow imposed on the people in that situation though they rarely advert to it."[22] The key here as Warren suggests is that people seldom bother to reflect how their freedom is being constantly restricted. Indeed, of its very nature teaching or any other goal-directed activity tends to restrict freedom more than formless happenings. Perhaps the strategy which restricts learner freedom most is the transmission strategy which derives from the proclamation theory. In a learning situation structured by this strategy, the learner has only two options: to pay attention or not to pay attention. In the structured learning strategy, where the learners interact with all the aspects of the learning environment, the choices available to the learners are much greater, and therefore freedom is enhanced. Cognitive pedagogical methods are seldom regarded as limitations on learner freedom because man has become accustomed to such limitations down through the centuries. Yet affective-directed and lifestyle pedagogical practices are condemned by some as limitations on learner freedom—principally because these practices represent newer pedagogical emphases which most people have not yet learned to exclude from their conceptualized parameters of freedom restrictors. Yet what can be more restrictive of learner freedom than the absolute cognitive brainwashing which is the transmission strategy or lecture technique? What should be borne in mind in any consideration of environmental limitation on learner freedom is that the environment promotes rather than determines. Even in the tightest conceivable design of operant conditioning, behaviorism, the environment seldom if ever "elicits" behavior in an all-or-nothing fashion of a reflex.[23] The structured learning situation as an improper restriction on learner freedom is a false issue which blinds the teacher and the curriculum builder to the real, basic pedagogical questions at hand.

An interesting sidenote about the point just made above is that some of the "new theology" is exploring the positive and fecundating impact of the environment as shaping man in its embrace. Indeed, some contemporary theologians are suggesting that theology has to become more environment-centered and more environment-pointed if it is to be relevant and fruitful to man in his concrete existential situation.[24] To be sure one wonders how there can be a viable theology of Jesus without placing the interactions of the God-Man with his environment at or near the very center.

For the religion teacher to structure the learning environment is to toll the death knell of the old pipeline system of learning whereby the teacher transmitted or imparted or presented the Good News to the learners. Gone will be the all too common mode of religious instruction in which the teacher sits or stands (depending on his notion of a herald) in front of a number of students in a single room presenting them with facts of a verbal-rational nature. By structuring all aspects of the learning environment, the religion teacher has at his disposal a pedagogical practice of vast potency and usefulness.

The biblical story of the Emmaus incident (Luke 24:13-35) is instructive concerning the differential effects of varying environments. The lecture-discussion environment, even when the lecturer or discussion leader was so eloquent and persuasive a teacher as Jesus, failed to elicit recognition on the part of the disciples of the true identity of Jesus. It was only when the environment was changed to a more nonverbally-oriented, lifestyle-directed situation of breaking bread at a table in a local inn did these men perceive who the stranger was.[25]

I should like to emphasize that environments merely facilitate; they do not produce effects automatically. It is not enough simply to structure a learning environment of the kind which will optimally facilitate the attainment of the desired learning objectives. The end result depends on the way the structured learning environment is utilized. Proper positioning of classroom furniture or an affective classroom climate help and indeed are vital to optimum facilitation, but neither produces effective learning automatically. Everything depends on what the teacher does with and in the shaped environment. The chairs might be in a close circle with the teacher occupying one of them in the fashion of an equal group member; however, if the teacher uses the lecture technique or authoritarian pedagogical practices, the potential advantages of this structured environment are nullified. The effective teacher is one who is sensitive to how he can most successfully structure the environment and best utilize pedagogical practice to enable the environment to exert its potential impact. At bottom, then, teacher behavior is the key to effective learning.

Teacher Behavior

Teacher behavior consists of those discrete observable pedagogical actions specifically designed to produce a desired learning outcome in another individual. A series or pattern of interconnected teacher behaviors is an instructional practice. Teaching is a series of pedagogical transactions: it is behavioral exchange of one kind or another.

Amazing as it may seem, teacher behavior has received far less attention than its central role in pedagogy would seem to require. Though there were a few important empirical investigations made of teacher behavior prior to the 1950's, it was not until late in that decade that educationists began directing their research efforts in any massive or concentrated way to this key variable in the instructional process. Indeed, in the area of religious education, virtually no critical examination of or exploration into ongoing teacher behaviors seems to have been undertaken. Religious educators have for centuries been content to issue pious but useless platitudes like "teaching is letting the Spirit blow where he wills" or "Christ is the real teacher," and to let the matter go at that.

Before the 1950's most of the attention of researchers was directed toward teacher personality characteristics. To be sure the personality characteristics of the teacher do have an effect on his pedagogical behavior; yet it is much more to the point and far more useful to directly investigate teacher behavior. I should like to observe in this connection that research on teacher behavior is not done as an end in itself but rather as a means toward developing and sharpening those teaching behaviors found to correlate most positively with pedagogical effectiveness.

Individual, discrete teacher behaviors do not stand in isolation, existing like some disconnected pedagogical atoms. Rather each teacher incorporates his individual, discrete pedagogical behaviors into an integrated teaching style. The function of teaching style is to organize discrete pedagogical behaviors into an overall pattern so that the behaviors reinforce each other in a chained manner. It should be emphasized that a teaching style is merely the arrangement of discrete teaching behaviors; it is not "mysterious" but can be analyzed and broken down into its constituent individual "atoms" of pedagogical behaviors. The taxonomy of the teaching act which I present in Chapter 4 spells out and clarifies the hierarchical interconnection between teaching behaviors and various levels of teaching style and beyond. As a result of their investigations, Jacob

Getzels and Herbert Thelen identify three basic kinds of teaching style, namely the nomothetic, the idiographic, and the transactional. The nomothetic style is one in which teacher behaviors are oriented toward the requirements of the institution, the role, and the expectation rather than on the requirements of the learner as a person of uniqueness and of needs. Teaching is targeted toward the handing down of what is known to those who do not as yet know. The idiographic style is one in which teacher behaviors are pointed toward the requirements of the learner as a person of uniqueness and of needs rather than toward the requirements of the institution, the role, and the expectation. Teaching is targeted toward helping the learner learn what he wants to learn. The transactional style is one in which teacher behaviors are pointed both toward the requirements of the learner as a person and the requirements of the institution. Teaching is targeted both toward helping the learner learn what he wants to learn and what the institution wants him to learn.[26] The celebrated pioneering empirical research by Harold Anderson discovered two different types of teaching style, the dominative and the integrative. In general the dominative style tends to be teacher-centered whereas the integrative is learner-centered.[27]

Teacher behaviors individually and as embedded in a pedagogical style are situated in functional contexts. David Ryans has identified five major functional contexts into which teacher behaviors fall: (1) motivating-reinforcing behavior; (2) presenting-explaining-demonstrating-structuring behavior; (3) organizing-planning-managing behavior; (4) evaluating behavior; (5) counseling-advising behavior.[28]

Teaching is not some amorphous, pseudomystical, spooky affair which somehow takes place in the instructional act. Rather teaching is a social activity involving teachers, learners, subject matter content, and environment, all in dynamic interaction. Hence the direct study of the teaching act can be fruitfully conducted by empirical means. Through the use of social-science methodology, researchers are able to identify and understand teacher behavior. Without a way of objectively describing the nature of the pedagogical dynamic, religion teachers in the past had no guide to capturing or harnessing the elusive phenomenon of their instructional behavior, the climate it creates in the learning situation, and its effect on the learner's attitudes and achievement. Now thanks to the burgeoning of detailed empirical investigations into the events in the lesson, we are beginning to be in a more favorable position to assist the religion teacher in making his professional behavior more effective.

Content analysis of the behavioral events taking place in the teaching-learning situation forms the basic methodology used by most current investigators of the pedagogical dynamic. Content analysis is any research technique for making inferences by objectively and systematically identifying specified characteristics of communications.[29] Thus content analysis represents an organized and planned investigation for assembling the data contained in communications, classifying or quantifying them to measure the concepts of other material under study, examining their patterns and interrelationships, and interpreting the findings.[30] Although not a research method *sui generis,* content analysis is distinguishable from other investigative techniques in at least two ways. First, its data (in contrast to census reports, for example) are the verbal, nonverbal, or other symbols which make up the content of communications. Second, (in contrast to literary criticism, for example) it aims to be exact and repeatable and to minimize any vagueness or bias resulting from the judgments of a single researcher. Like any other social-science technique, content analysis is objective, systematic, and undertaken within the context of some overall guiding theory.[31] Bernard Berelson identifies three situations calling for the use of content analysis: (1) when the investigator is curious about the content itself; (2) when he seeks inferences about the producers of or actors on the content; (3) when he seeks to understand the persons or audience who would use or are using the content.[32]

Interaction analysis typically is the kind of content analysis research which is utilized in the investigation of the teaching-learning dynamic in general and of teacher behavior in particular. As its name implies, interaction analysis examines the interactive behaviors among the four major cluster variables involved in the pedagogical act. In the teaching-learning dynamic one cannot speak simply of the teacher nor simply of teachers and learners and environment and subject matter content, but rather of all four in interaction.[33] Teaching is after all a social activity. Interaction analysis is a research technique for capturing quantitative and qualitative dimensions of observable classroom behavior and for ascertaining broader patterns into which these behaviors fall. For example, when the teacher says, "Please take your seats and give me your attention," the students manifest certain consequent responding behaviors which are a result of this teacher antecedent verbal behavior. In terms of affecting an overall pattern of student behavior, the teacher's verbal behavior in this instance centralizes authority, restricts social access, and causes a shift in the goal orientation of each student.[34] Interaction analysis thus provides an objective and factual record of both the kinds and the incidence of the behavioral events occurring in the teaching-learning act.

Two characteristics of interaction analysis are worthy of especial note. First, interaction analysis is nonjudgmental. It does not give a verdict on whether or not a particular classroom behavior is right or wrong, good or bad; it merely records the behavior. In interaction analysis it is behaviors which are being recorded, not teachers or students being judged. It often happens that the data gathered from interaction analysis research are correlated with the attainment of desired learning outcomes in order to judge which teacher behaviors are effective and which are ineffective in this regard. But in this case the data themselves are not judgmental; rather they are correlated with other data and then put to later judgmental use. A second noteworthy characteristic of interaction analysis is that it is subject-matter free. In other words interaction analysis does not depend for its validity, reliability, or effectiveness on the kind of subject matter content which is being taught or learned. Interaction analysis can be employed with equal success in any kind of subject matter content including religion.

Several types of instrumented coding systems have been devised to achieve accurate and reliable recordings of classroom behavior.[35] The coding systems receiving the greatest attention are the rating system, the sign system, and the category system. The rating system is one in which the observer, recorder, or other person scrutinizing the behavioral event assesses specified classroom behaviors in terms of some overall estimate, such as a five-point scale ranking behaviors from superior to poor. Often though not always the rating is made after the termination of the pedagogical event.[36] In contrast the sign system is one in which the observer or recorder uses a preprepared checklist of a relatively large number of specific behaviors to tally his observations or recordings. For example, the sign system might specify that the observer check off such observed teacher or student behaviors as "slump," "yawn," "works with students," "asks questions of students," and so on.[37] Finally, there is the category system in which a preprepared list of items (representing large chunks or patterns of highly similar kinds of behaviors) are drawn up so as to be mutually exclusive and exhaustive of all the behavioral options available in a given type of behavior (for example, verbal behavior).[38]

Viewed from a broader perspective, rating systems can be classified as low-inference measures while sign systems and category systems are representative of high-inference measures. (Inference in this case refers to the conceptual process intervening between the objective behaviors observed or recorded and the classification or coding of these behaviors on the instrument). In other words in a rating system, the observer is required to infer more in order to arrive at scores than he is with either a sign system or a category system. Rating systems, then, are high-inference measures because they lack behavioral specificity. Items like "enthusiasm," "helpful to students," or "clarity of presentation" require that the observer or recorder infer these constructs from a series of specific behaviors. The observer or recorder must also infer the frequency of such behavior in order to record whether it occurs "often," "sometimes," or "never." Sign systems and category systems, on the other hand, are low-inference measures because the items in these instruments focus on specific, denotable, distinguishable, and relatively objective behaviors such as "teacher praises student," "teacher repeats student's idea," and because these behaviors are recorded as frequency counts. But as Barak Rosenshine states, the distinction among these three systems based on inference level is not watertight since rating systems sometimes include low-inference items.[39]

While rating systems offer greater flexibility than do sign systems or category systems because they include high-inference variables, nonetheless the use of low-inference measures seems to be gaining the ascendancy both in teacher training and in educational research precisely because they do offer greater low-inference specificity. As compared with high-inference items, low inference data offer greater specific suggestions to the teacher in terms of improving his own pedagogical behavior. Category systems in particular are coming to be the most widely used form of interaction analysis. As of 1970 at least 140 observational category systems had been developed.[40] Anita Simon and Gil Boyer were able to edit a fifteen-volume anthology on classroom observation instruments alone.[41]

Category systems of classroom interaction analysis utilize direct or indirect observation of the behavioral events. Direct observation occurs when an observer or team of observers personally witnesses the pedagogical act either by being physically present in the classroom or by watching the instructional transaction through a one-way vision screen. Indirect observation is that in which the observer or team of observers examines an exact record of the instructional transaction. A written record (for example, a transcript of the verbal classroom events) while of some help is the least potent of all indirect observations in that it records only the verbal and cognitive aspects of the lesson. An audio record (for example, a tape recording of the instructional transaction) is somewhat more effective but still is limited in value because it records primarily verbal and cognitive behaviors, only a portion of the affective behaviors, and no nonverbal or other kinds of relevant overt behaviors at all. An audiovisual record (for example, a videotape recording of the teaching-learning act) is the most useful of all indirect observations since it records virtually all the verbal, nonverbal, cognitive, affective, and lifestyle aspects of the pedagogical interaction. For this reason videotape is gaining wider and wider acceptance in preservice and inservice programs designed to improve teacher behavior through interaction analysis or other kinds of behavioral awareness systems. In the instructional technology laboratory which I established in 1970 at the University of Notre Dame in connection with our doctoral program in religious instruction, I utilize three television cameras and videotape recorders in order to obtain a record of all aspects of the pedagogical transactions occurring in the entire teaching-learning environment. Effective use of interaction analysis systems calls for trained observers to insure the validity and reliability of the data gathered. Programs now exist in which observers can be trained in the use of interaction analysis in a comparatively short time.

Perhaps the most serious limitation of interaction analysis systems currently being used in exploring the pedagogical act is that they are typically one-factor instruments. But as I indicate many times throughout this book, the instructional act is characterized by a dynamic interaction of four major cluster variables, namely the teacher, the learner, the subject matter content, and the environment. Further, there are many dimensions or axes on which interaction among and within the four major cluster variables takes place, for example, the verbal and nonverbal dimensions. To date there has not been any interaction analysis system yet devised for investigating the teaching-learning dynamic which integrates all these variables and axes into one composite picture of the instructional act. Despite the highly significant impact of the instructional environment on the shape, direction, and efficacy of learning, no category system thus far developed explores the effects of the physical environment on teacher or learner behavior. Few systems specify the level of cognitive, affective, or lifestyle behavior of either teacher or students.[42] To illustrate: two teachers might be teaching the same high school religion· unit and be coded as having identical percentages of various types of question; yet teacher A might be asking the student about the meaning of sacramental signification while teacher B is inquiring about which items a family should have in the sickroom when the priest calls to administer the sacrament of the sick. There has been little or no effort to develop an interaction analysis category system which allows for a coded-item matching of the levels of teacher or learner cognitive and affective behaviors with those developed by Benjamin Bloom and David Krathwohl in their taxonomies of cognitive and affective objectives respectively. Most interaction analysis systems explore only the verbal dimension of the pedagogical act on the assumption that a teacher's verbal behaviors are representative of his other kinds of behaviors. Recognizing the limitations of the one-factor approach, some researchers—notably James Gallagher and his associates, Karl Openshaw, and Frederick Cyphert—have constructed multifactor interaction analysis systems. Yet such instruments are not widely used; indeed, the one-factor system developed by Ned Flanders together with other systems derived from it, such as that developed by Edmund Amidon (a former student of Flanders) are the instruments most widely utilized.

Interaction analysis systems even with the limitations described above make a significant and empirically proven contribution to both an understanding of and an improvement in the teaching process. Barak Rosenshine suggests some potential and/or actual benefits from the use of interaction analysis systems: (1) they assess the variability of classroom behavior either within or between instructional programs; (2) they measure the agreement between classroom behavior and certain instructional criteria; (3) they describe what occurs in the implementation of instructional materials; and (4) they ascertain the relationships between observed classroom behavior and instructional outcomes.[43] Inasmuch as interaction analysis has great serviceability in enabling the teacher to become aware of his own pedagogical behavior and thereby improve it, I shall devote the remainder of this chapter to a brief overview of some of the major and/or more widely used interaction analysis systems. Also I shall restrict my treatment to category systems of interaction analysis since these are coming to be much more popular than rating systems or sign systems.

Four main axes run throughout the category systems of interaction analysis thus far developed. As the term clearly denotes, the verbal-nonverbal axis indicates whether the classroom behaviors being analyzed are exclusively verbal, nonverbal, or a combination of both. The temporal-episodic axis points to whether the functional division employed to separate classroom behavior into analyzable units is made on a temporal basis (for example, every x number of seconds), or on an episodic basis (for example, each overall logical unit or behavior pattern), or a combination of the two. The cognitive-affective axis shows whether the classroom behaviors analyzed are exclusively cognitive or affective or a combination of both. Finally, there are the one-factor and multi-factor axes which I have discussed previously. Types of one-factor systems include the sole use of any one end of the verbal-nonverbal, temporal-episodic, cognitive-affective axes, as well as use of other single kinds of variables such as classroom climate. The vast majority of interaction analysis category systems available to date are of the verbal, temporal, cognitive, and one-factor varieties.

The most celebrated and widely used system for classroom interaction analysis is the one developed by Ned Flanders. This system is verbal, temporal, cognitive-affective, and one-factor. Borrowing from Robert Bales's work on group interaction analysis in general and from Harold Anderson's use of category systems in researching classroom behavior in particular, Flanders developed his system out of social psychological theory. The purpose of the Flanders instrument is to examine the effect of classroom social climate on students' academic achievement and on their attitudes. To accomplish this purpose, the Flanders system measures the incidence and pattern of the teacher's control over the students' freedom of action. The instrument primarily distinguishes those acts of the teacher which increase students' freedom of action and those which decrease their freedom of action.

There are ten behavioral categories in the Flanders interaction analysis system:

Category #1: Accepts Feeling: accepts and clarifies the feeling tone of the students in a nonthreatening manner. Feelings may be positive or negative. Predicting or recalling feelings are included.
Category #2: Praises or Encourages: praises or encourages student action or behavior. Jokes that release tension, not at the expense

of another individual, nodding head or saying "um hm?", or "go on" are included. *Category #3: Accepts or Uses Ideas of Student:* clarifying, building, or developing ideas suggested by a student. As the teacher brings more of his own ideas into play, shift to category five. *Category #4: Asks Questions:* asking a question about product content or procedure with the intent that a student answer. *Category #5: Lecturing:* giving facts or opinions about content or procedure; expressing his own ideas, asking rhetorical questions. *Category #6: Giving Directions:* directions, commands, or orders to which a student is expected to comply. *Category #7: Criticizing or Justifying Authority:* statements intended to change student behavior from nonacceptable to acceptable pattern; bawling someone out; stating why the teacher is doing what he is doing; extreme self-reference. *Category #8: Student Talk—Response:* a student makes a predictable response to teacher. Teacher initiates the contact or solicits student statement and sets limits to what the student says. *Category #9: Student Talk—Initiation:* talk by students which they initiate. Unpredictable statements in response to teacher. Shift from 8 to 9 as student introduces his own ideas. *Category #10: Silence or Confusion:* pauses, short periods of silence and periods of confusion in which communication cannot be understood by the observer.[44]

It should be noted that no scale or value rating is implied by these category numbers. Each category number is classificatory; that is, it designates a particular kind of communication behavior or interaction event. Further the categories are defined behaviorally, not judgmentally or speculatively.

The first seven categories deal with teacher talk while categories 8 and 9 center on student talk. On teacher talk the instrument distinguishes between talk of an indirect influence kind (categories 1, 2, 3, 4), and talk of a direct influence type (categories 5, 6, 7). In this way the incidence and kind of teacher influence on student behavior can be assessed.

The Flanders system is relatively simple to use and interpret. During the observation of the classroom interaction, a tally representing one of the ten category numbers is recorded every three seconds. At the conclusion of the observation (usually twenty minutes after the observation commenced), the tallies are inserted into a ten-by-ten matrix. Deciding which cell represents the proper one to put the tally is determined by the antecedent-consequent behavioral relationship—a lecture (category #5) followed by a teacher question (category #4) would be a 5-4, and inserted in the cell which represents the intersection between row 10 and column 5 on the 10x10 matrix (which of course contains 100 cells). The matrix is then plotted and analyzed to identify basic patterns of verbal interaction and teacher influence which occurred in the teaching-learning situation. Of especial importance is that the large variety of interpretations generated from this matrix is of a dynamic rather than a static sort because the matrix reveals which antecedent teacher behaviors generated which consequent student behaviors, and in what overall pattern of influence. There emerges from the matrix, then, a motion picture rather than a series of slides of what happened during the observed portion of the pedagogical act. Since the Flanders system is basically a one-factor system, the motion pictures are more in the form of X-ray film than of full-color pictures in which all the actors and props are fully recognizable.

It is not enough, therefore, to indicate that a teacher lectures fifty percent of the time or that he questions the students fifteen percent. In terms of understanding the pedagogical dynamics (motion picture) of the class, we must know when he uses the lecture or the questions and also with which other pedagogical behaviors he combines this usage. Only in this way will the antecedent-consequent pattern of the pedagogical act emerge, and only in this way can we ascertain the pattern of teacher influence. In terms of discovering the interaction patterns of the instructional act, we can read the matrix in one of two general ways: (1) the interconnections of category pairs, for example, 4-8; (2) loadings in large blocks of cells, for example, many tallies in a square encompassing the 1, 2, and 3 rows and columns. In terms of the first of these, the meaning of frequent entries in the 5-4 cell is that the teacher is interjecting questions throughout his lecturing. Repeated entries in the 5-7 cell, used when the lecture technique is broken by criticism, indicates the teacher is attempting to maintain order and control while he is lecturing. A heavy loading in the 4-6 and 4-5 cells suggests that the teacher is directing the students to answer his questions or he is employing an extended lecture technique following these questions, possibly to explain these further. A heavily loaded 4-8 cell indicates that the teacher has asked many direct questions—questions which inherently limit the range of student response. The use of a modified question-answer pattern is revealed by many tallies in the 4-8, 8-2, 2-4, and 3-4 cells. This pattern shows that the teacher asked a question and then encouraged or accepted student ideas before asking a second question. Frequent use of a 4-10 combination reveals periods of silence following teacher questions.[45]

Loadings in large blocks of cells also reveal the pattern of teacher-student interaction which took place in the observed portion of the lesson. A significant loading encompassing all the 1, 2, and 3 rows and columns points to a pattern of indirect rather than direct teacher influence. A large percentage of tallies occurring in the 4 and 5 rows and columns (the so-called "content cross") shows there was heavy emphasis on subject matter content during the lesson. Loadings in the 1-1, 2-2, 3-3, 3-4 and so on cells (called "steady state cells") indicate that a specific verbal act was maintained for more than three seconds. Many other combinations of loadings in the Flanders instrument reveal the different natures of the interactive pedagogical behaviors which occurred.

The degree to which teacher influence in the lesson was direct or indirect is found by computing the I/D ratio. (I stands for indirect teacher influence, D for direct teacher influence). The I/D ratio takes in all seven teacher-talk categories and is determined by dividing the total of the tallies in categories 1, 2, 3, and 4 by the total of the tallies in 5, 6, and 7. Most persons who work with the Flanders system prefer the modified i/d ratio which ignores categories 4 and 5 (asking questions and lecturing). The modified ratio is thus independent of communication patterns (like drill) which are unique to subject matter content. The modified i/d ratio thus is 1+2+3 divided by 6+7.

Like other kinds of interaction analysis category systems, the Flanders instrument is used not just to identify certain kinds of interactive behaviors or pedagogical patterns, but to improve teaching practice. Hence it is relevant here to mention some of the findings which utilization of the Flanders system has produced.

As a result of research using his interaction analysis system, Ned Flanders formulated the so-called "rule of the two-thirds." This rule states that in the average lesson someone is talking two-thirds of the time; two-thirds of that time the person talking is the teacher; and two-thirds of teacher talk is of the direct-influence type (lecture, giving directions, criticism, or justifying authority). Flanders also found that no teacher exhibits a pure influence pattern, that is, no teacher manifests only direct influence or only indirect influence over his students. Rather, each teacher mixes his direct-indirect behavior patterns. Hence one prominent variation among teachers is the degree to which they mix these. Using his interaction analysis category system instrument, Flanders discovered that teachers who used more indirect verbal patterns stimulated higher scholastic achievement in their students than did teachers whose patterns of verbal behavior were more direct.[46] Subsequent research by other investigators using the Flanders instrument came to the same conclusions. Further under indirect teacher influence students gained more constructive and independent attitudes than under the direct pattern. Classrooms which were scored high on student fondness of the teacher, level of motivation, lack of anxiety, and fair use of rewards and punishment were characterized by indirect teacher influence patterns while classrooms which were scored low in these areas tended to feature direct teacher influence patterns. Indirect teachers were more flexible than direct teachers in that they made more dramatic changes in their patterns of influence in the various time-use activity categories. However, in terms of all these data, it should be underscored that the effectiveness of the teacher's indirect and direct influence patterns was not an automatic or isolated affair; rather it was contingent upon its meshing with the other three major cluster variables in the learning situation, namely, student, subject-matter content, and environment. Thus direct and indirect teacher verbal behavior resulted in differential effects according to the clarity of the goal and on the dependent or independent personality configuration of the student. Also certain subject-matter content areas seemed to elicit differential teacher behaviors on the direct-indirect axis, with the most indirect mathematics teachers having a larger composite i/d ratio than the most indirect social studies teachers.

Another category system in use is the Verbal Interaction Category System (VICS).[47] This system is a modified version of the Flanders instrument and was designed and constructed by Edmund Amidon. VICS is verbal, temporal-episodic, cognitive-affective, and one-factor. A category is tallied every time a verbal behavior changes and every three seconds in any verbal behavior that lasts longer than three seconds. The categories in VICS are as follows: *Category #1:* teacher presents information or opinion; *Category #2:* teacher gives directions; *Category #3:* teacher asks narrow question; *Category #4:* teacher asks broad question; *Category #5:* teacher accepts student (a) ideas (b) action behavior (c) feeling; *Category #6:* Teacher rejects student (a) ideas (b) action behavior (c) feeling; *Category #7:* Student responds to teacher (a) predictably (b) unpredictably; *Category #8:* Student responds to another student; *Category #9:* Student initiates talk to teacher; *Category #10:* Student initiates talk to another student; *Category #11:* Silence; *Category Z:* Confusion. Tallying is done by straight numbers (for example, 2) or by numbers and postscripts (for example, 5b or 3Z).

There are four general category classes in VICS: teacher-initiated talk (categories 1, 2, 3, 4); teacher response (categories 5, 6); student response (categories 7, 8); student-initiated talk (categories 9, 10)—category 11 and the Z category are each in a class by itself. Though similar to the Flanders system on many counts, VICS does differ in some respects from the one by Amidon's former professor. Direct as opposed to indirect teacher influence is not a dimension of VICS; teacher categories are in terms of initiation and response. Unlike the Flanders system, VICS provides for differentiating the type of teacher question. In the area of student talk, VICS adds the dimensions of predictable and unpredictable response. VICS also separates the categories of silence and confusion. Finally, VICS distinguishes teacher response in terms of acceptant or rejecting responses and further specifies each of these in terms of ideas, action behaviors, and feelings. VICS has seventeen categories to Flanders ten and thus is more cumbersome to use; however, Amidon contends that his instrument furnishes more information than that of Flanders, thanks to the VICS modification and additional categories. Research investigations using the VICS have indicated that this category system is able to identify the verbal behavior patterns of superior teachers, and that these patterns do differ markedly from the verbal patterns of other teachers.[48]

Another verbal interaction analysis system derived from that of Flanders is the one constructed by John Hough.[49] Hough's system is verbal, temporal, cognitive-affective, and one-factor. Hough expands the number of categories in the original Flanders instrument to sixteen in order to obtain finer discriminations in teacher and student verbal behavior.

An interaction analysis category system similar to Flanders's in its examination of teacher control and student freedom in the classroom, but dissimilar in its basic approach to ascertaining this control and freedom, is the revised Provo Code developed by Marie Hughes and her associates.[50] The revised Provo Code is verbal, episodic, cognitive-affective, and one-factor. It utilizes thirty-three categories appropriately subsumed under seven major classes of teacher functions. Controlling functions include: (1) structure; (2) standard set; (3) regulate; (4) judge. Imposition of the teacher include: (5) regulaty self; (6) moralize; (7) teacher estimate of need; (8) inform appraisal; (9) inform. Under facilitating functions are the categories (10) checking; (11) demonstrating; (12) clarifying procedure. Included in functions that develop subject-matter content are (13) resource; (14) stimulate; (15) structure, turn back; (16) content-agree; (17) clarify; (18) evaluate. Functions which serve as response are (19) meets request; (20) clarify personal; (21) interprets; (22) acknowledges teacher mistake. Falling into the classification of functions of positive affectivity are (23) support; (24) solicitous; (25) encourage; (26) does for personal. As functions of negative affectivity there are (27) admonish; (28) reprimand; (29) accuse; (30) threaten; (31) negative response personal; (32) verbal futuristics; and (33) ignore. Under many of these categories, which are defined operationally and behaviorally, are types of verbal controlling behaviors appropriate to the category involved. Thus, for example, under category 3, standard set, are subcategories of recall, teacher edict, group developed, and universal. The revised Provo Code examines a wide range of teacher behaviors and in a manner more detailed and quite different from other interaction analysis category systems. It has been used with success; however, because of its complexity, it has not been widely used.

Perhaps the best known interaction analysis verbal category system seeking to examine the socioemotional climate or affective atmosphere of the pedagogical act is the one developed by John Withall.[51] The Withall system is verbal, temporal-episodic, affective, and one-factor. After a detailed analysis and subsequent telescoping of teacher statements in classroom situations, John Withall devised a seven-category system for measuring affective classroom climate. *Category #1:* Learner-supportive statements that have the intent of reassuring or commending the pupil. *Category #2:* Acceptant and clarifying statements having the intent to convey to the pupil the feeling that he was understood and help him elucidate his ideas and feelings. *Category #3:* Problem-structuring statements or questions which proffer information or raise questions about the problem in an objective manner with the intent to facilitate the learner's problem solving. *Category #4:* Neutral statements which comprise polite formalities, administrative comments, verbatim repetitions of something that has already been said. No intent inferrable. *Category #5:* Directive or hortative statements with intent to have a pupil follow a recommended course of action. *Category #6:* Reproving or disparaging remarks intended to deter the pupil from continued indulgence in his present "unacceptable" behavior. *Category #7:*

Teacher self-supporting remarks intended to sustain or justify the teacher's position or course of action. Categories 1, 2, and 3 are learner-centered; categories 5, 6, and 7 are teacher-centered; category 4 is neutral. By analyzing the incidence and pattern of teacher verbal interaction in terms of this seven-category system, it is possible to get a fairly good picture of the affective climate or emotional atmosphere of the teaching-learning act. From research utilizing his own system, Withall found that a sustained pattern of teacher-centered verbal behavior produced disruptive anxiety and reduced the learner's subsequent capability to recall the material under study. The reverse held true in student reactions to learner-centered teaching. The investigator concluded that providing opportunities for free choice and expression leads to the attainment of the desired learning outcome; also the teacher's verbal expression of understanding facilitates problem-solving on the part of students.

The verbal interaction analysis systems I have treated thus far have been primarily time-based in implementation, for example, in the Flanders system the unit of behavior delimited for study was arbitrarily set at whatever verbal behavior occurred within three-second intervals. Some specialists in the teaching-learning act believe it is more fruitful to examine pedagogical behavior in terms of units composed of episodes in which a particular type of behavior is sustained for a period of time. Episodes, they contend, form more natural units than does a predetermined arbitrary number of seconds or minutes. In an episodic system a unit is determined by examining the pedagogical transaction and ascertaining when a particular sustained behavior began and when it terminated. The two most significant episodic interaction analysis systems are the ones developed by Arno Bellack and his associates and by B. Othanel Smith and Milton Meux.

Bellack's system[52] is verbal, episodic, cognitive, and in some ways multi-factor. In developing this system, Bellack and his associates consciously and systematically worked out of a combination of gaming theory and linguistic analysis theory (of the Wittgenstein variety). It focuses on two main verbal activities: what the speaker does pedagogically with the words he speaks, and what he is saying in terms of subject-matter content. In terms of the first of these two foci, the Bellack system provides four episodic categories. *Category #1: Structuring.* Structuring moves establish the context for subsequent behavior by either launching or halting-excluding verbal interaction between students and teachers. For example, a teacher might launch a lesson with a structuring move which focuses attention on a specified subject-matter topic. *Category #2: Soliciting.* Moves which are designed to elicit a verbal response, to encourage the person(s) addressed to attend to something, or to elicit a nonverbal response. Examples of soliciting moves are questions, commands, and requests. *Category #3: Responding.* These moves have a reciprocal relationship to soliciting moves and occur only in relation to them. As such they serve to fulfill the expectation of soliciting moves. For example, student answers to a teacher's question is a responding move. *Category #4: Reacting.* These moves are occasioned by a structuring, soliciting, responding, or prior reacting move, but are not directly elicited by them. The pedagogical function of reacting moves is to modify (by clarifying, synthesizing, or expanding) and/or to rate (positively or negatively) what has been said previously. Reacting and responding moves differ in that a responding move is always directly elicited by a solicitation while preceding moves serve only as the occasion for reactions. For example, the teacher's rating of a student's response is considered a reacting move. The first two categories are classed as initiating moves; the last two are reflexive moves.

The second focus of the Bellack system is on what the speaker is saying in terms of subject-matter content. There are four categories in this area. *Category #1: Substantive with associated.* These cognitive meanings refer to the subject matter of the lesson, for example, specific concepts such as the sacrament of baptism and generalizations involving, for example, the relationship between sin and justice. *Category #2: Substantive-logical.* These are meanings which refer to the cognitive processes involved in dealing with subject matter content, such as defining, interpreting, explaining, opining. *Category #3: Instructional with associated.* These meanings pertain to such matters as assignments, materials, and routine classroom procedures which are part of the instructional process. *Category #4: Instructional-logical.* These meanings relate to distinctively didactic verbal learning processes such as those involved in positive and negative rating, explaining procedures, and giving directions.

In coding the verbal behaviors of a particular lesson, the Bellack system overlays one set of categories on the other. Units of discourse are determined by analyzing the flow of classroom communication and ascertaining when a particular pedagogical move started and when it ended, or when the class began to deal with a particular subject-matter content and when it finished its consideration of this content.

Use of the Bellack system yields many significant data about what takes place in the instructional act. For example, in one investigation[53] which utilized the Bellack system, Arno Bellack and his associates found that pedagogical moves occur in certain cyclical patterns or combinations which the researchers dubbed "teaching cycles." In this study the teacher initiated eighty-five percent of the teaching cycles. Teaching cycles of a given logical type tended to occur in clusters of two or more. A teaching cycle constituting a specific pattern of pedagogical moves tended to be followed by the same pattern to a greater extent than was indicated by the overall distribution of cycle types occurring in the total lesson. Teachers typically followed a soliciting-responding interchange with a reacting move. Unusual teaching cycles such as those involving reactions to structuring and soliciting moves tended to be initiated more by the pupil than by the teacher.

On the basis of the data derived from this study, Bellack and his associates were able to formulate five general rules for what he calls the classroom game. First, the basic verbal maneuvers employed by both teacher and pupil are pedagogical moves, either of the initiating variety (structuring or soliciting) or of the reflexive type (responding and reacting). Second, the teacher is the most active player in the game. He makes the most moves and speaks the most frequently. His speeches typically are the longest. In general he speaks three times more than all the students combined. Third, in the subject-matter field investigated, the major part of the classroom game is played with substantive cognitive meanings specified by the teacher's structuring of the game. From time to time, however, players are allowed to depart from this general focus. Fourth, players usually employ the empirical mode of thought (for example, fact-stating, explaining) in dealing with the substantive subject matter content. The analytic mode (for example, defining terms, interpreting statements) is used with much less frequency. Fifth, wins or losses are gauged on a relative interactive basis rather than on an absolute norm. Thus, for example, the teacher's winnings are determined by the amount and degree of pupil performance. Consequently while the teacher controls the game, nonetheless he is dependent upon the pupils for winning.

A second important episodic interaction analysis system is the one developed by B. Othanel Smith and Milton Meux.[54] The Smith-

Meux system is verbal, episodic, cognitive, and one-factor. It is one of the most cognitively-based of all existing interaction analysis instruments. The focus of the Smith-Meux system is "logical operations," that is the forms which verbal behavior takes as the teacher shapes the subject-matter content during the instructional act. Therefore this system concentrates exclusively on the logical aspects of the pedagogical act. The guiding hypothesis of the Smith-Meux instrument is that logical operations overtly or covertly determine both teacher and learner activity in the classroom.

Episodic units of analysis are ascertained by locating "entries" taking place in the course of the pedagogical act. Smith and Meux define an entry as a remark which serves to launch a new unit of verbal logical transactions. The instrument distinguishes between two main types of verbal logical activity, namely the monologue in which only one person speaks for an extended period of time and the dialogue.[55] While there is only one kind of monologue, there are two distinct patterns of dialogue. In the reciprocating pattern a back and forth alternation occurs between two or more speakers after the entry. In the coordinate pattern, each successive speaker responds more or less directly to the entry rather than to the remarks of the immediately preceding speaker. By virtue of its pivotal and controlling function, the entry serves as the basis for the determination of the categories to be examined. There are thirteen categories in the Smith-Meux system of logical operations occurring during the pedagogical act: (1) defining; (2) describing; (3) designating; (4) stating; (5) reporting; (6) substituting; (7) evaluating; (8) opining; (9) classifying; (10) comparing and contrasting; (11) conditional inferring; (12) explaining: (a) mechanical explaining; (b) causal explaining; (c) sequent explaining; (d) procedural explaining; (e) teleological explaining; (f) normative explaining; (13) directing and managing classroom.

Smith and Meux's category system is useful in identifying, describing, and evaluating the logical activities which take place in the classroom. It may therefore prove to be of significant assistance to theologically-oriented religious educators who tend to be principally concerned with more effectively facilitating product and process cognitive outcomes in religion class. Religious educators of a social-science orientation also might wish to use the Smith-Meux system to advantage in helping religion teachers sharpen the logical and cognitive aspects of their pedagogical activity.

All the interaction analysis category systems I have discussed so far are centered around verbal behavior in the classroom. But words constitute only one kind of the total behavioral exchange taking place in the instructional act. To be sure the underlying rationale for exclusive focusing on verbal behaviors is that this type of communication is sufficiently representative of the totality of behavioral contours found in the pedagogical act. Thus Ned Flanders, for example, states that verbal communication constitutes an adequate sample of the teacher's overall influence pattern. Yet it would seem that in some ways the verbal behaviors of teacher and students might fail to reveal much of the real essence or functioning of the pedagogical act. There is a great deal of difference between a lecture or asking questions when the teacher uses a soft tone of voice as against a harsh one or a tentative vocal expression as contrasted with an absolutist one. Yet on the Flanders instrument these important vocal attributes—I do not say "nuances"—are all recorded as "5" or "4" respectively. While words sometimes mask the teacher's true feelings and attitudes, his nonverbal behaviors make these quite transparent to the students and indeed elicit highly significant nonverbal (and sometimes verbal) reactions and responses. Thus it not infrequently happens that nonverbal communication in the classroom is more significant to both pupils and teachers than is verbal communication. This is particularly true for ghetto children and for other individuals coming from deprived socioeconomic neighborhoods. Therefore it is regrettable that more attention has not been given to constructing sophisticated and useful interaction analysis category systems of nonverbal behavior. Two such systems are in existence, however, namely, the Galloway system[56] and the Grant-Hennings system.[57] I shall restrict my discussion to the Galloway system.

The Galloway instrument is a seven-category system. *Category #1:* Enthusiastic support; *Category #2:* Helping; *Category #3:* Receptivity: *Category #4:* Pro forma; *Category #5:* Inattentive; *Category #6:* Unresponsive; *Category #7:* Disapproval. Under *each* of the seven categories are the following subdivisions: (a) facial expression; (b) action or movement; (c) vocal language. In this sense, then, there are twenty-one categories in the Galloway system. Main categories 1, 2, and 3 are classified as encouraging communication, while main categories 5, 6, and 7 are classified as inhibiting communication. Main category 4 is neutral. The Galloway system measures only teacher nonverbal communication; in this respect it is highly one-factor in design. However, the Galloway system is a useful instrument for examining the significant and influential nonverbal communications occurring during the pedagogical act.

An attempt to develop a multi-factor interaction analysis system was made by Karl Openshaw and his associates.[58] This system analyzes and categorizes four factors contained in each teaching-learning "encounter," namely the source or origin of the encounter, the direction of the encounter, the sign or mode of the encounter (for example, speaking, gesturing, writing), and the function of the encounter (for example, structuring, developing). Each of the four categories is divided into subcategories; in the function category there are both subcategories and sub-subcategories.

Conclusion

Teaching religion is a complex matter involving four major cluster independent variables (teacher, learner, subject-matter content, and environment), a dependent variable (the goal or objective), and a host of pedagogical practices to render the ongoing and dynamic relationships among all these elements as fruitful as possible in terms of facilitating the attainment of desired learning outcomes. A theory of teaching and its encapsulation in the teaching model presented earlier in this chapter help the religion teacher to radicate his particular instructional behaviors in the only soil which will support and nourish his educational practice, namely the soil of sound and adequate theory. A careful scrutiny of the antecedent-consequent dimensions of his teaching acts as revealed through various inter-action analysis systems will enable the religion teacher to become aware of his pedagogical behaviors so that he may more effectively control them in order to make his own instructional activity more successful. Because the teaching theory, the teaching model, and the systems of interaction analysis are all value-neutral, these three devices can be used as effectively in the teaching of religion as in the teaching of any other kind of content.

To indicate that the teaching process is a complex activity is not by any means to assert that it is wrapped in veils upon veils of mystery. Teaching is a process made up of a series of identifiable and improvable acts. These acts are chained in an antecedent-consequent fashion. The sooner religious instruction "despookifies" the teaching act and concentrates on identifying and improving the teacher's pedagogical behavior, the sooner will the Lord, the church, the teacher, and the learner reap the harvest.

TOWARD A REDIRECTION

"Come, my friends
'Tis not too late to seek a newer world."
  —Alfred Lord Tennyson[1]

Religion teaching is basically no different from any other kind of teaching. Nor is the learning of religion basically different from any other kind of learning. Recognition of these fundamental facts, so long explicitly or implicitly denied by religious educationists and educators, makes it possible for the entire field of religious instruction to come to new life and fruitfulness. It has been empirically demonstrated that certain antecedent instructional practices yield certain consequent outcomes. Moreover, we know that particular kinds of outcomes are promoted more efficiently by one pedagogical technique than by another. We also know that variables such as the student's expectancy, attitudes, intelligence, socioeconomic status and so forth do have a pronounced effect on the way he learns any reality (including religion). An awareness that the facts of teaching and the facts of learning are basically the same for all branches of instruction should have a positive and freeing effect on religious educators. No longer need they hide in a self-erected pedagogical ghetto, shutting themselves off from all the new and vivifying advances occurring in the educational world at large. Religious instruction is an intimate part of the entire educational fabric; it is not a swatch apart and separate from it. In short, if religious instruction is to come of age, it must perforce utilize each and every significant advance made in the theory and practice of teaching.

Teaching as Bringing About Desired Change

To teach is to cause learning. Therefore to teach is to bring about a desired change in the learner. Consequently the first job of the religion teacher (or curriculum builder) is to arrive at a decision concerning the nature of the change which should come to pass as a result of the educational activity he provides.[2] To make this decision at the outset is a necessary but not a sufficient precondition for effective teaching. Once the basic decision on outcome has been made, it is important to identify quite carefully and precisely the kind of behavior(s) involved in this outcome so that the learner can be furnished with a pedagogy which optimally facilitates the attainment of that kind of behavior.[3] Identification of the outcome-behavior entails a task analysis of the instructional objective. An analysis of the component tasks involved in this objective suggests to the teacher what he must do pedagogically to structure the learning situation so as to best enable the learner to master each of these components and thereby attain the objective. Thus the religion teacher (or curriculum builder) always asks the question "What is it I want the learner to be able to do as a result of my pedagogical activity?" This capability must be stated unambiguously, specifically, and behaviorally. By "capability" I mean the demonstrated ability of the learner to perform certain particular functions under specific conditions. For example, a capability might be the manifested ability to solve a series of problems testing the learner's understanding of the nature of sacrament in selected Christian denominations. A statement of an objective is useful and pedagogically valid only to the extent that it indicates precisely what the learner must be able to do or perform when he is demonstrating his mastery of the objective.[4] Earlier in this book I pointed out that learning is only a construct, an inference from performance. Unless the learner performs in a specified manner we have no indication that he has learned—after all, we cannot jump under his skin to determine the degree to which he has mastered desired cognitive, affective, or lifestyle objectives. This suggests to the religion teacher that learning objectives must be performance objectives; it tells the curriculum builder that his curriculum must be a performance curriculum. Further, a satisfactory statement of performance objectives must delineate the minimum standard or quality of this behavior which will be accepted as evidence that the teaching has been successful or completed.

The term "teaching" connotes effectiveness in pedagogy, that is, the teacher's effecting the attainment of some educational objective. It is only when the learner performs a behavior which represents this objective or part of it that the teacher can state with some confidence that his pedagogy has been effective. The nature of the performance will be determined by the nature of the objective, for example, a cognitive objective will naturally require the student to perform a cognitive behavior. To facilitate teacher effectiveness, therefore, it is helpful if not necessary for both himself and the curriculum builder to specify instructional objectives in performance terms. There are many types of cognitive, affective, and lifestyle performance outcomes which the religion teacher seeks, both from the product content aspect (for example, knowledge of the historical events of 1517, or understanding of the theology of baptism) and from the process content viewpoint (for example, response differentiation, association, multiple discrimination, and class concepts).[5] Teaching effectiveness (and teacher competence), therefore, is a multifactor variable rather than a single-factor one.

The specification of performance objectives and teacher behaviors most correlated to the probable effecting of these objectives will do much to eradicate a great deal of the irrelevant and diversionary pedagogical platitudes which have for so long blunted if not actually negated the effectiveness of religion teaching. One such platitude is that "if the teacher knows his subject matter sufficiently, he can teach it."[6] A distinguished Catholic purveyor of this platitude suggests that an improvement in religious instruction can come solely from an improvement in the teacher's theological understanding; an increase in the teacher's behavioral skill to facilitate learner performance is in no way helpful or fruitful.[7] Platitudes of this sort divert attention from teaching effectiveness by ignoring learner performance of the subject-matter objectives and the necessary pedagogical behaviors on the part of the teacher to bring about the requisite student performance. Teaching is an art-science—it requires skillful deployment of teacher behaviors to bring about the learner's performance of specified objectives. Another platitude of little help to religion teachers is the one often used by a Protestant religious educationist: "We are not in the business, after all, of communicating certain factors or modifying certain behavior patterns or of facilitating certain interpersonal relationships, so much as of siding with God in changing the world."[8] This platitude is as misleading as it is fuzzy. What does a student do when he sides with God? How does the teacher—or anyone else for that matter—know when the student is siding with God? What pedagogical behaviors does the teacher employ to help the learner side with God? In the end, the religion teacher will only know that the learner is siding with God when he is performing certain cognitive, affective, or lifestyle behaviors which are hypothesized to be positively correlated with "siding with God." Such consequent learner behaviors are the result of certain antecedent teacher pedagogical behaviors.

The performance objectives in the religion curriculum or religion lesson should be objectives related to religious instruction and not to theological instruction. Teaching religion, as I noted in an earlier chapter, is quite different from teaching theology. Teaching religion involves the deliberative and purposeful facilitation of cognitive, affective, and lifestyle outcomes. Toward this end, the integralist goal of the religion program, as distinct from the intellectualist or moralist goal, is the appropriate one.

Teaching Theory

There is nothing more important for religious instruction than a good and useful theory. At the broadest level, the most useful theory for religious instruction is social-science theory. At the intermediate level, at the level involved in the here-and-now flow of teaching, teaching theory is the most useful.

Theory is so crucial for religious instruction because in the final analysis, pedagogical practice is the application of a theory. Theory gives direction to action. The religion teacher's decision to select or not to select a given pedagogical practice is explicitly or implicitly determined by the instructional theory out of which he operates. The teaching theory, for example, will generate different pedagogical practices than the blow "theory" or the authenticity "theory" or the witness "theory."

Pedagogical practices, whether they be methods or techniques or steps or whatever, are simply specific isolated instances and therefore can only take on generalizable meaning to the extent that they are inserted into a broader theoretical framework. It is not enough that Mr. Brown, the senior religion teacher, has found technique X was effective at 10:00 A.M. on March 4; this is only one isolated instance, and as such gives no indication as to whether this technique will work for him in the afternoon, or on April 10, or whether it will work in Mrs. Larsen's class. By seeking a broader behavioral principle which explains the effectiveness of technique X (for example, an affective student response is secured through the teacher's deployment of an affective pedagogical stimulus), and by then radicating this principle into an even wider theoretical base (for example, learning is effected through an interaction of the teacher, learner, subject matter content, and environment), technique X becomes useful to Mr. Brown or to Mrs. Larsen in Chicago, or to Miss Cole in Hubbles Corners, Wyoming.

In every religion program there are effective teachers. The explanation frequently offered is that they are effective teachers because they have learned the "tricks of the game" from years of experience. But "tricks" need to be memorized, and the more there are, the harder it is to teach and to learn them. Principles deriving from theory are fewer and are more easily learned and taught. Principles derived from theory will produce the "tricks" if consciously and logically applied. Principles generate newer and more motile "tricks," but "tricks" alone do not generate other different "tricks." When effective teaching techniques are raised to an order of generalizability by inserting them into a theoretical framework, they become capable of providing pedagogical assistance for other religion teachers.[9] Improvement in the quality of religious pedagogy is least productive when it lacks a theoretical framework and merely seeks to establish a correlation between an outcome and some other instructional variable. It is from teaching theory that we can develop fruitful ideas of which factors in the instructional act need to be influenced, and in what direction.

The teaching model I presented in the previous chapter makes the teaching theory which it illustrates more graphic. The teaching model suggests that the instructional act is a dynamic interaction among teacher, learner, subject-matter content, and environment. Each of these variables must be understood and specified by the religion teacher if he wishes to shape the conditions which maximize the probability of learning. A prime task of the religion teacher is that he not only be aware of the general principle of the shaping of actual experience by environing conditions, but that he also recognize the specific concrete properties of the four major variables involved in the instructional act.[10] The teacher must be cognizant of the antecedent-consequent relationship present in his pedagogical behaviors; he should also be able to control his behaviors so that the most fruitful antecedent-consequent relationship may occur. In his pedagogical activity, he should integrate in a harmonious and conscious manner the elements of the instructional taxonomy, namely approach, style, strategy, method, technique, and step. The empirical findings on learning also provide the teacher with an indispensable source of information on how to vary his behaviors in terms of the learner element in the teaching model. When the religion teacher has more information about how a person learns and about this particular learner, he is in a far better position to more effectively shape and target his own instructional behaviors. The research shows that when teachers are supplied with information concerning their students and integrate this information into their own pedagogical behaviors, learning is enhanced.[11] Subject-matter content is the third critical variable in the teaching model. In terms of religion as subject-matter (in contradistinction to theology as subject-matter), there are product and process contents, cognitive-affective-lifestyle contents, conscious and unconscious contents, theological and nontheological contents. The Bloom taxonomy of cognitive objectives and the Krathwohl taxonomy of affective objectives furnish the religion teacher with invaluable assistance for sharpening and improving the attainment of cognitive-affective, product-process subject-matter outcomes. Finally, the environment constitutes an instructional variable whose extraordinary potency for inducing desired learnings is exceeded only by the typical religion teacher's nonuse of this variable. The research which I adduce in Chapter 6 amply demonstrates the high-level influence which the environment assumes in the teaching-learning process.

Teaching theory, whether in itself or as illustrated graphically in the teaching model, clearly suggests that the structured-learning-situation strategy is the most effective pedagogical strategy for bringing about desired learning outcomes. Indeed, it is not too much to say that the teaching model indicates that the structured-learning-situation strategy is the only adequate strategy for religion teaching. Now that this strategy has been identified, it remains the work of religious educationists and educators to begin to analyze the nature and function of the pedagogical task and how this task shapes and is shaped by the other three major variables present in the instructional dynamic. If the quality of religious instruction is to improve markedly, such an analysis must receive one of the top priorities in the galaxy of concerns articulated by religious education associations.

Evaluation of Religious Instruction

Probably no branch of education has less to do with sophisticated evaluation than does the field of religious instruction.[12] Yet as

David Hunter cogently reminds us, "to refuse to submit ourselves and our [religious education] work to evaluation is to put ourselves in the place of God, who alone is judge of quick and dead and in need of no judgment Himself."[13] A lack of evaluation, or even meaningless evaluation, is ruining the cutting edge of educational innovation.[14]

Why is sophisticated and rigorous evaluation so often lacking in religion teaching? Several basic reasons can be adduced. First, the theories of instruction in which most of contemporary religious education is rooted militate against if not actually disvalue totally any kind of evaluation. For example, the blow "theory" (which is probably the most widely accepted "theory" of religious instruction in Catholic circles) quite naturally denies the need, effectiveness, or validity of evaluation. After all, how can man evaluate the blowing Spirit? Secondly, religious instruction, as a budget analysis of any Christian denomination bears out, is typically a low-priority undertaking of the church. Sunday School teachers, CCD workers, and many of the administrative staffs of religious instruction programs are composed of well-meaning but professionally untrained personnel. These individuals lack the skills and often the inclination to engage in any sort of meaningful evaluation, to say nothing of sophisticated evaluation. Finally, there is the implicit or explicit conception that the outcomes of religious instruction cannot really be measured since they are spiritual and hence outside the competence of any evaluation system.

Adequate evaluation is indispensable for the improvement of religious instruction. How, then, can we overcome the obstacles and barriers which have prevented evaluation? Several tactics are available. First, religious instruction must be radicated in a theory of teaching rather than in the blow "theory" or the witness "theory" or any other unidimensional "theory." The teaching theory makes heavy and integral use of feedback data as a means of altering pedagogical behavior; and evaluation of religious instruction provides one of the most accurate and objective—and therefore one of the most helpful—kinds of feedback. Second, the entire religious instruction enterprise must be placed on a professional base. The present system of well-meaning but professionally untrained personnel, inadequate budgets, and low-level priority can have no result other than a deemphasis and indeed an outright denigration of evaluation. Third, religious instruction must be de-spookified. Religious behaviors are not some sort of vague, amorphous, spooky phenomena, but rather an identifiable set of behaviors. If religious behaviors were not identifiable, then how would it be possible for religious educators or churchmen or theologians to be able to identify the religious person or the just man? Can we not observe the difference between a religious man and a sinful man by his cognitive, affective, and lifestyle behaviors? To be sure, the whole notion and meaning of sin are wiped out when one insists that it is impossible to identify and assess the quality of an individual's behaviors. "You will be able to tell them by their fruits" (Matthew 7:16), that is by their behaviors. Fourth, cooperation of religion teachers and program administrators must be obtained if evaluation is to take place. If teachers and administrators mistrust the nature or goals of evaluation or fail to see its value, even the most sophisticated evaluation system will be unsuccessful. Quite frequently religion teachers and administrators perceive evaluation as a threat to them. This suggests that the evaluator and his associates work with teachers and administrators in a nonthreatening manner. This can best be accomplished by presenting them with an objective summarization of their pedagogical and facilitational behaviors indicating simply what took place antecedently and consequently in the instructional act. In other words, the evaluation should be made in a nonjudgmental manner. Once the teacher or administrator sees the actual consequences of his facilitational behavior, he himself can make his own discoveries and reach his own conclusions about which pedagogical changes he can and should make to reduce any discrepancy between his own instructional intent and his pedagogical actions.[15]

If evaluation of religious instruction is to be effective, it must be put on an operational base. Goals or objectives of religious instruction can best be operationalized by converting them into behavioral objectives or performance outcomes. A behavioral objective is a statement of pedagogical goals which describe desired learner performance and indicate the way in which this performance is to be developed.[16] Robert Mager suggests the following steps in composing behavioral objectives: (1) identify the terminal behavior by name, that is, specify the particular kind of behavior which will be accepted as evidence that the learner has achieved the objective; (2) define the desired behavioral outcome further by describing the important and significant conditions under which the behavior can be predicted or expected to occur; (3) specify the criteria of acceptable performance by describing the level of performance which is considered acceptable.[17] This sort of operationalizing of the desired learning objectives into behavioral or performance terms makes significant evaluation possible—evaluation which provides the teacher with the necessary feedback both on whether a particular learner has reached the desired goal and on how the teacher can best perform his instructional task in the future.

Evaluation must be scientific rather than impressionistic. In 1970 a Catholic religious educator wrote an article entitled "Evaluating Christian Experience Programs".[18] An analysis of this article reveals that there was no real evaluation going on at all—instead, it was simply a compilation of the author's impressionistic opinions and subjective perceptions of what he believed to be the effectiveness of his program. But evaluation without objective validity is not evaluation, and indeed diverts the attention of the religion teacher away from evaluation. (Parenthetically, it is interesting to note that the author of this article adopts the theological approach to religious instruction.)

Without true scientific, objective evaluation the religion teacher is isolated from systematic reliable information about his own pedagogical behavior and the consequences of that behavior. Yet, if religious instruction is to move forward, it must make heavy use of scientific, objective evaluation which puts the teacher or administrator in constant touch with his own instructional behavior.

Improving Religion Teaching

A major need in contemporary religious instruction is careful and systematic attention to pedagogical practice. It should be noted at the outset that while most teachers do possess an explicit or at least implicit educational philosophy, nonetheless the values inherent in this philosophy are not necessarily correlated with their instructional behavior. It is quite possible that the findings of a 1953 study in this connection are still applicable today. In this study the investigator found that while the responses of elementary school teachers to a checklist of educational beliefs tended to be consistent with contemporary educational philosophy, the actual classroom observations of these same teachers indicated a discrepancy between their beliefs and their pedagogical practices.[19] The implication of this study is that in order to upgrade the quality of instructional behavior, it is more efficacious to concentrate directly on the improvement of the teacher's preservice or inservice instructional behavior rather than to simply feed him strong dosages of educational philosophy or theology.

What I observe in the previous paragraph ought not to be construed as a diminution or a contradiction of what I wrote earlier about the axial importance of pedagogical theory for pedagogical practice. There is, after all, a vast difference between pedagogical philosophy and pedagogical theory, and only confusion results when the two are equated. Indeed, the directive role which pedagogical theory has for pedagogical practice is so great that it is practically impossible to downplay it. Consider, for example, the following incisive comment from a Catholic college professor who works in attempting to significantly improve the inservice training of religion teachers in the midwest:

> One of the biggest difficulties we found with religious coordinators is their inability to single out [instructional] variables and understand how they relate. Hypotheses, predictability, universals, sets and subsets are a foreign language [to them]. Every one of these coordinators wants to be "human" and "spread the Good News." Yet few, if any, want to realize that *human* and *spreading* are complex operations that require behavioral components. They just will not attempt to analyze or measure or hypothesize about these components. Everything is just heaped together. We have many women coordinators. I just wonder if the avoidance of analysis is a female trait.[20]

It is possible, and indeed quite probable that these religious educators were operating out of the blow theory or the witness theory or the dedication theory; had they adhered to the teaching theory, they would have been deeply interested and involved in behavioral analysis of the pedagogical act.

An improvement in the practice of religious instruction necessitates the conscious application of teaching theory as well as the harmonious, integrated insertion of a particular pedagogical practice into the taxonomy of the teaching act which I outlined in Chapter 4. Only in this way will all the six hierarchical elements of the taxonomy successfully work together to produce optimally effective pedagogical techniques.

The systematic and empirically-verified overall design of religious instruction practice is still in its infancy, primarily because of the heavy preponderance in former times of pious educational platitudes, fuzzy instructional thinking, inappropriate theoretical anchorages, and poor behavioral analysis. Those attempts which were made to design instructional practice typically were neither based on a comprehensive teaching theory nor on principles deriving from the findings of learning and teaching. Too often the designer of a pedagogical practice based the entire practice on a single appealing principle, ignoring all the other aspects of the teaching-learning dynamic. If religious instruction is to advance, very high priority must be given to the systematic design and implementation of pedagogical practice.

The key to designing and improving religious instructional practice lies in behavioral analysis of the pedagogical event and in subsequent behavioral control by the religion teacher. Although most of the religion teacher's instructional time is spent with learners, the complicated nature of professional pedagogical behavior is typically taken for granted. It is seldom analyzed scientifically. And when a behavioral analysis of the pedagogical event does take place, it is typically centered on the behavior of the learners, with little mention or attention to the complex antecedent elements of the teacher's pedagogical behavior.

A Model for the Improvement of Religion Teaching

What is urgently needed in religious instruction, then, is a model for preservice and inservice teacher improvement. Such a model, when applied in local parish or regional or diocesan situations can give those officially charged with the leadership in religious instruction the wherewithal to inaugurate continuous and continual preservice and inservice programs for their religion teachers.

An underlying postulate for this kind of program is that training in instructional improvement is useful and valuable to the extent that the religion teacher himself can be involved personally and intimately at every level of the training. Behavioral analysis and behavioral control of the instructional act must primarily and ultimately be coordinated with the religion teacher's pedagogical behavior in an actual teaching-learning situation.

Below I offer a model for preservice and inservice training of religion teachers in the acquisition and improvement of their pedagogy. This model incorporates training in both behavioral analysis and behavioral control.

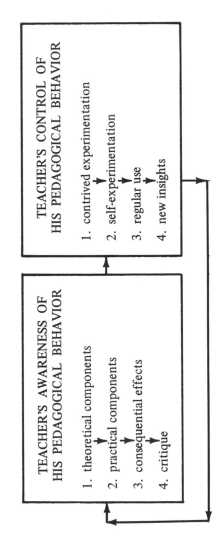

The left panel centers around enhancing the religion teacher's behavioral analysis of the pedagogical act while the right panel deals with heightening the teacher's pedagogical skill (control of his behaviors). The model plainly shows the flow of activities necessary to enable the religion teacher to optimally control his own instructional behaviors for the purpose of facilitating the desired learning outcomes. This model is of particular importance because it specifies how the teacher or administrator can concretely close the gap between the teacher's intention and the effectiveness of his action.

In the left panel, the teacher is first helped to become aware of the theoretical components operating in the religion lesson. He is enabled to identify which are the learning outcomes he desires his pupils to attain. He is assisted in ascertaining the degree to which these outcomes are rooted and operationalized in his own behavior, in the activities he has provided for the learners, in the type and arrangement of the subject-matter content, and in the total environment in which his teaching takes place. From this initial analysis, the teacher is then aided in critically analyzing what is actually taking place interactively in the instructional act. What is the flow of communication among teacher, learner, subject-matter content, and environment? The religion teacher is helped to identify observable and inferential operations occurring in the pedagogical dynamic. This analysis of the practical components generates a self-sharpening activity, namely that of focusing attention on the consequential effects of the teacher's pedagogical behaviors as they interact with the learner, the subject-matter content, and the environment. Teacher behaviors are antecedent, and as such produce certain consequential effects on the learner, subject-matter content, and environment. Since student learning is a function of the teacher's pedagogical behaviors, the analysis of this antecedent-consequent relationship is of utmost importance in the improvement of religious instruction. To round off the left panel, the first three stages of analysis lead the teacher to critique his own pedagogical performance in terms of whether the desired learning outcomes (consequences) which he had intentionally hoped to effect were indeed effected as a result of his pedagogical behaviors (antecedents). Behavioral analysis of this kind generates insight into which antecedent teacher behaviors were effective and which were ineffective in bringing about the desired consequential learner behaviors. This sort of behavioral critique, when properly handled by the teacher or supervisor, tends to lead to a program which will improve the teacher's control of his pedagogical behavior.

In the right panel of my model, the teacher experiments with his own pedagogical behavior first in a contrived setting and then in a setting more congruent with the typical classroom situation. During this experimentation he tries out certain pedagogical behaviors (antecedents) and works toward shaping and honing them in such a way as to be highly predictive of achieving the desired learning outcomes (consequences). In the contrived experimentation phase he tries out and works at performing particular instructional behaviors under specially-created unique conditions deliberatively designed to give the teacher focused and concentrated practice in the specified pedagogical behaviors. For example, the contrived environment might be a microteaching laboratory, and the specified pedagogical behavior might be a probing question or nonverbal communication. The self-experimentation phase might take place in a practicum situation simulating very closely a regular learning setting, or it might occur in the teacher's actual classroom. In either case, the teacher tries out and further experiments under natural conditions with the specified pedagogical behavior that he practiced in the contrived environment. In the third phase of the right panel he incorporates this by-now mastered pedagogical practice into his regular repertoire of pedagogical behaviors, using it as appropriate. Regular use of this practice will itself tend to lead the teacher to new analytical insights into his entire pedagogical practice; this in turn will lead upward to a new awaring of his pedagogical behavior. It is for this reason that there is an arrow in the model leading from "new insights" in the right panel to the entire left panel.

Two general aspects of this model deserve mention. First, it has a built-in feedback loop. This is crucial if there is to be a continuous, self-generating program for the improvement of religion teaching. Second, this model for the improvement of religion teaching incorporates the elements of the model of the teaching act which I offered in the preceding chapter. There can be no effective model or program for the improvement of religious instruction which does not incorporate the model of the teaching act.

The model for the improvement of religious instruction must be applied in actual practice if it is to yield the desired results. This model generates five practical and sequential steps which the religion teacher or supervisor[21] uses to apply the model and thereby improve the quality of religion teaching. *Step #1* consists in the systematic observation of the teacher's pedagogical behaviors and behavior patterns as he interacts with learners, subject-matter content, and environmental variables in the actual classroom situation. *Step #2* is the objective recording of the systematically observed teacher behaviors and behavior patterns. Many recording systems are available, including the interaction analysis procedures discussed in the previous chapters, videotape or audiotape devices, and so forth. *Step #3* is the purposeful feedback to the teacher of the objective data derived from the recorded observations. This feedback is objective in the sense that the actual recorded behaviors or behavior patterns, rather than subjective impressions of these behaviors are given to the teacher. The feedback is purposeful in that it is offered to the teacher in such a way that it will of itself generate in him an awareness of the antecedents and consequences of the pattern of behaviors which occurred in the actual classroom situation. The feedback may be furnished to the teacher by one person or by a group of persons, depending on which most effectively facilitates heightened behavioral awareness on the part of the teacher. *Step #4* is that of behavioral instruction or practice in a particular teaching skill or set of skills. This behavioral practice may take on one of two forms. It may consist of practice in reinforcing teaching behaviors which the recording showed are successful, inserting these pedagogical behaviors into new forms or patterns of instructional practice. Or it may consist of practice designed to modify existing teaching behaviors which the recording indicated are unsuccessful. In some cases, step #4 might be omitted when the originally recorded teaching behavior was successful and it would appear unwise to have the teacher either reinforce this behavior or place it into a wider configuration of behaviors. In any event, behavior training should occur only after the teacher has first manifested that he possesses an adequate level of behavioral awareness of what took place in the recorded classroom dynamic. There are many effective forms of behavioral training for pedagogical skills, such as microteaching, for example. *Step #5* is instruction in pedagogical principles and theory. This step is crucial if the awared and practiced pedagogical behavior is to be put into a framework which simultaneously makes this practice meaningful and enables it to spin-off new fruitful practices. Step #5 is typically omitted in theoretical treatments and in practical programs for teacher improvement; this accounts somewhat for the limited success which some of these programs have over the long term. When no theoretical anchorage or framework is given to the teacher, he will tend to assess his newly-acquired pedagogical skills on the basis of previously-held positions rather than on the basis of that aspect of teaching theory most germane to his newly-acquired pedagogical skill.[22]

It is at once apparent that steps 1, 2, and 3 refer to training the teacher in behavioral awareness; step 4 pertains to training in behavioral control, and step 5 is concerned with behavioral inference.

The transformation and upgrading of religious instruction are contingent upon the quality of preservice and inservice training programs. To prepare religion teachers in behavioral awareness and behavioral control is no easy matter. Religion teachers tend to teach as they were taught, and from a pedagogical perspective they typically were taught badly. The research data suggest that practice teaching seems to be the one element of preservice training most correlated with eventual and continued success in teaching;[23] nonetheless the one element either completely missing from or woefully underrepresented in graduate programs in religious education is that of practice in pedagogical behavior. This unfortunate state of affairs doubtless stems from the theological approach to religious instruction which holds that the teacher's knowledge of theology is the necessary and sufficient condition for effective religion teaching. If this present book means anything, it is that to have a yeasting and fruitful impact, religious instruction must be enfleshed in high-level and continuous preservice and inservice programs of behavioral analysis and control of the teaching act. Improved pedagogical skill far more than improved theological understanding is the key to more effective religion teaching now and in the years to come.

Many and proven are the ways of facilitating behavioral analysis and behavioral control in preservice and inservice training programs. I will briefly discuss four of the more significant ones: interaction analysis, microteaching; practicum experiences; internship experiences; and the teacher performance center.

Interaction Analysis. Considerable research has been done comparing the pedagogical effectiveness of student teachers who are trained in interaction analysis with matched teachers not so trained. Gertrude Moskowitz's review of the pertinent research concludes that training in interaction analysis typically produces beneficial change in one's teaching behavior. Student teachers who were trained in interaction analysis were found to be more effective in their student-teaching experiences than those not so trained.[24] A review of the research by Ernest Lohman and his associates indicates that preservice teachers who were trained in interaction analysis used significantly more verbal behaviors found to be associated with higher student achievement. Conversely, these same preservice teachers used significantly fewer behaviors which the research has concluded are correlated with lower student achievement.[25] Jeffrey Kirk's study discovered that preservice elementary school teachers trained in interaction analysis exhibited a wider and more fluid verbal pattern than teachers lacking this training.[26] An investigation which followed up preservice teachers four to twelve months after they had been trained in interaction analysis disclosed that these teachers used significantly more indirect verbal teaching behaviors and significantly less direct verbal teaching behaviors than those who were not so trained.[27] A review of the research indicates that preservice teachers trained in interaction analysis used significantly more verbal behaviors found to be associated with more positive pupil attitudes toward their teachers and toward school in general.[28] Norma Furst's investigation concluded that there was more student talk in classes taught by preservice secondary-school teachers trained in interaction analysis as compared with classes taught by preservice teachers not so trained. She also discovered that compared with teachers conventionally trained, the teachers trained in interaction analysis evidenced more frequent use of behaviors which accepted student ideas and less use of behaviors which rejected student ideas.[29] A study by Richard Zahn concluded that preservice teachers trained in interaction analysis had more positive attitudes toward teaching after their preservice experience than those who had not undergone this training. This held true regardless of the attitude of the cooperating field teacher.[30] An investigation by John Hough and Edmund Amidon found that over a semester's period of time, preservice teachers trained in interaction analysis became more empathic in their relationship with their pupils than those teachers not so trained. These researchers also discovered that the trained preservice teachers became more objective in their use of data about students and more experimental in their use of pedagogical practice than untrained teachers.[31] The data indicate that preservice teachers trained in interaction analysis differ significantly from those not so trained in the following ways: less direct teacher talk; less lecturing; less direction-giving; less extended teacher talk; more indirect teacher talk; more acceptance and clarification of student talk; more extended indirect teacher talk; more spontaneous student talk.[32]

The effectiveness of training in interaction analysis is not automatic or equal with all preservice teachers; it varies according to the personality configuration of the individual. Thus it has been discovered that the more authoritarian, rigid, and dogmatic a preservice or inservice teacher is, the less he will benefit from training in interaction analysis.[33] This finding has obvious ramifications for clerical and religious preservice or inservice teachers. Yet even here the picture is not really bleak since the above-cited investigations conclude that except for the extremely dogmatic and authoritarian personality types, the verbal behaviors of teachers possessing more than the average but less than extreme dogmatic and authoritarian personality configurations have been rendered more pedagogically effective through training in interaction analysis.

In one of the rare empirical studies on religion teaching, Raymond Whiteman found that use of interaction analysis combined with appropriate supervisory feedback produced enhanced and more effective teacher verbal behavior patterns along the lines of the data cited in the previous paragraph.[34] Whiteman's data clearly indicate the applicability of interaction analysis training for religion teaching, and also serve to reinforce my earlier statement that there is no basic difference between so-called "secular" teaching and learning, and "religious" teaching and learning. Church authorities charged with the responsibility of heightening preservice and inservice training of religion teachers might profitably utilize training in interaction analysis.

Microteaching. Microteaching is a teacher-training technique in which an individual practices a specified focused pedagogical skill in an instructional setting where all the normal classroom variables are telescoped into one small teaching unit. Dwight Allen and Kevin Ryan list five essential characteristics of microteaching. First, microteaching is real teaching. Though the instructional setting is a contrived one, nonetheless bona fide teaching does take place. Second, microteaching telescopes the normal classroom variables. Class size, number of learners, scope of subject-matter content, and time are all reduced. Third, microteaching focuses on the accomplishment of a particular pedagogical skill. It concentrates on the teacher's practicing a specified skill until he has achieved mastery of it. Such skills include probing questions, planned repetition, recognition of attending behaviors, reinforcement of student participation, and so forth. Fourth, microteaching allows for increased control of practice. Far more than in the regular classroom setting, the normal instructional variables can be structured and arranged so as to enable the teacher to sustain his pedagogical attention on the practice and mastery of just one instructional skill. Microteaching units are generally five to ten minutes in length; thus the teacher can practice and repractice his skill over and over again to the point of mastery. Finally, microteaching greatly expands the customary knowledge-of-pedagogical-results. Microteaching is done under the direction of an instructional supervisor, and is typically videotaped. Following the practice session, teacher and supervisor clinically analyze the video-tape. In such a clinical, supportive setting the teacher can first analyze his instructional behavior and then try it out anew in the microteaching setting to more effectively control this behavior.[35] There is considerable research evidence to suggest that microteaching improves teacher performance and effectiveness;[36] this doubtless is a major explanation for the use of microteaching in over half the nation's university-based teacher-training programs.[37] Surely micro-teaching should be a staple in the preservice and inservice programs for religious instruction in every diocese in the country as well as in university programs in religious education.

Practicum. A practicum is a laboratory situation in which peda-gogical theory and pedagogical practice are fused into a series of continuous, integrated practical instructional tasks which are per-formed, clinically analyzed, and related to pedagogical theory, and then performed again. A practicum is a purposefully and delibera-tively contrived experience which enables the preservice or inservice teacher to perceive, experience, and control the antecedent-consequent relationships of his instructional behavior. A practicum is generally situated in a laboratory setting in which all the instructional variables can be optimally arranged and structured with maximum ease. In the typical practicum situation, the following sequential steps are featured: (1) examination of teaching theory in general and of aspects of this theory which apply to the practice situation at hand; (2) establishment of the practice situation; (3) specification of the pedagogical behavior to be practiced; (4) observation of a skilled specialist performing the specific behavior; (5) performance of the specified behavior; (6) feedback of informa-tion about the performance; (7) modification and correction of the performance in the light of the feedback. The feedback consists in recordings of the performed behavior (written transcripts, audio-tapes, videotapes, and so on) followed by clinical analysis of the behavior which examines the antecedent-consequent pedagogical chaining of the performance in light of both teaching theory and the effectiveness of the performed behavior in bringing about the desired learning outcome.

There are many types of practice experiences which can take place in a practicum situation. Interaction analysis and microteaching are just two kinds of such experiences. Every helping profession has its practicum: medicine, the law, psychology, and so forth. If religion teaching is to move forward and improve, it is imperative that diocesan and local authorities establish laboratory settings in which practicum experiences can be put into continuous operation for the training of both preservice and inservice religion teachers.

Internship. The internship is that graduated and carefully supervised pedagogical field work undertaken concomitantly with university course work through which the present or future religion teacher supplements the other aspects of his in-university educational experience.[38] In a well-run internship program, the intern is supervised by both a university person in the religious education department and by an especially effective practitioner in the instructional or administrative field setting in which the intern is working. The internship experience is typical for the preservice program. In the internship program, the intern undergoes a wide variety of professional experiences, each designed to (1) sharpen relevant educational practices; (2) integrate these practices into a broad, harmonious pedagogical style; and (3) incorporate these practices into a framework of pertinent educational theory. There are seven sequential steps involved in the internship experience; these are the same as the steps in the practicum; however, in the internship the pacing is different from that which occurs in the practicum, for example, the observation stage is typically of longer duration in the internship than in the practicum. The prime distinction between the internship and the practicum is that the former is done in the field while the latter is done in the laboratory. Both the internship and the practicum have as their focus the clinical analysis and control of the religion teacher's pedagogical behaviors in an instructional setting. Hence any effective preservice and inservice program for religion teachers should include vigorous practicum and internship experiences.

Teacher Performance Center. The teacher performance center is a pedagogical laboratory in which (1) any aspect of pedagogical behavior can be recorded and analyzed through the use of currently available devices, and (2) the teacher can practice and sharpen the control of this behavior. The teacher performance center functions very much like a practicum; the major difference is that the teacher performance center is broader than a practicum in that it is housed in a diocesan or regional setting as well as in a university, and also that it is a continuous opportunity rather than simply a supervised course given at a designated time. In a teacher performance center, a religion teacher can at any time use any available videotape and analytical instruments to clinically analyze his pedagogical skills and work on their improvement. He can do this alone or with the help of an instructional supervisor if he so desires. It is safe to say that establishing and maintaining a well-equipped teacher performance center probably represents the most effective single concrete provision a diocese or region can make to enhance the quality of religion teaching within its jurisdiction.

Behaviorism and Behavioralism

Much of this book has been devoted to an examination of the teacher's behavior, and the consequences which this behavior has for subsequent learner behavior. What I have been suggesting constantly is that the key to more effective religious instruction is that the teacher identify, analyze, and control his pedagogical behavior for the purpose of bringing about optimal learning. To coin an expression, this is a behavioral emphasis. It seeks to make conscious and explicit those pedagogical behaviors which every religion teacher engages in. By raising these pedagogical behaviors to the level of consciously and explicitly recognized behaviors, it is possible to sharpen their use and hence render religious instruction more effective.

I should note that there is a vast difference between behavioralism and behaviorism. Behavioralism is a concerted effort to study, analyze, and harness human behavior of a cognitive, affective, or lifestyle variety. Behaviorism, by way of contrast, is a major theoretical school of psychology which contends that (1) all human behavior is simply a one-to-one relationship between a particular physical stimulus and a given response; (2) learning is the result solely of conditioned responses; (3) data drawn from experiential or introspective sources are worthless; (4) there is no reference or connection between behavior and mind or consciousness. Behaviorism typically takes a monistic, atomistic, and mechanistic view of human behavior. It tends to be consistent with a materialist philosophical system, though not necessarily so. John Broadus

Watson, Clark Hull, and B. F. Skinner are prominent exponents of behaviorism.

Behavioralism is much broader than behaviorism. Every theoretical school, like every thoughtful practitioner of a facilitational art-science (for example, teaching, counseling, administering) is behavioralistic because, by its very nature, a facilitational art-science is oriented around behavior. After all, facilitational activities are antecedent behaviors which yield desired consequent behaviors. The antecedent behaviors of the facilitator are purposive ones; they are deliberatively targeted to most effectively bring about the desired learning outcome. All behaviorists are behavioralists, but not all behavioralists are behaviorists. The position advocated in this book, together with the other two volumes in the trilogy, is one of behavioralism, not behaviorism.

Professionalism

If religious instruction is to move ahead along the lines suggested in this book, it must first of all become a professional activity. For present purposes, professionalism in religious instruction can be said to involve five characteristics: (1) sound theoretical framework; (2) adequate financial allocation; (3) sufficient support services and facilities; (4) research and data base; (5) trained personnel. Practices are applications or enfleshments of theory; thus a practice will be no more effective than the worth or usefulness of the theory it explicitly or implicitly enacts. Yet with but a very few exceptions, there has been too little adequate theorizing about the nature of religious instruction or about the nature of the teaching act. Second, religious instruction—both Catholic and Protestant—has been typically characterized by a scandalous lack of financial support from the denominations and churches. Notwithstanding, these same churches concomitantly expect and demand great results from the religious instruction programs which they sponsor. This strange attitude is reminiscent of the lyrics of a song popular in America during the early 1970's: "they put a nickel in and they want a dollar song." Third, support services and facilities in terms of a network of religious education are urgently needed if the work of religious instruction is to grow and bear fruit. Fourth, data banks and research instruments must be erected and utilized if the work of religious instruction is to be effective. Research activities should not be conducted in isolation, but must be a part of a regular program of development. Finally, religion teachers must be carefully selected, well-trained, full-time professional workers. As David Hunter cogently remarks, no one sends his child to a dentist whose training never went beyond reading a book on dentistry, or to public schools in which teachers simply had good will but no formal preservice and inservice training.[39] All religion teachers should hold a master's degree in religious instruction. (High echelon administrators of religious education programs should by the same token have attained the doctorate in this field.) Protestant and Catholic churches are only deluding themselves if they think they can continue to operate their religious instruction programs on a nonprofessional basis and have them effective. Church leaders must candidly ask themselves: "How valuable is our religious instruction program?" The real answer to this question can be determined by assessing their commitment to the program in terms of the five criteria I have just discussed.

Pelagianism and Semi-Pelagianism

It might be argued that the social-science approach to religious instruction is Pelagian. It will be recalled that Pelagianism was a fifth-century heresy which was "not primarily concerned with abstract problems of theology, but with Christian living."[40] The typical notion of Pelagianism is that it represents a radical affirmation of "the moral strength and self-sufficiency of man's free will. Man, relying entirely on his own power, can always will and do the good, even when in act, he neither wills nor does it."[41] In Pelagianism, man's will, not God's grace, basically accounts for a person's good acts. The purpose of grace is merely to aid man in doing what he can do by himself. Grace, therefore, is external to man.

On a somewhat more sophisticated plane, it might also be argued that the social-science approach to religious instruction is Semi-Pelagian. This heresy is associated with a fifth-century monk named Cassian. While downplaying and possibly repudiating Pelagianism, it nonetheless does assign a greater role to man's will than to God's grace. In contrast to Pelagianism, Semi-Pelagianism conceives of grace as interior. Semi-Pelagianism holds that the meritorious acts which God produces in man can also be produced by man himself. Man can achieve merit, or at least desire it to a certain degree by his own unaided actions.

The specter of Pelagianism and Semi-Pelagianism hangs like a pall over some modern religious educationists and theologians who are attempting to heal the wound brought on by a false separation of "natural" and "supernatural" in so much of Christian thought. David Hunter is quite perturbed at a duality he perceives between developing an effective kind of religious instruction and a lapse into a man-dependent Pelagianism. His solution, while sensitive and on the right track, is nevertheless not the final answer. Hunter notes that "the resulting tension between grace and free will, between faith and works, is a part of the essential nature and paradox of the Christian life."[42] For Gregory Baum, Pelagianism causes a special problem because of this Canadian theologian's rejection of an extrinsicist God. In an admirable and compelling effort to square his doctrine with anti-Pelagianism, Baum takes pains to emphasize that God's gratituousness is at the heart of the human condition, and that the Gospel explicitly repudiates the willful man. Yet in his attempt to save his theology from the charge of Pelagianism, Baum does lapse into a kind of vague amorphousness which suggests more of a last-ditch rescue endeavor than a carefully-thought out, well-reasoned effort. Thus Baum is led to say that "some things precious to man can be produced by will power or merited by personal effort, but important things just happen to man."[43] One is hard put to reconcile this statement of Gregory Baum with the way nature works—a nature which Baum himself contends is an arena for the workings of a God deeply intrinsic to the world. In nature there is nothing which "just happens"—there is always an antecedent-consequent chaining.

Nowhere does the social-science approach to religious instruction imply or maintain that the religion teacher can be or is effective without God. Nor does the structured learning situation strategy suggest in any fashion that learning can be facilitated without God's presence and power in each and every aspect. Nor does this approach in any way hint that human nature is totally good in itself or is free from taint of original sin in whatever form this sin may be considered. The social-science approach to religious instruction is value-free in terms of any and all specific theological positions. It can accommodate a Pelagian, an Augustinian, a Thomist, a Jansenist, or an advocate of the new theology. In any event, the social-science approach is definitely compatible with orthodox theology, whether old or new. In these terms, the issue is not whether God works intrinsically in man or in the teaching-learning dynamic, but how he works. In my own view, nature, teaching, learning, and man are not separated in any way over against God; rather nature is nature and can only be nature because of the presence, power, and being of God in all nature. Wherever teaching and learning take place, God is intimately and existentially present in every zone of the process. Nature is not nature alone—it is graced nature, or perhaps more precisely, grace-full nature. To say "nature" is at once to mention an aspect of God.[44] The laws of teaching and learning are not somehow apart from the laws of God. Teaching is effective when and only when it is true to the dynamics of its own nature; but to be true to its own nature is to be automatically true to the existential presence and ongoing activity of the God who is so existentially commingled with this nature as to make it a God-full nature. Because nature is the immediate object and milieu of human activity, a person is usually most true to God when he is chronologically first true to nature. Attempts to be chronologically first true to an unseen God has typically resulted in historical tragedies and in personal frustrations. Now all this is as different from Pelagianism as it is different from pantheism. To use the social-science approach to make religion teaching more effective is to be more true to God, since it is more in accord and harmony with the natural rhythm of the facilitation of learning in which the power of God flows as initiation, enablement, fruition, and completion.

Despookification of Religious Instruction

The research data on teaching and learning adduced throughout this book, all set in a backdrop of a God-full nature, suggest that effective religion teaching ought not to be explained in terms of any amorphous, spooky conception of the mysterious workings of God in the religious instruction act. Effective teaching is effective teaching, whether this be mathematics teaching, literature teaching, or religion teaching. The research has shown that teacher behavior does make a significant difference in the kind and amount of learning which takes place. Further, specific teacher behaviors do tend to elicit specific predictable learner behaviors. To posit a spooky explanation for religion teaching, to assert that its effectiveness is due to God mysteriously floating and operating in the pedagogical dynamic, is to divert attention from the very area in which attention is needed, namely the improvement of teaching. Spookifying religious instruction, as is so frequently done, seriously cripples any attempt to create a more effective religious pedagogy. To be sure, a despookification of religious instruction is the basic prerequisite and precondition for undertaking the fashioning of a truly successful program of religious instruction.

CONCLUSION

This book represents an application of the social-science approach to the pedagogical dynamic of teaching religion. This book also suggests that in the fashioning of a new religious instruction, the first step is to radicate the teaching of religion in a social-science framework. Just as the theological approach represents the adequate framework for theologizing, so does the social-science approach constitute the proper framework for religion teaching. Placing religious instruction in a social-science framework will do much to eliminate a good deal of its present fuzziness, a fuzziness typically caused by its being grounded in a foreign soil, namely theology. Social science is the genuine *métier* for religion teaching; it is here that religion teaching can truly achieve its potential. The isolation of religious instruction from the mainstream of general education and of social science accounts in part for the great fuzziness and amorphousness and spookiness which plague it. Apropos of this, Eugene Hemrick writes concerning his experiences working with inservice religion teachers in the field:

> [There is] much good will but very little controlled planning or sense of [pedagogical] direction. Goal setting is poorly operationalized, cause-effect relationships seldom put down on paper, and hypotheses are foreign language to most [religion teachers]. They still want the package with all the goodies they can take home and communicate to their students.[45]

It is only from a social-science base that a theory and practice unique to teaching can be developed.

With his usual perceptive insight, André Godin believes that the following observations are valid concerning religious instruction in both the United States and Europe: new ideas are rarely adopted on the basis of their empirically-demonstrated worth; they are seldom the object of systematic methodological evaluation; they "simply burst in from other areas of life."[46] Whatever reforms and realignments have taken place in religious instruction in the past few years are typically due not to data on teaching and learning, but rather to widespread discontent with religious instruction or to social and ecclesiastical pressures from outside. When a field such as religious instruction does not have from within the proper foundation or adequate machinery to generate improvements on the basis of empirical data on its effectiveness, one can only wonder if the field is either a nonentity or is bankrupt in its present framework. I believe that religious instruction is far from being a nonentity. The problem lies in the fact that its present framework, the theological approach, is by its own nature an inadequate base for religion teaching. It is not that the theology has been bad; rather it is that theology has been asked to do too much. Theology cannot tell us the most effective way to split the atom or how best to write poetry or how to teach religion. These are jobs for physical science and literary science and social science respectively.

In a kind of resistance to the social-science approach, some religious educators advance the fallacious argument that religious dimensions of teaching and learning are inaccessible to scientific investigation, and that the social-science approach is therefore inadequate for religion teaching. This argument fails because it ignores the very obvious fact that religion is a human phenomenon and therefore is amenable to empirical as well as to nonempirical investigation. To be sure, subjective phenomena are more difficult to examine than so-called objective phenomena, but this is far different from saying that subjective phenomena cannot be discerned and examined.[47] Indeed, if a person's religiosity cannot be assessed, then how can anyone, priest or layman, parent or educator make a valid assertion as to whether another person is religious or not, or even if he himself is religious? It is an irony of logic that those religious educators who oppose the social-science approach because they believe religious behavior cannot be scientifically discerned are actually espousing a form of that very behaviorism which gave rise to their presupposition. Behaviorism, it will be recalled, concentrates its attention exclusively on objective phenomena, contending that subjective phenomena cannot be examined and therefore most probably do not exist.

Merton Strommen reminds us that social science is not some kind of new authority opposed to theological science. Rather, social science is another way of listening to God and understanding his revelation.[48] Much of the improvement in certain sectors of the world has come through the use of theological science, but much of the improvement in other sectors has resulted from an application of social science and natural science and so forth. The task is to match the right science with the right sector. For religious instruction, the correct match is social science.

In our era there exists an urgent need in the area of religious instruction, namely a reconstruction of the entire field from basic theory right on down to the most particularized pedagogical step. A firstfruit of the social-science approach to religious instruction is the bringing to pass of such a basic reconstruction. To become truly effective, religious instruction must go social science; it can no longer postpone its appointment with history or with itself.

NOTES–CHAPTER I

1. Albert Camus, *The Plague,* translated by Stuart Gilbert (New York: Modern Library, 1948), p. 58.
2. See, for example, Thomas Aquinas, De Veritate, q. 11, a.1, ad.1. In the *Shape of Religious Instruction* (Dayton, Ohio: Pflaum/Standard, 1971) I make the crucial distinction among the discrete educational activities of instruction, guidance, and administration. To reinforce what I stated in the "Preface," *The Shape of Religious Instruction* lays the basic foundations for the social-science approach to religious instruction; consequently a familiarity with this work is necessary or at least very helpful for an adequate understanding of the present volume.
3. To be sure there are some current investigators of the teaching process who conceptualize teaching as the aiming or the intending by the teacher to bring about learning, rather than the actual effecting of the desired learning outcome. Nevertheless, the long-standing pedagogical, psychological, and philosophical tradition has been to regard teaching not simply in terms of the intentions of the teacher but rather in terms of the causation of learning. If teacher intention were the criterion of teaching, then in one sense every teacher would be *eo ipso* effective, which is patently absurd. On this point of teaching as teacher intentionality, see Ronald T. Hyman, "Introduction," in Ronald T. Hyman, editor, *TEACHING: Vantage Points for Study* (Philadelphia: Lippincott, 1968), pp. 7-8.
4. Anyone even vaguely familiar with scholarly investigation into the teaching-learning act knows that "behavior" is the generic term used to indicate *any* activity of the human organism. Yet it would appear that all too many Catholic religious educationists are not yet aware of this rather basic usage. These men seem to believe that the word "behavior" is simply a contraction of "overt behavior." Quite possibly this defect in understanding is due to the fact that the majority of Catholic religious educationists are theologians who have little or no background in education or social science. For a representative example of this mentality, see Michael Donnellan, "Review," in *The American Ecclesiastical Review,* CLV, (November, 1971), p. 210.
5. See Sylvester Wevitavidanelage, "New Directions in Catechetics in the Missions," in Alois Müller, editor, *Catechetics for the Future* (New York: Herder and Herder, 1970), pp. 77-83.
6. Gerard Sloyan, *Speaking of Religious Education* (New York: Herder and Herder, 1968), p. 67.
7. See, for example, Ivan Illich, *De-Schooling Society* (New York: Harper & Row, 1971).

8. "Hip-pocket data" is a term I employ to mean impressionistic data which an individual has gathered primarily from his own experience, filtered through his own perceptual system, and typically encoded by himself into a general law of behavior presumed to hold true for classes of individuals or situations. The individual sits on these data, absorbing them in the process; from time to time he proceeds to whip the data out of his hip pocket when he needs to explain phenomena.

9. At least one well-executed empirical study has concluded that the majority of Catholic and non-Catholic adults surveyed felt their children needed religious instruction programs in formal settings. This finding was particularly true of the Catholic respondents. John D. Donovan and George F. Madaus, "The Quality of Religious Education: An Interdenominational View," in *The Living Light*, VII, (Fall 1970), pp. 43-56.

10. James Michael Lee, *The Shape of Religious Instruction*, p. 7.

11. Marist House, located in La Porte, Indiana, was forced to close down because of strong opposition from several local pastors and lack of support by the bishops.

12. I say "can have" because some empirical investigations of Catholic schooling suggest that while such experiences seem to have an enhancing effect upon the learner's religious knowledge and incidence of religious practice, nonetheless they do not appear to have a marked deep positive effect on his religious behavior. See, for example, Andrew M. Greeley and Peter H. Rossi, *The Education of Catholic Americans* (Chicago: Aldine, 1966).

13. On this point, see Gabriel Moran, *Design for Religion* (New York: Herder and Herder, 1970), p. 78.

NOTES—CHAPTER II

1. E. M. Forster, *A Passage to India* (New York: Harcourt, Brace and World, 1924), p. 257.

2. It should be observed that many writers and speakers on this topic have tended to equate schooling with the actual classroom or learning situation itself, whether that situation is religion class, mathematics class, or history class. Hence there is validity, or at least usefulness, in applying their conceptualizations to the primary proximate purpose of religious instruction.

3. See, for example, Vincent Edward Smith, *The School Examined: Its Aims and Content* (Milwaukee: Bruce, 1960). For Smith, the school is identified solely with "learning from a teacher in the strict sense" (p. 33 footnote).

4. Neil G. McCluskey, *Catholic Viewpoint in Education*, 2d ed.

(Garden City, N.Y.: Doubleday, 1962), pp. 60-61.

5. Kevin O'Brien *The Proximate Aim of Education* (Milwaukee: Bruce, 1958); see also Barbara Zulinska, *Ad Resurrectionem: New Perspectives in Catholic Education,* translated by Mary Gertrude (Trenton, N.J.: White Eagle, 1962).

6. James Michael Lee, *The Purpose of Catholic Schooling* (Dayton, Ohio: National Catholic Educational Association and Pflaum/Standard, 1968).

7. James Michael Lee, *The Shape of Religious Instruction* (Dayton, Ohio: Pflaum/Standard, 1971), p. 11. See also Randolph Crump Miller, "The Objective of Christian Education," in Marvin J. Taylor, editor, *An Introduction to Christian Education* (Nashville, Tenn.: Abingdon, 1966), pp. 94-104; also Paul H. Vieth, *How to Teach in the Church School* (Philadelphia: Westminster, 1937), pp. 14-16.

8. See Charles Y. Glock, "On the Study of Religious Commitment," in *Religious Education,* research supplement, LVII (July-August 1962), pp. s-98–s-110. In the third category I have substituted the word "affective" for Glock's term "experiential."

9. Reginald A. Neuwien, editor, *Catholic Schools in Action: A Report* (Notre Dame, Ind.: University of Notre Dame Press, 1966).

10. Andrew M. Greeley and Peter H. Rossi, *The Education of Catholic Americans* (Chicago: Aldine, 1966).

11. John D. Donovan and George F. Madaus, "The Quality of Religious Education: An Interdenominational View," in *The Living Light,* VII, (Fall, 1970), pp. 43-56.

NOTES–CHAPTER III

1. Hermann Hesse, *Demian,* translated by Michael Roloff and Michael Lebeck (New York: Harper & Row, 1965), p. 46.

2. An educationist is a scholar who specializes in the scientific aspects of the theory and practice of education, while an educator is a practitioner of the art-science of education.

3. Gabriel Moran, *Design for Religion* (New York: Herder and Herder, 1970), p. 91.

4. For a fuller treatment of the distinction between theology and religion, see James Michael Lee, *The Shape of Religious Instruction* (Dayton, Ohio: Pflaum/Standard, 1971), pp. 249-253.

5. G. van Ackeren, "Theology," in *New Catholic Encyclopedia,* volume XIV (New York: McGraw-Hill, 1967), p. 39.

6. Emil Brunner, *Truth as Encounter,* translated by Amandus W. Loos and David Cairns (Philadelphia: Westminster, 1943), p. 113.

7. This point can easily be exemplified in an examination of the 1971 document on the permanency of the priesthood and apostolic succession, a document drawn up by a team of "old" and "new" American Catholic theologians. See Bishops' Subcommittee -on the Systematic Theology of the Priesthood—"Final Reports—Excerpts," *National Catholic Reporter*, VII, (October 8, 1971), p. 14.
8. This point is also made by Edward Schillebeeckx in his *Revelation and Theology*, volume I. translated by N. D. Smith (New York: Sheed and Ward, 1967), pp. 93-100.
9. See Karl Barth, *The Word of God and the Word of Man*, translated by Douglas Horton (New York: Harper Torchbacks, 1957), p. 54.
10. Edward George Bozzo, "Theology and Religious Experience," in *Theological Studies*. XXXI (September 1970). p. 435.
11. Kenneth D. Eberhard, "Involving Students in Theological Thinking," in *The Living Light*, VII (Winter 1970), pp. 67-68.
12. Paul Tillich, *Systematic Theology*, volume I (Chicago: University of Chicago Press, 1951), p. 3.
13. See the perceptive essay by Thomas F. O'Meara and Donald M. Weisser, "Afterword: The End of Theology?" in Thomas F. O'Meara and Donald M. Weisser, editors, *Projections: Shaping of an American Theology for the Future* (New York: Doubleday, 1970), pp. 217-228. Both O'Meara and Weisser have been deeply influenced by Tillich's thought, especially with respect to the theologian's basic task of reflecting and articulating the "living import" of theology in contemporary culture.
14. This type of existential mediatorship is beyond the scope, range, and capabilities of theology precisely because of the kind of science theology is. A comparative analysis of the fundamentally different forms of prediction, verification, facilitation, empirical control, and so forth bears this out. For a fuller treatment, see James Michael Lee, *The Shape of Religious Instruction*, pp. 101-224; also James Michael Lee, "Prediction in Religious Instruction," in *The Living Light*, in press. John van der Beek reminds me that theology is a cognitive mediator while religious instruction is a more fully existential mediator.
15. This definition is substantially the same as that given by Otto Semmelroth in his article "Mediatorship," in Karl Rahner et al., editors, *Sacramentum Mundi: An Encyclopedia of Theology*, volume IV (New York: Herder and Herder, 1969), p. 9. I am treating in this section of the mediation process in general and not specifically of Jesus Christ as mediator. On the latter point, see Emil Brunner, *The Mediator*, translated by Olive Wyon (Philadelphia: Westminster, 1947).

16. See "mediator" in Karl Rahner and Herbert Vorgrimler, *Theological Dictionary*, translated by Richard Strachan (New York: Herder and Herder, 1965), p. 281.

17. See James Michael Lee, "Religious Education: What Is It?" in *Discovery: A Forum for High School Religion Teachers*, published by the Webster Division of McGraw-Hill, I (March 1968), pp. 1-3.

18. For a representative example of this mentality, see Josef Goldbrunner, "Catechetical Method as Handmaid of Kerygma," in Johannes Hofinger, editor, *Teaching All Nations: A Symposium on Modern Catechetics*, revised and partly translated by Clifford Howell (New York: Herder and Herder, 1961), pp. 108-121.

19. In *The Shape of Religious Instruction* I discuss more fully the notion of religious instruction as messenger boy.

20. For a representative example, see Randolph Crump Miller, *The Clue to Christian Education* (New York: Scribner's, 1950), p. 8.

21. As I will suggest in a later chapter, "method" is a precise term and is not used correctly here. But since "method" is the term typically employed by religious educationists in treating of this duality, I shall retain the usage in this instance.

22. This concept of religious instruction as mediation is a highly fruitful one, and I hope someone will mine its riches more fully than limited space permits here. It is a sophisticated concept and consequently requires sophisticated analysis. As such it is probably beyond the ken of a mentality such as that represented in Michael Warren's "All Contributions Cheerfully Accepted," in *The Living Light*, VII (Winter 1970), pp. 26-28. Used with permission of Our Sunday Visitor.

23. I am conceptualizing "theologizing" to mean both one's reflection and the expression of that reflection from a theological vantage point. Thus theologizing can take place in theological activity properly considered (within the parameters and according to the methodological norms of theological science) or in various levels of everyday living.

24. For a representative and unequivocal treatment of this view, see James D. Smart, *The Teaching Ministry of the Church* (Philadelphia: Westminster, 1954).

25. I am not implying in this statement that there are two different theologies. Rather, there is only one theology, the configuration of which is influenced and to a degree shaped by the functional relationship in which it is situated. Configuration, of course, consists in the specific arrangement of the parts of a given whole.

26. Gabriel Moran, *Theology of Revelation* (New York: Herder and

Herder, 1966), p. 35.

27. I am not here using "relation" in the same way as Martin Buber does in his *I and Thou* (New York: Scribner's, 1958).

28. Two taxonomies of educational objectives, one for cognitive outcomes and the other for affective outcomes have already been developed. See Benjamin S. Bloom et al., *Taxonomy of Educational Objectives: Handbook I: Cognitive Domain* (New York: McKay, 1956); David R. Krathwohl, Benjamin S. Bloom, and Bertram B. Masia, *Taxonomy of Educational Objectives: Handbook II: Affective Domain* (New York: McKay, 1964).

29. Gabriel Moran, *Catechesis of Revelation* (New York: Herder and Herder, 1966), p. 71.

30. *Ibid.,* pp. 143-145. I have never found a single theologian who has satisfactorily worked his way out of this dilemma. To be sure, most persons who explicitly or implicitly adhere to the proposition that religious instruction is at bottom theological instruction seem never even to have seriously thought about this problem. Michael Warren is in this category. See Michael Warren, "All Contributions Cheerfully Accepted," pp. 20-33.

31. On this point see James Michael Lee, *Principles and Methods of Secondary Education* (New York: McGraw-Hill, 1963), pp. 270-274. Joint curricular decision-making should take place on all educational levels. In practice the most numerous experiments in this area have been in childhood education.

32. Gabriel Moran, *Catechesis of Revelation,* p. 144.

33. *Ibid.,* p. 70 and p. 68.

34. These teachers do, of course, say that the goal of religious instruction is Christian living. But when asked to indicate what Christian living is, they typically reply that it is the putting into practice, either now or usually later, of theological product content. Thus such teachers do in fact subscribe to the theological theory and not to social-science theory.

35. The toolbox metaphor is Brian Simpson's.

36. Gabriel Moran is an example of a blow theorist; to an extent so is Michael Warren.

37. Gabriel Moran, *Theology of Revelation,* p. 139.

38. I am indebted to Robert O'Gorman for drawing my attention to this point and for elaborating on it in his usual clear manner.

NOTES—CHAPTER IV

1. Margery Williams, *The Velveteen Rabbit* (Garden City, N.Y.: Doubleday, n.d.), p. 20.

2. John Dewey, *Democracy and Education* (New York: Macmillan, 1916), pp. 194-195. Italics deleted.

3. For earlier treatments of this point, see my essay "The *Teaching of Religion*," in James Michael Lee and Patrick C. Rooney, editors, *Toward a Future for Religious Education* (Dayton, Ohio: Pflaum/Standard, 1970). See also James Michael Lee, *Principles and Methods of Secondary Education* (New York: McGraw-Hill, 1963).

4. Marshall McLuhan, *Understanding Media: The Extensions of Man* (New York: McGraw-Hill, 1964).

5. Michael Warren, "All Contributions Cheerfully Accepted," in *The Living Light*, VII (Winter 1970), p. 26.

6. Gabriel Moran, "The Future of Catechetics," in *The Living Light*, V (Spring 1968), pp. 9-10.

7. Gabriel Moran, *Catechesis of Revelation* (New York: Herder and Herder, 1966), p. 38.

8. John Dewey, *Democracy and Education*, pp. 194-195.

9. Sara Little, *The Role of the Bible in Contemporary Christian Education* (Richmond, Va.: Knox, 1961), p. 174.

10. For a more complete discussion of religious instruction as messenger boy, see James Michael Lee, *The Shape of Religious Instruction* (Dayton, Ohio: Pflaum/Standard, 1971), pp. 246-248.

11. Josef Goldbrunner, "Catechetical Method as Handmaid of Kerygma," in Johannes Hofinger, editor, *Teaching All Nations: A Symposium on Modern Catechetics*, revised and partly translated by Clifford Howell (New York: Herder and Herder, 1961), p. 108.

12. Michael Warren, "Evaluating 'Christian Experience' Programs," in *The Living Light*, VII (Spring 1970), p. 92.

13. Frank B. Norris, "The Catechetics Course in the Major Seminary," in Johannes Hofinger and Theodore C. Stone, editors, *Pastoral Catechetics* (New York: Herder and Herder, 1964), p. 222.

14. Johannes Hofinger, *The Art of Teaching Christian Doctrine*, 2d ed. (Notre Dame, Ind.: University of Notre Dame Press, 1962), p. 64.

15. Sara Little, *The Role of the Bible in Contemporary Christian Education*, p. 7.

16. James C. Smart, *The Teaching Ministry of the Church* (Philadelphia: Westminster, 1954).

17. See Ronald T. Hyman, "Introduction," in Ronald T. Hyman, editor, *TEACHING: Vantage Points for Study* (Philadelphia: Lippincott, 1968), pp. 1-12.

18. Pierre Babin, *Methods*, translated and adapted by John F. Murphy (New York: Herder and Herder, 1967), p. 20.

19. Michael Warren, "All Contributions Cheerfully Accepted," p. 31.

20. Johannes Hofinger, *The Art of Teaching Christian Doctrine*, 2d ed., p. 63.
21. Randolph Crump Miller, *Education for Christian Living* (New York: Prentice-Hall, 1956), p. 9.
22. See James Michael Lee, "The Third Strategy: A Behavioral Approach to Religious Instruction," Parts 1, 2, and 3 in *Today's Catholic Teacher*, September 1969, pp. 10-12, 14, 27; October 1969, pp. 14-19; November 1969, pp. 22-27.
23. See James Michael Lee, *Principles and Methods in Secondary Education*, pp. 286-296.
24. Gerard S. Sloyan, "Catechetical Crossroads," in *Religious Education*, LIX (March-April 1964), p. 146.
25. John Dewey, *Democracy and Education*, p. 199.
26. Robert M. Gagné, "Instruction and the Conditions of Learning," in Laurence Siegel, editor, *INSTRUCTION: Some Contemporary Viewpoints* (San Francisco: Chandler, 1967), p. 309.
27. See Pauline S. Sears and Ernest R. Hilgard, "The Teacher's Role in the Motivation of the Learner," in National Society for the Study of Education, *Theories of Learning and Instruction*, Sixty-third Yearbook, part I (Chicago: University of Chicago Press, 1964), p. 194.
28. George B. Leonard, *Education and Ecstasy* (New York: Dell, 1968).
29. Pierre Babin, *Methods*, p. 19.
30. André Godin, "Importance and Difficulty of Scientific Research in Religious Education: The Problem of the 'Criterion'," in *Religious Education*, research supplement, LVII, (July-August 1962), p. s-167.
31. Merton P. Strommen, editor, *Research on Religious Development* (New York: Hawthorn, 1971).
32. André Godin, "Importance and Difficulty of Scientific Research in Religious Education," p. s-166. I substituted the word "teachers" for "professors" since the context appears to indicate that Richard Marius, the translator of Godin's article, rendered the word *"professeurs"* into the English "professors" without taking into account the culture-bound meaning of the original French word.
33. For a representative example of this type religion series, operating without a conscious empirically-verified research base, see Janaan Manternach and Carl J. Pfeifer, *Life, Love, Joy*, prepared under the auspices and direction of the National Center, Confraternity of Christian Doctrine.
34. Strangely Berard Marthaler, himself a theoretician, does not seem to understand this point. It would appear that he regards the usefulness of theory as reserved only for intellectuals, with

little relevancy for the workaday religion teacher. Quite the opposite, of course, is true. A religion teacher's effectiveness is in direct proportion to the explanatory and predictive power of the theory on which he consciously and unconsciously bases his very practical methodology and technique. See Berard L. Marthaler, "Review," in the *National Catholic Reporter,* VIII, (November 19, 1971), p. 8.

NOTES–CHAPTER V

1. Robert Bolt, *A Man for All Seasons,* Act 2 (New York: Random House, 1960), p. 92.
2. For a fuller discussion of the nature and function of theory, see James Michael Lee, *The Shape of Religious Instruction* (Dayton, Ohio: Pflaum/Standard, 1971), pp. 135-136, and 156-159.
3. On this point see Dwayne Huebner, "Curricular Language and Classroom Meanings," in James B. MacDonald and Robert R. Leeper, editors, *Language and Meaning* (Washington, D.C.: Association for Supervision and Curriculum Development, 1966), pp. 17-26.
4. Vladimir Ilyich Lenin, "What is to be Done?" in Henry M. Christman, editor, *Essential Works of Lenin* (New York: Bantam Books, 1966), p. 69.
5. B. Othanel Smith et al., *Teachers for the Real World* (Washington, D.C.: American Association of Colleges for Teacher Education, 1969), p. 28.
6. See James Michael Lee, "Prediction in Religious Instruction," in *The Living Light,* IX (Summer, 1972), pp. 43-54.
7. Ernest R. Hilgard, "A Perspective on the Relationship between Learning Theory and Educational Practices," in National Society for the Study of Education, *Theories of Learning and Instruction,* Sixty-third Yearbook, Part I (Chicago: University of Chicago Press, 1964), p. 411.
8. Paolo Freire, *Pedagogy of the Oppressed,* translated by Myra Bergman Ramos (New York: Herder and Herder, 1970), p. 119.
9. An examination of the programs of most universities offering the M.A. degree in religious education will readily confirm this fact.
10. Buford Stefflre and Kenneth Matheny, "Counseling Theory," in Robert L. Ebel, editor, *Encyclopedia of Educational Research,* 4th ed. (New York: Macmillan, 1969), p. 258.
11. There are theologians who maintain that church finance, church administration, and indeed church law and church history are part of theological science. See, for cxample, Virgilius Ferm, *A Protestant Dictionary* (New York: Philosophical Library, 1951),

p. 255; see also Donald E. Miller, "Religious Education as a Discipline: Christian Education as a Contextual Discipline," in *Religious Education,* LXII, (September-October 1967), p. 419; and [Yves] M. -J. Congar, "Théologie: ses divisions," in A. Vacant, E. Mangenot, and E. Ammann, editors, *Dictionnaire de Théologie Catholique,* tome 15, partie I (Paris: Letouzey et Ané, 1946), column 493.

12. Catholic curriculum builders, untrained as they generally are in education, typically fail to provide the teacher with any consistent set of instructional behaviors ordered on a taxonomic scale. Consequently the teachers' manuals they produce for use with their curricula are at best only minimally useful. See for example, the teacher's manual for the curriculum composed by Janaan Manternach and Carl J. Pfeifer entitled *Life, Love, Joy.*

13. Randolph Crump Miller, *The Clue to Christian Education* (New York: Scribner's, 1950), pp. 1-17.

14. Michael Warren takes this position. See Michael Warren, "All Contributions Cheerfully Accepted," in *The Living Light,* VII, (Winter, 1970), pp. 27-28.

15. See for example, Nels F. S. Ferré, *A Theology for Christian Education* (Philadelphia: Westminster, 1967), p. 171.

16. Karl Barth, *Church Dogmatics,* volume IV, part 3, 2nd half, translated by G. W. Bromiley (Edinburgh: Clark, 1962), p. 871.

17. Wayne Rood, "On *Christian* Religious Education," in *The Living Light,* VII, (Winter 1970), p. 9.

18. William Bedford Williamson, *Language and Concepts in Christian Education* ((Philadelphia: Westminster, 1970), p. 126.

19. Norman E. Wallen and Robert M. W. Travers, "Analysis and Investigation of Teaching Methods," in N. L. Gage, editor, *Handbook of Research on Teaching* (Chicago: Rand McNally, 1963), p. 465.

20. See Kenneth W. Spence, "Theoretical Interpretations of Learning," in S. S. Stevens, editor, *Handbook of Experimental Psychology* (New York: Wiley, 1951), pp. 690-691.

21. Robert M. Gagné, *The Conditions of Learning* (New York: Holt, Rinehart, and Winston, 1965).

22. It is for precisely this reason that I devoted a whole chapter in *The Shape of Religious Instruction* to the nature and relationship of the natural and the supernatural.

23. A. Morrison and D. McIntyre, *Teachers and Teaching* (Baltimore: Penguin, 1969), p. 57.

24. David P. Ausubel, "A Cognitive-Structure Theory of School Learning," in Laurence Siegel, editor, *INSTRUCTION: Some Contemporary Viewpoints* (San Francisco: Chandler, 1967), p. 213.

25. On this point see James Collins, "Introduction," in Thomas Aquinas, *The Teacher,* translated by James V. McGlynn (Chicago: Regnery Gateway, 1954), p. viii.
26. James Michael Lee, *Principles and Methods of Secondary Education* (New York: McGraw-Hill, 1963), p. 229.
27. The metaphor is Othanel Smith's. B. Othanel Smith, *Teachers for the Real World,* p. 35.
28. N. L. Gage, "Theories of Teaching," in National Society for the Study of Education, *Theories of Learning and Instruction,* p. 273.
29. N. L. Gage, "Theories of Teaching," p. 269. I have substituted the phrase "theory of teaching" for Gage's original "science and technology of teaching" because I believe Gage's phraseology does not accurately express his thesis, and indeed blurs it.
30. Ernest R. Hilgard, "A Perspective on the Relationship between Learning Theory and Educational Practices," in National Society for the Study of Education, *Theories of Learning and Instruction,* p. 402.
31. Ernest R. Hilgard, "A Perspective on the Relationship between Learning Theory and Educational Practices," p. 402.
32. Robert Glaser, "Learning," in Robert L. Ebel, editor, *Encyclopedia of Educational Research,* p. 706.
33. This analogy is drawn from N. L. Gage, "Paradigms for Research on Teaching," in N. L. Gage, editor, *Handbook of Research on Teaching* (Chicago: Rand McNally, 1963), p. 133.
34. Wayne Rood, "On *Christian* Religious Education," p. 11.
35. On this point, see N. L. Gage, "Paradigms for Research on Teaching," p. 133. The effects to which theory directly addresses itself are not, of course, specific effects; lower-order elements of the theory perform this function.
36. Sanford C. Erickson, "The Zigzag Curve of Learning," in Laurence Siegel, editor, *INSTRUCTION: Some Contemporary Viewpoints,* p. 143.
37. On this point, see Hans L. Zetterberg, *On Theory and Verification in Sociology* (Totowa, N.J.: Bedminster, 1965), p. 166.
38. See Chris D. Kehas, "Theoretical Formulations and Related Research," in *Review of Educational Research,* XXXVI, (April 1966), pp. 207-218.
39. Edmund J. Amidon and John B. Hough, "Chapter Overview," in Edmund J. Amidon and John B. Hough, editors, *Interaction Analysis: Theory, Research and Application* (Reading, Mass.: Addison-Wesley, 1967), p. 2.
40. As a consequence Murphy's book is virtually useless except as a sort of running account of what occurred in one teacher's classroom. Unfortunately too, Murphy hopelessly lumps to-

gether without distinction his own perceptions and the objective classroom events, making what could have been a highly useful book an even more useless one. Any student teacher would have known better. John F. Murphy, *The Catechetical Experience* (New York: Herder and Herder, 1968).

41. Louis M. Smith and William Geoffrey, *The Complexities of an Urban Classroom: An Analysis Toward a General Theory of Teaching* (New York: Holt, Rinehart and Winston, 1968).

42. Jerome Bruner, *Toward a Theory of Instruction*, p. 40.

43. *Ibid.*, pp. 40-42. Regrettably Bruner, a cognitive psychologist, adopts an almost exclusively intellectualist product-content orientation. This is inadequate as the *sole* base for identifying an all-embracing theory of instruction. Consequently I have expanded the dimensionalities of each of his four features in such a way as to include the entire range of instructional contents, namely product and process contents, cognitive and affective and lifestyle contents, verbal and nonverbal contents.

44. See David P. Ausubel, "A Cognitive-Structure Theory of School Learning," in Laurence Siegel, editor, *Instruction: Some Contemporary Viewpoints*, p. 213. I would take issue with Ausubel in his contention that teaching is just an application of or extension into the concrete of learning theory.

45. Elizabeth Steiner Maccia distinguishes four major kinds of theory: formal theory, event theory, valuational theory, and praxiological theory. See Elizabeth Steiner Maccia, "Curriculum Theory and Policy," Bureau of Educational Research and Services, The Ohio State University, 1965.

NOTES—CHAPTER VI

1. Ernest Hemingway, *For Whom the Bell Tolls* (New York: Scribner's, 1940), p. 11.

2. See Thomas Aquinas, *Expositio in Librum Beati Dionysii Divinis Nominibus*, cap. II, lect. 4. In Marietti edition (Torino, 1950), #176.

3. Learning findings are, of course, quite similar to and in many instances identical with laws of learning. See James Michael Lee, *The Shape of Religious Instruction* (Dayton, Ohio: Pflaum/Standard, 1971), pp. 154-156.

4. Ernest Hilgard, *Theories of Learning*, 2d ed. (New York: Appleton-Century-Crofts, 1956), p. 5.

5. Neal E. Miller and John Dollard, *Social Learning and Imitation* (New Haven, Conn.: Yale University Press, 1941), p. 21.

6. This definition and its elaboration are given in James Michael Lee, *Principles and Methods of Secondary Education* (New

York: McGraw-Hill, 1963), pp. 136-137.

7. Ronald Goldman, *Religious Thinking from Childhood to Adolescence* (London: Routledge and Kegan Paul, 1964), p. 66.

8. Norman E. Wallen and Robert M. W. Travers, "Analysis and Investigation of Teaching Methods," in N. L. Gage, editor, *Handbook of Research on Teaching* (Chicago: Rand McNally, 1963), p. 500.

9. James Michael Lee, *Principles and Methods of Secondary Education*, p. 144.

10. Jeffrey Keefe, "The Learning of Attitudes and Values," in James Michael Lee and Patrick C. Rooney, editors, *Toward a Future for Religious Education* (Dayton, Ohio: Pflaum/ Standard, 1970), pp. 30-54.

11. Bernard Berelson and Gary A. Steiner, *Human Behavior: An Inventory of Scientific Findings* (New York: Harcourt, Brace and World, 1964), p. 562.

12. Pierre Caillon, "The First Seven Years Are the Ones That Count," translated by Edward M. Bradley, in *Religious Education*, LXIII, (May-June 1968), p. 173. Earlier memories tend either to be the rare exceptions which prove the rule or, more typically, false memories.

13. John Bowlby, "The Nature of the Child's Tie to His Mother," in *International Journal of Psycho-Analysis*, XXXIX, Part 5 (1958) pp. 350-373.

14. René Spitz, *The First Year of Life* (New York: Norton, 1965).

15. Bruno Bettleheim, *The Empty Fortress* (New York: Free Press, 1967).

16. Bernard Berelson and Gary A. Steiner, *Human Behavior: An Inventory of Scientific Findings*, p. 75.

17. Benjamin S. Bloom, *Stability and Change in Human Characteristics* (New York: Wiley, 1964).

18. Lawrence Kohlberg, "Development of Moral Character and Moral Ideology," in Martin L. Hoffman and Lois Wladis Hoffman, editors, *Review of Child Development Research*, Volume I (New York: Russell Sage Foundation, 1964), p. 392.

19. *Ibid.*

20. Ira J. Gordon, "Social and Emotional Development," in Robert L. Ebel, editor, *Encyclopedia of Educational Research*, 4th ed. (New York: Macmillan, 1969), pp. 1222-1223.

21. Robert R. Sears, Eleanor E. Maccoby, and Harry Levin, *Patterns of Child Rearing* (Evanston, Ill.: Row, Peterson, 1957).

22. Bernard Berelson and Gary A. Steiner, *Human Behavior: An Inventory of Scientific Findings*, p. 66.

23. Robert F. Peck and Herbert Richek, "Adolescence," in Robert L. Ebel, editor, *Encyclopedia of Educational Research*, pp. 47-48.
24. Bernard Berelson and Gary A. Steiner, *Human Behavior: An Inventory of Scientific Findings*, p. 76.
25. Wesley C. Becker et al., "Factors in Parental Behavior and Personality as Related to Problem Behavior in Children," in *Journal of Consulting Psychology*, XXIII, (April, 1959), pp. 107-118.
26. Kurt Lewin, Ronald Lippitt, and Ralph K. White, "Patterns of Aggressive Behavior in Experimentally Created 'Social Climates'," in *Journal of Social Psychology*, X: *Bulletin of the Society for the Psychological Study of Social Issues*, May 1939, pp. 271-299.
27. Boyd McCandless, *Children and Adolescents* (New York: Holt, Rinehart and Winston, 1961), pp. 357-404.
28. Robert R. Sears et al., "Some Child-Rearing Antecedents of Aggression and Dependency in Young Children," in *Genetic Psychology Monographs*, XLVII, (May 1953), p. 214.
29. Leonard D. Eron et al., "Social Class, Parental Punishment for Aggression, and Child Aggression," in *Child Development*, XXXIV, (December 1963), pp. 849-867.
30. Donald W. MacKinnon, "Violation of Prohibition," in Henry A. Murray, *Explorations in Personality* (New York: Oxford, 1938), p. 498.
31. James J. Gallagher, "Gifted Children," in Robert L. Ebel, editor, *Encyclopedia of Educational Research*, p. 539.
32. Benjamin Fine, *1,000,000 Delinquents* (Cleveland: World, 1955), p. 151.
33. Leonard Berkowitz, *The Development of Motives and Values in the Child* (New York: Basic Books, 1964), p. 71.
34. Alfred L. Baldwin, Joan Kalhorn, and Fay Huffman Breese, "Patterns of Parent Behavior," *Psychological Monographs*, LVIII, no. 3 (1945), pp. 1-75.
35. Robert F. Peck and Robert J. Havighurst, *The Psychology of Character Development* (New York: Wiley, 1960).
36. John K. Coster, "Attitudes Toward School of High School Pupils from Three Income Levels," in *Journal of Educational Psychology*, XLIX, (April 1958), p. 65.
37. Robert J. Havighurst and Fay H. Breese, "Relation between Ability and Social Status in a Midwestern Community: III: Primary Mental Abilities," in *Journal of Educational Psychology*, XXXVIII, (April 1957), pp. 241-247.
38. Eleanor E. Maccoby, Patricia K. Gibbs, and Human Development Laboratory Staff, "Methods of Child-rearing in Two

Social Classes," in Celia Stendler, editor, *Readings in Child Behavior and Development,* 2d ed. (New York: Harcourt, Brace and World, 1964), pp. 272-287.

39. Jo Ann Stiles and Boyd McCandless, "Child Development," in Robert L. Ebel, editor, *Encyclopedia of Educational Research,* p. 121.

40. See James Michael Lee, "Catholic Education: The Winds of Change," in *Ave Maria,* CVII, (April 13, 1968), pp. 6-9, 29-31.

41. Robert F. Peck and Robert J. Havighurst, *The Psychology of Character Development.*

42. Andrew M. Greeley and Peter H. Rossi, *The Education of Catholic Americans* (Chicago: Aldine, 1966).

43. Ronald L. Johnstone, *The Effectiveness of Lutheran Elementary and Secondary Schools as Agencies of Christian Education* (St. Louis: Concordia, 1966).

44. Donald Arthur Erickson, "Differential Effects of Public and Sectarian Schooling on the Religiousness of the Child," unpublished doctoral dissertation, University of Chicago, 1962.

45. Sarah Frances Anders, "Religious Behavior of Church Families," in *Marriage and Family Living,* XVII, (February, 1955), pp. 54-57.

46. For a report of this study, see David O. Moberg, "Religious Practices," in Merton P. Strommen, editor, *Research on Religious Development* (New York: Hawthorn, 1971), p. 561.

47. Robert F. Peck and Robert J. Havighurst, *The Psychology of Character Development.*

48. B. F. Skinner, *Beyond Freedom and Dignity* (New York: Knopf, 1971), pp. 19-20.

49. Paul B. Maves, "Religious Development in Adulthood," in Merton P. Strommen, editor, *Research on Religious Development,* p. 782.

50. Sloan Wayland, "Social Context and the Adolescent," *What Shall the High School Teach?, Association for Supervision and Curriculum Development,* Fifty-sixth Yearbook (Washington: ASCD, 1956), p. 28.

51. E. B. Reutter, "The Sociology of Adolescence," in *American Journal of Sociology,* XLIII, (November 1937), pp. 414-427.

52. Robert F. Peck and Herbert Richek, "Adolescence," p. 44.

53. Benjamin S. Bloom, *Stability and Change in Human Characteristics,* (New York: Wiley, 1964).

54. Bernard Berelson and Gary A. Steiner, *Human Behavior: An Inventory of Scientific Findings,* p. 606.

55. Hortense Doyle, "The Self-Concept Studied in Relation to the Culture of Teen-age Boys and Girls in Canada, England, and the United States," unpublished doctoral dissertation, St.

Louis University, 1960.

56. James Michael Lee, *Principles and Methods in Secondary Education*, p. 531.

57. James S. Coleman, *The Adolescent Society* (New York: Free Press, 1961).

58. Irvin J. Lehman, "Some Socio-cultural Differences in Attitudes and Values," in *Journal of Educational Sociology*, XXXVI (September 1962), pp. 1-9.

59. Alice Wessel and M. Rita Flaherty, "Changes in CPI Scores after One Year in College," in *Journal of Psychology*, XVII, (January 1964), pp. 235-238.

60. Marie Francis Kenoyer, "The Influence of Religious Life on Three Levels of Perceptual Processes," unpublished doctoral dissertation, Fordham University, 1961.

61. Robert McKay Brooks, "The Former Major Seminarian: A Study of Change of Status," unpublished doctoral dissertation, University of Notre Dame, 1960.

62. For a review of the research, see James Michael Lee and Nathaniel J. Pallone, *Guidance and Counseling in Schools: Foundations and Processes* (New York: McGraw-Hill, 1966), pp. 317-320.

63. Edwin J. Thomas and Clifford F. Fink, "Effects of Group Size," in *Psychological Bulletin*, LX, (July 1963), pp. 371-384.

64. Robert F. Bales et al., "Structure and Dynamics of Small Groups," in Joseph B. Gittler, editor, *Review of Sociology: Analysis of a Decade* (New York: Wiley, 1957), pp. 391-417.

65. Jack R. Gibb, "The Effects of Group Size and Threat Reduction upon Creativity in a Problem-solving Situation." Paper presented at the Convention of the American Psychological Association, 1951.

66. Bernard Berelson and Gary A. Steiner, *Human Behavior: An Inventory of Scientific Findings*, p. 358.

67. D. W. Taylor and W. L. Faust, "Twenty Questions: Efficiency in Problem Solving as a Function of Size of Group," in *Journal of Experimental Psychology*, XLIV (November 1952), pp. 360-363.

68. Philip Slater, "Contrasting Correlates of Group Size," in *Sociometry*, XXI (June 1958), pp. 129-139.

69. R. C. Ziller, "Group Size: A Determinant of the Quality of Group Decisions," in *Sociometry*, XX, (September 1957), pp. 165-173.

70. Gwendolyn McConkie Cannon, "Kindergarten Class Size: A Study," in *Childhood Education*, XLIII, (September 1966), pp. 9-11.

71. William C. Kvaraceus, *Juvenile Delinquency* (Washington,

D.C.: Department of Classroom Teachers, National Education Association, 1958), p. 4.

72. James S. Coleman, *The Adolescent Society.*

73. Morton Deutsch, "The Effects of Co-operation and Competition upon Group Process," in Dorwin Cartwright and Alvin Zander, editors, *Group Dynamics: Research and Theory,* 3d ed. (New York: Harper & Row, 1968), pp. 461-482.

74. Merrill Roff, "Childhood Social Interactions and Young Adult Conduct," in *Journal of Abnormal and Social Psychology,* LXIII, (September 1961), pp. 333-337.

75. Samuel H. Cox, "Family Background Effects on Personality Development and Social Acceptance," Cooperative Research Contract No. OE 2-10-051, United States Office of Education, 1966.

76. S. B. Sells and Merrill Roff, "Peer Acceptance-Rejection and Personality Development," Cooperative Research Contract No. OE 2-10-05, United States Office of Education, 1966.

77. A. Morrison and D. McIntyre, *Teachers and Teaching* (Baltimore: Penguin, 1969), pp. 125-126.

78. S. E. Asch, "Effects of Group Pressure upon the Modification and Distortion of Judgments," in Harold Guetzkow, editor, *Groups, Leadership and Men: Research in Human Relations* (Pittsburgh: Carnegie Press, 1951), pp. 177-190.

79. Monroe Lefkowitz, Robert R. Blake, and Jane Srygley Mouton, "Status Factors in Pedestrian Violation of Traffic Signals," in *Journal of Abnormal and Social Psychology,* LI, (November 1955), pp. 704-706.

80. Herman Turk, Eugene L. Hartley, and David M. Shaw, "The Expectation of Social Influence," in *Journal of Social Psychology,* LVIII, (October 1962), pp. 23-29.

81. W. Lloyd Warner and Paul S. Lunt, *The Social Life of a Modern Community* (New Haven, Conn.: Yale University Press, 1941).

82. Refia Uğurel-Şemin, "Moral Behavior and Moral Judgment in Children," in *Journal of Abnormal and Social Psychology,* XLVII (April 1952), pp. 463-474.

83. Bernard Spilka, "Research on Religious Beliefs: A Critical Review," in Merton P. Strommen, editor, *Research on Religious Development,* pp. 498-500. Spilka notes that "criterion problems plague this research."

84. David O. Moberg, "Religious Practices," pp. 577-578.

85. Clement Cosgrove, "A Study of the Extent and Relationship between the Theoretical Knowledge and Practical Knowledge of Religious and Moral Truths and Principles among Catholic Elementary School Children," unpublished doctoral disserta-

tion, Fordham University, 1955.
86. Jack McClellan, "Creative Writing Characteristics of Children," unpublished doctoral dissertation, University of Southern California, 1956.
87. Jerome S. Bruner and Cecile C. Goodman, "Value and Need as Organizing Factors in Perception," in *Journal of Abnormal and Social Psychology*, XLII, (January 1947), pp. 33-44.
88. Bernard Berelson and Gary A. Steiner, *Human Behavior: An Inventory of Scientific Findings*, p. 639.
89. R. Srivastava and T. Peel, "Human Movement as a Function of Color Stimulation" (Topeka, Kans.: The Environmental Research Foundation, 1968, mimeographed).
90. Faber Birren, *Color Psychology and Color Therapy* (New Hyde Park, N.Y.: University Books. 1961).
91. Kurt Goldstein, "Some Experimental Observations Concerning the Influence of Colors on the Function of the Organism," in *Occupational Therapy and Rehabilitation*, XXI, (June 1942), pp. 147-151.
92. D. B. Harmon, "Lighting and the Eye," in *Illuminating Engineering*, XXXIX, (September 1944), pp. 481-500.
93. Cited in Faber Birren, *Color Psychology and Color Therapy*, pp. 272-276.
94. John W. Black, "The Effect of Room Characteristics upon Vocal Intensity and Rate," in *Journal of Acoustical Society of America*, XXII, (March 1950), pp. 174-176.
95. A. H. Maslow and Norbett L. Mintz, "Effects of Esthetic Surroundings: I. Initial Effects of Three Esthetic Conditions upon Perceiving 'Energy' and 'Well-being' in Faces," in *Journal of Psychology*, XLI, (April 1956), pp. 247-254.
96. Norbett L. Mintz, "Effects of Esthetic Surroundings: II. Prolonged and Repeated Experience in a 'Beautiful' and an 'Ugly' Room," in *Journal of Psychology*, XLI, (April 1956), pp. 459-466.
97. R. F. Srivastava and L. R. Good, "Patterns of Group Interaction in Three Architecturally Different Psychiatric Treatment Environments" (Topeka, Kan.: The Environmental Research Foundation, 1968, mimeographed).
98. Robert Sommer and Hugh Ross, "Social Interaction in a Geriatric Ward," in *International Journal of Social Psychiatry*, IV, (Autumn 1958), pp. 128-133.
99. Robert Sommer, "Studies in Personal Space," in *Sociometry*, XXII, (September 1959), pp. 247-260.
100. Clifford J. Drew, "Research on the Psychological-Behavioral Effects of the Physical Environment," in *Review of Educational Research*, XLI, (December 1971), pp. 447-465.

101. Carl Pfeifer, to cite just one example, seems to suggest that the use of differential environments to achieve differential learning outcomes is too bothersome and too impractical for the religion teacher. The research cited in this section exposes the superficiality and indeed the lack of learning-centeredness in Pfeifer's remark. See Carl J. Pfeifer, "Review," in *The Living Light*, VII, (Winter 1970), p. 134.

102. George B. Leonard, *Education and Ecstasy* (New York: Dell, 1968), pp. 19-20. Leonard is a popular essayist rather than a professional educationist; however, his book presents in highly readable form a rather good review of some relevant research on effective learning.

103. William H. Bexton, Woodburn Heron, and T. H. Scott, "Effects of Variation in the Sensory Environment," in *Canadian Journal of Psychology*, VIII, (June 1954), pp. 70-76.

104. Benjamin Bloom et al., *Compensatory Education for Cultural Deprivation* (New York: Holt, Rinehart and Winston, 1965).

105. Wayne Dennis, "Causes of Retardation Among Institutional Children: Iran," in Celia B. Stendler, editor, *Readings in Child Behavior and Development* (New York: Harcourt, Brace and World, 1964), pp. 93-101; see also William Goldfarb, "Psychological Privation in Infancy and Subsequent Adjustment," in *American Journal of Orthopsychiatry*, XV, (April 1945), pp. 247-255.

106. Benjamin Bloom, "Race and Social Class as Separate Factors Related to Social Environment," paper presented at the convention of the American Psychological Association, 1963.

107. Edith M. Dowley, "Early Childhood Education," in Robert L. Ebel, editor, *Encyclopedia of Educational Research*, p. 317.

108. Leon J. Yarrow, "Separation from Parents during Early Childhood," in Martin L. Hoffman and Lois W. Hoffman, editors, *Review of Child Development and Research*, pp. 89-136.

109. Norman E. Wallen and Robert M. W. Travers, "Analysis and Investigation of Teaching Methods," p. 499.

110. B. F. Skinner, *Science and Human Behavior* (New York: Macmillan, 1958).

111. Carl R. Rogers, *Client-Centered Therapy* (Boston: Houghton Mifflin, 1951).

112. H. J. Eysenck and S. Rachman, *The Causes and Cures of Neurosis* (London: Routledge and Kegan Paul, 1965).

113. Edgar Dale, *Audio-Visual Methods in Teaching*, revised edition (New York: Holt, Rinehart and Winston, 1954), pp. 42-56.

114. Yvonne Sayegh and Wayne Dennis, "The Effect of Supplementary Experiences upon the Behavioral Development of Infants in Institutions," in *Child Development*, XXXVI,

(March 1965), pp. 81-90.

115. John Dewey, *Experience and Education* (New York: Macmillan, 1938).

116. Michael G. Lawler, "Let's Take a Look—Again—at Experience," in *Religious Education*, LXVI, (September-October 1971); pp. 341-347.

117. Lee J. Cronbach, *Educational Psychology*, 2d ed. (New York: Harcourt, Brace and World, 1963), p. 342.

118. Bernard Berelson and Gary A. Steiner, *Human Behavior: An Inventory of Scientific Findings*, p. 181.

119. John Withall, "The Development of a Technique for the Measurement of Social-Emotional Climate in Classrooms," in *Journal of Experimental Education*, XVII, (June 1949), p. 347.

120. Benton J. Underwood, "Laboratory Studies of Verbal Learning," in National Society for the Study of Education, *Theories of Learning and Instruction*, Sixty-third Yearbook, Part I (Chicago: University of Chicago Press, 1964), p. 142.

121. Bernard Berelson and Gary A. Steiner, *Human Behavior: An Inventory of Scientific Findings*, p. 166. See also James Michael Lee, *Principles and Methods of Secondary Education*, p. 154.

122. David P. Ausubel, "A Cognitive-structure Theory of School Learning," in Laurence Siegel, editor, *Instruction: Some Contemporary Viewpoints* (San Francisco: Chandler, 1967), p. 209.

123. Glenn Terrell, Jr., and Wallace A. Kennedy, "Discrimination Learning and Transposition in Children as a Function of the Nature of the Reward," in *Journal of Experimental Psychology*, LIII, (April 1957), pp. 257-260; Glenn Terrell, Jr., Kathryn Durkin, and Melvin Wiesley, "Social Class and the Nature of the Incentive in Discrimination Learning," in *Journal of Abnormal and Social Psychology*, LIX, (September 1959), pp. 270-272.

124. Bernard Berelson and Gary A. Steiner, *Human Behavior: An Inventory of Scientific Findings*, pp. 261-267.

125. James Michael Lee, *Principles and Methods of Secondary Education*, p. 154.

126. Charles M. Lucas and John E. Horrocks, "An Experimental Approach to the Analysis of Adolescent Needs," in *Child Development*, XXXI, (September 1960), pp. 479-487.

127. National Association of Secondary-School Principals, *Planning for American Youth*, revised edition (Washington: The Association, 1951), p. 9.

128. Robert Havighurst, *Developmental Tasks in Education*, 2d ed.

(New York: Wiley, 1952).
129. James Michael Lee, *Principles and Methods of Secondary Education*, pp. 167-170.
130. Robert K. Merton, *Mass Persuasion* (New York: Harper & Brothers, 1946).
131. This is a highly complex psychological and philosophical issue and I can do no more than raise the point.
132. For a brief discussion of the structured learning strategy, see James Michael Lee, "The *Teaching* of Religion," in James Michael Lee and Patrick C. Rooney, editors, *Toward a Future for Religious Education* (Dayton, Ohio: Pflaum/Standard, 1970), pp. 55-92.
133. Bernard Spilka and Paul H. Werme, "Religious and Mental Disorders: A Research Perspective," in Merton P. Strommen, editor, *Research on Religious Development*, pp. 473-474.
134. Theories explaining reinforcement are many and varied; one only has to think of classical conditioning and operant conditioning theories, or more generally of behaviorism and gestaltism. Space does not permit a detailed comparison of these theories, or of the different terminology they employ (for example, cognitive theorists typically refer to reinforcement as "feedback"). But a brief word might be in order concerning the distinction between classical conditioning theory and operant conditioning theory. The primary distinction is that in classical conditioning the organism's response has no environmental effects, whereas in operant conditioning the learned response does have effects upon them and can therefore be truly adaptive to the situation. Respondent behavior is elicited reflexively by particular stimuli while operant behavior is emitted by the organism without having any particular identifiable eliciting stimulus. B. F. Skinner was one of the first to make this clear distinction between elicited behavior (basis of classical conditioning theory) and emitted behavior (basis of operant conditioning theory). Operant conditioning refers to a kind of behavior under the control of its consequences, for example, rewards and punishments. Elicited behavior (for example, reflex response of closure and meaning when the eye reads a particular word on a page) tends to be less free and less under the conscious control of the individual than emitted behavior (the choice-response an individual can make to answer or not to answer a ringing telephone). Elicited behavior, then, is under the direct control of the stimulus, while emitted behavior is under the control of environmental contingencies varying in intensity and power. Despite the divergent theories of reinforcement, it is an established fact

that a behavior is acquired as a result of a contingent response of an organism to a consequent event. There may be a few neo-Rogerians who would attempt to deny this fact of learning; yet an examination of their own therapeutic methods reveals that they not only employ specific reinforcers (for example, verbal reinforcers such as "um-mm" and nonverbal reinforcers such as head-nodding) but also generalized reinforcers (conveying to the patient or client the feeling that the therapist has unconditional and positive regard for him). For an extended treatment of conditioning theory, see Ernest R. Hilgard and Donald G. Marquis, *Conditioning and Learning,* revised by Gregory A. Kimble (New York: Appleton-Century-Crofts, 1961).

135. Robert Glaser, "Learning," in Robert L. Ebel, editor, *Encyclopedia of Educational Research,* p. 712.
136. Douglas H. Lawrence and Leon Festinger, *Deterrents and Reinforcements: The Psychology of Insufficient Reward* (Palo Alto, Calif.: Stanford University Press, 1962).
137. Lee J. Cronbach, *Educational Psychology,* p. 492.
138. Secondary reinforcement in the system of operant conditioning is analogous to the higher-order conditioning of the classical theory. It should be noted that there is no complete consensus among psychologists on what precisely constitutes primary and secondary reinforcers.
139. Ernest R. Hilgard, *Introduction to Psychology,* 3d ed. (New York: Harcourt, Brace and World, 1962), p. 262.
140. Dewey Lipe and Steven M. Jung, "Manipulating Incentives to Enhance School Learning," in *Review of Educational Research,* XLI, (October 1971), p. 257.
141. Gilbert Sax, "Concept Formation," in Robert L. Ebel, editor, *Encyclopedia of Educational Research,* p. 198. This finding holds true not only for concept learning but for virtually all other kinds of learning as well.
142. Ernest R. Hilgard and Donald G. Marquis, *Conditioning and Learning.*
143. Dewey Lipe and Steven M. Jung, "Manipulating Incentives to Enhance School Learning," pp. 270-271.
144. Robert G. Packard, "The Control of 'Classroom Attention': A Group Contingency for Complex Behavior," in *Journal of Applied Behavior Analysis,* III, (Spring 1970), pp. 13-28.
145. Harry Helson, *Adaptation Level Theory* (New York: Harper & Row, 1964).
146. There are also other forms of reinforcement schedules including the tandem schedule, the rate-reinforcement schedule, the multiple schedule, the concurrent schedule, and perhaps most

importantly, the chained schedule. Space limitations preclude more than a mere mention of these variations. See G. S. Reynolds, *A Primer of Operant Conditioning.* (Glenview, Ill.: Scott, Foresman, 1968), pp. 59-93.

147. B. F. Skinner, *Science and Human Behavior* (New York: Macmillan, 1953), pp. 99-106.
148. B. F. Skinner, *Beyond Freedom and Dignity,* p. 179.
149. Ernest Hilgard and Donald G. Marquis, *Conditioning and Learning,* p. 166.
150. Bernard Berelson and Gary A. Steiner, *Human Behavior: An Inventory of Scientific Findings,* p. 144.
151. James Michael Lee and Nathaniel J. Pallone, *Guidance and Counseling in Schools: Foundations and Processes,* p. 266.
152. *Ibid.*
153. William S. Verplanck, "The Control of the Content of Conversation: Reinforcement of Statements of Opinion," in *Journal of Abnormal and Social Psychology,* LVI, (November 1955), pp. 668-676.
154. Don R. Thomas, Wesley C. Becker, and Marianne Armstrong, "Production and Elimination of Disruptive Behavior by Systematically Varying Teacher Behavior," in *Journal of Applied Behavior Analysis,* I, (Spring 1968), pp. 35-45.
155. Elizabeth B. Hurlock, "An Evaluation of Certain Incentives Used in School Work," in *Journal of Educational Psychology,* XVI, (March 1925), pp. 145-149.
156. Harold W. Stevenson and Leila C. Snyder, "Performance as a Function of the Interaction of Incentive Conditions," in *Journal of Personality,* XXVIII, (March 1960), p. 1.
157. Bonnie B. Tyler, "Expectancy for Eventual Success as a Factor in Problem-solving Behavior," in *Journal of Educational Psychology,* XLIX, (June 1958), p. 167.
158. G. G. Thompson and C. W. Hunnicutt, "Effect of Repeated Praise or Blame on the Work Achievement of Introverts and Extroverts," in *Journal of Educational Psychology,* XXXV, (May 1944), pp. 257-266.
159. Gerald R. Levin and John J. Simmons, "Response to Praise by Emotionally Disturbed Boys," in *Psychological Reports,* XI, (August 1962), p. 10.
160. Dewey Lipe and Steven M. Jung, "Manipulating Incentives to Enhance School Learning," pp. 249-280.
161. Lee J. Cronbach, *Educational Psychology,* p. 492.
162. James M. Hedegard, "An Overview of Historical Formulations," in Laurence Siegel, *Instruction: Some Contemporary Viewpoints,* p. 11.
163. Robert Glaser, "Learning," p. 715.

164. See Kenneth H. Wodtke and Bobby R. Brown, "Social Learning and Imitation," in *Review of Educational Research,* XXXVII, (December 1967), pp. 514-538.

165. B. Othanel Smith, "Discipline," in Robert L. Ebel, editor, *Encyclopedia of Educational Research,* p. 294.

166. Jacob S. Kounin and Paul V. Gump, "The Comparative Influences of Punitive and Nonpunitive Teachers upon Children's Conceptions of Misconduct," in *Journal of Educational Psychology,* LII, (February 1961), p. 49.

167. Sheldon Glueck and Eleanor Glueck, *Unravelling Juvenile Delinquency* (Cambridge, Mass.: Harvard University Press, 1950), p. 132.

168. John W. M. Whiting and Irvin L. Child, *Child Training and Personality* (New Haven, Conn.: Yale University Press, 1953).

169. B. F. Skinner, *Beyond Freedom and Dignity,* p. 62.

170. See, for example, Roger V. Burton, Eleanor E. Maccoby, and Wesley Allinsmith, "Antecedents of Resistance to Temptation in Four-Year-Old Children," in *Child Development,* XXXII, (December 1961), pp. 689-710.

171. Francis L. Harmon, *Principles of Psychology,* revised edition (Milwaukee: Bruce, 1951), p. 536.

172. William A. Kelly, *Educational Psychology,* 4th ed. (Milwaukee: Bruce, 1956), pp. 290-292.

173. Marion Panyan, Howard Boozer, and Nancy Morris, "Feedback to Attendants for Applying Operant Techniques," in *Journal of Applied Behavioral Analysis,* III, (Spring 1970), pp. 1-4.

174. R. Vance Hall, Diane Lund, and Deloris Jackson, "Effects of Teacher Attention on Study Behavior," in *Journal of Applied Behavior Analysis,* I, (Spring 1968), pp. 1-12.

175. David P. Ausubel, "A Cognitive-Structure Theory of School Learning," p. 256.

176. Hani Van De Riet, "Effects of Praise and Reproof on Paired-Associate Learning in Educationally Retarded Children," in *Journal of Educational Psychology,* LV, (June 1964), pp. 139-143.

177. Hershel Berkowitz, "Effects of Prior Experimenter-Subject Relationships on Reinforced Reaction Time of Schizophrenics and Normals," in *Journal of Abnormal and Social Psychology,* LXIX, (November 1964), pp. 522-530.

178. See Ruben M. Baron, "Social Reinforcement Effects as a Function of Social Reinforcement History," in *Psychological Review,* LXXIII, (November 1966), pp. 527-539.

179. Wallace A. Kennedy and Herman C. Willcutt, "Praise and Blame as Incentives," in *Psychological Bulletin,* LXII, (November 1964), pp. 323-332.

180. G. M. Della Piana and N. L. Gage, "Pupils' Values and the Validity of the Minnesota Teacher Attitude Inventory," in *Journal of Educational Psychology*, XLVI, (March 1955), pp. 167-178.
181. Lee J. Cronbach, *Educational Psychology*, p. 491.
182. Ernest R. Hilgard and David H. Russell, "Motivation in School Learning," in National Society for the Study of Education, *Learning and Instruction*, Forty-ninth Yearbook, Part I (Chicago: University of Chicago Press, 1950), p. 48.
183. Leonard Berkowitz, *The Development of Motives and Values in the Child*, pp. 81-82.
184. B. F. Skinner, *Beyond Freedom and Dignity*, p. 68.
185. M. E. Highfield and A. Pinsent, "A Survey of Rewards and Punishments in Schools," reported in A. Morrison and D. McIntyre, *Teachers and Teaching*, pp. 140-141.
186. Donald H. Kausler, "Aspiration Level as a Determinant of Performance," in *Journal of Personality*, XXVII, (September 1959), pp. 346-351.
187. Bernard Berelson and Gary A. Steiner, *Human Behavior: An Inventory of Scientific Findings*, p. 81.
188. Leonard Berkowitz, *The Development of Motives and Values in the Child*, p. 40.
189. David C. McClelland et al., *The Achievement Motive* (New York: Appleton-Century-Crofts, 1951), pp. 275-333.
190. A. Morrison and D. McIntyre, *Teachers and Teaching*, p. 128.
191. *Ibid.*, pp. 126-130.
192. Bernard C. Rosen, "Family Structure and Achievement Motivation," in *American Sociological Review*, XXVI, (August 1961), pp. 574-585.
193. Leonard Berkowitz, *The Development of Motives and Values in the Child*, p. 41.
194. David C. McClelland, *The Achieving Society* (Princeton, N.J.: Van Nostrand, 1961), pp. 404-406.
195. Robert F. Peck and Herbert Richek, "Adolescence," in Robert L. Ebel, editor, *Encyclopedia of Educational Research*, p. 47. See also Pauline S. Sears and Ernest R. Hilgard, "The Teacher's Role in the Motivation of the Learner," in National Society for the Study of Education, *Theories of Learning and Instruction*, Sixty-third Yearbook, Part I (Chicago: University of Chicago Press, 1964), p. 187.
196. Charles McArthur, "Personality Differences between Middle and Upper Classes," in *Journal of Abnormal and Social Psychology*, L, (May 1955), pp. 247-254.
197. See, for example, Bernard C. Rosen, "Race, Ethnicity and the Achievement Syndrome," in *American Sociological Review*,

XXIV, (February 1959), pp. 47-60.

198. Leonard Berkowitz, *The Development of Motives and Values in the Child*, pp. 24-25.

199. Gerhard Lenski, *The Religious Factor* (Garden City, N.Y.: Doubleday, 1961), p. 270.

200. Nathaniel J. Pallone, "Religious Authority and Social Perceptions: A Laboratory Exploration in Social Influence," in *Journal of Social Psychology*, LXVIII, (April 1966), pp. 229-241.

201. Francis A. Yeandel, "Social Authority and Social Perception: A Laboratory Study of the Effect of Pressure to Conform Perceptually Applied by Religious and Military Authority Surrogates," unpublished doctoral dissertation, University of Notre Dame, 1966.

202. Annette Walters and Ritamary Bradley, "Motivation and Religious Behavior," in Merton P. Strommen, editor, *Research on Religious Development*, p. 606.

203. John Tracy Ellis, "American Catholics and the Intellectual Life," in *Thought*, XXX, (Autumn 1955), pp. 351-388; see also Thomas F. O'Dea, *American Catholic Dilemma: An Inquiry into the Intellectual Life* (New York: Sheed & Ward, 1958).

204. Seymour Warkov and Andrew M. Greeley, "Parochial School Origins and Educational Achievement," in *American Sociological Review*, XXXI, (June 1966), p. 412.

205. John D. Donovan, *The Academic Man in the Catholic College* (New York: Sheed & Ward, 1964), pp. 151-168.

206. Albert J. Mayer and Harry Sharp, "Religious Preference and Worldly Success," in Richard D. Knudten, editor, *The Sociology of Religion* (New York: Appleton-Century-Crofts, 1967), pp. 344-345.

207. Seymour Warkov and Andrew M. Greeley, "Parochial School Origins and Educational Achievement," p. 414. The impact of the Second Vatican Council might provide fresh new data on the entire question raised in this section. But it would appear that within the Catholic Church it has been chiefly the intellectual and religious elite who by and large have been influenced by Vatican II. One can recall, for example, a study made in a heavily-Catholic New England diocese during the last year of the Council; the majority of the Catholics surveyed at that time had never even heard of the Council, and less than ten percent knew what the major issues were before Vatican II. Hence it is not at all certain or even probable that an updating of some of the survey data I mention here will yield contradictory results. In fact, some of the studies I cite, such as those

of Pallone, Yeandel, Donovan, and Mayer and Sharp were conducted during or following Vatican II.

208. Walter Mischel and Joan Grusec, "Waiting for Rewards and Punishments: Effects of Time and Probability on Choice," in *Journal of Personality and Social Psychology*, V, (January 1967), p. 24. In one sense delayed gratification is a form of delayed reinforcement.

209. Leonard Berkowitz, *The Development of Motives and Values in the Child*, p. 35.

210. Walter Mischel, "Delay of Gratification, Need for Achievement and Acquiescence in Another Culture," in *Journal of Abnormal and Social Psychology*, LXII, (May 1961), pp. 543-552.

211. Walter Mischel, "Preference for Delayed Reinforcement and Social Responsibility," in *Journal of Abnormal and Social Psychology*, LXII, (January 1961), pp. 1-7.

212. Roy W. Fairchild, "Delayed Gratification: A Psychological and Religious Analysis," in Merton P. Strommen, editor, *Research on Religious Development*, pp. 179-180.

213. Jeanne Block and Barclay Martin, "Predicting the Behavior of Children under Frustration," in *Journal of Abnormal and Social Psychology*, LI, (September 1955), pp. 281-285. Some psychologists, notably of a psychoanalytic or psycho-therapeutic bent, like to call the ability to defer gratification "ego control" or "ego strength" although the terms are not coextensive.

214. Walter Mischel, "Preference for Delayed Reinforcement and Social Psychology."

215. B. Othanel Smith et al., *Teachers for the Real World* (Washington, D.C.: American Association of Colleges for Teacher Education, 1969), p. 90.

216. Robert Rosenthal and Lenore Jacobson, *Pygmalion in the Classroom: Teacher Expectation and Pupils' Intellectual Development* (New York: Holt, Rinehart and Winston, 1968). There is some dispute raging on certain methodological aspects of the Rosenthal and Jacobson study; further, while the body of research clearly indicates that teacher expectancy distinctly affects pupil performance, there is some controversy over whether teacher expectancy substantially affects I.Q. On this point see Janet D. Elashoff and Richard E. Snow, editors, *Pygmalion Reconsidered* (Worthington, Ohio: Jones, 1971).

217. J. Philip Baker and Janet L. Crist, "Teacher Expectancies: A Review of the Literature," in *Pygmalion Reconsidered*, pp. 48-64.

218. A. Morrison and D. McIntyre, *Teachers and Teaching*, pp. 103-105.

219. Kenneth Clark, *Dark Ghetto: Dilemmas of Social Power* (New York: Harper, 1965).
220. For a review of the research, see David G. Ryans, "Motivation in Learning," in National Society for the Study of Education, *The Psychology of Learning*, Forty-first Yearbook, Part II (Chicago: University of Chicago Press, 1942), pp. 318-319.
221. For a complete account of this research investigation, see F. J. Roethlisberger and William J. Dickson, *Management and the Worker* (Cambridge, Mass.: Harvard University Press, 1939).
222. F. J. Ryan and James S. Davie, "Social Acceptance, Academic Achievement, and Academic Aptitude among High School Students," in *Journal of Educational Research*, LII, (November 1958), pp. 101-106.
223. Ned A. Flanders, "Personal-Social Anxiety as a Factor in Experimental Learning Situations," in *Journal of Educational Research*, XLV, (October 1951), pp. 100-110.
224. A. Morrison and D. McIntyre, *Teachers and Teaching*, p. 128.
225. E. Paul Torrance, "Current Research on the Nature of Creativity," in *Journal of Counseling Psychology*, VI (Winter 1959), pp. 309-311.
226. Leonard Berkowitz, *The Development of Motives and Values in the Child*, p. 43.
227. Bonnie B. Tyler, "Expectancy for Eventual Success as a Factor in Problem-solving Behavior," in *Journal of Educational Psychology*, XLIX, (June 1958), p. 171.
228. For a summary of these three investigations, see David Elkind, "The Child's Conception of His Religious Identity," in *Lumen Vitae*, XIX, (December 1964), pp. 635-646.
229. Ronald T. Hyman, "Overview of Section Three," in Ronald T. Hyman, editor, *Teaching: Vantage Points for Study* (Philadelphia: Lippincott, 1968), p. 147.
230. Morton T[rippe] Kelsey, "The Place of Affect in Religious Education: Psychodynamics of Affectivity and Emotion," in *Lumen Vitae*, XXVI (March 1971), p. 71.
231. Mary Agnita Spurgeon, "Implications of Teacher-Pupil Relations in the Supervision of Sister Teachers," unpublished doctoral dissertation, Fordham University, 1959, p. 151.
232. Herbert T. Olander and Helen M. Kleyle, "Differences in Personal and Professional Characteristics of a Selected Group of Elementary Teachers with Contrasting Success Records," in *Educational Administration and Supervision*, XLV, (July 1959), pp. 191-195.
233. Anna Porter Burrell, "Facilitating Learning through Emphasis on Meeting Children's Basic Emotional Needs," in *Journal of Educational Sociology*, XXIV, (March 1951), pp. 381-393.

234. Harold H. Anderson and Helen M. Brewer, "Studies of Teachers' Classroom Personalities. I. Dominative and Socially Integrative Behavior of Kindergarten Teachers," in *Applied Psychology Monographs,* no. 6, July 1945; Harold H. Anderson and Joseph E. Brewer, "Studies of Teachers' Classroom Personalities. II. Effects of Teachers' Dominative and Integrative Contacts on Children's Classroom Behavior," in *Applied Psychology Monographs,* no. 8, June 1946; Harold H. Anderson, Joseph E. Brewer, and Mary Frances Reed, "Studies of Teachers' Classroom Behaviors. III. Follow-up Studies of the Effects of Dominative and Integrative Contacts on Children's Behavior," in *Applied Psychology Monographs,* no. 11, December 1946.

235. Hugh V. Perkins, "The Effects of Social-Emotional Climate and Curriculum on Group Learning of In-service Teachers," unpublished doctoral dissertation, University of Chicago, 1949.

236. Kurt Lewin, Ronald Lippitt, and Ralph K. White, "Patterns of Aggressive Behavior in Experimentally Created 'Social Climates'," pp. 271-299. Often this study is cited as one which simply demonstrates the effects of autocratic versus laissez-faire versus democratic leadership. However, a closer examination of the study reveals that the behavior of the autocratic leader was high in negative affect as contrasted to the leader's behavior during laissez-faire and democratic leadership sessions. Consequently, this study also manifests the results of the leader's affective behavior on group learning and performance.

237. Ned A. Flanders, *Interaction Analysis in the Classroom: A Manual for Observers,* revised edition (Ann Arbor, Mich.: School of Education, University of Michigan, 1966), pp. 53-54. The broad grouping of direct and indirect affective teacher behaviors are my construction from the original Flanders system.

238. Raymond Whiteman, "The Differing Patterns of Behavior as Observed in Teachers of Religion and Teachers of Mathematics and Social Studies," unpublished seminar project, University of Notre Dame, 1971.

239. O. L. Davis and Drew C. Tinsley, "Cognitive Objectives Revealed by Classroom Questions Asked by Social Studies Student Teachers," in Ronald T. Hyman, editor, *Teaching: Vantage Points for Study,* p. 143.

240. Carl R. Rogers, *On Becoming a Person* (Boston: Houghton Mifflin, 1961); see also Carl R. Rogers, *Freedom to Learn* (Columbus, Ohio: Merrill, 1969).

241. James E. Dittes, "Galvanic Skin Response as a Measure of a

Patient's Reaction to the Therapist's Permissiveness," in *Journal of Abnormal and Social Psychology*, LV, (November 1957), pp. 295-303.

242. Jeffrey Keefe, "The Learning of Attitudes and Values," in James Michael Lee and Patrick C. Rooney, editors, *Toward a Future for Religious Education*, p. 45.

243. Martin L. Hoffman, "Development of Internal Moral Standards in Children," in Merton P. Strommen, editor, *Research on Religious Development*, pp. 211-263.

244. Bernard Berelson and Gary A. Steiner, *Human Behavior: An Inventory of Scientific Findings*, pp. 75-77.

245. Albert Bandura and R. H. Walters, *Adolescent Aggression* (New York: Ronald, 1959).

246. David C. McClelland, *The Achieving Society*.

247. Harold M. Skeels, *Adult Status of Children with Contrasting Early Life Experiences: A Follow-up Study* (Chicago: University of Chicago Press, 1965).

248. Harry F. Harlow and Robert R. Zimmerman, "The Development of Affectional Responses in Infant Monkeys," in *Proceedings of the American Philosophical Society*, CII. (1958), pp. 501-509.

249. Morton T[rippe] Kelsey, "The Place of Affect in Religious Education: Psychodynamics of Affectivity and Emotion," p. 80.

250. *Ibid.*, pp. 68-80.

251. James Hillman, *Emotion: A Comprehensive Phenomenology of Theories and Their Meanings for Therapy* (Evanston, Ill.: Northwestern University Press, 1964).

252. Michael Warren, "All Contributions Cheerfully Accepted," in *The Living Light*, VII, (Winter 1970), p. 31.

253. Raymond Whiteman, "The Differing Patterns of Behavior as Observed in Teachers of Religion and Teachers of Mathematics and Social Studies."

254. Robert O'Gorman, "The Nature and Meaning of the Affective Domain," in *Lumen Vitae*, XXVI, (March 1971), pp. 81-88.

255. Many of these research investigations are reported in Edmund J. Amidon and John B. Hough, editors, *Interaction Analysis: Theory, Research and Application* (Reading, Mass.: Addison-Wesley, 1967).

256. Personal interview with Raymond Whiteman, February 4, 1972.

257. Gordon W. Allport, "Attitudes," in Carl A. Murchison, Editor, *A Handbook of Social Psychology* (Worcester, Mass.: Clark University Press, 1935), p. 810.

258. David Krech and Richard S. Crutchfield, *Theory and Practice*

of *Social Psychology* (New York: McGraw-Hill, 1948), p. 152.
259. George G. Stern, "Measuring Noncognitive Variables in Research on Teaching," in N. L. Gage, *Handbook of Research on Teaching*, p. 404.
260. James Michael Lee, *Principles and Methods of Secondary Education*, p. 176.
261. Dale B. Harris, "How Children Learn Interests, Motives and Attitudes," National Society for the Study of Education, *Learning and Instruction*, Forty-ninth Yearbook, Part I (Chicago: University of Chicago Press, 1950), pp. 140-141.
262. Jeffrey Keefe, "The Learning of Attitudes, Values, and Beliefs," pp. 34-35.
263. J. B. Cooper and J. L. McGaugh, "Attitude and Related Concepts," in Marie Jahoda and Neil Warren, editors, *Attitudes* (Baltimore: Penguin, 1966), p. 26.
264. Gordon W. Allport, "Attitudes," p. 806.
265. Jerome M. Levine and Gardner Murphy, "The Learning and Forgetting of Controversial Material," in *Journal of Abnormal and Social Psychology*, XXXVIII, (October 1943), pp. 507-517. A similar kind of study by Donald Fitzgerald and David Ausubel placed emphasis on the cognitive infrastructure of the attitude as a powerful element facilitating or hindering the learning of material opposed to the learner's attitudes. See Donald Fitzgerald and David P. Ausubel, "Cognitive versus Affective Factors in the Learning and Retention of Controversial Material," in *Journal of Educational Psychology*, LXIII, (April 1963), pp. 73-84.
266. I am here following the analysis which Solomon Asch makes in his "Attitudes as Cognitive Structures," in Maria Jahoda and Neil Warren, editors, *Attitudes*, pp. 34-36.
267. One can only speculate whether it is indeed this way which Michael Warren (attitudinally conditioned in favor of the theological approach to religious instruction and against the social-science approach) takes to hard research data (facts) I presented in those earlier works which he has bothered to read. Warren alleges that pre-1960 social-science data (facts) are outdated. The truth of the matter is that many of the classic investigations were conducted before 1960. Some types of culture-bound survey data do become outdated; however, only rarely do I cite such material, and when I do, I am quick to point this out. To be sure, a very large number of pre-1960 facts are as relevant today as they were at the time they were unearthed by the researchers. See Michael Warren, "All Contributions Cheerfully Accepted," p. 32.
268. Could it be that Michael Warren also is utilizing this device

when he asserts that the application of social-science data to religious instruction is extremely limited? *Ibid.*

269. Ole R. Holsti, *Content Analysis for the Social Sciences and Humanities* (Reading, Mass.: Addison-Wesley, 1969), p. 88.

270. Charles F. Cannell and James C. MacDonald, "The Impact of Health News on Attitudes and Behavior," in *Journalism Quarterly*, XXXIII, (Summer 1956), pp. 315-323.

271. Shirley A. Star and Helen MacGill Hughes, "Report of an Educational Campaign: The Cincinnati Plan for the United Nations," in *American Journal of Sociology*, LV, (January 1950), pp. 389-400.

272. Bernard Berelson and Gary A. Steiner, *Human Behavior: An Inventory of Scientific Findings*, pp. 562-564.

273. Daniel Katz and Ezra Stotland, "A Preliminary Statement to a Theory of Attitude Structure and Change," in Sigmund Koch, editor, *Psychology: A Study of a Science: Formulations of the Person and the Social Content*, volume III (New York: McGraw-Hill, 1959), pp. 423-475.

274. Jeffrey Keefe, "The Learning of Attitudes, Values, and Beliefs," p. 31.

275. Robert F. Peck and Robert J. Havighurst, *The Psychology of Character Development*.

276. Jeffrey Keefe, "The Learning of Attitudes, Values, and Beliefs," p. 53.

277. Robert J. Havighurst and Barry Keating, "The Religion of Youth," in Merton P. Strommen, editor, *Research on Religious Development*, p. 714.

278. Edwin D. Starbuck, *The Psychology of Religion* (New York: Scribner's, 1899).

279. Michael Argyle, *Religious Behavior* (Glencoe, Ill.: Free Press, 1959).

280. See Erik H. Erikson, *Identity: Youth and Crisis* (New York: Norton, 1968), pp. 128-141. Erikson also views adolescent love as a matter of identity more than a matter of sexuality. "To a considerable extent adolescent love is an attempt to arrive at a definition of one's identity by projecting one's diffused self-image on another and by seeing it thus reflected and gradually clarified. That is why so much of young love is conversation." (p. 132).

281. David Elkind and Sally Elkind, "Varieties of Religious Experience in Young Adolescents," in *Journal for the Scientific Study of Religion*, II, (Fall 1962), pp. 102-112.

282. Robert J. Havighurst and Barry Keating, "The Religion of Youth," p. 714.

283. Winifred G. Baker and William A. Koppe, *Children's Religious*

Concepts (Schenectady, N.Y.: Union College, 1959); also Hanford D. Wright and William A. Koppe, "Children's Potential Religious Concepts," in *Character Potential*, II, (February 1964), pp. 83-90.

284. P. J. Lawrence, "Children's Thinking about Religion: A Study of Concrete Operational Thinking," in *Religious Education*, XL, (March-April 1965), pp. 111-116.

285. See, for example, Atlee L. Stroup, *Marriage and the Family: A Developmental Approach* (New York: Appleton-Century-Crofts, 1966), pp. 219-368; Talcott Parsons and Robert F. Bales, *Family Socialization and Interaction Process* (New York: Free Press, 1955); Rose Laub Coser, editor, *The Family: Its Structure and Functions* (New York: St. Martin's, 1964), pp. 251-383.

286. See, for example, James Michael Lee and Nathaniel J. Pallone, *Guidance and Counseling in Schools: Foundations and Processes*, pp. 392-413.

287. Paul B. Maves, "Religious Development in Adulthood," in Merton P. Strommen, editor, *Research on Religious Development*, p. 782.

288. Leonard Berkowitz, *The Development of Motives and Values in the Child*, p. 70.

289. See, for example, Solomon E. Asch, "Studies of Independence and Conformity: I. A Minority of One against a Unanimous Majority," in *Psychological Monographs*, LXIII, No. 9 (1956).

290. Elizabeth Douvan, *A Study of Adolescent Boys* (Ann Arbor, Mich.: Institute for Social Research, University of Michigan, 1955).

291. Stephen B. Withey, "The Influence of the Peer Group on the Values of Youth," in *Religious Education: Research Supplement*, LVII, (July-August 1962), p. 2-41.

292. Bernard Berelson and Gary A. Steiner, *Human Behavior: An Inventory of Scientific Findings*, p. 566.

293. Robert C. Bealer and Fern K. Willets, "The Religious Interests of American High School Youth," in *Religious Education*, LXII, (September-October 1967), p. 442.

294. Jeffrey Keefe, "The Learning of Attitudes, Values, and Beliefs," p. 48.

295. Robert F. Peck and Robert J. Havighurst, *The Psychology of Character Development*.

296. H. H. Remmers and D. H. Radley, *The American Teenager* (Indianapolis, Ind.: Bobbs-Merrill, 1957).

297. Michael Argyle, *Religious Behavior*.

298. John T. Fox, "Authoritarianism and the St. Ambrose College Student," in *Religious Education*, LX, (July-August 1965), p. 276.

299. James E. Dittes, "Religion, Prejudice, and Personality," in Merton P. Strommen, editor, *Research on Religious Development,* p. 367.
300. *Ibid.,* p. 378.
301. Paul F. Secord and Carl W. Backman, *Social Psychology* (New York: McGraw-Hill, 1964).
302. E. W. J. Faison, "Experimental Comparison on the Effectiveness of One-sided and Two-sided Mass Communications on the Influence of Economic Attitudes," as cited in *ibid.,* p. 139.
303. Irving L. Janis and Seymour Feshbach, "Effects of Fear-arousing Communications," in *Journal of Abnormal and Social Psychology,* XLVIII, (January 1953), pp. 78-92.
304. Jum C. Nunnally and Howard M. Bobren, "Variables Governing the Willingness to Receive Communications on Mental Health," in *Journal of Personality,* XXVII, (March 1959), pp. 38-45.
305. See James Michael Lee, "Catholic Education in the United States," in James Michael Lee, editor, *Catholic Education in the Western World* (Notre Dame, Ind.: University of Notre Dame Press, 1967), pp. 307-308.
306. Robert F. Peck and Robert J. Havighurst, *The Psychology of Character Development.*
307. A typical restricted notion of teaching is that it is primarily a cognitive, verbal transaction between student and teacher.
308. See, for example, Abraham Kroll, "The Teacher's Influence upon the Social Attitude of Boys in the Twelfth Grade," in *Journal of Educational Psychology,* XXV, (March 1934), pp. 274-280.
309. Austin de M. Bond, *An Experiment in the Teaching of Genetics* (New York: Bureau of Publications, Teachers College, Columbia University, 1940).
310. See, for example, Louis E. Raths, Merrill Harmin, and Sidney B. Simon, *Values and Teaching* (Columbus, Ohio: Merrill, 1966).
311. Ira N. Brophy, "The Luxury of Anti-Negro Prejudice," in *Public Opinion Quarterly,* IX, (Winter 1945-46), pp. 456-466.
312. Morton Deutsch and Mary Evans Collins, *Interracial Housing: A Psychological Evaluation of a Social Experiment* (Minneapolis: University of Minnesota Press, 1951).
313. John Harding and Russell Hogrefe, "Attitudes of White Department Store Employees toward Negro Co-workers," in *Journal of Social Issues,* VIII, (January 1952), pp. 18-28.
314. Kenneth B. Clark, "Desegregation: An Appraisal of the Evidence," in *Journal of Social Issues,* IX, (April 1953), pp. 2-76.
315. Jack W. Brehm, "Attitudinal Consequences of Commitment in

Unpleasant Behavior," in *Journal of Abnormal and Social Psychology*, LX, (May 1960), pp. 379-383.

316. Melvin L. DeFleur and Frank R. Westie, "Verbal Attitudes and Overt Acts," in *American Sociological Review*, XXIII, (December 1958), pp. 667-673.

317. See, for example, Milton Rokeach, *Beliefs, Attitudes, and Values* (San Francisco: Jossey-Bass, 1968).

318. Jeffrey Keefe, "The Learning of Attitudes, Values, and Beliefs," p. 49.

319. James Michael Lee, *Principles and Methods of Secondary Education*, pp. 314-315.

320. Richard A. Schmuck and Matthew D. Miles, *Organization Development in Schools* (Palo Alto, Calif.: National, 1971).

321. For a detailed discussion of this point, see Patrick C. Rooney, "Religious Instruction in the Context of Catholic Schooling," in James Michael Lee and Patrick C. Rooney, editors, *Toward a Future for Religious Education*, pp. 5-29.

322. This study is cited in Edmund J. Goebel, "Making the High School Truly Catholic," in Michael J. McKeough, editor, *The Administration of the Catholic High School* (Washington: The Catholic University of America Press, 1948), p. 169.

323. Bernard Berelson and Gary A. Steiner, *Human Behavior: An Inventory of Scientific Findings*, p. 439.

324. Marie Edmund Harvey, "A Study of Religious Attitudes of a Group of Catholic College Women," unpublished master's thesis, Fordham University, 1954, pp. 46-49.

325. This study is cited in Robert Hassenger, "Impact of Catholic Colleges," in Robert Hassenger, editor, *The Shape of Catholic Higher Education* (Chicago: University of Chicago Press, 1967), p. 123.

326. Philip Jacob, *Changing Values in College* (New Haven, Conn.: Hazen Foundation, 1956).

327. Robert Hassenger, "Impact of Catholic Colleges," pp. 103-161.

328. Benjamin S. Bloom, J. Thomas Hastings, and George F. Madaus, *Handbook on Formative and Summative Evaluation of Student Learning* (New York: McGraw-Hill, 1971).

329. For a review of the relevant research, see James E. Dittes, "Two Issues in Measuring Religion," in Merton P. Strommen, editor, *Research on Religious Development*, pp. 91-102.

330. See Martin L. Hoffman, "Development of Internal Moral Standards in Children," in *ibid.*, pp. 252-254.

331. Hugh Hartshorne and Mark A. May, *Studies in the Nature of Character: volume I. Studies in Deceit* (New York: Macmillan, 1928).

332. Wesley Allinsmith, "Moral Standards II: The Learning of Moral

Standards," in Daniel R. Miller and Guy E. Swanson, editors, *Inner Conflict and Defense* (New York: Holt, Rinehart and Winston, 1960), pp. 141-176.

333. Martin L. Hoffman, "Development of Internal Moral Standards in Children," p. 253.

334. Leonard Berkowitz, *The Development of Motives and Values in the Child*, pp. 60-61.

335. Jean Piaget, *The Moral Judgment of the Child*, translated by Marjorie Gabain (New York: Free Press, 1965).

336. See, for example, Charles Franklyn Preston, "The Development of Moral Judgment in Young People," unpublished doctoral dissertation, University of Toronto, 1962, pp. 22-40.

337. See, for example, Urie Bronfenbrenner, "The Role of Age, Sex, Class and Culture in Studies of Moral Development," in *Religious Education*, research supplement, LVII, (July-August 1962), p. s-3.

338. Piaget himself is unclear on this point.

339. For example, his sample was both very small and unrepresentative and did not utilize the standard statistical treatment.

340. For a summary of these investigations, see David Elkind, "The Child's Conception of His Religious Identity," in *Lumen Vitae*, XIX, (December 1964), pp. 635-646.

341. Ronald Goldman, *Religious Thinking from Childhood to Adolescence*.

342. Lawrence Kohlberg, "Stages of Moral Development," in C. M. Beck, B. S. Crittenden, and E. V. Sullivan, Editors, *Moral Education: Interdisciplinary Approaches*. (Toronto: University of Toronto Press, 1971), pp. 23-92.

343. Doug Sholl, "The Contributions of Lawrence Kohlberg to Religious and Moral Education," in *Religious Education*, LXVI (September-October 1971), pp. 364-365.

344. André Godin, one of Europe's foremost psychologists of religion, merits special mention and credit as one of the earliest Continental Catholic scholars to use rigorous social-science methodology in investigating religious phenomena. Often misunderstood and unappreciated by European Catholic religious educationists who characteristically operate out of a theological worldview, Godin has done more than perhaps any other European Catholic scholar to open up Continental religious education to the modern world as regards social science.

345. André Godin and S. Marthe, "Magic Mentality and Sacramental Life," in André Godin, editor, *Teaching the Sacraments and Morality* (Chicago: Loyola University Press, 1965), pp. 121-139.

346. André Godin and Bernadette Van Roey, "Immanent Justice and Divine Protection in Children of 6 to 14 Years," in *Lumen Vitae*, XIV, (March 1959), pp. 129-148.

347. R. H. Thouless and L. B. Brown, "Petitionary Prayer: Belief in its Appropriateness and Causal Efficacy among Adolescent Girls," in *Lumen Vitae*, XIX, (June 1964), pp. 298-310.

348. Diane Long, David Elkind, and Bernard Spilka, "The Child's Conception of Prayer," in *Journal for the Scientific Study of Religion*, VI, (April 1967), pp. 101-109.

349. Christian Van Bunnen, "The Burning Bush: The Symbolic Implications of the Bible Story among Children 5-12 Years," in *Lumen Vitae*, XIX, (June 1964), pp. 325-338.

350. Godelieve de Valensart, "Modern Religious Pictures: Spontaneous Choices and Understanding of Symbols among Children, Five to Twelve Years Old," in *Lumen Vitae*, XXII, (September 1967), pp. 487-502.

351. Jean-Pierre Deconchy, *Structure génétique de l'idée de Dieu* (Bruxelles: Lumen Vitae Press, 1967); see also Jean-Pierre Deconchy, "The Idea of God: Its Emergence between Seven and Sixteen Years: A Semantic Approach Using Free Associations," in *Lumen Vitae*, XIX, (June 1964), pp. 285-296.

352. Arnold Gesell and L. B. Ames, *Youth: The Years from Ten to Sixteen* (New York: Harper & Brothers, 1956).

353. Merton P. Strommen, "Introduction," in Merton P. Strommen, editor, *Research on Religious Development*, p. 110.

354. This in no way detracts from Piaget's genius.

355. Leonard Berkowitz, *The Development of Motives and Values in the Child*, p. 48.

356. Duncan MacRae, "A Test of Piaget's Theories of Moral Development," in *Journal of Abnormal and Social Psychology*, XLIX (January 1954), pp. 14-18.

357. Urie Bronfenbrenner, "The Role of Age, Sex, Class, and Culture in Studies of Moral Development," p. s-4.

358. M. R. Harrower, "Social Status and Moral Development," in *British Journal of Educational Psychology*, IV (February 1934), pp. 75-95.

359. Urie Bronfenbrenner, "The Role of Age, Sex, Class, and Culture in Studies of Moral Development," p. s-4.

360. Albert Bandura and Frederick J. McDonald, "Influence of Social Reinforcement and the Behavior of Models in Shaping Children's Moral Judgments," in *Journal of Abnormal and Social Psychology*, LXVII, (September 1965), pp. 274-281.

361. Edith M. Dowley, "Early Childhood Education," in Robert L. Ebel, editor, *Encyclopedia of Educational Research*, p. 324.

362. Bernard Spilka, "Research on Religious Beliefs: A Critical

Review," in Merton P. Strommen, editor, *Research on Religious Development*, pp. 485-520.

363. Robert F. Peck and Robert J. Havighurst, *The Psychology of Character Development;* also Leonard Berkowitz, *The Development of Motives and Values in the Child*, p. 76.

364. Martin L. Hoffman, "The Role of the Parent in the Child's Moral Growth," in *Religious Education* Research Supplement, LVII, (July-August 1962), pp. s-18–s-33.

365. Donald W. MacKinnon, "Violation of Prohibition," p. 498.

366. Justin Aronfreed, "Internal and External Orientation in the Moral Behavior of Children," paper read at the annual convention of the American Psychological Association, 1960.

367. Wesley Allinsmith, "Moral Standards: II: The Learning of Moral Standards," pp. 141-176.

368. Leonard Berkowitz, *The Development of Motives and Values in the Child*, pp. 90-91.

369. Bernard Berelson and Gary A. Steiner, *Human Behavior: An Inventory of Scientific Findings*, p. 77.

370. For a review of this research, see Ira J. Gordon, "Social and Emotional Development," in Robert L. Ebel, editor, *Encyclopedia of Educational Research*, p. 1226.

371. Robert R. Sears, Eleanor E. Maccoby, and Harry Levin, *Patterns of Child Rearing*.

372. Martin L. Hoffman, "The Role of the Parent in the Child's Moral Growth," in *Religious Education* Research Supplement, LVII, (July-August 1962), pp. s-29–s-30.

373. Robert R. Sears, Eleanor E. Maccoby, and Harry Levin, *Patterns of Child Rearing*.

374. Urie Bronfenbrenner, "The Role of Age, Sex, Class, and Culture in Studies of Moral Development," p. s-7.

375. Clement Cosgrove, "A Study of the Extent and Relationship between Theoretical Knowledge and Practical Knowledge of Religious and Moral Truths and Principles among Catholic Elementary School Children," p. 295.

376. Justin Aronfreed, "The Nature, Variety, and Social Patterning of Moral Responses to Transgression," in *Journal of Abnormal and Social Psychology*, LXIII, (September 1961), pp. 223-240.

377. Laura Dolger and Janet Ginandes, "Children's Attitudes Toward Discipline as Related to Socioeconomic Status," in *Journal of Experimental Education*, XV, (December 1946), pp. 161-165.

378. Urie Bronfenbrenner, "The Role of Age, Sex, Class, and Culture in Studies of Moral Development," pp. s-3–s-17.

379. Bernard Spilka, "Research on Religious Beliefs: A Critical Review," p. 495.

380. Leonore Boehm, "The Development of Conscience: A Comparison of Students in Catholic Parochial Schools and in Public Schools," in *Child Development*, XXXIII, (September 1962), pp. 591-602.
381. Alfred C. Kinsey, Wardell B. Pomeroy, and Clyde E. Martin, *Sexual Behavior in the Human Male* (Philadelphia: Saunders, 1948); Alfred C. Kinsey et al., *Sexual Behavior in the Human Female* (Philadelphia: Saunders, 1952).
382. E. Terry Prothro, "Arab Students' Choices of Ways to Live," in *Journal of Social Psychology*, XLVII, (February 1958), pp. 3-7.
383. James Michael Lee, "The *Teaching* of Religion," in James Michael Lee and Patrick C. Rooney, editors, *Toward a Future for Religious Education*, pp. 72-73.
384. Leonard Berkowitz, *The Development of Motives and Values in the Child*, p. 66.
385. David Elkind, "Research and Evaluation in Religious Instruction," in James Michael Lee and Patrick C. Rooney, editors, *Toward a Future for Religious Education*, p. 223.
386. David Elkind, "The Child's Conception of His Religious Identity," p. 646.
387. This investigation is cited in Oliver E. Graebner, "Research in Religious Development: Child Concepts of God," in *Religious Education*, LIX, (May-June 1964), p. 240.
388. Janaan Manternach and Carl J. Pfeifer, *Life, Love, Joy* (Morristown: N.J.: Silver Burdett, 1968-). I center my attention on this series because it is produced under the auspices and direction of the American Catholic bishops and hence represents—in theory at least—the curriculum most in congruence with the mind of the American episcopate. In terms of curriculum validity, other Catholic textbook series are no better.
389. *Ibid.* Teacher's Manual, p. 7.
390. Lawrence Kohlberg, "Development of Moral Character," p. 426.
391. Urie Bronfenbrenner, "Soviet Methods of Character Education: Some Implications for Research," in *American Psychologist*, XVII, (August 1962), pp. 550-565.
392. Leonard Berkowitz, *The Development of Motives and Values in the Child*, p. 54.
393. Justin Aronfreed, "The Nature, Variety, and Social Patterning of Moral Responses to Transgressions."
394. André Godin and Bernadette Van Roey, "Immanent Justice and Divine Protection," p. 147.
395. Leonard Berkowitz, *The Development of Motives and Values*

in the Child, pp. 42-43, 95-96.

396. Justin Aronfreed, "The Nature, Variety, and Social Patterning of Moral Responses to Transgressions."

397. See Herbert J. Klausmeier and J. Kent Davis, "Transfer of Learning," in Robert L. Ebel, editor, *Encyclopedia of Educational Research*, p. 1484.

398. There is still disagreement about which comprehensive theory best explains the data on transfer.

399. Methodologically speaking, the specification and measurement of gross task characteristics are exceedingly difficult to make, especially in complex tasks. Hence the bulk of the research has been concerned with investigating stimulus similarity; recently, however, response characteristics are being researched with increased frequency.

400. Herbert J. Klausmeier and J. Kent Davis, "Transfer of Learning," pp. 1486-1487.

401. *Ibid.*, p. 1489.

402. Concepts based on a relatively large number of facts also seem to be retained more easily and longer. William P. McDougall, "Differential Retention of Course Outcomes in Educational Psychology," in *Journal of Educational Psychology*, XLIX, (April 1958), pp. 53-60.

403. Herbert Klausmeier and J. Kent Davis, "Transfer of Learning," p. 1489.

404. Jack E. Kittell, "An Experimental Study of the Effects of External Direction during Learning on Transfer and Retention of Principles," in *Journal of Educational Psychology*, XLVIII, (November 1957), p. 404.

405. G. M. Haslerud and Shirley Meyers, "The Transfer Value of Given and Individually Derived Principles," in *Journal of Educational Psychology*, XLIX, (December 1958), p. 297.

406. Herbert Klausmeier and J. Kent Davis, "Transfer of Learning," p. 1489.

407. Henry C. Ellis, *The Transfer of Learning* (New York: Macmillan, 1965), p. 51.

408. Robert M. W. Travers, *Essentials of Learning*, 2d ed. (New York: Macmillan, 1967), p. 260.

409. Henry C. Ellis, *The Transfer of Learning*, p. 73.

410. Robert C. Craig, *The Transfer Value of Guided Learning* (New York: Bureau of Publications, Teachers College, Columbia University, 1953).

411. Henry C. Ellis, *The Transfer of Learning*, p. 72.

412. D. H. Holding, "Transfer between Difficult and Easy Tasks," *British Journal of Psychology*, LIII, (November 1963), pp. 397-407.

413. Bernard Berelson and Gary A. Steiner, *Human Behavior: An Inventory of Scientific Findings,* p. 164.
414. Jaime Castiello, *A Humane Psychology of Education* (New York: Sheed & Ward, 1936), p. 172.
415. Ray Mars Simpson, "Attitudes toward the Ten Commandments," in *Journal of Social Psychology,* IV, (May 1933), pp. 223-230.
416. Carmen V. Diaz, "A Study of the Ability of Eleventh-grade Girls to Apply the Principles of the Moral Law to Actual and Hypothetical Life Situations," unpublished doctoral dissertation, Fordham University, 1952.
417. Hugh Hartshorne and Mark A. May, *Studies in the Nature of Character, I.: Studies in Deceit.*
418. Charles Y. Glock, "On the Study of Religious Commitment," in *Religious Education,* Research Supplement, LVII, (July-August 1962), pp. s-98—s-110.
419. For a further discussion of the religion class as a laboratory for Christian living, see James Michael Lee, *The Shape of Religious Instruction,* pp. 81-88.
420. See Robert J. Kibler, Larry L. Barker, and David T. Miles, *Behavioral Objectives and Instruction* (Boston: Allyn and Bacon, 1970).
421. Henry C. Ellis, *The Transfer of Learning,* p. 74.
422. David F. Ausubel, "A Cognitive-Structure Theory of School Learning," pp. 239-240.

NOTES–CHAPTER VII

1. Daniel Pezeril, *Rue Notre Dame,* translated by A. Gordon Smith (New York: Sheed & Ward, 1953), p. 50.
2. One has only to listen to evaluations of teacher effectiveness made by many Protestant and Catholic religious education directors to realize how widespread is the adherence to the personality theory.
3. E. Schillebeeckx, *Christ, the Sacrament of the Encounter with God,* translated by Paul Barrett, revised by Laurence Bright and Mark Schoof (New York: Sheed & Ward, 1963), p. 166.
4. J. W. Getzels and P. W. Jackson, "The Teacher's Personality and Characteristics," in N. L. Gage, editor, *Handbook of Research on Teaching* (Chicago: Rand McNally, 1963), pp. 506-582.
5. See, for example, Josef Andreas Jungmann, *Handing on the Faith: A Manual of Catechetics,* translated and revised by A. N. Fuerst (New York: Herder and Herder, 1959), p. 75.
6. A. Morrison and D. McIntyre, *Teachers and Teaching* (Balti-

more: Penguin, 1969), p. 42.

7. These data apply to the use of Biological Sciences Curriculum Study (BSCS) materials. However, the process is easily extrapolatable to the area of religious instruction. James J. Gallagher, *Teacher Variation in Concept Presentation in BSCS Curriculum* (Urbana, Ill.: Institute for Research on Exceptional Children, University of Illinois, 1966).

8. Edward M. Hanley, "Review of Research Involving Applied Behavior in the Classroom," in *Review of Educational Research*, XL, (December 1970), p. 617.

9. James Michael Lee and Nathaniel J. Pallone, *Guidance and Counseling in Schools: Foundations and Processes* (New York: McGraw-Hill, 1966), p. 298.

10. Carleton Washburne and Louis M. Heil, "What Characteristics of Teachers Affect Children's Growth?" in *School Review,* LXVIII, (Winter 1960), pp. 420, 428.

11. Wilbert McKeachie et al., "Student Affiliation, Motives, Teacher Warmth, and Academic Achievement," in *Journal of Personality and Social Psychology,* IV, (October 1966), pp. 457-461.

12. S. E. Asch, "Effects of Group Pressure upon the Modification and Distortion of Judgments," in Harold Guetzkow, editor, *Groups, Leadership, and Men: Research in Human Relations* (Pittsburgh: Carnegie Press, 1951), pp. 177-190.

13. Jerome Kagan and Paul H. Mussen, "Dependency Themes on the TAT and Group Conformity," in *Journal of Consulting Psychology,* XX, (February 1956), pp. 29-32.

14. Norman Livson and Paul H. Mussen, "The Relation of Control to Overt Aggression and Dependency," in *Journal of Abnormal and Social Psychology,* LV, (July 1957), pp. 66-71.

15. Edmund Amidon and Ned A. Flanders, "The Effects of Direct and Indirect Teacher Influence on Dependent-Prone Students Learning Geometry," in *Journal of Educational Psychology,* LII, (December 1961), pp. 286-291.

16. Norman M. Chansky, "The Attitudes Students Assign to Their Teachers," in *Journal of Educational Psychology,* XLIX, (February 1958), pp. 13-16.

17. George G. Stern, "Measuring Noncognitive Variables in Research on Teaching," in N. L. Gage, editor, *Handbook of Research on Teaching,* p. 417.

18. *Ibid.,* see also James Michael Lee, *Principles and Methods of Secondary Education* (New York: McGraw-Hill, 1963), pp. 253-254.

19. A. Morrison and D. McIntyre, *Teachers and Teaching,* pp. 46-47.

20. Robert F. Peck, "Personality Patterns of Prospective Teachers," in *Journal of Experimental Education*, XXIX, (December 1960), pp. 169-175.

21. Thomas J. McCarthy, "Personality Traits of Seminarians," in *Studies in Psychology and Psychiatry from the Catholic University of America*, volume 5, no. 4, 1942. McCarthy utilized the Bernreuter instrument.

22. Rayner Van Vurst, "An Investigation into the Relationship between Selected Personality Traits and Reactions to Frustration among Religious Seminarians and Lay Students," unpublished master's thesis, University of Detroit, 1964. Van Vurst used the Edwards Personal Preference Schedule.

23. George C. Stern, Morris L. Stein, and Benjamin S. Bloom, *Methods in Personality Assessment* (New York: Free·Press, 1956).

24. James E. Dittes, "Psychological Characteristics of Religious Professionals," in Merton P. Strommen, *Research on Religious Development* (New York: Hawthorn, 1971), p. 449.

25. George Hagmaier and Eugene C. Kennedy, "Psychological Aspects of Seminary Life," in James Michael Lee and Louis J. Putz, editors, *Seminary Education in a Time of Change* (South Bend, Ind.: Fides, 1965), pp. 254-285. It may be that newer seminary and novitiate environments do or will produce different personality tendencies. This, however, still remains to be seen.

26. Raymond H. Potvin and Antanis Suziedelis, *Seminarians of the Sixties: A National Survey* (Washington: Center for Applied Research in the Apostolate, 1969), p. 53; James E. Dittes, "Psychological Characteristics of Religious Professionals," pp. 422-460.

27. *Ibid.*, pp. 429-432.

28. Frances F. Fuller, Oliver H. Bown, and Robert F. Peck, *Creating Climate for Growth* (Austin, Tex.: University of Texas, Hogg Foundation for Mental Health, 1967), p. 21.

29. B. Othanel Smith et al., *Teachers for the Real World* (Washington: American Association of Colleges for Teacher Education, 1969), p. 84.

30. Gregory Baum, *Man Becoming: God in Secular Experience* (New York: Herder and Herder, 1970), pp. 50-51.

31. Marshall McLuhan, *Understanding Media: The Extensions of Man* (New York: McGraw-Hill, 1964), p. 319.

32. Josef Goldbrunner, "Catechesis and Encounter," in Josef Goldbrunner, editor, *New Catechetical Methods* (Notre Dame, Ind.: University of Notre Dame Press, 1965), p. 43.

33. Charles Bidwell, "Sociology of Education," in Robert L. Ebel,

editor, *Encyclopedia of Educational Research,* 4th ed. (New York: Macmillan, 1969), p. 1243.

34. E. Schillebeeckx, *Christ, the Sacrament of the Encounter with God,* p. 174.

35. B. Othanel Smith et al., *Teachers for the Real World,* p. 82.

36. One of the most clear and charming rationales I have ever heard for the authenticity theory was from Christianne Brusselmanns, the Belgian religious educationist, during a lengthy discussion in the study of my home in the early spring of 1968.

37. Carl R. Rogers, "The Facilitation of Significant Learning," in Laurence Siegel, editor, *Instruction: Some Contemporary Viewpoints* (San Francisco: Chandler, 1967) p. 45.

38. For a discussion of the mediational role of religious instruction as against the once posited content-method duality, see Chapter 3.

39. A. Morrison and D. McIntyre, *Teachers and Teaching,* p. 109.

40. See B. F. Skinner, *Beyond Freedom and Dignity* (New York: Knopf, 1971), pp. 12-13.

41. Carl R. Rogers, "The Facilitation of Significant Learning," p. 45.

42. Gabriel Moran, *Catechesis of Revelation* (New York: Herder and Herder, 1966), p. 121.

43. Wayne R. Rood, *The Art of Teaching Christianity* (Nashville, Tenn.: Abingdon, 1968), p. 49.

44. William Reedy, "The Mystery of Christ," in Johannes Hofinger and Theodore C. Stone, editors, *Pastoral Catechetics* (New York: Herder and Herder, 1964), p. 111. Italics deleted.

45. Augustin Gruber, *Praktisches Handbuch der Katechetik,* 7th ed., quoted in Josef Jungmann, *Handing on the Faith, A Manual of Catechetics,* p. 246.

46. S. Anita Stauffer, "Identification Theory and Christian Moral Education," in *Religious Education,* LXVII, (January-February 1972), pp. 60-61.

47. Albert Bandura and Richard H. Walters, *Social Learning and Personality Development* (New York: Holt, Rinehart and Winston, 1963), p. 89.

48. Percival M. Symonds, *Dynamic Psychology* (New York: Appleton-Century-Crofts, 1949), p. 240.

49. Carter V. Good, editor, *Dictionary of Education,* 2d ed. (New York: McGraw-Hill, 1959), p. 278.

50. Lawrence Kohlberg, "Moral Development and Identification," in National Society for the Study of Education, *Child Psychology,* Sixty-second Yearbook, Part I (Chicago: University of Chicago Press, 1963), p. 296.

51. Urie Bronfenbrenner, "The Study of Identification through Interpersonal Perception," in Renato Tagiuri and Luigi Petrullo, editors, *Person Perception and Interpersonal Behavior* (Palo Alto, Cal.: Stanford University Press, 1959), pp. 118-122.
52. Urie Bronfenbrenner, "The Study of Identification through Interpersonal Perception," p. 112.
53. Neal E. Miller and John Dollard, *Social Learning and Imitation* (New Haven, Conn.: Yale University Press, 1941).
54. Kenneth H. Wodtke and Bobby R. Brown, "Social Learning and Imitation," in *Review of Educational Research*, XXXVII, (December 1967), pp. 526-527.
55. Albert Bandura, Dorothea Ross, and Sheila A. Ross, "A Comparative Test of the Status Envy, Social Power, and Secondary Reinforcement Theories of Identificatory Learning," in *Journal of Abnormal and Social Psychology*, LXVII, (December 1963), pp. 527-534.
56. Robert R. Sears, "Identification as a Form of Behavior Development," in Dale B. Harris, editor, *The Concepts of Development* (Minneapolis, Minn.: University of Minnesota Press, 1957), p. 153.
57. Judy F. Rosenblith, "Learning by Imitation in Kindergarten Children," in *Child Development*, XXX, (March 1959), pp. 69-80.
58. Robert R. Sears, "Identification as a Form of Behavior Development," pp. 159-160.
59. Nevitt Sanford, "The Dynamics of Identification," in *Psychological Review*, LXII, (March 1959), pp. 106-108.
60. Lee J. Cronbach, *Educational Psychology* 2d ed. (New York: Harcourt, Brace and World, 1963), p. 426.
61. Stuart M. Stoke, "An Inquiry into the Concept of Identification," in *Journal of Genetic Psychology*, LXXVI, (March 1950), p. 178.
62. André Godin, "Some Developmental Tasks in Christian Education," in Merton P. Strommen, editor, *Research on Religious Development*, pp. 139-140; also Beverly B. Allinsmith, "Expressive Styles: II. Directness with Which Anger Is Expressed," in Daniel R. Miller and Guy E. Swanson, editors, *Inner Conflict and Defense* (New York: Holt, Rinehart and Winston, 1960), pp. 315-336.
63. Leonard Berkowitz, *The Development of Motives and Values in the Child* (New York: Basic Books, 1964), pp. 82-83.
64. Albert Bandura and Frederick J. McDonald, "Influence of Social Reinforcement and the Behavior of Models in Shaping Children's Moral Judgments," in *Journal of Abnormal and*

Social Psychology, LXVII, (September 1963), pp. 274-281.

65. Leonard Berkowitz, *The Development of Motives and Values in the Child,* p. 73.

66. Paul H. Mussen, John J. Conger, and Jerome Kagan, *Child Development and Personality,* 2d ed. (New York: Harper & Row, 1963), p. 263.

67. Michael Warren, "All Contributions Cheerfully Accepted," in *The Living Light,* VII, (Winter 1970), p. 30.

68. M. Virgine, "A Survey Course in Catechist Formation," in Johannes Hofinger and Theodore C. Stone, editors, *Pastoral Catechetics,* p. 272.

69. For example, there is the case of Robert Duryea, a West Coast priest who served as pastor of a West Coast suburban church at the same time he was married (for seven years) and had a son (whom he named Paul in honor of the reigning Pontiff). Such a "marriage," according to Catholic moral theology and canon law, is mortally sinful and carries with it automatic excommunication. Yet empirical evidence—albeit of a non-tightly controlled type—furnished by a formal statement issued by the parish council and the staff workers at this church indicated that Duryea was an effective priest and educator. The vast majority of Duryea's parishioners also felt that Duryea was a successful priest. See Earl Caldwell, "Coast Priest Married 7 Years, Dismissed and Excommunicated," in *The New York Times,* April 15, 1971, p. 30; also Lester Kinsolving, "Priest Married for Seven Years," in *The National Catholic Reporter,* VII, (April 23, 1971), pp. 1 and 11. It is common knowledge among historians of the American Church that a certain nineteenth-century Catholic bishop who was widely acknowledged as a particularly effective educator and promoter of educational causes had a lady friend for quite a few years.

70. The force of this argument varies directly with the degree to which the denomination holds to the principle of general revelation.

71. Nevitt Sanford, "The Dynamics of Identification," pp. 106-118.

72. See B. F. Skinner, *Beyond Freedom and Dignity,* p. 92.

73. N. L. Gage, "Theories of Teaching," in National Society for the Study of Education, *Theories of Learning and Instruction,* Sixty-third Yearbook, Part I (Chicago: University of Chicago Press, 1964), pp. 278-279.

74. Pauline S. Sears and Ernest R. Hilgard, "The Teacher's Role in the Motivation of the Learner," in *ibid.,* p. 204.

75. George S. Stern, "Measuring Noncognitive Variables in Research on Teaching," in N. L. Gage, editor, *Handbook of*

Research on Teaching, p. 425.
76. Michael Warren, "All Contributions Cheerfully Accepted," p. 30.
77. Pierre Babin, *Methods,* translated and adapted by John F. Murphy (New York: Herder and Herder, 1967), p. 99.
78. David G. Ryans, *Characteristics of Teachers* (Washington: American Council on Education, 1960).
79. Pauline S. Sears and Ernest R. Hilgard, "The Teacher's Role in the Motivation of the Learner," p. 209.
80. O. Hobart Mowrer, *Learning Theory and the Symbolic Processes* (New York: Wiley, 1960); Judy F. Rosenblith, "Learning by Imitation in Kindergarten Children," p. 71.
81. Sara Little, *The Role of the Bible in Contemporary Christian Education* (Richmond, Va.: Knox, 1961), p. 168.
82. Wayne R. Rood, *The Art of Teaching Christianity,* p. 74.
83. Gabriel Moran, *Catechesis of Revelation,* p. 67. I have substituted the words "religion teacher" for "catechist" since I believe the former to be more historically correct as well as more ecumenically understandable.
84. A possible contender for this dubious honor is the dedication theory.
85. See Emil Brunner, *Truth as Encounter,* translated by Amandus W. Loos and David Cairns (Philadelphia: Westminster, 1943), pp. 74-75.
86. Gabriel Moran, *Catechesis of Revelation,* p. 117.
87. T. W. Dean, "The Training of Adolescents to Prayer," in *Lumen Vitae,* XVIII, (June 1963), p. 242.
88. Michael Warren, "All Contributions Cheerfully Accepted," p. 30. Warren espouses both the blow theory and the witness theory.
89. Gabriel Moran, *Catechesis of Revelation,* pp. 116-117. I have substituted the words "religious instruction" and "religion teacher" for "catechesis" and "catechist" for reasons previously indicated.
90. Morris L. Cogan, "The Behavior of Teachers and the Productive Behavior of Their Pupils," in *Journal of Experimental Education,* XXVII, (December 1958), pp. 89-124.
91. Ronald Lippitt, "An Analysis of Group Reaction to Three Types of Experimentally Created Social Climates," unpublished doctoral dissertation, University of Iowa, 1940.
92. A. Morrison and D. McIntyre, *Teachers and Teaching,* p. 116.
93. Everett W. Bovard, "Interaction and Attraction to the Group," in *Human Relations,* IX, (November 1958), pp. 481-489.
94. James Michael Lee, *The Shape of Religious Instruction* (Dayton, Ohio: Pflaum/Standard, 1971), p. 196.

95. Jean Le Du and Marcel van Caster, *Experiential Catechetics,* translated by Denis Barrett (Paramus, N.J.: Newman, 1960), p. 2.

96. Gerard S. Sloyan, *Speaking of Religious Education* (New York: Herder and Herder, 1968), p. 70.

97. Roger Shinn, "Christian Education as Adoption," in *Religious Education,* LVII, (March-April 1962), p. 89.

98. Gregory Baum, *Man Becoming: God in Secular Experience,* p. 249.

99. André Godin, "Some Developmental Tasks in Christian Education," p. 111. Godin has for years been interested in this central problem of criteria in religious instruction. See his landmark article, "Importance and Difficulty of Scientific Research in Religious Education: The Problem of the 'Criterion'," translated by Richard Marius in *Religious Education,* Research Supplement, LVII, (July-August 1962), pp. s-166–s-174.

100. Charles F. Melchert, "Educational Theory and Religious Education: The Significance of Marc Belth for Religious Education," in *Religious Education,* LXIV, (July-August 1969), p. 264.

101. S. Anita Stauffer, "Identification Theory and Christian Moral Education," p. 67.

102. See Martin Buber, *I and Thou,* 2d ed., translated by Ronald Gregor Smith (New York: Scribner's, 1958), also Martin Buber, *Between Man and Man,* translated by Ronald Gregor Smith (London: Routledge and Kegan Paul, 1947).

103. Reuel L. Howe, *The Miracle of Dialogue* (Greenwich, Conn.: Seabury, 1953).

104. Wayne R. Rood, *The Art of Teaching Christianity,* pp. 18-26.

105. *Ibid.,* p. 27.

106. David R. Hunter, from *Christian Education as Engagement* © by the Trustees of the Lester Bradner Fund. Used by permission. (New York: Seabury, 1963), p. 19.

107. See William H. Stavsky, "Using the Insights of Psychotherapy in Teaching," in *The Elementary School Journal,* LVIII, (October 1957), pp. 28-35.

108. Wayne R. Rood, *The Art of Teaching Christianity,* p. 148; Pierre Babin, *Methods,* p. 42.

109. James Michael Lee and Nathaniel J. Pallone, *Guidance and Counseling in Schools: Foundations and Processes,* pp. 135-136.

110. A. Morrison and D. McIntyre, *Teachers and Teaching,* pp. 175-176.

111. Carl R. Rogers, "Significant Learning: In Therapy and in

Education," in *Educational Leadership*, XVI, (January 1959), p. 235.
112. David R. Hunter, *Christian Education as Engagement*, p. 20.
113. Wayne R. Rood, *The Art of Teaching Christianity*, p. 31.
114. *Ibid.*, pp. 80-88.
115. *Ibid.*, p. 74.
116. *Ibid.*, p. 37.
117. David R. Hunter, *Christian Education as Engagement*, p. 16.
118. *Ibid.*, p. 19.
119. Wayne R. Rood, *The Art of Teaching Christianity*, p. 29.
120. Alfred McBride, *Catechetics: A Theology of Proclamation* (Milwaukee: Bruce, 1966), p. 13.
121. On the structured learning situation strategy, see James Michael Lee, "The *Teaching* of Religion," pp. 56-64.
122. Horace B. English and Ava Champney English, *A Comprehensive Dictionary of Psychological and Psychoanalytical Terms* (New York: Longmans, 1958), p. 270.
123. See Louise L. Tyler, "The Concept of an Ideal Teacher-Student Relationship," in *Journal of Educational Research*, LVIII, (November 1964), pp. 112-117.
124. David R. Hunter, *Christian Education as Engagement*, p. 26.
125. It seems axiomatic that our present knowledge of effectiveness of past teaching acts is correlated with past actions.
126. David R. Hunter, *Christian Education as Engagement*, pp. 78-79. Hunter made this statement in relation to teacher trainers in orientation sessions, but it appears to hold true also as a general pedagogical device in his view.
127. See Johannes Hofinger, *The Art of Teaching Christian Doctrine: The Good News and Its Proclamation*, 2d ed. (Notre Dame, Ind.: University of Notre Dame Press, 1962), pp. 6-7.
128. Johannes Hofinger, "Stages Leading to Faith and Their Role in the Catechesis of the Faithful," in Johannes Hofinger and Theodore C. Stone, editors, *Pastoral Catechetics*, pp. 144-159.
129. Johannes Hofinger, *The Art of Teaching Christian Doctrine: The Good News and Its Proclamation*, p. 67. Hofinger tends to base his pedagogy around the Munich Method.
130. Marcel van Caster, *The Structure of Catechetics*, translated by Edward J. Dirkswager, Jr., Olga Guedetarian, and Nicolas Smith (New York: Herder and Herder, 1965), p. 185.
131. Josef Goldbrunner, "Catechetical Method as Handmaid of Kerygma," in Johannes Hofinger, editor, *Teaching All Nations: A Symposium on Modern Catechetics*, revised and partly translated by Clifford Howell (New York: Herder and Herder, 1961), p. 112.
132. Alfred McBride, *Catechetics: A Theology of Proclamation*, p. vii.

133. Gabriel Moran, *Catechesis of Revelation*, p. 100. Here Moran seems to equate preaching and pulpit, and religion teaching and the lecture.
134. Gabriel Moran, *Design for Religion* (New York: Herder and Herder, 1970), pp. 16-17.
135. Josef Goldbrunner, "Catechetical Method as Handmaid of Kerygma," p. 111.
136. *Ibid.*, p. 113.
137. Josef Andreas Jungmann, *Handing on the Faith: A Manual of Catechetics.*
138. See James Michael Lee, *The Shape of Religious Instruction*, pp. 36-42.
139. Alfred McBride, *Catechetics: A Theology of Proclamation*, p. 150.
140. "General Conclusions," in Johannes Hofinger, *Teaching All Nations: A Symposium on Modern Catechetics*, p. 398.
141. James Michael Lee, *The Shape of Religious Instruction*, *passim*.
142. James Michael Lee, "The *Teaching* of Religion," p. 92.
143. James Michael Lee, *Principles and Methods of Secondary Education*, p. 242.
144. Wayne R. Rood, *The Art of Teaching Christianity*, pp. 204-205.
145. For a fuller discussion of the nature and source of the teacher's authority, see Walter Doyle, "A Professional Model for the Authority of the Teacher in the Educational Enterprise," unpublished doctoral dissertation, University of Notre Dame, 1967.
146. Robert M. Gagné, "Instruction and the Conditions of Learning," in Laurence Siegel, editor, *Instruction: Some Contemporary Viewpoints*, p. 292.
147. Laurence Siegel and Lila Corkland Siegel, "The Instructional Gestalt," in *ibid.*, pp. 261-290; also Herbert Wahlberg, "A Model for Research on Instruction," in *School Review*, LXXVIII, (February 1970), pp. 185-200.
148. See B. Othanel Smith, et al., *Teachers for the Real World*, p. 69.
149. Ted W. Ward and John E. Ivey, Jr., "Improvement of Educational Practice," in Robert L. Ebel, editor, *Encyclopedia of Educational Research*, p. 626.
150. For a short explanation of the relation of feedback to the teaching-learning process, see C. Kyle Packer and Toni Packer, "Cybernetics, Information Theory and the Educative Process," in *Teachers College Record*, LXI, (December 1959), pp. 134-142. For a more detailed analysis, see Norbert Wiener,

Cybernetics: Control and Communication in the Animal and the Machine, 2d ed. (New York: M.I.T. Press and Wiley, 1961).

151. Robert M. Gagné, "Instruction and the Conditions of Learning," p. 295.

152. The structured learning situation strategy is discussed in James Michael Lee, "The *Teaching* of Religion," in James Michael Lee and Patrick C. Rooney, editors, *Toward a Future for Religious Education* (Dayton, Ohio: Pflaum/Standard, 1970), pp. 55-92.

153. Norman E. Wallen and Robert M. W. Travers, "Analysis and Investigation of Teaching Methods," in N. L. Gage, editor, *Handbook of Research on Teaching,* p. 491.

154. David R. Hunter, *Christian Education as Engagement,* pp. 32-33.

155. For a further treatment of this crucial point, see James Michael Lee, *The Shape of Religious Instruction,* pp. 223-234.

156. David R. Hunter, *Christian Education as Engagement,* p. 45.

157. On this last point, see Jean Le Du, "Catechesis and Pre-Catechesis," in Jean Le Du and Marcel van Caster, *Experiential Catechetics,* pp. 61-62.

158. Wayne R. Rood, *The Art of Teaching Christianity,* p. 12.

159. *Ibid.,* p. 46.

160. For such a worldview, see James D. Smart, *The Teaching Ministry of the Church* (Philadelphia: Westminster, 1954), p. 24.

161. John Withall, "The Development of a Technique for the Measurement of Social-Emotional Climate in Classrooms," in *Journal of Experimental Education,* XVII, (March 1949), pp. 347-361.

162. Gregory Baum, *Man Becoming: God in Secular Experience,* p. 8.

163. See James Michael Lee, "The *Teaching* of Religion," pp. 56-64; also Gabriel Moran, *Design for Religion,* pp. 16-17.

164. James Michael Lee, *The Shape of Religious Instruction.*

NOTES–CHAPTER VIII

1. Wolfgang Amadeus Mozart, *Die Zauberflöte,* Act II, libretto by Emanuel Schikaneder, translation mine.

2. I am indebted to Canice Connors for the felicitous phrase "to manage the process of change." See Canice Connors, "Managing the Processes of Change—Concern of CCD Institute," in *CCD News and Notes: Diocese of Pittsburgh,* IV, (October 1971), p. 1.

3. Wayne R. Rood, "On *Christian* Religious Education," in *The*

Living Light, VII (Winter 1970), p. 7.

4. This particular terminology is borrowed from Walter Doyle's rather thorough analysis of the teacher as a professional. See Walter Doyle, "A Professional Model for the Authority of the Teacher in the Educational Enterprise," unpublished doctoral dissertation, University of Notre Dame, 1967, especially p. 123.

5. *Ibid.* I have substituted the word "physiology" throughout this quote for the word "biology" which appears in the original Doyle text.

6. See James Michael Lee, "Prediction in Religious Instruction," in *The Living Light,* IX (Summer 1972) pp. 43-54.

7. William B. Michael, "Prediction," in Robert L. Ebel, editor, *Encyclopedia of Educational Research,* 4th ed. (New York: Macmillan, 1969), p. 982.

8. J. P. Guilford, *Fundamental Statistics in Psychology and Education,* 4th ed. (New York: McGraw-Hill, 1965), pp. 356-357.

9. See, for example, James D. Smart, *The Teaching Ministry of the Church* (Philadelphia: Westminster,1954), p. 167.

10. Wayne R. Rood, *The Art of Teaching Christianity* (Nashville, Tenn.: Abingdon, 1968), p. 178.

11. Gabriel Moran, *Theology of Revelation* (New York: Herder and Herder, 1966), p. 147.

12. Michael Warren, "Evaluating 'Christian Experience' Programs," in *The Living Light,* VII (Spring 1970), p. 86.

13. John Dewey writes that "the method of teaching is the method of an art, of action intelligently directed by ends." John Dewey, *Democracy and Education* (New York: Macmillan, 1916), p. 200.

14. For the phraseology of (2) I am indebted to Marshall McLuhan, *Understanding Media: The Extensions of Man* (New York: McGraw-Hill, 1964), p. 254.

15. See Clyde E. Curran, "Artistry in Teaching," in *Educational Theory,* III (April 1953), pp. 134-149.

16. Wayne R. Rood, "On *Christian* Religious Education," pp. 6-7.

17. See James Michael Lee, *Principles and Methods of Secondary Education* (New York: McGraw-Hill, 1963), pp. 229 and 270.

18. Thomas Aquinas, *De Veritate,* q. X, a. 8.

19. C. Ellis Nelson, *Where Faith Begins* (Richmond, Va.: Knox 1967), p. 63.

20. See John Julian Ryan, *Beyond Humanism* (New York: Sheed & Ward, 1950), pp. 32-47.

21. Randolph Crump Miller, *Biblical Theology and Christian Education* (New York: Scribner's, 1956), p. 33.

22. Lewis J. Sherrill, *The Gift of Power* (New York: Macmillan, 1955), p. 78.

23. Marcel van Caster, *The Structure of Catechetics*, translated by Edward J. Dirkswager, Jr., Olga Guedetarian, and Nicolas Smith (New York: Herder and Herder, 1965), p. 205.
24. Maria Montessori, *The Montessori Method*, translated by Anne E. George (Cambridge, Mass.: Bentley, 1965).
25. I am drawing this analogy from N. L. Gage, Philip J. Runkel, and B. B. Chaterjee, *Equilibrium Theory and Behavior Change: An Experiment in Feedback from Pupils to Teachers* (Urbana, Ill.: Bureau of Educational Research, College of Education, University of Illinois, 1960), p. 3.
26. John C. Whitehorn and Barbara J. Betz, "A Study of Psychotherapeutic Relationships between Physicians and Schizophrenic Patients," in *American Journal of Psychiatry*, CXI, (November 1954), pp. 321-331.
27. Carl R. Rogers, "The Characteristics of a Helping Relationship," in *Personnel and Guidance Journal*, XXXVII, (September 1958), p. 7.
28. B. Othanel Smith et al., *Teachers for the Real World* (Washington: American Association of Colleges for Teacher Education, 1969), p. 90.
29. For a further discussion of this point, see James Michael Lee, *Principles and Methods of Secondary Education*, pp. 269-285.
30. Michael Warren, "All Contributions Cheerfully Accepted," in *The Living Light*, VII, (Winter 1970), p. 30.
31. See, for example, Wayne R. Rood, *The Art of Teaching Christianity*, p. 51.
32. Some foreign substances were formerly called "negative catalysts" because they retarded the rate of chemical reaction. However, it has since been discovered that such substances are themselves changed in the reaction and are therefore not true catalysts. Hence the term "catalyst" is reserved for a foreign substance which speeds up the reaction without itself undergoing change.
33. Johannes Hofinger, *The Art of Teaching Christian Doctrine: The Good News and Its Proclamation*, 2d ed. (Notre Dame, Ind.: University of Notre Dame Press, 1962), p. 64.
34. See John Dewey, *Experience and Education* (New York: Macmillan, 1938), pp. 38-39.
35. See Morris L. Cogan, "Theory and Design of a Study of Teacher-Pupil Interaction," in *Harvard Educational Review*, XXVI, (Fall 1956), pp. 315-342.
36. Paulo Freire, *Pedagogy of the Oppressed*, translated by Myra Bergman Ramos (New York: Herder and Herder, 1970), p. 67. Unfortunately Freire appears to limit his notion of dialogue to the verbal and cognitive rather than to the totally existential.

37. Wayne R. Rood, *The Art of Teaching Christianity*, p. 160. Interestingly, it is this same Rood who argues that a teacher is a catalyst—surely a contradiction of his notion of the teacher as one who crosses over to the learner's side and is changed in the dialogical process.
38. Thomas Aquinas, *De Veritate*, q. XI, a. 1.
39. See, for example, Ephesians 1:23; Colossians 1:24; Ephesians 4:10; and James 2:22, together with exigetical commentaries on these texts.
40. Ned A. Flanders, "Teacher Influence, Pupil Attitudes, and Achievement," in Ronald T. Hyman, *Teaching: Vantage Points for Study* (Philadelphia: Lippincott, 1968), p. 265.
41. John C. Whitehorn and Barbara J. Betz, "A Study of Psychotherapeutic Relationships between Physicians and Schizophrenic Patients," p. 331.
42. The most mature, most effective, and most personal of Catholic priests and Protestant ministers I have met in my life have been those who unselfishly place their personalities totally at the service of their priestly or ministerial function. These men have very interesting and fascinating personalities and are exciting to be with. I cannot help but think of Edward Heston, Brendan Forsyth, Jack Welch, and Harold Burgess in this regard.
43. George B. Leonard, *Education and Ecstasy* (New York: Dell, 1968), p. 2.

NOTES—CHAPTER IX

1. W. Somerset Maugham, *Of Human Bondage* (New York: Random House Modern Library, 1915), p. 130.
2. Benjamin S. Bloom, "Testing Cognitive Ability and Achievement," in N. L. Gage, editor, *Handbook of Research on Teaching* (Chicago: Rand McNally, 1963), p. 389.
3. For a further discussion on this point, see Robert M. Gagné, *The Conditions of Learning* (New York: Holt, Rinehart and Winston, 1965).
4. Maria Montessori, *The Montessori Method,* translated by Anne E. George (Cambridge, Mass.: Bentley, 1965), p. 225.
5. Michael Scriven, "The Methodology of Evaluation," in Ralph W. Tyler, Robert M. Gagne, and Michael Scriven, editors, *Perspectives on Curriculum Evaluation* (Chicago: Rand McNally, 1967), pp. 39-83.
6. James Michael Lee, *The Shape of Religious Instruction* (Dayton, Ohio: Pflaum/Standard, 1971), pp. 158, 302-303.
7. This definition was drawn from David G. Ryans, "Teacher Behavior: Theory and Research: Implications for Teacher Edu-

cation," in *Journal of Teacher Education*, XIV, (September 1963), pp. 277-278.

8. See Bruce J. Biddle, "Teacher Roles," in Robert L. Ebel, editor, *Encyclopedia of Educational Research*, 4th ed. (New York: Macmillan, 1969), p. 1442.

9. C. Ellis Nelson, "Religious Instruction in Protestant Churches," in James Michael Lee and Patrick C. Rooney, editors, *Toward a Future for Religious. Education* (Dayton, Ohio: Pflaum/ Standard, 1970), p. 157. Italics deleted. Also I have changed the word "child" to "learner."

10. Kenneth Benne and Paul Sheets, "Functional Roles of Group Members," in *Journal of Social Issues*, IV, (Spring 1948), pp. 41-49.

11. Gale E. Jensen, "The Social Structure of the Classroom Group: An Observational Framework," in *Journal of Educational Psychology*, XLVI, (October 1956), pp. 362-374.

12. Robert Glaser, "The Design of Instruction," in National Society for the Study of Education, *The Changing American School*, Sixty-fifth Yearbook, Part II (Chicago: University of Chicago Press, 1966), pp. 219-220.

13. Bruce J. Biddle and Raymond S. Adams, "Teacher Behavior in the Classroom Context," in Laurence Siegel, editor, *Instruction: Some Contemporary Viewpoints* (San Francisco: Chandler, 1967), p. 102.

14. Wayne R. Rood, *The Art of Teaching Christianity* (Nashville, Tenn.: Abingdon, 1968), p. 66.

15. John C. Jahnke, "A Behavioristic Analysis of Instruction," in Laurence Siegel, editor, *Instruction: Some Contemporary Viewpoints*, p. 183.

16. John Dewey, *Democracy and Education* (New York: Macmillan, 1916), p. 24.

17. Didier Piveteau, "Biblical Pedagogics," in James Michael Lee and Patrick C. Rooney, editors, *Toward a Future for Religious Education*, p. 110.

18. B. F. Skinner, *The Technology of Teaching* (New York: Appleton-Century-Crofts, 1968).

19. J. Richard Suchman, "Inquiry Training: Building Skills for Autonomous Discovery," in *Merrill Palmer Quarterly*, VII, (July 1961), pp. 147-169. See also Lee S. Shulman and Evan R. Keislar, editors, *Learning by Discovery: A Critical Appraisal* (Chicago: Rand McNally, 1966).

20. John Dewey, *Democracy and Education*.

21. Maria Montessori, *The Montessori Method*.

22. Michael Warren, "All Contributions Cheerfully Accepted," in *The Living Light*, VII, (Winter 1970), p. 29.

23. B. F. Skinner, *Beyond Freedom and Dignity*, pp. 96-97.
24. See, for example, Thomas F. O'Meara and Donald M. Weisser, "Afterword: The End of Theology?" in Thomas F. O'Meara and Donald M. Weisser, editors, *Projections: Shaping an American Theology for the Future* (Garden City, N.Y.: Doubleday, 1970), pp. 217-228.
25. Carroll Stuhlmueller observes that the phrase "their eyes were opened" (Luke 24:31) occurs only eight times in the entire new testament, and always means a deeper understanding of revelation. Carroll Stuhmueller, "The Gospel According to Luke," in Raymond E. Brown, Joseph A. Fitzmyer, and Roland E. Murphy, editors, *The Jerome Biblical Commentary*, vol. II (Englewood Cliffs, N.J.: Prentice-Hall, 1968), p. 163.
26. Jacob W. Getzels and Herbert A. Thelen, "The Classroom Group as a Unique Social System," in National Society for the Study of Education, *The Dynamics of Instructional Groups*, Fifty-ninth Yearbook, Part II (Chicago: University of Chicago Press, 1960), pp. 53-82.
27. Harold H. Anderson, "The Measurement of Domination and of Socially Integrative Behavior in Teachers' Contacts with Children," in *Child Development*, X, (June 1939), pp. 73-89.
28. David G. Ryans, "Teacher Behavior Theory and Research: Implications for Teacher Education," p. 275.
29. Ole R. Holsti, *Content Analysis for the Social Sciences and Humanities* (Reading, Mass.: Addison-Wesley, 1969), p. 14.
30. Matilda White Riley and Clarice S. Stoll, "Content Analysis," in David L. Sills, editor, *International Encyclopedia of the Social Sciences*, vol. III (New York: Macmillan and Free Press, 1968), p. 370.
31. No general theory of communication is universally accepted by social scientists as of this writing. Nonetheless each content analyst does select explicitly or at least implicitly some theory which does serve to guide and anchor and give meaning to his data.
32. Bernard Berelson, *Content Analysis in Communications Research* (New York: Free Press, 1952).
33. Paulo Freire, *Pedagogy of the Oppressed*, translated by Myra Bergman Ramos (New York: Herder and Herder, 1970), p. 123.
34. Ned A. Flanders, "Diagnosing and Utilizing Social Structures in Classroom Learning," in National Society for the Study of Education, *The Dynamics of Instructional Groups*, p. 204.
35. David M. Medley and Harold E. Mitzel, "Measuring Classroom Behavior by Systematic Observation," in N. L. Gage, editor, *Handbook of Research on Teaching*, pp. 247-328.
36. H. H. Remmers, "Rating Methods in Research on Teaching, in

ibid., pp. 329-378. An example of the use of the rating system is David G. Ryans, *Personality Characteristics of Teachers* (Washington: American Council on Education, 1960).

37. An example of the use of the sign system is the Observation Schedule and Record (OScAR). See Donald M. Medley and Harold E. Mitzel, "A Technique for Measuring Classroom Behavior," in *Journal of Educational Psychology*, XLIX, (April 1958), pp. 86-92.

38. Probably the most celebrated and widely-used category system is that of Flanders. See Ned A. Flanders, *Interaction Analysis in the Classroom: A Manual for Observers*, rev. ed. (Ann Arbor, Mich.: School of Education, University of Michigan, 1966).

39. Barak Rosenshine, "Evaluation of Classroom Instruction," in *Review of Educational Research*, XL, (April 1970), pp. 280-282. The comparison I present in this paragraph of these different systems closely follows Rosenshine's treatment.

40. *Ibid.*, p. 283.

41. Anita Simon and E. Gil Boyer, editors, *Mirrors for Behavior: An Anthology of Classroom Observation Instruments*, vols. I-XV (Philadelphia: Research for Better Schools, 1967-).

42. Fortunately a few researchers such as Hilda Taba are developing interaction analysis systems which address themselves to this critical variable.

43. Barak Rosenshine, "Evaluation of Classroom Instruction," p. 288.

44. Ned A. Flanders, *Interaction Analysis in the Classroom: A Manual for Observers*, rev. ed., p. 7. This paragraph was taken intact from Flanders.

45. Edmund Amidon and Ned Flanders, "Interaction Analysis as a Feedback System," in Edmund J. Amidon and John B. Hough, editors, *Interaction Analysis: Theory, Research and Application* (Reading, Mass.: Addison-Wesley, 1967), p. 140. This Amidon-Hough volume and a book edited by Ronald Hyman represent two of the most helpful anthologies of various kinds of interaction analysis category systems. See Ronald T. Hyman, *Teaching: Vantage Points for Study* (Philadelphia: Lippincott, 1968).

46. Ned A. Flanders, "Some Relationships among Teacher Influence, Pupil Attitudes and Achievement," in Edmund J. Amidon and John B. Hough, editors, *Interaction Analysis: Theory, Research and Application*, p. 229.

47. Edmund Amidon and Elizabeth Hunter, "Verbal Interaction in the Classroom: The Verbal Interaction Category System," in *ibid.*, pp. 141-149.

48. See, for example, Edmund Amidon and Michael Giammetteo,

"The Verbal Behavior of Superior Elementary Teachers," in *ibid.*, pp. 186-188.
49. John B. Hough, "An Observational System for the Analysis of Classroom Interaction," in *ibid.*, pp. 150-157.
50. Marie M. Hughes, "What is Teaching? One Viewpoint: Addendum—The University of Utah Revision of the Provo Code for the Analysis of Teaching," in Ronald T. Hyman, editor, *Teaching: Vantage Points for Study*, pp. 271-284.
51. John Withall, "The Development of a Technique for the Measurement of Social-Emotional Climate in Classrooms," in *Journal of Experimental Education*, XVII, (March 1949), pp. 347-361. In some ways the instrument was the forerunner of the Flanders system.
52. Arno Bellack et al., *The Language of the Classroom* (New York: Teachers College Press, 1966).
53. See *ibid.*
54. B. Othanel Smith, *A Study of the Logic of Teaching* (Urbana, Ill.: Bureau of Educational Research, University of Illinois, 1962).
55. Smith and Meux term the dialogue as "episode." To avoid confusion in terminology, I have substituted the term "dialogue" for "episode."
56. Charles M. Galloway, "Nonverbal Communication in Teaching," in *Educational Leadership*, XXIV, (October 1966), pp. 55-63.
57. Barbara M. Grant and Dorothy Grant Hennings, *The Teacher Moves: An Analysis of Non-verbal Activity* (New York: Teachers College Press, 1971).
58. Karl Openshaw et al., *The Development of a Taxonomy for the Classification of Teacher Classroom Behavior* (Columbus, Ohio: The Ohio State Research Foundation, 1966). See especially pp. 52-55.

NOTES—CHAPTER X

1. Alfred Lord Tennyson, *Ulysses.*
2. I would hope that this decision would be arrived at jointly by the religion teacher, the parents, the learner(s), and persons representing the larger church community.
3. Robert Glaser, "The Design of Instruction," in National Society for the Study of Education, *The Changing American School*, Sixty-fifth Yearbook, Part II (Chicago: University of Chicago Press, 1966), p. 219.
4. Robert F. Mager, *Preparing Instructional Objectives* (Palo Alto, Cal.: Fearon, 1962), p. 13.
5. Both these product and process objectives happen to be forms

of cognitive objectives.

6. Marc Belth disposes of this platitude. See Marc Belth, *Education as a Discipline* (Boston: Allyn and Bacon, 1965), pp. 54-58.

7. Gabriel Moran, *Design for Religion* (New York: Herder and Herder, 1970), pp. 62-63.

8. Wayne R. Rood, "On Christian Religious Education," in *The Living Light*, VII, (Winter 1970), p. 11.

9. Edward M. Hanley, "Review of Research Involving Applied Behavior in the Classroom," in *Review of Educational Research*, XL, (December 1970), p. 618.

10. John Dewey, *Experience and Education* (New York: Macmillan, 1938), p. 35.

11. A. Morrison and D. McIntyre, *Teachers and Teaching* (Baltimore: Penguin, 1969), pp. 176-177.

12. By "sophisticated" here I mean the taking into account of the attainment of performance objectives as a function of the four major independent variables in the teaching model.

13. David R. Hunter, *Christian Education as Engagement* (New York: Seabury, 1963), pp. 98-99.

14. Ian Westbury, "Curriculum Evaluation," in *Review of Educational Research*, XL, (April 1970), pp. 239-240.

15. See Walter Doyle, *Supervision: Key to Effective Teaching* (Dayton, Ohio: NCEA and Pflaum/Standard, 1969).

16. Margaret Ammons, "Objectives and Outcomes," in Robert L. Ebel, editor, *Encyclopedia of Educational Research* (New York: Macmillan, 1969), p. 911.

17. Robert F. Mager, *Preparing Instructional Objectives*.

18. Michael Warren, "Evaluating Christian Experience Programs," in *The Living Light*, VII, (Spring 1970), pp. 84-93.

19. W. A. Oliver, "Teachers' Educational Beliefs versus Their Classroom Practices," in *Journal of Educational Research*, XLVII, (September 1953), pp. 47-55.

20. Personal correspondence from Eugene Hemrick, November 15, 1971.

21. The scientific study of supervision has gained momentum in recent years, after decades of languishing in the doldrums of idle talk, nonproductive checklists, and managerial dicta. For new currents in supervision, see Robert Goldhammer, *Clinical Supervision* (New York: Holt, Rinehart and Winston, 1969); Morris L. Cogan, "Clinical Supervision by Groups," in Association for Student Teaching, *The College Supervisor*, Forty-third Yearbook (Cedar Falls, Iowa: The Association, 1964); Walter Doyle, *Supervision: Key to Effective Teaching*.

22. Robert F. Peck, "Promoting Self-Disciplined Learning: A Researchable Revolution," in B. Othanel Smith, editor, *Research*

in Teacher Education (New York: Prentice-Hall, 1971), p. 92.

23. Don Davies and Kathleen Amershek, "Student Teaching," in Robert L. Ebel, editor, *Encyclopedia of Educational Research*, pp. 1376-1387.

24. Gertrude Moskowitz, "The Attitudes and Teaching Patterns of Cooperating Teachers and Student Teachers Trained in Interaction Analysis," in Edmund J. Amidon and John B. Hough, editors, *Interaction Analysis: Theory, Research and Application* (Reading, Mass.: Addison-Wesley, 1967), p. 272.

25. Ernest E. Lohman, Richard Ober, and John B. Hough, "A Study of the Effect of Pre-Service Training in Interaction Analysis on the Verbal Behavior of Student Teachers," in *ibid.*, p. 347.

26. Jeffrey Kirk, "Elementary School Student Teachers and Interaction Analysis," in *ibid.*, p. 305.

27. Ernest E. Lohman, Richard Ober, and John B. Hough, "A Study of the Effect on Pre-Service Training in Interaction Analysis on the Verbal Behavior of Student Teachers," p. 359.

28. *Ibid.*, p. 347.

29. Norma Furst, "The Effects of Training in Interaction Analysis on the Behavior of Student Teachers in Secondary Schools," in Edmund J. Amidon and John B. Hough, editors, *Interaction Analysis: Theory, Research and Application* (Reading, Mass.: Addison-Wesley, 1967), pp. 326-327.

30. Richard D. Zahn, "The Use of Interaction Analysis in Supervising Student Teachers," in *ibid.*, p. 297.

31. John B. Hough and Edmund Amidon, "Behavioral Change in Student Teachers," in *ibid.*, pp. 308-309, 313.

32. Ernest E. Lohman, Richard Ober, and John B. Hough, "A Study of the Effect on Pre-Service Training in Interaction Analysis on the Verbal Behavior of Student Teachers," pp. 355-358.

33. John B. Hough and Edmund Amidon, "Behavioral Change in Student Teachers," p. 308; see also Richard D. Zahn, "The Use of Interaction Analysis in Supervising Student Teachers," p. 297.

34. Raymond Whiteman, "The Differing Patterns of Behavior as Observed in Teachers of Religion and Teachers of Mathematics and Social Studies," unpublished seminar project, University of Notre Dame, 1971.

35. Dwight Allen and Kevin Ryan, *Microteaching* (Reading, Mass.: Addison-Wesley, 1969), pp. 1-9.

36. Ned A. Flanders, "Introduction," in *ibid.*, p. xiv.

37. *Ibid.*, p. xiii.

38. James Michael Lee, "Overview of Educational Problems in Seminaries: II—Administration," in James Michael Lee and Louis J. Putz, editors, *Seminary Education in a Time of Change*

(Notre Dame, Ind.: Fides, 1965), p. 123.
39. David R. Hunter, *Christian Education as Engagement*, p. 66.
40. John Ferguson, *Pelagius* (Cambridge, England: Heffer, 1956), p. 159. This is one of the finest works on the subject available in the English language. See also Torgny Bohlin, *Die Theologie des Pelagius und Ihre Genesis* (Uppsala, Sweden: Lundequistaka, 1957). Ferguson notes that "much that has been written about Pelagius is a loose expression of a general impression and is not based upon a detailed examination of his views" (p. 182).
41. F. Cayré, *Manual of Patrology and History of Theology*, vol. I, translated by H. Howitt (Paris: Desclée, 1927), p. 391.
42. David R. Hunter, *Christian Education as Engagement*, p. 21.
43. Gregory Baum, *Man Becoming: God in Secular Experience* (New York: Herder and Herder, 1970), p. 128.
44. By "aspect" here I do not mean a part of God but a manifestation of God. A cause is somehow in its effect; the more pervasive the cause, the more pervasive will it be in its effect.
45. Personal correspondence from Eugene Hemrick, Feb. 1, 1972.
46. André Godin, "Some Developmental Tasks in Christian Education," in Merton P. Strommen, editor, *Research on Religious Development* (New York: Hawthorn, 1971), p. 110.
47. On this point, see James E. Dittes, "Two Issues in Measuring Religion," in *ibid.*, p. 82.
48. Merton P. Strommen, editor, "Introduction," in *ibid.*, pp. xviii-xix.

valuational, 308
Theory of instruction, 6; 47-57; 272-274; *see also* Theory and practice
features of, 54-55
functions of, 53-54
help to teacher, 51-53
and instructional practice, 55-57; 272-274
and learning, 6; 47-50; 57
learning findings, relation to, 6; 57
learning theory, contrasted to, 47-50
as praxiological theory, 57
Theory of learning, 43-50
help to teacher, 45-47
limitations of for instructional practice, 47-50
theological and social science, 43-45
Christian learning theory, 43-45
Theory and practice, 26-27; 39-43; 149-151; 273; 304-305
nature of theory, 39-43
in religious instruction, 149-151
usefulness of theory to practice, 26-27; 39-43; 273; 304-305
Transactional teaching, 250
Transfer of learning, 141-147
definition of, 141
findings on, 142-144
effects, 142-144
importance of, 142
practice and, 143-144
principles and facts, 143-144
level of, 142

horizontal, 142
vertical, 142
significance of, 144-148
Holy Spirit and, 145
maximizing probability, 146-147
task similarity, 146
types of, 141
negative, 141
positive, 141
zero, 141
Translation stage of religious instruction, 18-19
Transmission strategy, 25; 79; 117; 147; 175; 219; 221; 225; 237; 239; 241; 247; 278; *see also* Proclamation "theory" of religious instruction

Values, 107; *see also* Attitudes
Videotape, 104; 254

Withall Interaction Analysis System, 262-263
Witness "theory" of religious instruction, 164-174; 215; 239; 272; 275